African American Religion

African American Religion

Varieties of Protest and Accommodation

SECOND EDITION

HANS A. BAER
AND MERRILL SINGER

The University of Tennessee Press • Knoxville

Library of Congress Cataloging-in-Publication Data

Baer, Hans A., 1944–
African American religion : varieties of protest and accommodation / Hans A. Baer and Merrill Singer.— 2nd ed.
p. cm.
Includes bibliographical references and index.
ISBN 1-57233-186-0 (pbk. : alk. paper)
1. African Americans—Religion. I. Singer, Merrill. II. Title.
BR563.N4 B34 2002
277.3'082'08996073—dc20   2002000249

Contents

Illustrations

Tables

Preface to the Second Edition

$\mathcal{T}$he renaissance in the scholarly study of African American religion in the United States to which we alluded in the preface of *African American Religion in the Twentieth Century* has continued on in a variety of settings, including books, anthologies, articles, and presentations at conferences. New historical research has been done on various aspects of African American religion in the formation and development of African American denominations (Campbell 1995; Montgomery 1993) and African American missionary societies (Fitts 1993) during the nineteenth century as well as leading African American clerics (Seraile 1998; Martin 1999) during that time period. As Sernett (1997: 3) observes, "African American religious studies as a specialty within the American Academy of Religion is nearly a quarter-century old and has yielded rich and varied harvest." In contrast to the past when scholars have tended to focus their studies on unconventional religious groups and movements within the African American community, various significant studies have been conducted on the Black mainstream churches (Irvin 1992; Gregg 1993; Higginbotham 1993; Pitts 1993; Sawyer 1994; Taylor 1994; Lakey 1996; Sernett 1997; Billingsley 1999) and Black mainstream ministers (Haywood 1993; Frady 1996). Continuing fascination with African American Islam has prompted the publication of several biographies on three leading figures in its history, namely Elijah Muhammad (Gardell 1996; Clegg 1997; Evanzz 1999), Malcolm X (Perry 1991; Dyson 1995; Caro 1996, 1998), and Louis Farrakhan (Mayida 1996; Levinsohn 1997).

We have been gratified with the widespread acceptance and course adoption of *African American Religion in the Twentieth Century*, which remains the only broad overview of African American religion in its multifaceted organizational aspects in a textbook form. Shortly following the publication of our volume, Larry G. Murphy, J. Gordon Melton, and Gary L. Head (1993) published the *Encyclopedia of African American Religions*, which provides numerous short essays on African American religious groups and personalities. In addition to incorporating materials that have been published since 1992 into *African American Religion* we have added two new chapters—"African Religious Healing and Folk Medicine" and "African American Sacred Music"—because of their significance as part and parcel of the African American religious experience. We hope that our colleagues and students in African American religious studies will find this revised and expanded volume to be a valuable resource in both their teaching and research.

Preface

African American religion developed within the larger context of American capitalism. It emerged initially under slavery and mercantile capitalism during the antebellum period. Although African American religion underwent some institutionalization during this period under the aegis of the independent black church movement, its development in the form of a wide array of organized sects and denominations occurred after the Civil War and concurrent with the development of industrial capitalism in both the North and the South. From its very beginnings, African American religion has exhibited a contradictory nature. On the one hand, the slave masters attempted to use religion as a means of urging peoples of African ancestry to be compliant agricultural workers and house servants and to seek their salvation in a nebulous afterlife. The frequent portrayal of African American religion as otherworldly is, however, a facile generalization. Peoples of African ancestry shaped European American Christianity into its various forms, as well as in some cases Judaism and Islam, to meet their own needs and to serve as the single social institution that for many generations they could call their own. African American religion to a large extent is a reworked Christianity that has its own character, style, and outlook, but one which incorporated elements of African religion. Even Judaic and Islamic sects in the African American community exhibit a syncretism of these two religious traditions.

According to E. Franklin Frazier (1974: 44), African American religion has historically functioned as a "refuge in a hostile white world." African Americans have utilized religion as a way of creating space in addressing the vagaries of racism and class stratification. At one level, the Black church constitutes, as Du Bois (1967: 201) argues, a center of social life, a primary vehicle of communication, and an organizer of entertainment and amusement in the African American community. Black churches have often served as mutual-aid societies, which help their members survive crises associated with illness or death. Black ministers frequently established a school along with a church, and Black denominations created seminaries, colleges, and universities following the Civil War. In pursuing these activities, African American religion often exhibited an accommodative dimension by attempting to create an acquiescent space for Blacks in a racist society, whether it was in the rural areas of the South or the cities of the industrial North.

At another level, however, African American religion has acted as a form of self-expression and resistance to a white-dominated society. Indeed, one scholar goes so far as to argue that African American churches constitute the "most activist sector of American religion" (Fowler 1985: 311). Black denominations based in the antebellum North were active in the abolition movement. During various periods, Black ministers served as federal and state officials, state legislators, and U.S. congresspeople, and one was even elected a U.S. senator. Recently, the Rev. Jesse Jackson has run for the U.S. presidency and garnered a notable number of votes in primary elections. Further, many Black churches have sponsored political debates held in their sanctuaries and served as rallying centers for political and economic reform. As Marable observes, "From Reconstruction to Black Power, many significant political figures engaged in Black liberation struggles were either ministers or were profoundly influenced by religion: Nat Turner, Henry H. Garnet, David Walker, Elijah Muhammad, Malcolm X, Andrew Young, Jesse Jackson, John Lewis and hundreds more. The most influential minister in twentieth century American society, Black or white, was Martin Luther King, Jr." (Marable 1983: 196). Indeed, Dr. King was without doubt the most widely known and admired African American in U.S. history.

Scholars from a variety of disciplines, including history, religious studies, political science, sociology, and anthropology, have recognized the central significance of religion in African American culture. Scholarly studies on African American religion in the United States can be traced back to W. E. B. Du Bois's *The Negro Church* (1903b). More extensive examinations of African American religion—despite the existence of path-making studies such as Benjamin E. Mays and Joseph R. Nicholson's *The Negro Church* (orig. 1933; 1968), and Carter G. Woodson's *The History of the Negro Church* (1945)—appeared in the wake of the civil rights movement in which numerous Baptist and Methodist churches throughout the South played a significant role. A renaissance has occurred in the study of African American religion in the United States over the last two decades. The concern of scholars with the religious forms created and embraced by African Americans has been swept from the still waters of sporadic interest into a gathering billow of excited attention with a degree of suddenness that at times has marked upsurges in the complexity of the subject matter. In 1971 a group of Black churchpeople established the Society for the Study of Black Religion. This growing scholarly interest has perhaps been best exemplified by the activities of the Afro-American Religious History Group within the American Academy of Religion since the creation of the group in 1973. The ever-growing scholarly commitment to understanding the religious life of African Americans has already produced a bountiful harvest of new books and journal articles. To date, however, the revival has focused mostly on comprehending African American religion as it was evolving during the late eighteenth and nineteenth centuries rather than the present century. Sociologists and anthropologists have been devoting increasing attention to African American religious practices during the modern period, in contrast to historians who have concentrated their efforts on its early development. Drawing on both of these lines of inquiry, a major concern of this book is in situating contemporary African American religion in relation to the contexts of its development across the last several hundred years. As we shall demonstrate, African American religion has never been static, and its dynamism emerges in part from its role as succor and inspiration for a people struggling both to survive and to advance under harsh and changing social circumstances.

Several scholars have provided us with broad overviews of African American religion (Washington 1960, 1973; Frazier 1974; Wilmore 1983a; Lincoln 1984; Lincoln and Mamiya 1990), although no one has yet written a comprehensive account of it on the scale of Sidney Ahlstorm's *A Religious History of the American People* (1975). Most of these scholars focus on general aspects of the mainstream denominations in the Black community and in some cases present a pejorative treatment of more unconventional religious groups. Ironically, detailed scholarly accounts of the mainstream denominations, such as the National Baptist Convention, USA, or the African Methodist Episcopal church, are virtually nonexistent. Nevertheless, most social scientific examinations of African American religion, including those by Johnson (1934, 1941), Dollard (1937), Powdermaker (1967), Lewis (1955), Hamilton (1972), Dougherty (1978), Mukenge (1983), and Beck (1989), refer, often indirectly, to the Baptist and, to a lesser degree, the Methodist churches that claim the allegiance of the majority of church-going Blacks. The richest accounts of specific Black religious movements focus on Black Islam (Lincoln 1962; Essien-Udom 1962; Marsh 1984),

Black Judaism (Brotz 1970; Singer 1979, 1982), Garveyism (Burkett 1978), Black Pentecostalism (Williams 1974; Paris 1982), Father Divine's Peace Mission (Hoshor 1936; Parker 1937; Harris 1971; Burnham 1979; Weisbrot 1983), and Black Spiritualism (Kaslow and Jacobs 1981; Baer 1984).

Despite a growing literature on various aspects of the subject during the twentieth century, our book is the first comprehensive overview that covers this period and attempts to recognize the diversity of forms that African American religion takes. In undertaking this massive effort, we have drawn from two major sources. The first of these comes from a large assortment of books, articles, newspaper accounts, and unpublished theses and dissertations—many of which are not readily available to the general reader. The second of these sources is our own ethnographic fieldwork on Black religion and ethnomedicine, particularly within the Spiritual movement (Baer 1981, 1984, 1985, 1988) and the Original Hebrew Israelites (Singer 1979, 1982, 1985, 1988). Our approach to interpreting African American religion is primarily social scientific, but it also incorporates a strong historical orientation. While in most cases we refer to congregations and individuals by their actual names, as is standard practice in ethnography, we refer to some congregations and individuals by pseudonyms because certain social scientists whose works we cite, including our own, did so. We were both trained as cultural anthropologists, but, except for our understanding of religion as a cultural system, our perspective is similar to that of many sociologists. Our book should be of interest to scholars and teachers concerned with African American studies (especially African American religion), the anthropology and sociology of religion, and religious studies. This volume, we believe, should prove a useful introduction to historians as they begin to give greater consideration to the history of African American religion during the twentieth century.

The organizational framework for this book began over lunch at the 1979 American Anthropological Association Meeting in Cincinnati. Having carried out research with contrasting African American sects, we were struggling to fit the group we had studied into a larger framework. None of the existing typologies of African American religious organizations seemed adequate. Over the course of an increasingly animated discussion, a new typology began to take shape in rough form on the only paper readily at hand, a somewhat crumpled napkin. During the next few months, we refined our initial thinking and in the following year published our model in the journal *Anthropological Quarterly* (Baer and Singer 1981). In a series of subsequent articles on specific African American religious groups and in a book on

African American Spiritual churches by Baer (1984), we made reference to the typology. Still, the sense remained that a full application of the typology to the wide range of religious groups in the African American community would make a contribution to the better understanding of these important social phenomena.

In contrast to many scholarly studies of African American religion, which assume the presence of a divine intervention in its development, our approach is methodological agnosticism. As McGuire aptly observes, "Sociology [and anthropology] must necessarily 'bracket' (i.e., methodologically set aside) the crucial question: To what extent is this action also from God? This does not mean that sociology [or anthropology] treats religious behavior and experience as 'merely' interpretation. Nevertheless, whatever else they may be, religious behavior and experience are also human and are therefore proper subjects for sociological [and anthropological] research and understanding" (McGuire 1987: 5). As social scientists, we recognize that religion is an integral part of sociocultural systems and as such often motivates human beings to act as if supernatural forces have a reality of their own.

In our efforts to understand the significance of African American religion, we are indebted especially to the leaders and members of various congregations that we visited and interviewed, particularly those within the Spiritual movement and the Original Hebrew Nation. Baer's participation in the following National Endowment for the Humanities events contributed to his deeper appreciation of the complexity of African American religion: the Institute on Afro American Religious History (directed by Professors Albert J. Raboteau and David Wills) at Princeton University in summer 1984, the Seminar on the Black Protest Movement in the Twentieth Century (directed by Professor August Meier) at Kent State University in summer 1985, and the Institute on African American Culture (directed by Professor Gloria Dickinson) at Trenton State College in summer 1987. We are also thankful to Gayraud S. Wilmore, Stephen Glazier, Monika Helwig, and Michael Kleine for having read earlier drafts of this manuscript either in full or in part. We appreciate the support that Carol Orr has given us in our work on African American religion. Finally, we would like to acknowledge Stella Capek and Lani Davison, social scientists in their own right, who have afforded us the support and encouragement to make this book possible.

As critical anthropologists, we hope that our efforts will contribute to a fuller appreciation of the richness of African American religion and the strategies that Black people have adopted in their search for hope and dignity in a society that has treated them and continues to treat them brutally. Perhaps their intense humanity and their capacity to face what Charles H. Long (1971: 60) terms the "'hardness' of life," part of which is described in this book, will inspire others to join in the struggle not only for their liberation but also for that of all peoples who are the victims of oppression and degradation.

Introduction

Varieties of Protest and Accommodation

Regardless of the time period, African American culture has been characterized by a considerable degree of diversity along regional, class, and, of particular interest to us here, religious lines (Green 1970; Baer and Singer 1981). The extent of this variability to a great extent escaped notice for three reasons. First, African Americans until recently received little significant notice in the mainstream media, in education, in the social sciences, in the humanities, and in what so innocently and quaintly has been termed "polite society." Second, most of the attention that has been given has been shaped by the tendency of whites and white institutions to project an image of African Americans that blurs sharp differences. Variability, in fact, is in deep contradiction to the racist tendency to create simplifying categories as well as the underlying economic need to control African American labor and deploy it *en masse* for the marginal "dirty work" that keeps the system running. Finally, in responding to threat and slander from the dominant society, African American intellectuals—most of whom until this century have been preachers—have been compelled to stress unity and commonality rather than the celebration of diversity. As a consequence, the myriad expressions of African American religiosity have been compressed in scholarly understanding into a number of major types and a few peripheral and largely unattended variants, a pattern that can be seen in the tendency to equate African American religion with the "Black church." While this concept may have a certain heuristic value, it is misleading in its implication that the religious experience among Blacks has been uniform or monolithic. Lost in this tendency has been a full appreciation of the creative potential of African Americans to mobilize their religious feelings to meet diverse challenges, as well as a comprehensive understanding of the very place of religion in African American life and identity.

Nonetheless, the development of Black religion, especially during the twentieth century, has taken a multiplicity of interrelated streams. Wilmore captures a sense of the growing diversification of African American religion around the turn of century in the following remarks:

> *The period between 1890 and the Second World War was one of the luxuri-*
> *ant growth and proliferation of many forms of black religion in the United*
> *States and Africa that challenged the bourgeoisification of the mainline black*
> *denominations. Black Holiness and Pentecostalism, arising from the southern*
> *folk religion pressure-cooked in the teeming ghettos of the North, mixed in fas-*
> *cinating combinations with some of the black consciousness and nationalistic*
> *tendencies. . . . Garveyism, as a religious movement, is one of the permuta-*
> *tions of these converging and polarizing aspects of black religion and radical-*
> *ism.* (Wilmore 1983a: 152)

Even earlier social scientists, such as Jones (1939), Fauset (1971), and Drake and Cayton (1945), gave us an appreciation for religious pluralism among Black Americans. Ulf Hannerz, a Swedish anthropologist, portrays the continuation of this bountiful complexity through his vivid description of the Black sections of Washington, D.C., during the 1960s:

> *The ghetto has many streets like Winston Street, with the same kinds of row*
> *houses, occasionally a larger apartment house, and many of the small busi-*
> *nesses—the groceries, the barber shops, the liquor stores. There is a high*
> *turnover among these, as many of them are rather unsuccessful operations,*
> *and there are often vacant premises. Some of these become the homes of store-*
> *front churches which advertise their services and Sunday school programs in*
> *the erstwhile shop windows, most of which are white painted or covered by self-*
> *adhesive plastic imitations of stained glass. The diversity of their names*—The
> Full Speed Gospel, Church of God in Christ, The Peaceway Temple,
> The Miracle Temple of Truth, The Christian Home Penecostal [sic]
> Holiness Church of God of Americans, The Maranatha Gospel Gospel
> Hall, The Solid Rock Church of God in Christ, The Way Back to
> Pentecostal Church, The Full Gospel Tabernacle Church of the Liv-
> ing God *and a multitude of other combinations—is one pointer of their inde-*
> *pendence of older, large, and well-established churches. These storefront*
> *churches, "Spiritual," "Holiness," or "Sanctified," have small congregations*
> *of perhaps a couple dozen members and are led by preachers who may be male*
> *or female but are more often male. The tiny congregations usually have no or*
> *little connection with any other church.* (Hannerz 1969: 27–28)

In addition to exemplifying the variety and richness of the African American experience, religion is a significant dimension of African American culture because of what it can tell us about the position and condition of Black people in the United States. In commenting upon the "dialectic of accommodation and resistance" of Blacks during antebellum times, Genovese (1974: 659) observes that their "protonational consciousness" was "expressed primarily through a religious sensibility, that enabled a mass of oppressed individuals to cohere as a people." Through religion, as Genovese observes, African Americans found a voice, indeed multiple and variegated voices, to speak not only of their spiritual quest and fulfillment but of their earthly trials and social yearnings as well. In this interplay of worldly and otherworldly images and attributes, African Americans constructed their identity as a people. Consequently, African American politics has always had and continues to have a decidedly religious slant, while African American religion is deeply political.

In exploring this theme, which is central to this book, it must be stressed that the relationship between religion and political consciousness is paradoxical and often contradictory. While Karl Marx's assertion that religion is the "opium of the people" is well known, it is little understood Marx was also cognizant of the emancipatory potential of religion. In the main, Marx viewed religion as "the self-consciousness and self-feeling of a man who has either not yet found himself or has already lost himself again" (Marx and Engels 1964: 41). Although Marx recognized that throughout history ruling classes have used religion as a mechanism of social control, he nonetheless regarded it primarily as an attempt by the suffering masses to ease the pain, at least for the moment, of living in an exploitive, fragmented, and class-divided society. The bitter price that the masses must pay for the solace of religion is a form of "false consciousness" that obscures the real root of their suffering, namely a stratified social system. In this, religion may divert energy from the most political of tasks, the overthrow of oppression. Marx succinctly summarized the dual nature of religion in the following statement: "Religious distress is at the same time the *expression* of real distress and the *protest* against real distress. Religion is the sigh of the oppressed creature, the heart of a heartless world, just as it is the spirit of the unspiritual situation" (Marx and Engels 1964: 42; emphasis in original).

Unfortunately, Marx had very little further to say about the protest function of religion. It was actually Friedrich Engels more than Marx who elaborated upon the matter of religious protest. According to Engels, prior to the nineteenth century, class struggles had been "carried out under religious shibboleths" and were usually "concealed behind a religious screen"

(Marx and Engels 1964: 98). This is precisely Cohn's (1970) argument regarding the revolutionary millenarianism that flourished among the unorganized and atomized sectors of both rural and urban European populations during the Middle Ages. Lacking institutionalized methods of voicing their grievances, they turned to religious prophets and miracle-working saints to mobilize their energies. The religious character of these moments, much like those among African Americans during the twentieth century, was conditioned by the social fragmentation of their adherents and the utility of religion as a cohesive force. African Americans have been able to come together in religion—although not in any particular religious group or church—as a shared sense of deep attachment to and experience of a spiritual presence and create a felt unity across their profound diversity. And unity, of course, is fundamental to the waging of social struggles of any kind.

Guided in part by Marx and Engels's recognition of the dual nature of religion, a significant debate in the literature on African American religion addresses the matter of whether it has been accommodative to white-dominated society or emancipatory for the Black masses (G. Marx 1967; Genovese 1974; Nelsen and Nelsen 1975; Raboteau 1978; Childs 1980; Marable 1981; Peck 1982). Unfortunately, assertions as to whether African American religion tends to be either an opiate or an inspiration for militancy (G. Marx 1967) often overlook the fundamental feature of concern to this study: the significant level of diversity that characterizes the religions of African Americans. For example, Nelsen and Nelsen (1975) operate with a concept of sectarianism that automatically associates it with otherworldliness, emotionalism, and political indifference. In reality, unconventional religious groups among African Americans vary considerably in their beliefs, attitudes, and behavioral patterns. Bearing this in mind, any attempt to address the juxtaposition of protest and accommodation in African American religion must be sensitive to the variety of configurations covered by this label. Furthermore, as Childs (1980: 25) so aptly observes, the "complexity of the black church cannot be unraveled until an approach is developed that weds empirical clarity with the philosophical willingness to accept contradiction as a critical aspect of social reality." Indeed, contradictions and contention are among the most fundamental of social realities.

In attempting to unravel the essence of African American religion, we rely upon Gramsci's concept of hegemony. We do not purport to further the theoretical development of this concept but attempt to apply it to our analysis of the juxtaposition of protest and accommodation in African American religion. As Marable (1983: 211) so aptly states, "The insights of Marxist theorist Antonio Gramsci . . . have particular merit" in efforts to elucidate the role of African American religion.

In the development of this concept, his most important contribution to social theory, Gramsci elaborated upon Marx and Engels's observation that the "ideas of the ruling class are, in every age, the ruling ideas." According to Gramsci (1971: 12), the supremacy of a social group may manifest itself in "two major superstructural 'levels': the one that can be called 'civil society,' and that of 'political society' or 'the State.'" These two levels correspond on the one hand to the "function of 'hegemony' which the dominant group exercises throughout the society and on the other hand to that of 'direct domination' or command exercised through the State and 'judicial' government. . . . The intellectuals are the dominant group's 'deputies' exercising the subaltern functions of social ideology and political government" (Gramsci 1971: 12). Whereas direct domination is realized through the coercive organs of the state apparatus (e.g., the parliament, the courts, the military, the police, etc.), hegemony, as Femia (1975: 30) observes, is "objectified in and exercised through the institutions of civil society, the ensemble of educational, religious, and associational institutions." In Salanini's (1981: 139) apt phrase, "civil society is based on consensus; political society on force."

"Hegemony" refers to the process by which one class exerts control of the cognitive and intellectual life of society by structural means as opposed to coercive ones. Hegemony is achieved through the diffusion of certain values, attitudes, beliefs, social norms, and legal precepts that, to a greater or lesser degree, come to permeate civil society. According to Bobock (1986: 7), "At base, hegemony is all about ideology. But it is ideology writ large: the idea of an all-encompassing dominant ideology whose scope extends throughout all social, cultural and economic spheres of a society." A consequence of hegemony is that the ruling class obtains the acquiescence of various subordinate groups to its dominance. Not surprisingly, ruling classes have preferred to establish their power, wealth, and status ideologically rather than by coercive force. Hegemony "performs functions that the military and policy machinery could never carry out: it mystifies power relations, public issues, and historical events; it encourages fatalism and passivity toward political action; it justifies various types of system-serving deprivation and sacrifice" (Boggs 1984: 161). In short, not only is hegemony effective, in the long run it is considerably less costly than raw coercion or even ideological domination because it does not automatically generate resentment. Rather, it hinges on "the consensual aspects of political control" (Femia 1981: 25).

In essence, as Bauman points out in the case of capitalist society, the worldview of the dominant group or ruling class is so thoroughly diffused and entrenched among the masses that it becomes the "commonsense" view of the entire society:

> *Capitalism, like any established system, has a powerful edge over any of its potential adversaries in that its very reality, the structure of the everyday situations which it creates for the individual, reaffirms and reinforces the capitalism-sustaining brand of commonsense even without an open intervention of refined intellectual arguments. It lends the habitual patterns of conduct a spurious air of naturalness and eternity; and it stamps everyday routine as rational behavior, having previously established the value of rationality as a supreme criterion of worthiness. Moreover, the ruling class can rely on the fact that its culture, once established, defines all imaginable improvement as an advance in acquisition of this very culture. Even a powerful thrust toward amelioration, therefore, can hardly fracture the cultural foundation of the current hegemony: if anything, it will rather reinforce it by adding a new strength and popularity to its constituent value-patterns.* (Bauman 1976: 68)

The arenas of ideological-cultural transmission are vast. Ruling classes utilize all institutional mechanisms through which perceptions are shaped—the mass media, the schools, the churches, conventional political parties, the family, and even medicine—to mold the beliefs, attitudes, and behavior of the masses of people. In modern capitalist societies, cultural hegemony in large measure is achieved and maintained through a subtle process of education, which involves not only the schools but also the mass media and popular literature. Since these agencies of socialization are generally, even if unobtrusively, controlled by the dominant group, it is not surprising that they communicate and reinforce its image of social reality.

Gramsci also believed that religion constitutes a significant component in the larger matrix of domination. In the case of his own country, Italy, he argued that the Catholic church taught that dignity and poverty are synonymous values. Religious hegemony limits "popular rebellion—for example, by instilling in the masses the idea of a 'natural' or 'God-given' character of existing structures and social relations (private property, the family), the importance of transcendental concerns over everyday, 'earthly' collective action, the 'moral' virtues of poverty and meekness, and the sacrosanct nature of all forms of established authority" (Boggs 1984: 76). African American religion, as we shall see, plays a similar role, a function we refer to as its accommodative dimension.

Yet, no class society is a formation of complete dominance, even hegemonic dominance. Dominated groups always offer resistance of one form or other to their oppression. As Scott (1990: 124) correctly observes, "much of the resistance to the dominant culture [takes] the form of religious heterodoxy and heresy." Religious groups achieve a certain degree of autonomy in advanced capitalist societies that allows them to pose challenges to the existing social system. As Bobock (1986: 60) observes, "A state is able to control whether religious organizations raise monies, use endowments, conduct ritual practices or organize their own education programmes; but once granted these freedoms, churches and religious movements may become important and effective sources of independent philosophy and of political criticism." As we attempt to demonstrate in this book, elements of protest have permeated African American religion, whether we are speaking about slave religion during the antebellum period or its various manifestations today. In the case of Italy, Gramsci himself regarded popular religious culture as "a kind of permanent and ineradicable *resistance*, implicit, mechanical and objective, to the hegemony based on Catholicism" (Schwimmer 1987: 88; emphasis in original). So too with African American religion in all of its startling variety. African American resistance of white domination is part of the very essence of what Genovese (1974) referred to as African American "religious sensibility." Marable adopts the term "Blackwater" to capture this vitalizing essence. "Blackwater," he writes, "is the consciousness of oppression, a cultural search for self-affirmation and authority" (Marable 1981: 40). Along the trail of this enduring search, this quest for both spiritual and social transformation, African American religious response to hegemony has taken many outward forms. The unity within this diversity, we argue, is the felt need to counter at the individual or group level, through personal salvation as social action, through occult rituals or political militancy, the twin insults of white racism and economic exploitation.

Our book focuses on African American religion during the present century, but we briefly examine its emergence under slavery and mercantile capitalism and its subsequent development in the decades following the Civil War so as to provide the context for understanding ongoing developments under industrial capitalism. As Marable (1981: 34) asserts, "Black Christianity, as well as the totality of the black religious experience within America, cannot be understood outside the development of white racism and capitalist exploitation." Thus, our discussion at all times locates Black religion in relation to the social and economic forces confronting the Black population. In this way, we strive to reveal the social essence of Black religion as a culturally produced structure that simultaneously offers some protection from the elements, provides a sheltered arena for personal development and expression, and allows a controlled level of protest of the external social world.

In chapter 1, we recognize at least three prevailing themes that have shaped African American religion, namely influences from African culture, influences from religious patterns in European American culture, and religious responses by Blacks to the racist and stratified nature of American society. Chapter 2 deals with the socioeconomic conditions that contributed to the growing variability of African American religion during the early decades of the twentieth century—a period when massive numbers of Blacks migrated from the rural areas of the South to the cities of both the North and the South. Chapters 3 through 6 are organized around a typology of Black sectarianism as a response to racial stratification that we have found useful in understanding the multifaceted and contradictory nature of African American religion (Baer and Singer 1981). Our typology, which we explain in greater detail in chapter 2, identifies four basic types of Black religious groups: (1) the mainstream denominations or established sects, (2) the messianic-nationalist sects, (3) the conversionist sects, and (4) the thaumaturgical sects.

Each chapter discusses the history, beliefs, social organization, and ritual content of various religious groups characteristic of a particular sectarian type. As will be shown, these types as well as specific groups within each type juxtapose elements of protest and accommodation in different degrees. Chapter 7 recognizes the existence of a "mixed type" that combines features of two or more of the four types delineated in our classificatory scheme. Furthermore, this chapter discusses the evolution that the various types of Black sects tend to follow. In our concluding chapter, we examine the syncretic nature and the counterhegemonic potential of African American religion. Here, we are concerned with exploring both the basis of the rich ideological, ritual, and organizational diversity reviewed in chapters 3 through 7 as well as with analyzing new developments as expressed in the Black Theology movement and the Rainbow Coalition headed up by Rev. Jesse Jackson.

I

The Cultural Background

$\mathcal{T}$he precise starting point of African American religion is probably impossible to establish, but we can safely assume, just as was the case for African religion, that it exhibited an instrumental orientation that attempted to empower its adherents with techniques for dealings with situations in the here and now. According to Mintz and Price (1976: 23), "We can probably date the beginnings of Afro-American religion from the moment that one person in need received ritual assistance from another who belonged to a different cultural group.'" African American religion resembled African religions in that it was "relatively permeable to foreign influences and tended to be 'additive' rather than 'exclusive' in [its] orientation toward other cultures" (Mintz and Price 1976: 23).

African American religion derives from many sources. Three are of particular importance: (1) influences from the African past, (2) borrowings from the patterns of European American culture, and (3) religious responses of African Americans to their subordinate status in a racist and stratified social system. Critical as it may be to the complete comprehension of African American religion, the first of these sources of influence continues to be the most difficult to establish with confidence. Some authorities, like W. E. B. Du Bois (1903a) and Melville J. Herskovits (1941), have argued that African American religion in the United States exhibits numerous African features. Conversely, E. Franklin Frazier (1949), while admitting the existence of African retentions in Latin America and the Caribbean, emphatically maintained that the destructive process of slavery in the United States, with the passing away of earlier generations born in Africa, seared all but vestigial traces of African culture from the collective consciousness of people of African ancestry in North America.

Given the diversity of African societies, particularly in West Africa and Central Africa, where the first slaves came from, it is evident that no single

African culture or religion could have remained intact in North America. Yet, as Raboteau observes,

> *The acculturative process was broader and more complex than simple retention or destruction of Africanisms. Elements of African behavior and belief could have been modified by contact with European culture and could have merged with it in a new syncretistic form. Conversely, European traits could have been shaped and reinterpreted by the slaves in the light of their African past. On the one hand, the similarity of some traits may make it difficult or even impossible to separate what is African from what is European in origin; on the other hand, this very commonality might have served to reinforce certain African elements while others withered under severe prohibition and attack.* (Raboteau 1978: 58–59)

As Raboteau stresses, and as we emphasize, African influences can be expected to be found, but normally only in syncretized form, blended with diverse non-African components in a unique configuration. Indeed, over the past two decades, a fair number of scholars have worked hard to demonstrate linkage to Africa, not only in Latin America and the Caribbean but also in the United States (Mitchell 1975; Simpson 1978; Sobel 1979; Walker 1972; Jules-Rosette 1980). These researchers itemized certain African religious concepts and practices—such as the pantheon of High God and lesser divinities; ancestor worship; initiation rites; spirit possession; healing and funeral rituals; magical rituals for seizing spiritual power; and ecstatic ceremonies enlivened by rhythmic dancing, drumming, and singing—that persist either in their original or modified form in the New World. Through the labor of these scholars, it is affirmed that the African roots of African American religion and culture were never fully nor effectively severed, however draconian the efforts of white society to do so. One response of a people dragged from their homes, transported forcibly to a strange and often cruel land, and maintained over centuries on the bottom rung of an exploitive social system evidently was to cling to cultural patterns that by their existence challenged the naturalness and certitude of day-to-day subordination.

However, a shortcoming of the ongoing efforts to demonstrate connections between the Old and New Worlds, however commendable the motivation, is that they exhibit a "grab bag" quality, often ignoring the subtle transformational processes involved. Furthermore, as Ahlo (1980: 44) rightly asserts, "the uncritical use of the religion and worldview of present-day Africans in such studies as we have rests upon an untenably static conception of African societies" that ignores changes that they have undergone since the seventeenth and eighteenth centuries, including changes wrought by European contact.

The Cultural Background

While we make occasional reference to probable African influences on African American religion in the United States, and do wish to shed light on their significance, our primary aim is not the excavation of African survivals but rather the explication of the actual character and diversity of religion as manifest among African Americans during the twentieth century. Ultimately, we believe that much of the originality and special richness of African American religion rests in the fact that it was forged by a people of African ancestry in the crucible of oppression, first during slavery and later under patterns of segregation, discrimination, brutalization, and economic exploitation. No doubt, African cultural elements were retained and effectively mobilized as part of African American response to life in the United States. We argue, however, that much of the current importance of these African elements derives not from their possible source but in the part they have played and continue to play in the crafting of special mechanisms for social survival, emotional comfort, and transcendent expression under the harshest of physical circumstances. Africanisms give a special temperament to African American religion, contributing features that help account for experiential differences between the religious lives of African and non-African Americans; but extensive syncretism, acculturation, and diffusion of African elements into white society limit the primacy of the search for origins in accounting for these patterns. The need to respond to racism and economic oppression, by contrast, is of such compelling urgency that its effect has closely shaped the very heart and soul of African American religion in all of its complexity.

The Impact of Slavery, Capitalism, and European American Christianity

The development of early African American religion must be viewed in the context of the vicissitudes of North American slavery between the seventeenth and nineteenth centuries. According to Hindess and Hirst (1975: 148), "slave production in the Americas appeared as a specialist agrarian region subordinate to the capitalist mode of production and the capitalist world market." Whereas slavery was the most developed form of production in ancient state societies, such as Greece and Rome, it was articulated with and subordinate to mercantile capitalism during the period of European expansion in the New World. In this context, slaves as human capital functioned as an important tool of production for the creation of surplus-value or profit.

Economies, however, never function in direct fiscal form. They are always mediated by symbolic systems capable of transforming cold economic relations into patterns of life and meaning that meet a basic human need for purpose, order, inspiration, and expression. Religion is one such symbolic system. And, with regard to slavery, Christianity played a critical role in sustaining this mode of exploitation as a component of peripheral capitalism. Five functions that Christianity performed on behalf of slavery are identifiable.

(1) It provided an ideological rationale for the enslavement of Africans and the social cohesion of white society:

(2) It was part of the deculturation process that the slaves were subjected to after arriving in the Americas;

(3) It had the effect of subduing and pacifying the slaves;

(4) It helped enhance the profitability of the slaves by ensuring their willingness to work hard under adverse conditions.

(5) It functioned to create uniformity among peoples of diverse cultural backgrounds.

Nonetheless, even though a black child was baptized after the arrival of the first slave ship at Jamestown, Virginia, most slaves in North America during the seventeenth and eighteenth centuries were unbaptized or nominal Christians (Du Bois 1903b: 10). Several factors initially impeded the process of slave conversion. Many slaveowners feared that baptism would make slaves free. This dilemma was resolved by the passage of legislation between 1664 and 1706 in at least six colonies denying that baptism changed the status of a slave (Raboteau 1978: 99). The Church of England established the Society for the Propagation of the Gospel in London in 1701 in order to minister not only to the American colonists but also to people of African ancestry. But due to a shortage of missionaries, only a relatively small number of slaves actually were instructed by the society's missionaries. Furthermore, since in the eyes of the Anglican church proper religious instruction required considerable time, many slaveowners considered conversion as uneconomical. The constant exhortations by the British government and the Bishop of London urging slaveowners to convert their slaves "frequently struck the planters as meddling by outsiders in affairs which only insiders could fully understand" (Jordan 1968: 209). In keeping with racist views, many slaveowners asserted that their slaves were intellectually incapable of understanding the subtleties of Christian dogma. Raboteau (1978: 102) suggests that "[t]he most serious obstacle to the missionary's access to the slaves was the slaveholder's vague awareness that a Christian slave would have some claim to fellowship, a claim that threatened the security of the master-slave hierarchy. Even after other fears had been removed by legislation or by argument, unease with the concept of spiritual equality between master and slave caused slave owners to reject the idea of Christianizing their slaves." Commonly, slaveowners voiced ever-present fears that conversion would make the slaves difficult to manage and perhaps even prompt them to rise up against their masters. Finally, an unknown number of slaves resisted attempts to convert them to the white God of the oppressor.

The missionaries attempted to dispel slaveowners' fears by arguing that converted slaves would be more industrious and docile laborers. In 1768 the Society for the Propagation of the Gospel defended slavery while pleading with the slaveowners to treat the slaves kindly as well as feed and clothe them adequately. For the most part, attempts to convert and give religious instruction to the slaves during the eighteenth century in North America were a failure.

Growing concern about conversion of blacks occurred during the Great Awakenings. By 1734–36, a revival in the vicinity of Northampton, Massachusetts, resulted in the conversion of some blacks (Raboteau 1978: 128). Many whites and a number of blacks joined the new evangelical churches—Methodist, Baptist, and Presbyterian—during the First Awakening. George Whitefield and many other evangelists traversed the length and breadth of the colonies, preaching the gospel to crowds that included African Americans. The First Awakening emphasized spiritual equality rather than racial equality, as is indicated by Whitefield's affirmation of slavery in a private letter to John Wesley in 1751 (Jordan 1968: 214). Large numbers of blacks did not join the Methodist and Baptist churches until after the American Revolution.

The Second Great Awakening (1770–1815) had an even more profound impact on African American religiosity than did the first. The New Light Presbyterians, the Separate Baptists, and the Methodists spread the evangelical message to the new southwestern frontier. The Great Western Revival, which was "inaugurated in 1800 by the Gasper River and Cane Ridge camp meetings in Kentucky, embraced blacks, who eagerly participated in the tumultuous exercises which became characteristic of frontier revivalism. The camp meeting proved to be a powerful instrument for accelerating the pace of slave conversions" (Raboteau 1978: 132). The Western Revival spread to surrounding states, including Virginia, North Carolina, South Carolina, Tennessee, and Georgia. Launched by the Presbyterians, the camp meeting became the focus of the Second Great Awakening and was quickly "adopted by other evangelical denominations and finally became a distinctly Methodist institution" (Ahlo 1980: 53).

American Methodism inherited a strong antislavery impulse from its founder, John Wesley. Indeed, Wesley urged the English reformer William Wilberforce to fight the slave trade until American slavery was completely eradicated (Richardson 1976: 51). Early Methodist preachers called for the abolition of slavery and demanded that all Methodist slaveholders free their slaves immediately. Methodist conferences between 1780 and 1784 condemned slavery as contrary to the Christian gospel. The Conference of 1784 even called for the excommunication of any member who purchased or sold a slave.

The Methodists were by no means the first religious group to oppose slavery. The Quakers are generally credited as being the staunchest opponents of slavery in the period prior to the American Revolution. Yet, as Philip S. Foner (1976: 10) so tellingly observes, "it is abundantly clear that the appeals of the antislavery Quakers went largely unheeded when they interfered with the demand for bound labor. In an era of economic expansion, Philadelphians, including Quakers, used slave labor for their manpower needs since the flow of white servants had declined, and not until white indentured laborers became available in sufficient number to meet their needs did the abolitionist appeals begin to produce more than a few dozen manumissions." Moreover, some Quaker societies conducted racially segregated religious meetings and buried black members in separate cemeteries (Cowing 1971: 114).

Contrary to the conventional view that abolitionism rested upon moral and religious grounds, it would be more correct to argue that it was the product of the complex interaction of material and ideological factors. During the mercantile period, there is little doubt that slavery was a significant element in the process of capital accumulation that led to the Industrial Revolution (Williams 1944). Despite this, the need of industrial capitalism for raw materials from and new markets in the colonies rapidly made slavery obsolete. Adam Smith conjectured as early as 1751 that chattel slavery retarded industrial development in the colonies and argued in 1776 in *The Wealth of Nations* that slave labor was more expensive than free labor. British capitalists began to recognize that the slave trade was impeding the economic development of the African continent. In addition to exploiting Africa as a crop-producing region for the home market, Britain desired to end the slave trade because its abolition would deny its European competitors, especially the French in the Caribbean, a source of labor (Wallerstein 1979).

These abolitionists believed in freedom of trade, of conscience and of wage contracts. Therefore they opposed slavery as being contrary to the word of God and to individual human dignity, as well as to one's God-given right to dispose of one's labor to best advantage. These arguments won the support of many religious groups, especially Quakers, at home and missionaries abroad. The latter viewed the slave trade as an obstacle to the diffusion of Christianity, and therefore favored the substitution in its place of "legitimate trade" in agricultural products. "Christianity, Commerce, and Civilization," they maintained, were interconnected and inseparable. (Stavrianos 1981: 197)

Across the Atlantic the emphasis on a diversified agricultural economy and the increasing availability of low-cost labor from Europe greatly contributed to the abolition of slavery in the North. During the colonial period many white craftsmen and mechanics in the cities supported the abolition of slavery since they perceived their slave counterparts as an economic threat (Foner 1974: 4). The emancipation of slaves in the North, however, resulted in their exclusion from most of the skilled trades—the beginning of the "split labor market," which has continued to the present day. In contrast, slavery did not die such an easy death in the South. Ironically, some southerners, including George Washington, believed that changing economic conditions coupled with the spirit of the American Revolution would spell the demise of slavery. In fact,

> *between 1782 and 1790 more than ten thousand Negroes were freed in Virginia alone. This was the period just following America's War for Independence, when there was much talk of liberty, equality, and freedom, and—what was very important—it was the period when worn-out tobacco lands made owning slaves no longer profitable. It was quite easy to convince a slaveholder, who was losing money on his slaves, that slavery was evil and should be abolished.* (Huberman 1960: 176)

Indeed, some Virginia planters did begin to wonder if slavery had exhausted its profitability. Many felt that they would be better off if their slaves were freed and even returned to Africa. Largely as a result of a strikingly high rate of increase of manumissions, the free black population in the United States increased from 59,557 to 186,466 between 1790 and 1810 (Frazier 1949: 55).

Such economic facts help to explain why evangelical preachers with antislavery sentiments proselytized among the African Americans of the Upper South during the Second Great Awakening. At the same time, many slaves saw that the ideology of the Second Awakening had implications beyond that of spiritual equality. In the camp meetings and in their aftermath, the slaves sometimes found themselves on the same social plane as their white brethren.

Ironically, technological innovations gave slavery a new lease on life. The invention of the power loom and the steam engine led to a tremendous increase in the demand for raw cotton. According to Woodman (1966: 5), "English imports jumped from an average of about one million pounds during the first half of the eighteenth century to about 56,000,000 pounds in

1800. Gradually the demand began to outstrip the traditional sources of English supply—the West Indies, the Isle of Bourbon, the Levant, and Brazil—and prices edged upward."

The Revolutionary War prevented Americans from immediately catering to the spiraling English demand for cotton. Following the war, however, planters in the Sea Islands area of South Carolina and Georgia began to grow long-staple, black-seed cotton. The growth of this variety was restricted to the coastal plain. The short-staple variety of cotton, grown in some inland areas of South Carolina and Georgia in the early 1790s, required tedious manual separation of its seeds. The appearance of Eli Whitney's cotton gin in 1793 suddenly made the production of short-staple cotton highly lucrative. It was not long before cotton production transformed the southern plantation economy as well as American capitalism generally. The new kingdom quickly spread to Alabama, Tennessee, Mississippi, Louisiana, Arkansas, and Texas. Cotton was grown by some small farmers, but its highest profit margin accrued from the use of slave labor. As a result of these developments, the Upper South discovered that its surplus slaves could be sold to the highest bidders in the expanding cotton lands to the southwest. In addition to the efforts by northern abolitionists, the campaign that resulted in congressional abolition of United States participation in the international slave trade in 1807 included the efforts of "groups in the Upper South seeking economic advantage from their slave surplus" (Geschwender 1978: 140).

With the exception of the Quakers, the early Methodists were the most ardent in their opposition to slavery. However, beginning with the general conference of 1784, the Methodist rules against slavery underwent a steady process of erosion. The initial abolitionism of the Baptists was never as great of a threat to the slaveholders as that of the Methodists because "they had no regular conferences at which constant declaration against slavery could be made" (Sernett 1975: 38). As the Baptists improved in social status and grew in numbers, they dropped their concern with the downtrodden and evolved into a mainstream southern denomination. As a result of these economically driven transformations, Christianity increasingly emerged as a vitalizing component of the second wave of slave-based production.

The Establishment of Plantation Missions

On December 2, 1832, Charles Colcock Jones, a Presbyterian minister, was appointed the first missionary of the Association for the Religious Instruction of Negroes—an organization established by planters in Liberty County,

Georgia. He authored a book, *Religious Instruction of the Negroes*, and a pamphlet, *Suggestions for the Religious Instruction of the Negroes*, both of which gained wide circulation and set the stage for the use of Christianity as a bulwark of the slave system.

In addition to instilling morals and obedience in the slaves, the missionaries, like Jones, contended that religious instruction would prevent the eruption of slave revolts, such as those led by Denmark Vesey in 1822 in Charleston, South Carolina, and by Nat Turner in Southampton County, Virginia, in 1831. As Cornelius (1999: 2) argues, "Missionaries perpetuated the image of a patriarchal slave system based on religious values and preparation of slaves and masters for a better future in this world and the next." Given the growing strength of the northern abolitionist movement, which included in its ranks many evangelical ministers, southern evangelicals offered religious instruction as evidence that slaveowners respected the humanity of their slaves. Abolitionists were blamed for the passage by the 1830s in most southern states of laws that forbade teaching slaves to read and write, restricted or banned preaching by blacks, and required white supervision of slaves' religious meetings. The prohibition on preaching by blacks, however, must have been welcomed by at least some white missionaries since they faced competition from popular black lay preachers conducting praise meetings.

The Methodists quickly emerged as leaders in the development of religious instruction among the slaves. The schisms along sectional lines among the Methodists in 1845 intensified efforts on behalf of plantation missions without arousing slaveowner animosity. In 1845 representatives from the Methodist, Presbyterian, and Episcopalian churches convened in Charleston, South Carolina, in order to foster missionary work among the slaves (Sernett 1975: 53). The Baptists had made many black converts, but they were latecomers in creating a systematic program of religious instruction among the slaves. Upon its establishment in 1845, however, the Southern Baptist Convention instructed its Board of Domestic Missions to provide religious outreach to black people.

A small portion of the northern clergy and laity became involved in religious instruction among the slaves, despite white southern hostility to outside interference. On September 2, 1846, the American Missionary Association was created in Albany, New York, for this purpose. As opposed to this organization, which denounced fellowship with slaveowners, the Southern Aid Society (formed on September 28, 1853 in New York City) "restricted its activities to the promotion of the Gospel and pledged to treat 'our Southern fellow-citizens and fellow-Christians with generous confidence . . . with paternal appreciation'" (Sernett 1975: 55).

It is difficult to infer the actual impact of the evangelical efforts among blacks during the antebellum period. Many slaves probably internalized the Christian message in one form or other even though they remained outside the formal structures of specific religious bodies. Conversely, some slaves clearly resented the message of subservience taught by the plantation missionaries and rejected it out of hand as "white man's religion." Many slaves viewed southern white religion as being hypocritical as a result of their comparison of the stated ideals of the Christian gospel with the behavior of their masters and mistresses. Some believed that their owners would be damned for their cruelty (Levine 1977: 34). Finally, black converts did not simply adopt Christianity as it was preached by white evangelicals. Rather, as we will see in greater detail later in this chapter, "[t]hey blended it with their own folk religion, partly African in origin, and thus created a message of love and mutual support, of their own worth as black people, and of their ultimate deliverance from bondage. Their Christianity served as a bulwark against the dehumanization inherent in slavery" (Genovese 1979: 6–7).

Religious Life in the Slave Community

As opposed to the "institutional church" that developed among free blacks, particularly in the North, during the antebellum period, Frazier (1974) referred to the religion of the slaves as the "invisible institution." Mechal Sobel (1979: xvii) contends, however, that the existence of at least partially independent black churches from the 1750s on "substantiate the thesis that the so-called hidden institution, the black church of the slave period, was not hidden at all; that the black church was a known and well-established institution." Yet it is important to note that many of these churches were located in towns and cities, and consequently had little direct impact upon the great majority of plantation slaves.

Patterns of Integration, Segregation, and Separatism in Slave Religion

Slaves worshipped in a wide variety of settings: with whites, with free blacks, exclusively with fellow slaves, and in private. Many slaveowners provided their slaves with passports to attend religious services in towns or on other plantations. Slaveowners were more likely to take house slaves and some of those with higher positions in the slave hierarchy to religious services at white churches than they were to take ordinary field workers. Slaves were required to sit in separate galleries on one side, in the rear, or in the balcony of the sanctuary. They were usually not expected to play an active role in the service, except perhaps in the singing of white hymns. "There were occasionally slaves who just could not 'behave themselves' and started 'shouting' in the middle of the service, but generally the experience seems to have been more or less uninspiring" (Ahlo 1980: 164). White preachers sometimes delivered a special sermon to the slave congregants immediately after the regular morning service or later in the afternoon. Needless to say, these sermons generally instructed the slave to "obey your masters." Blacks sometimes also had classes with one of their own as the leader or "watchman."

Since slaves often did not find services in white-controlled churches to be especially meaningful, they resented the requirement to attend. Despite this, others went voluntarily or found the trip into town an opportunity for a social outing and a reprieve from the oppressive routine of plantation life.

Because slaveowners often granted their slaves freedom of choice as to church membership, many of them flocked to the Baptist and Methodist churches. Several interpretations exist as to why the Baptists and Methodists found greater appeal among blacks than did the Episcopalians, Presbyterians, and Congregationalists. Herskovits (1941) asserted that the Baptists were especially attractive to African Americans because baptism by immersion resembled initiation rites associated with West African cults. Just as the water spirits induced devotees to jump into a stream, lake, or river, the Holy Spirit occasionally prompted a Christian convert to shout for joy upon emerging from the baptismal waters. In a somewhat similar vein, Sobel (1979: 107) argues that evidence for the "thesis that the black Baptists achieved a unique and extraordinarily significant synthesis of the African and Baptist cosmos rests on comparative analysis of their visions." The Methodists did not practice baptism by immersion, but they also shouted, emphasized the conversion experience, and continued the "holy dance." In contrast to such arguments, Genovese (1974: 107), who by no means denies the impress of African religion on African American religion, maintains that "the greatest advantage held by both Baptists and Methodists, with their particular strength in the countryside and in the cities respectively, was that they worked hard to reach the blacks and understood the need to enlist black preachers and 'assistants' to work with them." The Baptists with their organizational flexibility permitted a wide latitude in religious style. In reality, it seems plausible that both ritual compatibilities with West African religion and certain evangelical policies gave the Baptists and Methodists an edge over other Protestant groups in making converts among black people.

Whites were anxious to either supervise slave religious meetings on the plantation or have blacks attend integrated churches in the towns in the aftermath of the slave rebellions led by Vesey and Turner. But the numerical predominance of blacks in many congregations became increasingly annoying to their white members, who often found it difficult to control the exuberance of their alleged social inferiors. Consequently, as Genovese (1974: 235) observes, "[d]uring the last three decades of the antebellum period Baptists, Methodists, Presbyterians, and others accelerated, both by design and simply by taking the path of least resistance, the long-developing trend toward racial separation within the churches."

Given the racism of white Christians, the movement toward religious separatism was welcomed by both free blacks and slaves. Slaves frequently met for services apart from whites whenever the opportunity arose, despite the continuation of white-led or supervised religious meetings on the plantations. In addition to Sunday evening services, the slaves conducted religious meetings at the end of the work day one or even more times a week. That these services sometimes lasted until the early hours of the morning, rendering their participants rather exhausted in the performance of assigned labor, was probably more disturbing to the slaveowners than their actual occurrence. Such meetings were conducted in the slave quarters, "praise houses," "hush arbors," or, if greater seclusion was required, deep in the woods, swamps, or caverns. The slaves built the hush harbors of poles and brush in or near the slave quarters and used crude planks from small logs for seats (Cornelius 1999: 9). In keeping with the planters' fear of their clandestine nature, religious meetings sometimes indeed did provide a cover for "various forms of resistance, ranging from slave revolts to individual escapes" (Ahlo 1980: 157). In many cases, however, slaveowners exhibited relatively little concern with the nonwork lives of their labor force. In fact it was generally difficult to enforce laws prohibiting slaves' religious meetings conducted in the absence of whites.

In addition to religious meetings that were attended either exclusively by slaves or by slaves in the presence of one or two supervising whites, baptisms, marriage ceremonies, funerals, and annual revivals often involved greater numbers of whites (Raboteau 1978: 219). Camp meetings constituted high points in the religious life of the slaves. When the intensity of their religious fervor proved to be offensive to the whites present, the slaves removed themselves to a more secluded spot so that they could express themselves more fully and freely.

It is important to add that not all slaves in the United States accepted a version of Christianity. Some, if not many, continued to subscribe to traditional African beliefs or Islam (Raboteau 1978: 4–7). The existing evidence suggests that there was relatively little overt antagonism between Christian and non-Christian slaves, however (Ahlo 1980: 190).

The Black Church Independence Movement

Scholars referring to "independent" black churches during the antebellum period often fail to emphasize that independence is a matter of degree. As Wilmore (1983a: 74) observes, "Black people enjoyed no real freedom or equality of ecclesiastical status in either the North or the South. It never occurred to white Christians that the equality denied their brothers and sisters in civil society should at least be made available to them within the church." In referring to some of the congregations often cited as early independent black churches, such as those in and about Savannah, Georgia, and Williamsburg and Petersburg, Virginia, Sernett notes that their autonomy was often severely limited by the requirement that slaves who attended them had to receive a pass from their masters and by white involvement of one sort or another in their internal affairs. In his view, "if a particular congregation was composed primarily of free Negroes, had title to its place of worship, a black pastor, and could conduct its business affairs without harassment, it can be called 'independent'" (Sernett 1975: 112). It is highly doubtful whether very many black churches, at least in the South, enjoyed this degree of independence during the antebellum period. The emergence of "independent" black churches, however, became commonplace in the South after the Civil War, particularly in urban areas. Even those churches, while exercising a considerable control over their internal affairs, encountered limitations because of the unavoidable reliance upon white financial patronage.

Thus it seems appropriate to develop a classification of separate black churches that recognizes varying degrees of autonomy or self-regulation. The following list describes degrees of independence of black churches during the eighteenth and nineteenth centuries. Concrete examples of the types and subtypes of churches in this list will be given in the following discussion of black Baptist and Methodist churches during the eighteenth and nineteenth centuries.

A. Nonaffiliated black congregation

B. Church affiliated with a white-controlled association or denomination
   1. Black congregation pastored by white minister
   2. Black congregation pastored by a black preacher or minister but supervised by a white individual or committee

C. Church affiliated with a separate black church regional association

D. Church affiliated with a black national denomination

Most black churches in the South conformed to laws requiring them to be affiliated with white-controlled religious bodies, but "[m]any known independent black churches never joined any association. These ranged from 'private churches' where chapels were owned by black pastors, and which were as idiosyncratic as their owners chose to be, to very 'regular' Baptist churches such as Lott Carey's Providence Baptist Church. . . ." (Sobel 1979: 185). Furthermore, although after the Nat Turner rebellion of 1831 many black Baptist churches in Virginia and probably elsewhere were formally led by white preachers, unofficially they exerted considerable control over internal affairs and functioned on a quasi-independent basis.

Despite limits on their freedom, independent black churches constituted the one institution where black people were able to act as a community, especially in the South. As we will see in greater detail in chapter 3, the African Baptist and Methodist churches established during the nineteenth century embodied many of the functions and forms of what became the present-day mainstream congregations and denominations in the black community. These early churches provided:

(1) an arena for the formation, maintenance, and expression of African American culture;

(2) a social support network for participants, ranging from formal structures such as mutual aid and burial societies to informal ones that allowed for camaraderie and recreation;

(3) a set of honorable titles and awards not achievable in the larger society; and

(4) a context for the acquisition and practice of leadership and organizing skills that sometimes were transferred to social activism in the larger society.

Black Baptist Churches in the Eighteenth and Nineteenth Centuries

The appearance of separate black Baptist churches was an outgrowth of the First and Second Great Awakenings. More black people were attracted to the Baptists than to the Quakers, the Anglicans, Congregationalists, Presbyterians, and even the Methodists. African Americans functioned as full members in at least some early mixed Baptist churches and even preached to mixed or even predominantly white congregations, but the growing concern for respectability among white Baptists precluded any possibility of meaningful racial integration. According to Sobel (1979: 188), "[t]he earliest Southern Black churches generally began not as outgrowths of mixed churches but as independent Black churches. Blacks, generally converted at revivals, met together (very often in areas in which there were no white Baptist churches) and sought to become the body of Christ." While most early black Baptist churches were pastored by free people or ex-slaves, several of them were established by slaves. In some cases, in fact, slaveowners provided meeting places and financial support for the churches. Nevertheless, most of the early black Baptist congregations that emerged in the antebellum South fell under types A, B-1, and B-2 in the list above. Furthermore, separate black Baptist congregations were located primarily in towns and cities but drew from both free blacks and slaves in surrounding rural areas for membership.

Because of their emphasis on the autonomy of the local congregation, as opposed to the centralized ecclesiastical structure that the Methodists inherited from the Anglicans, it was easier for separate black Baptist congregations to emerge. Yet, as we will see in the next section, this decentralized feature was an important factor in preventing black Baptists from developing denominational structures until well after the Civil War. Once black Methodists broke completely from the Methodist Episcopal church, in contrast, they were able to erect denominational structures within a relatively short period of time.

Scholars have debated over which was the first "independent" black Baptist church in North America. One notable candidate for this distinction was a slave congregation established sometime after the Separate Baptist revival of 1735 on the plantation of William Byrd III near the present-day community of Mecklenburg, Virginia (Sobel 1979: 102). Both Sernett (1975: 111) and Raboteau (1978: 139–41), however, maintain that the Silver Bluff Church in South Carolina, established sometime between 1773 and 1775, was the earliest black Baptist church in North America. Due to events related to the American Revolution, in 1793 the congregation appears to have relocated itself as the First African Baptist Church of Augusta. Other early independent black Baptist churches were established in Savannah, Georgia, and in various parts of Virginia during the late eighteenth century.

The African-Baptist faith took root among northern blacks, many of whom were fugitive slaves and free blacks from the South, during the first decade of the nineteenth century. The earliest northern black Baptist churches —such as the Joy Street Baptist Church (established in 1805) in Boston, the Abyssinian Baptist Church (established in 1808) in New York City, and the First African Baptist Church (established in 1809) in Philadelphia—appear to have emerged as protests to discrimination in racially mixed congregations (Pelt and Smith 1960: 48–52).

Black Baptist churches in the Midwest were the first to organize separate black regional associations, despite their somewhat later appearance. The first of these was formed in September 1835 as the Providence Baptist Association by six Ohio churches, which were composed primarily of ex-slaves (Sobel 1979: 215–16). Like their white counterparts, these black associations were concerned with domestic missions, mutual aid, and educational activities. Above and beyond this, abolitionism was one of their major concerns, as is evidenced by the Providence Association changing its name to "the Providence Antislavery (Colored) Baptist Association." In 1840 a group of black churches, many of which retained membership in white-controlled associations, in New England and Middle Atlantic states created the American Baptist Missionary Convention. The Providence Association and the Wood River Association merged in 1853 to form the Western Colored Baptist Association.

Most black Christians worshiped with whites in racially mixed congregations, despite the existence of African Baptist churches in the antebellum South. According to Boles (1983: 201), "[n]orthern churchmen, however, saw the South after the war as a fertile mission field, with four million freedmen as possible converts. Northern churches rushed to establish southern branches of the African Methodist Episcopal Church, the African Methodist Episcopal Zion Church, and the Methodist Episcopal Church, North, for example." In response to racial discrimination, thousands of freed blacks withdrew from white-controlled congregations, associations, conventions, and denominations. Black Baptists from the North, many of whom were ex-slaves, were unable to conduct evangelical work as effectively as the African Methodists in the South because of the relatively decentralized nature of Baptist policy. Nevertheless, membership in black Baptist churches jumped rapidly with an influx of freed people.

After the Civil War, several fledging attempts to forge a national black Baptist denomination met with varying success. The northeastern-based American Baptist Missionary Convention merged with the western group to form the Consolidated Convention and held its first official meeting in Nashville, Tennessee, two years after the end of the Civil War (Washington 1986: 60–65). Following several damaging schisms, the collaboration unraveled and finally dissolved at its annual meeting in Cincinnati in 1879.

The growing ascendancy of nationalist sentiment among black Baptists, in large measure prompted by racist policies in the various white Baptist conventions with which they had cooperated in certain areas (e.g., missions, education, publishing), led to the consolidation of a black denomination uniting southern and northern Baptists in 1895 (Washington 1986: 182–85). The still-prominent National Baptist Convention, USA, Inc., came into existence in Atlanta after the adoption of a resolution before the 1894 meeting of the Baptist Foreign Mission Convention (established in 1880) in Montgomery, Alabama, to merge itself with the American National Baptist Convention (est. 1880) and the Baptist National Education Convention (est. 1893). The Foreign Mission, Home Mission, and Educational boards assumed the functions of these separate bodies.

Black Methodist Churches during the Eighteenth and Nineteenth Centuries

Black Methodists, although slower to found independent churches, were able to move toward denominational structures well before their Baptist brethren. It is important to mention, however, that the growth of both the African Methodist Episcopal church and the African Methodist Episcopal Zion church was limited and confined mainly to the North during the antebellum period.

The story of the African Methodists opens in post-revolutionary Philadelphia—a time and place that found churchgoing blacks scattered about in a diversity of religious groups but concentrated "in great numbers among the Methodists, and particularly at St. George's Church, where they formed a sizable segment of the membership" (George 1973: 40). Under the effective leadership of Richard Allen and Absalom Jones, two prominent black members of St. George's, a group of free blacks organized in May 1787 the Free African Society, a mutual aid organization dedicated primarily to providing members with proper burials and support for their widows and children. In tune with reigning values, the new society also urged its members to work hard and be thrifty so as to prosper, to practice marital fidelity, and to refrain from the consumption of alcohol. Due to discriminatory practices on the part of whites, members of the Free African Society made a final and historically celebrated break with St. George's Church sometime between 1787 and 1792 (George 1973; Sernett 1975). After severing ties with St. George's, the majority of schismatics favored joining the Episcopal church, despite Allen and Jones's announced preference to remain within the Methodist fold. Allen established a meeting place in a relocated blacksmith shop, which in short time was too small for its growing congregation. Upon completion of a larger building, the schismatics dedicated it as the African Episcopal Church of St. Thomas on July 17, 1794. Jones was ordained the deacon of the church in 1795 and the first black priest in the Protestant Episcopal church in 1804 (Richardson 1976: 73). Differences with Jones and his continued allegiance to the Methodism ultimately led Allen to start his own congregation, which was dedicated as the Bethel African Methodist Episcopal Church on July 29, 1794, by Bishop Francis Ashbury of the Methodist Episcopal church.

Rev. Daniel Coker, who had led the formation of another African Methodist congregation in Baltimore, and Richard Allen called a general meeting of concerned black Methodists in Philadelphia on April 9, 1816. Sixteen delegates from congregations in Baltimore; Philadelphia; Wilmington, Delaware; Attleborough, Pennsylvania; and Salem, New Jersey, resolved to unite as the African Methodist Episcopal (AME) church. After Coker refused nomination to serve as the bishop of the new denomination, Richard Allen was elevated to this status.

Prior to the end of the Civil War, the AME church found its most fertile fields in the North and Midwest. Whereas in 1826 the church had 7,937 members in three conferences (Philadelphia, Baltimore, and New York), by 1856 it numbered 19,437 members and had established the Ohio (1840), Canada (1840), Indiana (1855), and Missouri (1855) missions as well as several other foreign missions, especially in Haiti (Richardson 1976: 112). The AME church was banned from most areas of the antebellum South by slaveholders who feared that it would serve as an inspiration for slave revolts, but there is some evidence indicating that an AME congregation existed in Mobile, Alabama, as early as 1820 (Walker 1982: 20). Morris and Marcus Brown established a Methodist congregation among free blacks in Charleston, South Carolina, in 1816. However, when it was alleged that Morris Brown played a part in the Denmark Vesey insurrection of 1822, the Charleston church was closed and Brown was forced to flee and seek refuge in Philadelphia.

The racially mixed St. John's Street Church in New York City served as the focal point for the development of what eventually became the second major black Methodist denomination, namely the African Methodist Episcopal Zion church. Segregation in church facilities and lack of access to influential positions convinced several black members of St. John's in the late 1780s to obtain permission to conduct occasional prayer meetings by themselves. Although the church was incorporated on April 6, 1801, and controlled its own property, it continued to depend upon St. John's for ordained elders. In 1813 a trustee of Zion formed a second black Methodist congregation, called Asbury, that also continued to function under the jurisdiction of St. John's but eventually became affiliated with the AME church.

Apparently, a few ministers were dissatisfied with the refusal of the Methodist Episcopal church to ordain black preachers, but most members initially were not ready to sever ties with the parent body. Consequently, Zion and Asbury, along with separate black congregations from Long Island, New Haven, Easton (Pennsylvania), and the Wesleyan church (an AME break-off in Philadelphia) met in New York on June 21, 1821, and selected one of the Methodist bishops as their superintendent. When the 1824 general conference of the Methodist Episcopal church failed to grant the Zionites official recognition as a separate black conference, they finally announced their independence from the parent denomination (Norwood 1974: 174). By 1829 the Zionites were supporting conferences in New York and Philadelphia. On the eve of the Civil War, the African Methodist Episcopal Zion church (the qualifier "Zion" was finally added in 1856 to avoid confusion with the AME church) had some 4,600 members and had added the New England (1845), Allegheny (1849), Genesee (1849), and Baltimore (1859) conferences (Richardson 1976: 137).

The aftermath of the Civil War had an unparalleled impact on the growth of black church membership, transforming the region into a vast mission territory and enabling rapid increases in church memberships. The AME church particularly established itself in southern cities and AME Zion church found a geographic niche particularly in North Carolina. The AME Zion church created the North Carolina Conference in New Bern, North Carolina, in 1864 which in turn served as the basis for the Virginia Conference (1866), the South Carolina Conference (1867), the Georgia Conference (1867), and the Tennessee Conference (1872) (Martin 1999: 65). Approximately two-thirds of the black members of the Methodist Episcopal Church, South, separated themselves into other congregations and denominations (Dvorak 1991: 114). Whites in the Methodist Episcopal Church, South, disdainfully referred to the African Methodist churches and the Methodist Episcopal Church, North, as "political churches" (Dvorak 1991: 157). While both the AME church and the AMEZ church entered the South as bitter rivals, they also faced fierce competition from the Methodist Episcopal Church, North, and, after 1870, the Colored Methodist Episcopal church. The African Methodists did some proselytizing among the unchurched but concentrated upon gaining the black members of the Methodist Episcopal Church, South.

The two African Methodist denominations appealed to many freedpeople, but most black ministers of the Methodist Episcopal Church, South, were opposed to their efforts. The literacy requirements that the AME church had established for its ministers frightened many of those who "held their positions at the sufferance of the ME Church, South, which was not known for its advocacy of an educated black clergy" (Walker 1982: 75). Despite its later suspicions about the role of the African Methodist missionaries in politicizing southern blacks, initially some of its white ministers encouraged black congregations to join either the AME church or the AMEZ church so as to undermine the recruitment activities of the Methodist Episcopal Church, North, which they regarded as an agent of radical Republicanism. Ultimately, the ME Church, South, shifted tactics with respect to the ME Church, North, and the African Methodists by creating the structure for a rival black Methodist denomination. In December 1870, the first general conference of the Colored Methodist Episcopal church convened in Jackson, Tennessee, where two black bishops—Henry Miles and Richard H. Vanderherst —were elected. White missionaries affiliated with organizations such the American Baptist Home Mission and American Missionary Association also established black congregations (Montgomery 1993: 37).

Protest and Accommodation in Slave Religion and the Independent Black Church Movement

Sociological interpretations of slave religion, by and large, view it as having been primarily accommodative toward antebellum southern society. In observing that slave religion was characterized by emotionalism, fatalism, and submission, W. E. B. Du Bois (1903a) argued that the slave, "losing the joy of this world, eagerly seized upon the offered conceptions of the next." Stressing the otherworldliness of traditional Christianity that had been internalized by the slaves, Mays (1968) also asserted that their conception of God was compensatory. More recent studies of slave religion, by contrast, recognize its juxtaposition of elements of protest and accommodation (Harding 1969; Genovese 1974; Marable 1981). According to Genovese (1979: 7), the "moral content of black religion emerged to justify accommodation and compromise as a properly Christian response and simultaneously drew the teeth of political messianism and revolutionary millenialism." In his penetrating historical analysis of slave religion in the United States, Raboteau appears to give roughly equal weight to its twin accommodative and rebellious dimensions:

> *Slave religion has been stereotyped as otherworldly and compensatory. It was otherworldly in the sense that it held that this world and this life were not the end, nor the final measure of existence. It was compensatory to the extent that it consoled and supported the slaves worn out by the unremitting toil and*

capricious cruelty of the "peculiar institution." To conclude, however, that religion distracted slaves from concern with life and dissuaded them from action in the present is to distort the full story and to simplify the complex role of religious motivation in human behavior. It does not always follow that belief in a future state of happiness leads to an acceptance of suffering in this world. . . .

To describe slave religion as merely otherworldly is inaccurate, for the slaves believed that God had acted, was acting, and would continue to act within human history and within their own particular history as a peculiar people just as long ago he acted on behalf of another chosen people, biblical Israel. Moreover, slave religion had a this-worldly impact, not only in leading some slaves to acts of external rebellion, but also in helping slaves to assert and maintain a sense of personal value—even of ultimate worth. The religious meetings in the quarters, groves, and "hush harbors" were themselves frequently acts of rebellion against the proscriptions of the master. (Raboteau 1978: 317–18)

Though slaves were often depicted as a rather submissive and docile lot, in Herbert Aptheker's (1943) *American Negro Slave Revolts* a radically different view of slave protest emerges. It is difficult to determine exactly to what extent religious thought inspired rebellions among the slaves in the United States. Wilmore (1983a: 31), for one, feels that "there is good reason to believe that religion was considerably more involved than the most accessible records reveal." If one considers that a major source of information about the religion of the slaves was that left by the white missionaries who evangelized among them, it should not be surprising that the relationship between religion and rebellion was downplayed, if not totally neglected. On the other hand, it is imperative that we not exaggerate the revolutionary potential of the slave insurrections. According to Genovese (1970: 395), "[a]s many of Aptheker's critics have pointed out, most of the two hundred fifty revolts probably never happened, being the imagination of hysterical or self-serving whites, insignificant plots that never matured, or mere local disturbances of a questionable nature."

Little doubt can be raised, however, that religion played a critical part in the three most significant slave rebellions in North American history, namely those spearheaded by Gabriel Prosser, Denmark Vesey, and Nat Turner. In the months prior to the insurrection outside of Richmond in 1800, Prosser attempted to recruit followers by proclaiming that he had been aware since childhood of his divine election as a deliverer of his people. Viewing himself as the new Samson, Prosser believed he would lead the slaves in the establishment of a black Kingdom in Virginia. Vesey, an ex-slave who belonged to the Hampstead Church (a branch of the African

Methodist Association of Charleston), found a following among both free blacks and slaves. While not claiming to be a religious leader per se, in his recruitment activities for the rebellion of 1822, Vesey appealed to scriptures by likening the situation of the slaves to that of the ancient Israelites. Gullah Jack, one of Vesey's lieutenants and a well-known conjurer, mobilized those slaves who were closer to African religious traditions. Finally, in the slave rebellion of 1830 in Southampton County, Virginia, Nat Turner explicitly portrayed his mission in terms of the prophetic tradition of the Old Testament.

However, the prospects of a successful revolt of the sort that occurred in Haiti in the late eighteenth century were very poor in the United States. For one thing, whereas the slaves generally were in the clear majority in the Caribbean, they generally were not in most areas of the antebellum South. Furthermore, unlike the situation elsewhere, the southern planter was able to incite and mobilize racism to pit blacks and lower-class whites against each other. Additionally, a significant distinction existed between the religion of the slaves in the United States and those in other areas of the Americas. Genovese (1970: 402–3) contends that "religion (Islam, voodoo or Afro-Catholic syncretisms) proved to be an essential ingredient in slave cohesion and organized resistance throughout the hemisphere, but in the United States the enforced prevalence of Protestant Christianity played an opposite role." The southern ruling class utilized both legal and extra-legal coercion to maintain its dominance over blacks. As Genovese (1974) demonstrates in his application of Gramsci's concept of hegemony, the southern ruling class's ideology of paternalism, which relied heavily on religious rationales, served a more significant function in regulating the behavior if not the thinking of the slaves. Paternalism in the minds of the slaveowners justified their appropriation of the labor of peoples of African ancestry.

Indeed, slave owners were able to convince themselves that slavery was an uplifting experience for blacks, not only exposing them to proper work habits and self-discipline but bringing them to the saving grace of Christianity as well. In that blacks were thought to possess an innately childlike mentality and to be in danger of eternal damnation without the benefit of Christian indoctrination and baptism, the southern planters, with the assistance of their clerical supporters, embraced the idea that slaveholding constituted "a duty and a burden" and attempted to instill these same beliefs in their slaves. That the slaves internalized portions of the slaveowners' ideology is manifested by their belief that Jesus the Savior was a meek, humble, and compassionate figure with whom they could converse about their earthly sorrows. For the most part, they did not imagine him as a messiah-king bearing a bloodied sword and mounted on a noble steed who would lead them in liberating battle against their sinful oppressors. As a system of ideological hegemony, paternalism created a tendency for slaves to identify with their plantation community rather than with one another as a social class. It enabled the slaves to accept the slaveowners, at least tentatively and on principle, as brothers in Christ, while at the same time permitting them to recognize some of them as "good masters" and others as "bad masters."

Despite this set of arrangements and the fact that much of the African heritage of the slaves had been submerged or destroyed, the hegemonic control over their religion was in the end imperfect and partial. As Genovese (1974: 659) observes, "[t]he slaves' religion developed into the organized center of their resistance within accommodation; it reflected the hegemony of the master class but also set firm limits to that hegemony." The slaves were able to discover elements in Christianity that were consistent with their own aspirations and experience-shaped perception of reality. As Scott (1990: 124) noted, "much of the resistance to the dominant culture [takes] the form of religious heterodoxy and heresy." The slaves did not exhibit a simple unilateral acceptance of the whites' cosmology. Rather, as Levine (1977: 37) indicates, "[f]or the slave, Heaven and Hell were not [abstract] concepts but places which could well be experienced during one's lifetime; God and Christ and Satan were not symbols but personages with whom meetings or confrontations were quite possible." While heaven indeed might at times be constructed in otherworldly terms, it might be viewed, depending on the context, as Africa, Jerusalem, Canada, or some other sought-after earthly sanctuary. Jesus was a knowable helper who approached humans as imperfect beings rather than as condemned sinners. Most slaves found the notion that one could be punished for all eternity for some human shortcoming to be incomprehensible and unjust. In their construction of a theology of hope and survival, the slaves preserved their own sense of identity and dignity while resisting the psychological trauma of an oppressive social system.

As in the case of slave religion, interpretations of the role of black churches during the nineteenth century vary widely. For Frazier, the disenfranchisement, relegation to inferior schools, and subjection to mob violence that southern blacks underwent following Reconstruction forced them to seek sanctuary in their churches:

> *The Negro church with its own forms of religious worship was a world which the white man did not invade but only regarded with an attitude of condescending amusement. The Negro church could enjoy this freedom so long as it offered no threat to the white man's dominance in both economic and*

social relations. And, on the whole, the Negro's church was not a threat to
white domination and aided the Negro to become accommodated to an inferior
status. The religion of the Negro continued to be otherworldly in its outlook,
dismissing the privations and sufferings and injustices of this world as tempo-
rary and transient. The Negro church remained a refuge despite the fact that
the Negro often accepted the disparagement of Negroes by whites and the dom-
ination of whites. But all of this was a part of God's plan and was regarded
just as the physical environment was regarded. What mattered was the way h
was treated in the church which gave him an opportunity for self-expression
and status. (Frazier 1974: 51)

Frazier's emphasis on the accommodative dimensions of black churches
is countered by others who stress their emancipatory activities during the
nineteenth century. Wilmore refers to the independent black church movement as *"the first Black freedom movement"* (1983a: 78; emphasis in original)
and as "a form of Black insurrection against the most vulnerable and accessible form of institutionalized racism and oppression in the nation: the American churches." Indeed, especially in the North, representatives of black
churches were involved in antislavery, abolitionist, and proto–black nationalist movements. The Convention movement began as a secular adjunct of
northern black churches and opposed slavery, black emigrationism to Africa
as advocated by the American Colonization Society, and racial discrimination. Following a competition between the AME church and the AME Zion
church for its meeting place, Richard Allen presided over the first National
Negro Convention in 1830 at Mother Bethel Church in Philadelphia.
William Lloyd Garrison organized the Anti-Slavery Society on January 6,
1832, in the basement of the Joy Street Church with some of the members
of this famous black Baptist congregation participating in the event (George
1973: 76). AME and AME Zion churches served as stations in the underground railroad that assisted slaves in escaping to the North and Canada. All
of the black Baptist associations addressed some degree of opposition to
slavery, often in the form of resolutions.

But the abolitionism of the black churches was far from radical in tone.
As Sernett (1975: 150) observes, in their posture toward slavery Richard
Allen and Absalom Jones were "gradual emancipationists" who placed "their
trust in the wise providence of God, . . . looked to that day when all men
would be free, and urged the slaves to take comfort in the Gospel promises
until that time." It was not until 1856 that the general conference of the
AME church raised the issue of slavery to a central place on its agenda,
when the Bethelites discovered that some members held slaves until such
time that the latter could repay their purchase price. A resolution ranking

slavery as a greater evil than drinking barely passed at the annual meeting of the Western Colored Baptist Convention in 1859 (Washington 1986: 35). Militant clergymen such as Rev. Henry Highland Garnet, a Presbyterian who at the National Negro Convention in 1843 in Buffalo bravely counseled the slaves to rebel against their masters, were the exception rather than the rule. Furthermore, in contrast to a few high-status black clergymen belonging to the Episcopalian, Presbyterian, and Congregational churches, most ministers in charge of black congregations within white-controlled denominations were hobbled in their ability to protest publicly (Swift 1989).

Marable traces the roots of modern black politics to the activities of black religious leaders during the nineteenth century:

> *Hundreds of Black Methodist and Baptist ministers were active in electoral politics during Reconstruction. In 1865, for example, the presiding officer of the African Methodist Episcopal Zion Church, the Reverend J.W. Hood, issued a series of radical reforms for Blacks which included the right to vote. There were a large number of Black ministers elected to their respective state constitutional conventions in the late 1860s. . . . In the 1880s, Black ministers like attorney T. McCants Stewart, pastor of New York City's Bethel African Methodist Episcopal Church, served on that city's school board and championed the necessity for Black political independence. Many Black religious leaders supported Black nationalist programs, including C.H. Philips, editor of the Colored Methodist Episcopal Christian Index, and Henry M. Turner. Without exaggeration, it can be stated that almost every Black minister was something of a politician, and that every aspiring Black politician had to be something of a minister.* (Marable 1983: 197)

For example, James Walker Hood, an AME Zion clergyman, became a prominent political leader in North Carolina during and following the Civil War and participated in the Freedmen's State Convention in 1865 and the State Reconstruction Convention in 1867–1868 (Martin 1999: 79).

With the realization that Emancipation and Reconstruction had not ensured civil rights for African Americans, some black clergymen became advocates of black separatism. Henry McNeal Turner, an outspoken AME bishop from the South, vociferously advocated the return of at least some blacks to Africa. Further, he asserted that blacks should worship a black God and were not obligated to give their political allegiance to the United States.

As George (1973: 160) observes, political activism in black churches "revealed only a small, although very obvious, part of the total: the more substantial portion of [the black preacher's] ministry was less public in nature, and consisted of serving the needs of his congregation." If anything, the routine activities of the church, along with attempts to ensure its survival in the face of meager funds and white hostility, prevented greater attention to the important social issues of the day. With the reinstitution of restrictive black codes throughout the South in the late nineteenth century, political activities increasingly became relegated to the narrow confines of in-house church issues, a submerging of black church activism that was to last until the civil rights movement in the 1950s and 1960s.

In sum, black Christianity in the United States, from its birth in the camp meetings and the hush arbors of the slave period, can best be understood as a dialectical unity of protest and accommodation. Because it combines, and endlessly recombines, both elements in a contradictory and changing whole, African American religion is impossible to adequately characterize and is forever resistant to facile generalization. For every conclusion, there are contradictory moments and cases. For every summation, there are anomalous instances. Serving as it does a dual purpose as both shield and sword in an often harsh and always hostile environment, black religion has emerged as a sometimes stormy admixture of diverse responses to oppression and heartfelt yearning for both spiritual and material salvation.

II

Religious Diversification during the
Era of Advanced Industrial Capitalism

African American religion underwent a rapid process of diversification in
the early decades of the twentieth century, particularly with the appearance
of a wide array of new Holiness, Pentecostal, Spiritual, Islamic, and Judaic
sects. To a large extent, the baseline for this diversification was the "black
rural church." As an ideal type, the black rural church is embodied especially
in the black Baptist congregations but also in many of the black Methodist
congregations that existed and continue to exist in the countryside, towns,
and even small cities of the South. The rural church was the "sentimental
model" that the migrants hoped to participate in when they attended the
large mainstream congregations in the cities of the North and South. Since
they often felt marginal in the stratified mainstream congregations, a significant number of these lower-class migrants attempted to recreate the ethos
of the rural church in storefronts and converted residential buildings. In
many cases, services at first were held in the apartment or home of a
self-proclaimed religious leader before his or her congregation grew large
enough to financially support larger meeting quarters.

The migrants often established independent Baptist congregations or
exclusively lower-class Baptist congregations that sooner or later became
affiliated with one of the national Baptist denominations. Often, however,
the migrants were attracted to the "black gods of the metropolis"—the
charismatic prophets and messiahs of various emerging sectarian movements
(Fauset 1971). Charismatic, and sometimes flamboyant, individuals such
as W. D. Fard, Elijah Muhammad, Father Divine, Daddy Grace, Elder
Michauex, Bishop Cherry, and Prophet Jones are among the better known
of these religious figures, but countless minor "gods" captured the religious

imagination of the migrants. One of these lesser "gods" is Reverend Bobby E. Lawson, the "Royal Elect Ruler" of God's Elect Kingdom of Eternal Life (a storefront in Flint, Michigan, whose "First Annual Kingdom Jubilee" Baer attended during the summer of 1979).

The Black Rural Church

At the turn of the century, over 90 percent of African Americans resided below the Mason-Dixon line. While many southern cities underwent relatively rapid industrialization and population growth following the Civil War, blacks did not migrate to them in as great numbers as whites did. As Rose (1948: 64) notes, "The tradition persisted that Negroes could not operate machines, or at least that was the argument used to keep them out of the new occupations. Negroes lost out in many of the skilled occupations they had formerly held." In 1910 about 80 percent of southern blacks lived in rural areas (Marks 1985). Consequently, the vast majority of religiously active blacks were attending relatively small churches in the countryside, towns, and small cities of the South at the time the Great Migration began. Furthermore, nearly all black rural churches were and continue to be found in the South.

In attempting to capture the ethos of the black rural church as an ideal, the major part of this section discusses the denominational forms, the politico-religious organization, the religious and secular activities, and the role of the black rural church within the castelike system of the South. While we describe black rural churches as they existed prior to the civil rights movement, we will speak in the ethnographic present. The remainder of this section presents a postscript on the status of the black rural church since the civil rights movement.

It is important to note, however, that the black rural church was not a static institution during the first half of the twentieth century. Unfortunately, no one to date has conducted a detailed study of the changes that the black rural church underwent during this period. Nevertheless, some general patterns have been recorded. The out-migration of African Americans from the rural South to the cities of both the North and the South had a significant impact on the black rural church during the first half of the twentieth century. As a consequence, most black churches in the countryside have not had regular or full-time ministers. While out-migration contributed to an increase of this pattern during the twentieth century, it was not uncommon in earlier times. Some churches merged in order to deal with the shortage of ministers, but many continued to function despite heavy losses in membership. According to Raper (1936: 362), "A few Negro churches in Greene (Georgia) have been disbanded since 1922 because of the virtual depopulation of certain areas in the western half of the county, and many of the churches still intact are so weakened that they do not have Sunday services and now raise for their once-a-month preacher but a fraction of what they raised before the exodus."

Despite the general pattern of out-migration, not all churches underwent a decline of membership during the first half of the twentieth century. In his survey of 483 black rural churches, Felton (1952: 46) found that, from 1939 to 1949, 190 (39.3 percent) increased in membership whereas 57 (11.8 percent) remained stationary and 236 (48.9 percent) underwent a decline in membership. The revival appears to have undergone some decline in significance during the twentieth century. Mays and Nicholson (1933: 253) reported that in the early 1930s most ministers in their survey asserted that "the revival no longer causes large numbers of 'conversions.' It is now used largely for reviving the church membership."

Denominational Variation

Many of the smaller communities in the rural South exhibit both socioeconomic and religious homogeneity. The frequency of such a pattern contributes to the assertion among many southerners "that if a Negro is not a Baptist someone has been tampering with him" (Dollard 1937: 225). Many of the black Baptist churches in small southern communities are not affiliated with any of the national Baptist denominations. For example, Shrimp Creek (pseudonym), a village of some four hundred blacks located about fifteen miles south of Savannah, has five "independent small wooden Baptist churches" (Ottenberg 1959: 8).

Even in small black communities where denominational variation exists, its significance may be minimized. In some instances, Baptist and Methodist congregations in small black communities share the same building on alternate Sundays. The pattern of informal ecumenism between the Baptists and Methodists is further illustrated by the common practice of attending other churches on Sundays when one's own congregation is not conducting a service.

Denominational affiliation is more pronounced in towns and small cities, where it often reflects social status. As Johnson (1941: 155–56) observes, "Much of the rivalry between churches of the same or different denominations, and the uneconomical multiplication of churches and cults, traces back to this ferment of competition for social position and prestige within the Negro community." Nevertheless, even in these communities the significance of denominational variation is also de-emphasized. In Cottonville (pseudonym), a Mississippi town with six black churches (two Baptist, one Methodist Episcopal, one AME, one belonging to " a sect called the Christians," and one Church of God in Christ), "The unimportance of sectarianism is frequently stressed, both from the pulpit and in conversation among the laity. On fifth Sundays of the month an inter-denominational Sunday is held, in which all participate except the Church of God in Christ" (Powdermaker 1967: 233).

While a fair amount of cooperation and visiting occurs between Missionary Baptist and Methodist congregations, especially in the smaller communities, most Holiness, Pentecostal, and Primitive Baptist congregations hold themselves—and are held by others—at a distance from the conventional churches. In Cottonville, members of the Church of God in Christ, whose ecstatic rituals are considered excessive by the Baptists and Methodists, view themselves as being more spiritually minded than their detractors. On St. Simons Island off the Georgia coast during the late 1920s, "the initial handful of converts to 'holiness' did not originally intend either to renounce their memberships in the Baptist churches or to form a congregation or church of their own. But the Baptists objected to the shouting and dancing of the 'saints' in the midst of their otherwise decorous worship service, and the converts were forced out" (Goldsmith 1985: 93). In certain rural parts of the Upper South, black Primitive or "Hard Shell" Baptists, who stress the predestination, foot washing, and extreme congregational autonomy, refrain from interaction not only with other religious groups but with secular organizations such as Masonic lodges (Sutton 1983).

Politico-Religious Organization

The common responses to the shortage of ministers in the countryside have been intermittent scheduling of Sunday services and greater lay control over church affairs. As Mays and Nicholson (1933: 252) found in their survey of Sunday services in rural churches, most do not conduct services every Sunday. Of the 185 congregations in their sample, 10.8 percent of them held one service per month, 61.1 percent two services, 7.5 percent three services, 16.8 percent four services, and 3.8 percent eight services. Rural church membership varies widely depending in large part on local economic opportunities. For example, Richardson (1947: 49–51) found that, whereas 89.7 percent of the blacks (many of whom were small farm owners) in Northumberland County, Virginia, belonged to churches, only 10.0 percent of the blacks in Mississippi County, Arkansas (a predominantly tenant area), did so.

In Shrimp Creek, each church conducts a regular communion service with its visiting minister once a month (Ottenberg 1959: 12). The five Baptist congregations are served by four ministers (all of whom pastor Savannah churches), with two of them being served by the same minister. Some of the ministers also serve other rural churches near Savannah. In addition to the pattern of city ministers intermittently visiting outlying congregations, many rural churches are served by circuit preachers who may live in the countryside themselves. For example, Rev. Louis Cole (1901–81), a black Baptist preacher, for many years conducted services in the North Mississippi–West Tennessee area, visiting Gatewood Church every first Sunday, Mount Vernon every second Sunday, Mount Gilliam every third Sunday, and Lagoshen every fourth Sunday. "In addition, he visited many other churches as a guest, substitute or assistant—at revivals, weddings, funerals, baptizings, fund-raising programs and special annual services such as Mother's Day, Founder's Day, Men's Day, Children's Day, Appreciation Day, Homecoming Day" (Walker 1985: 51).

Due to the pattern of absentee ministry, lay leaders assume most of the responsibility for maintaining and operating the churches in the countryside. In Shrimp Creek, the deacons maintain control over the Baptist churches and, although ministers are selected by the congregation following guest sermons, exert considerable input in this decision (Ottenberg 1959). They also administer church finances, supervise collections, organize prayer services and various social activities, hold joint meetings with other churches, and act as "spiritual fathers" to those seeking a conversion experience or "vision" to join the church.

Positions of church leadership are correlated with financial means, age, and sex. In Kent (pseudonym), a small Piedmont milltown, "status in the church is often equated with faithfulness of contribution—and to some extent with amount" (Lewis 1955: 114). Similarly, most of the deacons in Shrimp Creek are descendants of the older well-established families and, while far from being affluent, "fall roughly into the middle or upper range of the economic level of the community" (Ottenberg 1959: 11).

Active church members in Missionary Baptist and Methodist churches generally belong to one or more of several age-graded and/or sexually exclusive auxiliaries such as Sunday schools, usher boards, choirs, and choral clubs. In addition to these organizations, Missionary Baptist churches have all-male deacon boards and all-female missionary societies, and the Methodists have boards of trustees, stewards, stewardesses, and deaconesses as well as missionary societies. The usher board, which often has junior and senior branches, is "one of the most prevalent, most active and most popular of rural church organizations" (Richardson 1947: 104).

Although nearly all ministers in rural areas are male, women greatly outstrip men in membership, attendance, and active participation. In his observations of three black Churches—the Field's Street Methodist Episcopal, the Mount Prospect African Methodist Episcopal Zion, and the Union Baptist—as well as in nearby churches of the hinterland of Kent, Lewis found that, "Despite the fact that nominal control and direction are in the hands of the men, women apparently contribute a larger share of the financial and moral support. Church politics is primarily a man's game, but the women wield great indirect power. In a recent, prolonged dispute in one of the churches, the women staged a coup and temporarily assumed authority as a means of forcing a truce between factions in the church" (Lewis 1955: 106). Women's auxiliaries also sponsor most of the church entertainments and "socials."

Religious and Social Events

In the typical rural black church, "the monthly [or bi-monthly] preaching service is the all important activity" (Raper 1936: 364). Since rural people have more difficulty seeing friends and acquaintances during the week than do town or city dwellers, the preaching service permits members and visitors to reestablish social bonds and to share information and gossip. The clothing of the congregants manifests the social nature of this event. Women wear their finest dresses, hats, hose, and jewelry. Men generally wear suits, even on hot humid summer days, although some of the younger men and adolescent males may wear only dress shirts and ties.

The Sunday preaching service, regardless of whether it occurs in a Baptist or Methodist church, almost invariably includes certain ritual events such as prayer, hymn-singing, testifying, "penny" and regular collections, the sermon, and the benediction, but the exact sequence in which these occur varies considerably from congregation to congregation (See Johnson [1934: 153–61] Powdermaker [1967: 249] and Ferris [1972] for accounts of services in rural black Baptist congregations). In each instance, however, the sermon, which occurs in the latter half of the service, functions as the focal ritual event of the service. Whereas ritual events prior to it collectively serve as a prelude to the climatic sermon, which may last over an hour, events afterwards are anticlimactic. Following Gennep (1960), it can be argued that pre-sermon events separate worshippers from the profane world whereas post-sermon ritual events reincorporate them back into this world. Separation is best exemplified in the testimony session, during which various members, especially women, review recent hardships in their lives and express their joy in being able to discard them, at least temporarily, since they are in the process of entering a sacred liminal period. More so than any other portion of the service, the sermon or "message" constitutes a liminal period during which the preacher may act out the journey to heaven or various members of the congregation become ecstatic or "shout."

> *The sermons of the average rural minister are long and repetitious. Phrases are emphasized by gestures and vehement expression. The congregation responds constantly with shouts of approval and conviction. It is expected that several persons, mostly women, will "get happy" and give expression to long hysterical seizures in the course of which they testify to their salvation, release some pent-up sorrow over deceased relatives, or bemoan a hard and hopeless life or the unjustified slander of their character in the community. The most emotional parts of the sermons are those which make reference to troubles and offer homely solace or inspired promise of reward or punishment by God, as the situation warrants.* (Johnson 1941: 143–44)

The sermon and associated events often last well over an hour. Reincorporation is symbolized by generally having the regular collection, which may take up to a half hour or even more, after the sermon.

Next to the preaching service, the Sunday school is theoretically the most important regularly scheduled religious event in the black rural church. Even on those Sundays when a minister preaches at the church, he does not generally supervise the Sunday school, and rarely attends. "If he arrives at the church before the Sunday school is over, it is not an uncommon sight to see him standing on the outside of the building visiting with men, waiting for the Sunday school to adjourn" (Felton 1952: 48). The Sunday school usually meets every week and consequently is run almost exclusively by laypeople. Attendance at the Sunday school is invariably less than at the preaching service and in many instances other religious and social events. In a survey of 105 rural Sunday schools in four southern counties, Richardson (1947: 108) found that "Six schools had but five members or less; twenty-six had between eleven and twenty members, and fifty-three . . . ranged between twenty and fifty members." The larger Sunday schools are age-graded into two or more classes. The principal teaching method includes reading, explaining, and commenting upon Biblical passages.

On those Sundays when the minister is absent, or during the week, church auxiliaries or even nonchurch groups, such as lodges, schools, and burial societies, conduct prayer meetings and special programs. According to Richardson (1947: 104), usher boards play an instrumental role in organizing "sings," to which groups from other churches are invited, as well as other recreational affairs. Women's auxiliaries periodically sponsor church entertainments such as chicken hunts, suppers, candy pulls, and fashion shows, which are attended not only by church members but also the larger community (Powdermaker 1967: 278–85). A major purpose of such events is the raising of funds for the church and for needy members.

Since many black people were introduced to Christianity at the revivals of the Great Awakenings during antebellum times, it should not be surprising that traditionally the revival constitutes the high point of the annual ritual cycle. Churches generally conduct revivals in the late summer or early fall after the harvest. Revivals, which may last as long as two weeks, often function as a homecoming day when former inhabitants of the community who have moved to other rural areas or even faraway cities return to their place of origin. As Hamilton and Ellison (1930: 25) report, "The typical revivalist is a man of extravagant gifts and unrestrained emotions [who] speaks fluently and loudly" and is an adept singer of songs "arranged to tunes which have a rhythmic swing." As a consequence, ecstatic behavior in the form of "shouting" and dancing is much more common during revivals than during regular religious services. While the Holiness and Pentecostal revivals tend to be the most exuberant, even members of some of the more sedate Baptist and Methodist congregations "get happy" on these occasions (see Dollard [1937: 253–56] and Powdermaker [1967: 253–56] for detailed accounts of revivals).

Traditionally, many young people joined the church under the emotional excitement of the revival. In the Baptist churches, baptisms by immersion at the bank of a river may occur as an aftermath of the revival. The converts wear white, shirtlike garments and white headpieces. While most of the baptized emerge out of the water calmly and matter-of-factly, some do so shouting for joy (See Dollard [1937: 236–39] for a detailed account of a baptism).

Funerals are extremely significant religious occasions that often prompt more ecstatic behavior than preaching services or even revivals (See Johnson [1934: 162–79] and Powdermaker [1967: 249–52] for detailed accounts of funerals). For many church members, a proper burial constitutes the most valued goal in their lives.

> *The basic pattern combines these essential steps: return of corpse to the home the evening before the funeral; on the day of the funeral body and funeral party are driven to the church. . . . The corpse is borne into the church while the church bell tolls and the choir sings or the minister utters an incantation; a song is sung by the choir and audience; a scripture reading and/or prayer is delivered by assisting minister or prominent church member; obituary, acknowledgement of flowers, messages, and testimonies by friends and neighbors are delivered; a*

eulogy is rendered by the pastor; final view of the remains is taken by the audience; internment follows, with male volunteers filling the grave after final rites.
(Lewis 1955: 109)

The Role of the Black Rural Church in the Southern Caste System

The role of the black church as it functioned in the countryside and small town of the South prior to the civil rights era must be considered in the larger context of the castelike system within which it was embedded. As Hraba (1979: 268) observes, "The racial caste system that followed Emancipation meant the exclusion of cheap black labor from nearly all trades save agrarian labor and domestic service, the segregation and exclusion of blacks from decent education, and the almost complete exclusion of blacks from the political process in the South." The defeat of the Populist movement, with its fragile white-black tenant alliance, in the 1890s heightened color-caste distinctions through an extension of Jim Crow laws and practices throughout the South. While many whites were economically little better off than the black masses, the few social privileges accorded under the caste system served to provide them with a sense of superiority over blacks. Conversely, many whites left the land for skilled and semi-skilled jobs in the textile mills and even some unionized trades. "The 1910 census reveals that over half of the gainfully employed blacks were in agriculture. More than half of the remainder (one-fourth of the total) were in domestic occupations. Thus on the eve of World War I, the vast majority of black Americans were located in the South and engaged in the production of agricultural staples. The position of blacks not engaged in agriculture had deteriorated greatly. Five out of every six southern artisans in 1865 were black, but only one in 20 was black in 1900" (Geschwender 1978: 169–70).

Blacks also held menial jobs in the lumber industry, coal mining, railroad maintenance, and tobacco factories—most of which were rurally based operations. In the cities and towns, the vast majority of black workers were concentrated in either domestic and personal service or in unskilled positions as porters, draymen, laundresses, and seamstresses (Baron 1971: 16). Similarly, blacks were restricted to the most menial positions in the growing southern textile industry.

In contrast to the existence of a small black middle class or petite bourgeoisie in the cities and, to a lesser degree, the smaller towns, socioeconomic differences among African Americans in the countryside were minimal. Despite marked racial inequalities in land tenure, the number of black-owned farms doubled between 1890 and 1910 due to financial loans that black farmers were able to obtain from black-owned banks (Marable 1981: 52–68). Unfortunately, the decline of cotton prices as a result of the closing of transatlantic commerce upon the outbreak of World War I, the coming of the boll weevil, soil erosion, and a general worsening of race relations in the South translated into the beginning of the demise of the African American land-owning class.

> *Changes in farm ownership were accompanied by changing patterns of tenancy. The number of Black tenants increased from 670,000 in 1910 to almost 700,000 in 1930 and then declined to approximately 500,000 in 1940. White tenants numbered less than 870,000 in 1910, increased to approximately 1,090,000 in 1930 and declined to 940,000 in 1940. The rate of increase in tenancy between 1910 and 1930 was less rapid for blacks than whites, just as the rate of decline between 1930 and 1940 was more rapid. Blacks made up over half the agricultural wage labor force in 1910, but accounted for less than half in both 1930 and 1940. They were driven out of cotton agriculture more rapidly than whites, regardless of status.* (Geschwender 1978: 177)

Given a declining agricultural economy, blacks became an easy target for white hostility. Coupled with the availability of jobs in northern industries created by World War I and the economic prosperity of the 1920s, these conditions propelled massive numbers of blacks to leave the rural areas of the South. As a result of this migration, as well as later ones, the black rural church underwent a tremendous decline in membership and resources.

As is the case for all religious groups in complex societies, the role of the black rural church has been and continues to be multifaceted and paradoxical. The black rural church constitutes the principal center of sociability and a major repository of the black cultural ethos. As Johnson (1934: 150) comments, "it offers the medium for a community feeling, singing together, praying together, and indulging in the formal expressions of fellowship." Black rural churches provide not only a locus for the renewal of social bonds but also a mechanism for assisting members in times of financial need, emergency, and personal sorrow. In the past, they played a major role in community-based education, and they still make regular contributions to Baptist and Methodist higher education funds. Programs are periodically conducted to raise funds for college students belonging to the local congregation. Religious services, social events, and fund-raising are openly recognized as forms of entertainment and opportunities for relaxation. In contrast to the grim puritanical tone of many white evangelical churches, black churchgoers unabashedly see no contradiction between their search for spirituality and having "fun" or a "good time." Although always conditioned by a strong sense of remaining within the bounds of respectability, black church behavior contrasts with its white counterpart in its reigning cultural definition of religious propriety.

In assessing the role of the black rural church within the context of the southern caste system, particularly prior to the civil rights movement, many scholars have argued that on balance it functioned as a cathartic mechanism and a "refuge in a hostile white world" (Frazier 1974: 50) that inadvertently maintained the status quo. Charles Johnson (1941: 169) contended that the black rural church is a "conservative institution" whose "greatest value appears to be that of providing emotional relief for the fixed problems of a hard life." In a similar vein, Powdermaker (1967: 285) asserted that it "serves as an antidote, a palliative, and escape" which tends to "counteract the discontents that make for rebellion." Obviously the black rural church served to alleviate many of the frustrations, anxieties, and fears emanating from economic exploitation and sociopolitical repression that blacks experienced under the castelike structure of the South.

Following Gramsci, it may also be argued that the black rural church constituted a hegemonic agency permitting the southern planter and merchant classes to dominate black people. This is not to say that white elites directly controlled activities that occurred in black churches in small towns and the countryside. In these settings, African Americans have exerted a considerable degree of autonomy over their religious affairs. It is often asserted that the "black church" is one institution over which African Americans are in full control (Powdermaker 1967: 223; Hamilton 1972). In reality, however, black control over churches in the rural South was restricted by the patronage system. As Myrdal (1962: 874) points out, "Poverty often makes the Negro church dependent upon white benefactors."

It was quite common for black ministers and congregations to obtain building materials and financial resources from white patrons in constructing or maintaining their churches in small towns and the countryside. In his study of Old City, Plantation Town, and their neighboring Mississippi counties, Davis (1940: 37–38) found that black ministers often initiated a "gift" relationship with influential whites and attempted to persuade them to assume a patriarchal stance toward the black community. A wealthy white woman stated that a leading black minister in Plantation Town had convinced the members of her social circle to make regular donations toward his salary. Officers of the women's auxiliaries in the four largest black churches in Plantation Town solicited funds for their ministers' salaries and church building funds from upper- and middle-class white women and white storekeepers. Davis, Gardner, and Gardner report the case of the treasurer of a black church and lodge near Old City who served as "patriarch-tenant-manager" over a local group of tenant farmers: "He has persuaded his landlord to make "advances" to tenants in cash rather than in supplies, so that tenants might be able to meet their financial obligations to the church and lodge. The "advancing" of from $12 to $15 every two weeks to a tenant-family provided a steady cash income for these organizations" (Davis, Gardner, and Gardner 1965: 246).

The obvious price that blacks paid for the patronage system was accommodation to the caste system. However, it is important to note that most black rural churches probably received little or no support from white patrons. What kept these churches in check? According to Davis (1940: 56), any black preacher in Plantation Town, Old City, and their hinterlands who attacked the caste system was "in acute danger of being driven out of the area, or whipped." Consequently, black ministers took great caution not to say anything that could be construed by whites as a condemnation of existing race relations. For the most part, however, black religious leaders and churchgoers probably rarely even conceived of the thought of challenging the status quo. As Femia (1981: 33) observes, "the exigencies of survival and day-to-day practicalities restrict mental (or ideological) development, and subordinate even the unwilling and rebellious to the logic and norms of the system."

In some instances, whites directly manipulated black ministers and congregations in order to ensure black subordination. For example, Davis (1940: 34) found that white planters and businessmen in Old City, Plantation Town, and their neighboring counties, with the collaboration of the Negro Business League, "attempted to use the Negro churches during the Great Migration to check the migration of Negroes." On the whole, such instances of direct pressure by whites upon black ministers to maintain the caste system were the exception rather than the rule. In his examination of a large number of sermons delivered by black preachers in the Old City area, Davis (1940: 46–48) recorded no instances of a black preacher attacking the caste system or suggesting any need for economic change. When blacks in Old City expressed outrage at the hanging of two blacks accused of murder, a black minister told his congregation that such sentiments were futile because "We ain't no more than a coon with a collar 'round his neck" (quoted in Davis 1940: 46). The minister of a large black church in the Plantation Town vicinity compared the relationship between his members and God to that between the black tenant and his white landlord.

The hegemonic role of black religion in inculcating the symbols of the color-caste system of the Old South is poignantly illustrated by the annual religious pageant entitled "Heaven is My Home," conducted by one of the leading black churches in Old City during the 1930s (Davis 1940: 67–69). Sponsored by the Old City Garden Club, the pageant was performed before separate black and white audiences. In 1934, about half of the annual income of the church came from the white-sponsored pageant.

> *The pageant represents the dogma of the spiritual and other-worldly Negro, and emphasizes both the humility and the native genius for song of the Negro actors. When the white sponsors had the Negro actors photographed by a news-reel company, they placed them in front of an ante-bellum plantation house, with a group of Negroes dressed in plantation clothes standing around them.*
>
> *The Negroes themselves symbolized the "whiteness" of God and Heaven by placing white or yellow-skinned Negroes in the roles of St. Peter, and the attendant angels. The patriarchal relationship of white to Negroes, and the latter group's humility and social subservience were expressed in the climax of the pageant when an old Negro woman played the role of a "mammy." This role proved the favorite of the white audiences, and was regarded by Negro church leaders as the chief reasons for the financial success of the entertain-ment. The white newspaper in Old City stated that the Negro "mammy" was the chief attraction of the pageant, and emphasized the fact that she was a for-mer slave. Sentiment for the old plantation relationship of Negroes to whites, and for the continuance of the subservient position of Negroes was organized around this figure.* (Davis 1940: 68–69)

The near-totality of the black rural church as a hegemonic institution under the castelike system is exemplified by a sermon entitled "The Poor-Rich and the Rich-Poor" recorded by Hortense Powdermaker. In this ser-mon, a leading black minister in the Cottonville area told a parable about a rich woman who was given her cook's shanty when she went to heaven whereas her cook received a big house for her service to God on earth. Some might interpret the sermon as a subtle critique of the caste system; Powdermaker (1967: 443) argues that it "supports the *status quo* by telling the poor—i.e., the Negroes—that their reward will be in heaven, and that they are rich in their poverty if they worship God." Yet, no stratified soci-ety, even one as rigid as the castelike system of the Old South, has exercised pure dominance. Dominated groups somehow manage to offer resistance to ruling classes or to hegemonic agencies and customs that indirectly fos-ter the ideas of the ruling classes. As opposed to the strong emphasis on eternal damnation characterizing many white fundamentalist or evangeli-cal religious groups, African American Christianity has always stressed the joys of the afterlife. As Powdermaker (1967: 246) notes, "Benevolent mercy rather than stern justice is the chief attribute of the Negro's God. . . . The accent has shifted from hell to heaven, from retribution to forgiveness, from fear to hope."

The Black Rural Church since the Civil Rights Movement

In his assertion that the "black church functioned as the institutional center of the modern civil rights movement," Morris (1984: 4) is by and large referring to the complex of black urban churches in the South rather than to its rural counterpart. Most of the prominent black ministers involved in the civil rights movement, such as Martin Luther King, Jr., and Ralph D. Abernathy of Montgomery, Fred Shuttlesworth of Birmingham, Kelly Miller Smith of Nashville, and Wyatt Tee Walker of Petersburg, Virginia, were leaders of urban congregations (Marable 1984: 71). The migration of blacks to the large and medium-sized cities of the South made it possible for the black urban churches to operate on a scale unattainable in the small cities, towns, and countryside. In contrast, as MacAdam (1982: 92) observes, "the rural church was, in most cases, organizationally weak and conservative in orientation. Both factors served to limit the effectiveness of the rural black church as an institutional vehicle of social change." Nonetheless, an unknown number of black rural churches did play a supportive role in the civil rights movement, and some were among the many southern black churches burned or bombed during the 1960s.

Since the early 1950s, little research has been done on black rural churches. The civil rights movement of the late 1950s and early 1960s transformed many aspects of everyday life in the rural South and eliminated terror as a primary mode of social control. While rural blacks have gained—at least in theory—certain civil rights, such as the legal right to vote, attend integrated public schools, and use public facilities, most of them continue to be subjected to economic exploitation, poverty, racial discrimination, and perhaps more so than before, structural unemployment. In many ways, black rural churches have remained as they were around the turn of the century. In the case of Promised Band, South Carolina,

> *Crossroads, Mt. Zion, and Jacob's Chapel were "the center of all the community" in the 1970's in much the same way as they had been for a century. Membership rates for all churches were high. Seventy-eight percent of the families at Promised Land attended church at least several times a month. . . .*
>
> *There was little realistic difference between being a Baptist or a Methodist at Promised Land. . . .Half the families divided their church loyalties between the two denominations, the result of marriages between Baptist and*

Methodist youths who, like their parents before them, refused to relinquish ties with a church that was second in importance only to their kinship bonds. Children from these households usually attended both churches alternative weeks. Methodist wives often helped serve dinner at Baptist homecomings and Baptist husbands were equally visible at Methodist events. (Bethel 1981: 263)

In a similar vein, Dougherty (1978: 34) reports that in Edge Crossing (pseudonym), a rural black community in north central Florida, the three local Baptist churches are the places where black people of all ages "come after relating with one another through the week in schools, homes, stores, shops, and work." Mt. Calvary Baptist Church holds services on the second and fourth Sundays of the month, St. Peter's on the third Sunday, and Oak Ridge on the first Sunday. On months with a fifth Sunday, the churches rotate responsibility for holding services.

The most extensive survey of black churches since the 1950s was completed recently by a team directed by C. Eric Lincoln and Lawrence H. Mamiya. The rural phase of the project consisted of interviews with 363 clergy who are the pastors of 619 churches in certain "Black Belt" counties of the South. Ongoing migration of blacks to urban areas has left the arrangement of the absentee pastorate intact. The development of interstate highways and improved roads since World War II "led to increased mobility by absentee pastors" (Lincoln and Mamiya 1990: 96). In contrast to Mays and Nicholson's (1933: 254) prediction that the "day of the professional evangelist" was drawing to a close, Lincoln and Mamiya learned that the revival continues to function as a major form of religious renewal. Of the 619 churches in their sample, 542 (87.9 percent) have at least one annual revival (Lincoln and Mamiya 1990: 107). Although many Baptist churches and the Church of God in Christ (Pentecostal) have a ban on women pastors, they permit women to be "evangelists," in which capacity they may preach at revivals or special religious meetings. As opposed to Felton's (1952) finding that only 12.8 percent of the churches in his sample were involved with the National Association for the Advancement of Colored People (NAACP), Lincoln and Mamiya (1990: 109) report that 50.1 percent of the rural churches in their sample are involved with civil rights organizations and activities. It is important to note, however, that the NAACP as well as various other moderate black civil rights organization are no longer regarded by white elites as a serious threat. At any rate, as Lincoln and Mamiya (1990: 113–14) so aptly assert, "Black rural churches became the first institutions to carry the hopes and dreams of an outcast people. If they were not always heroic institutions, they at least contributed to the survival of their people in the most extreme and violent circumstances."

Industrialization, Migration, and Urbanization: The Proletarianization of the Black Peasantry

At the beginning of the twentieth century, nine out of ten blacks in the United States were living in the South, the vast majority in the rural areas. For the most part, African Americans constituted a castelike stratum held in "debt peonage" (Silberman 1964: 46) by the quasi-feudal character of the rural economy. The black codes and other restrictive Jim Crow laws were used to control blacks and thereby provide a manageable and inexpensive labor force. Despite these oppressive conditions, African Americans inhabited a relatively stable society; and it was not until World War I, with black migration primarily to the urban North but also to the cities of the South, that blacks underwent a rapid process of proletarianization.

Several events provided the impetus for the northward relocation of what ultimately amounted to a half million blacks during or shortly after World War I. As Cox (1976: 58) observes, "on the whole, the 'push' of the Negro population from the rural South has been greater than the inducements or 'pull' of the cities." Prior to World War I, the industrial North had relied primarily on European immigrants for a cheap labor supply. An annual average of more than 900,000 immigrants entered the United States from Europe during the period 1910–14, but the onset of the war reduced the annual flow to about 100,000 (Geschwender 1978: 172). At the same time, World War I stimulated the economy and increased the demand for labor, a demand in large part fulfilled by the migration of southern blacks. In the South, the spread from Mexico of the boll weevil, as well as soil erosion and depletion, seriously cut into agricultural productivity. Other push factors included the severity of labor exploitation, the relocation of many agricultural endeavors in the West, and continued lynching and physical intimidation by terrorist organizations like the Ku Klux Klan. Despite the protests of southern businessmen and planters, anxious over the loss of their supply of cheap labor, African Americans began to look to the North as a land of opportunity.

> *Migration out of the countryside started in 1915 and swept to a human tide by 1917. The major movement was to Northern cities, so that between 1910 and 1920 the black population increased in Chicago from 44,000 to 109,000; in New York from 92,000 to 152,000; in Detroit from 6,000 to 41,000; and in Philadelphia from 84,000 to 134,000. That decade there was a net increase of 322,000 in the number of Southern born blacks living in the North, exceeding the aggregate increase of the preceding 40 years. A secondary movement took place to Southern cities, especially those with shipbuilding and heavy industry. . . .* (Baron 1976: 105)

After the war, African American migration to the cities continued. The war's end opened the floodgates once more to European emigration, and the 1920s saw the swelling of anti-foreigner hysteria, culminating in the passage of prohibitive immigration quota laws. Northern capitalists supported this legislation because a seemingly more compliant proletariat had been discovered in the rural South. While the North may have been presented by labor recruiters as the Promised Land, what most blacks found in Detroit, Chicago, Gary, Pittsburgh, Newark, New York, and other cities was considerably less inspiring. In the South they had occupied the lowest rungs of a rigid caste system; in the North—although theoretically possessing more legal rights—blacks (as well as to a lesser degree southern whites) came to occupy the lower echelon in a split labor market (Bonacich 1976). In this capacity, they were frequently used as "scabs" to break strikes and thwart labor-organizing drives. There were instances of cooperation between white workers and black workers during the early decades of the century, but competition for scarce jobs more often than not translated into hostile relations and provoked racist sentiments among white workers. At times this conflict was translated into race riots in which angry whites invaded black neighborhoods. It is important to note that "the riots did not grow out of the inherent racial prejudice of their participants, but rather developed directly from the friction caused by the ways in which black labor was put to use in the North" (Smith 1981: 343).

Analyses of racism (Reich 1971) show that it serves a number of vital functions for an expanding capitalist economy: it rationalizes lower-class living and working conditions; it divides the working class into competing sectors, thereby depressing wages and other benefits; and, because elements of the racist ideology are internalized by members of the pariah group, it keeps the most exploited segment of the working class dispirited and less openly rebellious. Faced with the choice between a minimal existence and starvation, African Americans were unwittingly used as strikebreakers at wages well below those won by white workers in their struggles with the capitalist class. Eventually an accommodation between black and white workers became institutionalized: whites came to occupy the professions and the skilled technical and craft positions while blacks were relegated by and large to semiskilled or unskilled occupations (or perpetual unemployment or underemployment) at the bottom of the labor hierarchy. In more recent decades some blacks have been able to make occupational advances, but the dual labor market essentially remains intact.

The generalization of racism beyond the economic realm—into housing, education, and other areas—ensures its credibility and effectiveness in the marketplace. Black migrants to the cities were consequently herded into decaying ghettos and provided with substandard schools and social services. In the case of Chicago, perhaps the most segregated of northern cities, blacks were systematically excluded from white sections of the city, drastically limited in their choice of jobs, and barred from many places of public accommodation. This discriminatory pattern developed in similar fashion throughout the urban North.

Although the flight of rural blacks into the cities of the North and the South never ceased, the Great Depression of the 1930s slowed the pace considerably. During this desperate period in American history, urban blacks were subjected to severe deprivation, with unemployment reaching devastating proportions and evictions commonplace in black ghettos. In some sections of Chicago's South Side, black unemployment stood at over 85 percent by 1931 (Gosnell 1937). In response to rising social unrest among various segments of the society, the federal government instituted various relief programs, with the Federal Emergency Relief Act having the most impact on poor blacks. Whereas approximately 22,000 black families had been receiving welfare in 1931, a year later this figure jumped to 48,000 (Botempts and Conroy 1966: 296). In 1933, 26.7 percent of urban blacks were on relief, compared with 9.6 percent of white city dwellers (Walters 1970: 91).

World War II ushered in a massive new influx of blacks to the cities. While the demand for labor in defense industries initiated this development, the technological innovations in agriculture spurred the heavy migrant flow after the war. During this period, capital-intensive production supplanted the traditional labor-intensive character of southern agriculture. Mechanical corn and cotton pickers, self-propelled combines, bulldozers, one-man hay balers, and other mechanical devices were introduced on a large scale. Furthermore, the increasing shift to cash crops such as soybeans, which require minimal hand labor, also served to eliminate the need for black agricultural workers. In addition, many black landowners were unable to compete with the better financed and more highly mechanized white-owned farms. During the 1940s just over 1.5 million blacks moved northward. During the 1950s and 1960s still another 2.9 million blacks migrated to the North (Sackey 1973: 42). By 1970 only 52 percent of African Americans were located in the South, and the majority of blacks in the North and the South were situated in urban areas (Baron 1976). Through this process, African Americans were transformed from an agrarian peasantry into a diversified urban proletariat.

In the process, their religious forms changed as well. As the primary institution available for responding to external threat and challenge, as well as internal aspiration and expression, the African American church was remade anew in the shadow of the Great Migration.

The Mainstream Churches and the Rise of the Storefronts and "Black Gods of the Metropolis"

By the turn of the century, what had become the "mainline" or "mainstream" churches in the African American community were well in place in the large and medium-sized cities of both the South and the North. In contrast to the relatively narrow range of denominational variation among

Table 1

*Denominational Variation among Black Churches
in Selected Cities around the Turn of the Century*

	Philadelphia[a]	Atlanta[b]	Chicago[c]
Episcopal	6	1	1
Presbyterian	3	1	2
Congregational	-	1	-
Christian	-	1	1
Roman Catholic	1	-	-
Adventist	-	-	1
Methodist Episcopal	6	4	2
Methodist Protestant	1	-	-
African Methodist Episcopal	14	14	9
African Methodist Episcopal Zion	3	-	1
Colored Methodist Episcopal	-	3	-
Union African Methodist Episcopal	1	-	-
Baptist	17	29	11
Total	**52**	**54**	**28**

SOURCE: Derived from Du Bois 1903b.
NOTES: [a]Census taken in 1897. [b]Census taken in 1901–2. [c]Census date unspecified.

black rural churches, black urban churches even at this time exhibited a fair degree of heterogeneity. As we will see in greater detail later, this heterogeneity became more pronounced during the period between the two world wars. Table 1 illustrates denominational variation among black churches in Philadelphia, Atlanta, and Chicago around the turn of the century.

As in the larger society, denominational affiliation reflected class differences in the black community. As Du Bois remarked at the beginning of the century,

> *At St. Thomas' (Episcopal) one looks for the well-to-do Philadelphians, largely descendants of favorite mulatto house servants, and consequently well-bred and educated, but rather cold and reserved to strangers or newcomers; at Central Presbyterian one sees the older, simpler set of respectable Philadelphians with distinctly Quaker characteristics—pleasant but conservative; at Bethel may be seen the best of the great laboring class—steady, honest people, well dressed and well fed, with church and family traditions; at Wesley will be found the new arrivals, the sightseers and the strangers to the city—hearty and easy-going people, who welcome all comers and ask few questions; at Union Bethel one may look for the Virginia servant girls and their young men; and so on throughout the city. Each church forms its own social circle, and not many stray beyond its bounds.* (Du Bois 1903b: 203–4)

Black congregations affiliated with white-controlled denominations catered to elite African Americans. In turn-of-the-century Atlanta, most members of the black Congregational, Episcopal, and Presbyterian congregations "are at least high school graduates, and a large per cent is composed of business and professional men and women" (Du Bois 1903b: 73). In contrast, the Methodist and Baptist churches exhibited considerable class variation, both from congregation to congregation and within congregations. In the case of Atlanta Methodists, "A great majority of the members of the smaller churches are common laborers and are quite poor. The members of the larger churches are in moderate circumstances, and although most of them are laborers, there is a fair per cent of artisans and business men among them" (Du Bois 1903b: 72). Although in general Baptists tended to be of a somewhat lower socioeconomic status than Methodists, the Baptists churches "were included among the most influential and wealthy churches of the city" (Du Bois 1903b: 73). On the whole, most black Baptists churches catered primarily to working- and lower-class people.

The period between 1900 and World War I saw an increase in the size of the existing black churches as well as the establishment of new congregations affiliated with the mainstream denominations as a result of the gradual but steady migration of rural blacks to the cities. As Gottlieb (1987: 201) observes, as elsewhere, "Black preachers [in Pittsburgh] were important gatekeepers for southern blacks in helping them find jobs, providing food and shelter in church buildings during emergencies, and organizing social or recreational programs." Furthermore, schisms within the older congregations, often initiated by working-class members who revolted against control by middle-class members, also often led to the creation of new congregations. In Chicago, "Most of the Baptist churches were offshoots of Olivet, the oldest and largest Negro Baptist church in the city, while the AME churches were generally founded by dissident parishioners from Quinn Chapel and Bethel Church" (Spear 1967: 91).

Even prior to World War I, some of the larger black congregations attempted to cater to the material needs of southern migrants. The most notable example was the Institutional Church and Social Settlement of Chicago, established in 1900 by Reverdy Ransom, who was destined to become one of the leading bishops of the African Methodist Episcopal church:

> *Institutional operated a day nursery, a kindergarten, a mothers' club, an employment bureau, a print shop, and a fully equipped gymnasium; it offered a complete slate of club activities and classes in sewing, cooking, and music; its Forum featured lectures by leading white and Negro figures; and its facilities were always available for concerts, meetings, and other civic functions. . . . The wide range of social activities was designed to attract lower-class Negroes without church affiliation and sophisticated Negroes who found Institutional's emphasis on the social gospel more appealing than the traditional preoccupation with sin and salvation.* (Spear 1967: 95–96)

In part due to the rise of secular social welfare agencies and lack of adequate finances, this innovative congregation declined before the end of the World War I era. The social services offered by some of the other large black churches were considerably more modest. Olivet Baptist Church in Chicago started a relief program for the unemployed in 1908 (Spear 1967: 92). Bethel AME was the first organization in Detroit to conduct an outreach program among black people by creating a social service department in 1911, and adding labor and housing bureaus a few years later (Kartzman 1973: 140).

Unconventional African American sects proliferated after World War I, but some of these groups began to emerge before the war. "A black congregation that held services in a converted frame residence on Chene Street became the First Church of God in Michigan in 1884, although it did not acquire a clergyman until 1917" (Kartzman 1973: 145). The Holiness Church of the Living God was formed in Detroit in August 1909 by Bishop J. B. C. Cummings (Kartzman 1973: 146). In Chicago, the Holy Nazarene Tabernacle Apostolic Church was founded in 1908 by Natties L. Thornton; the Church of Redemption of Souls, a Spiritualist congregation, was holding services on State Street by 1915 (Spear 1967: 96). In 1896 William S. Crowdy formed the Church of God and Saints, the first black Judaic sect in the United States, in Lawrence, Kansas. The initial step toward the Islamization of black religion occurred with the founding of the Moorish Science Temple by Noble Drew Ali in Newark in 1913 (Essien-Udom 1962).

The process of urbanization that accompanies capitalist expansion has repeatedly been demonstrated to have unsettling effects on rural migrants, not only in industrial societies but also in the Third World. Next to the family, the church—despite its accommodative dimensions—had been the most important institution among African Americans in the rural South. As Williams (1974: 9) observes, "The migration to cities created a social crisis, for it separated masses of blacks from their rural life style and destroyed the social organization which gave meaning to their segregated rural Southern society." Many migrants apparently found more-or-less comfortable niches in the large, well-established Baptist and Methodist congregations of the urban North and South. Olivet Baptist Church in Chicago grew from about four thousand members in 1915 to nearly nine thousand in 1920 (Spear 1967: 177). Many new congregations affiliated with established denominations also sprang up during this period. A survey of five selected northern cities between 1916 and 1926 indicated a 151 percent increase in the number of black Baptist churches and an 85 percent increase in the number of African Methodist Episcopal churches (Scheiner 1965: 99). Pilgrim, Progressive, Provident, Liberty, and Monumental Baptist churches were founded between 1916 and 1919 in Chicago and grew into relatively large congregations within a decade (Spear 1967: 178). In Cleveland, the number of black churches increased from 17 a few years before the Great Migration to 44 by 1918, 78 by 1921, and over 140 by 1933 (Kusmer 1976: 207).

However, the older Baptist and Methodist churches in the African American community simply did not have the resources necessary to meet the material needs of overwhelming numbers of poor migrants. Furthermore, many migrants who had enjoyed positions of leadership and responsibility in rural churches found themselves relegated to the sidelines of the large urban congregations. In addition to seeming more bureaucratic, impersonal, formal, and sedate than their counterparts in the South, the established congregations increasingly adapted themselves to the more secular concerns of a new black middle class (Frazier 1974). Lower-class migrants frequently found they were viewed with disdain by their more affluent northern-born communicants and threatened by their sophistication.

A common strategy adopted by the migrants to deal with this situation was to establish storefront and house churches. Many storefront churches called themselves "Baptist," but Spear (1967: 176) contends that in reality "they often closely resembled the Holiness churches in their uninhibited form of worship." Furthermore, many African American migrants were attracted to the Holiness, Pentecostal, Spiritualist or Spiritual, Judaic, Islamic, and other sects such as the Father Divine Peace Mission movement, and the African Orthodox church, which emerged in tremendous profusion not only in the industrial North but also in many cities of the South. Arthur Paris (1982: 27–28) cautions us not to lump all of the groups that occupied storefronts and house churches with "the welter of other spiritualist, nationalist, or neo-African groups that also used commercial space." The term "storefront" refers to a physical trait shared by many religious groups rather than a sociological category per se. Many substantial black Baptist and some black Methodist churches of today started out as storefront churches.

In their survey of black churches in twelve cities, Mays and Nicholson (1933: 313) found that 777 of a total of 2,104 church buildings that they surveyed were storefronts or converted residences. About half of the 777 storefront congregations were Baptists; many others were of the Holiness and Spiritual varieties. In reality, the percentage of storefront and house churches, at least in certain cities, may have been considerably higher. Also, Mays and Nicholson may very likely have missed many of these churches in their survey. In his survey of 278 black congregations in Chicago, Sutherland (1930: 47) found that 178 (64.0 percent) of them conducted services "in a single room in a vacant store or in an apartment building or in temporary tent quarters." Whereas 65.9 percent of 133 Baptist congregations worshipped in such settings, only 12 out of the 35 AME, AME Zion, and CME congregations did so (Sutherland 1930: 57). Drake and Cayton (1945: 633) found that in Bronzeville 66.4 percent of the "Holiness" congregations, 52.2 percent of the "miscellaneous" congregations, and 50.1 percent of the "Spiritualist" congregations were housed in storefronts. In his survey of 173 black storefront churches in the "Central Area" of Cleveland, Blackwell (1949) discovered that 79 were Holiness/Pentecostal, 71 Baptist, 17 Spiritual, 5 Methodist, and 1 Presbyterian. Given the poverty of the newly arrived migrants, the storefront served as temporary quarters before the congregation grew to such a size that it could afford to purchase or rent a larger noncommercial structure, often a church building being vacated by a white congregation whose members were fleeing to the suburbs.

Following Wallace's (1956) concept of revitalization movements, Harrison (1971: 244) describes storefront churches as "deliberate, conscious, organized efforts of migrants to create a more satisfying mode of existence by refurbishing rural religious behavior to an urban environment." While storefront churches in the black community attract many individuals, they originally emerged—even prior to the Great Migration—as a response to the needs of the rural migrants, and they still serve this function. As opposed to the anonymity of the large urban church, the storefront provides its members with a sense of belonging to a religious community in which the pastor knows them personally. Furthermore, the storefront church, as Frazier (1974: 59) observes, permits its members to worship with a "maximum of free religious expression" which generally includes shouting, holy dancing, and the singing of spirituals and other popular religious hymns.

In the midst of the social crisis faced by the migrants from the rural South, black religion became even more diversified than it had been before. As Nelsen and Nelsen (1975: 43) observe, "The story of the urban church in the postwar years is largely an epic of established black Protestantism trying to meet a major crisis with limited material resources and, all too often, with limited imagination as well—and of a restless population first searching for renewal at the old familiar altars, then turning to the storefronts, the Father Divines, the black Muslims in their quest for a religion that could make the new and strange burdens of urban life somehow tolerable." In the 1920s Harlem offered migrants houses of worship such as the Metaphysical Church of the Divine Investigation, Mt. Zion Pentecostal Church, St. Matthew's Church of the Divine Silence and Truth, Congregation of Beth B'Nai Abraham, the Temple of Luxor, Sanctified Sons of the Holy Ghost, and Live-Ever-Die-Never Church (Reid 1926; Osofsky 1965: 144). This process of diversification later would be accelerated by the insecurities induced by the Great Depression, which affected blacks even more adversely than it did whites. According to Wilmore (1983a: 162), "the Black community, by the end of the decade of the 1930s, was literally glutted with churches of every variety and description."

Tables 2 and 3 roughly indicate the diversification that occurred within African American religion during the 1920s and 1930s. Of the many unconventional religious groups found in the black urban neighborhoods, the Holiness, Pentecostal, and Spiritual churches were the main varieties. An examination of table 2 reveals that Holiness, Pentecostal and Spiritual congregations were more common in northern cities than in southern ones. Table 3 shows that, at least in Chicago, Holiness, Pentecostal and Spiritual churches increased in both numbers and in percentages of the total number

Table 2

Congregations Belonging to Selected Religious Bodies in Twelve Cities

	7 Southern Cities		5 Northern Cities		All 12 Cities	
	No.	% of total sample	No.	% of total sample	No.	% of total sample
Baptist	661	61.5	446	45.3	1,127	53.6
Methodist	209	20.0	160	16.3	369	17.5
Holiness/Pentecostal	95	8.8	244	23.7	339	16.1
Spiritual	36	3.3	78	7.6	114	5.4

SOURCE: Adapted from Mays and Nicholson (1933: 210–22).

Table 3

Black Congregations in Chicago, 1928 and 1938

Denomination or Sect	1928		1938	
	Number of Churches	Percent	Number of Churches	Percent
Baptist	133	45.1	215	45.3
Black Methodist	35	11.9	42	8.9
White-controlled groups	22	7.4	27	5.6
Community Churches, Inc.	3	1.0	10	2.1
Holiness/Pentecostal	56	19.0	107	22.6
Spiritual	17	5.8	51	10.7
Others	29	9.8	23	4.8
Total	295	100.0	475	100.0

SOURCE: Adapted from Sutherland (1930) and Drake and Cayton (1945).

of black churches between 1928 and 1938. Drake and Cayton (1945: 413) also found the "existence of a number of small denominations indigenous to Bronzeville and such all-Negro 'cults' as the African Orthodox church, the Christian Catholics, the Temple of Moorish Science, and numerous fly-by-night groups organized around enterprising but untrained preachers."

Lincoln and Mamiya (1990: 407) estimate that 80.6 percent of church-going African Americans belong to seven religious bodies—the National Baptist Convention, USA; the National Baptist Convention of America; the Progressive National Baptist Convention; the African Methodist Episcopal church; the African Methodist Episcopal Zion church; the Christian Methodist Episcopal church; and the Church of God in Christ. They estimate that 5.9 percent of churchgoing African Americans belong to "smaller black communions," 5.1 percent to "predominantly white Protestant groups," and 8.4 percent to the Roman Catholic church. In reality, the number of African Americans belonging to "smaller black communions"—a category that presumably includes conversionist sects other than COGIC (Church of God in Christ), messianic-nationalist sects, and thaumaturgical sects—may be greater than the figure reported by Lincoln and Mamiya in that membership statistics for many unconventional African American groups goes unreported. At any rate, table 4 presents the reported membership figures for major black religious bodies. There exists considerable variation in the last reported year for membership figures among these religious bodies. Furthermore, as tends to be the case for most religious bodies, the figures may be inflated. Unfortunately, membership figures for many unconventional black religious bodies are either difficult to obtain or unavailable.

Types of African American Religious Sects

To comprehend the nature of religious diversity in African American religion, we utilize a typology of black sectarianism (Baer and Singer 1981). In the process of conducting research on various relatively unknown religious groups in the black community, we concluded that there was a need for a typology that systematically recognizes the diversity of black religious groups while placing them in a shared context. We recognized that the content, structure, and variability of African American religion derives primarily from three sources: (1) influences from African cultures; (2) influences from religious patterns in European American culture; and (3) religious responses on the part of blacks to cope with their minority status in American society. Our typology focuses upon the third source, largely because it appears to be the overriding factor that has shaped all black religious groups in the United States. Yinger appears to concur with our assessment: "Negro sectarianism is a product of the same fundamental causes as sectarianism in general, but there are some special factors that have affected it. It can be understood only in the total context of the Negro's place in American society" (Yinger 1970: 324).

Table 4

Membership of Major Black Religious Bodies

Religious Body	Year	No. of Churches	Membership
National Baptist Convention, USA	1958	26,000	5,500,000
National Baptist Convention of America	1956	11,398	2,668,779
Progressive National Baptist Convention	1967	655	521,692
National Primitive Baptist Convention	1975	606	250,000
African Methodist Episcopal church	1981	6,200	2,210,000
African Methodist Episcopal Zion church	1987	6,060	1,220,260
Christian Methodist Episcopal church	1983	2,340	718,922
Church of God in Christ	1982	9,982	3,709,661
Church of God in Christ, International	1982	300	200,000

SOURCE: Adapted from Jacquet (1989: 238–45).

Our typology concerns only those religious movements and organizations composed primarily of black members, in keeping with our view that African American religion is largely a response to the racism and class stratification inherent in American society. Our typology does not include white-controlled religious organizations, such as the Catholic church, various mainstream Protestant denominations, the Seventh Day Adventists, and the Jehovah's Witnesses, which contain either predominantly black congregations or have black members scattered among various predominantly white congregations. There are, of course, many important questions that the presence of African Americans in such organizations raises. For example, why do blacks join predominantly white congregations, or why do they establish congregations affiliated with white-controlled religious groups? Or how do black congregations, such as the black Catholic churches common in southern Louisiana and central Kentucky, adapt the content of white-controlled religious organizations to the African American experience? We reserve some of these issues for the next chapter, which will look at the mainstream churches—both those affiliated with the established black denominations and those affiliated with white-controlled denominations.

For our typology of African American sectarianism, we chose two dimensions as axes. One axis considers the "strategies of social action" that black religious groups adopt in addressing their structural position in American society. In this regard, the response of a particular group may be instrumental; that is, it may focus on the attainment of concrete goals aimed at improving the objective material and social status of its adherents, or it may be expressive in that it releases the emotional tensions resulting from social oppression. The second axis considers the general "attitudinal orientation" of the members of various religious groups to the cultural patterns of the larger society, or more specifically to those of the dominant or majority group. A particular religious body may incorporate a positive orientation; that is, it may accept the overall values and behavioral patterns of the larger society. Or it may adopt a negative orientation in that it rejects or is repulsed by them, at least conditionally.

Figure 1 illustrates this typology in the form of a four-cell matrix. Each cell represents a different type of religious sect. While much of the sociology of religion is devoted to making fine-grained distinctions between "sect" and "cult," we dispense with these in our discussion. Instead, we emphasize the sectarian nature of African American religious groups in that they all exist unavoidably in a state of some tension with the larger society. This is so because the racial status of their adherents automatically insures both the experience of oppression, individually and/or collectively, and the resultant use of the religious group to respond in some fashion to this experience.

Mainstream Denominations

The established sects or mainstream denominations in the black community are committed, at least in theory, to a reformist strategy of social activism that will enable African Americans to become better integrated into the political, economic, and social institutions of the larger society. Many of the congregations of this type continue to exhibit a strong expressive side in worship activities, but they are strongly committed to various instrumental activities, such as lending support to various protests, raising funds to fight discrimination, and sponsoring college scholarships. Members of the mainstream denominations or established sects tend to accept the cultural patterns of the larger society and want to share in the benefits of the "American Dream."

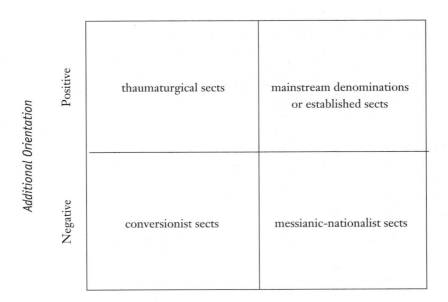

Fig. 1. Religious responses to the larger society among African Americans.

The mainstream denominations are drawn primarily from two religious movements. The first movement included groups of free blacks who separated from predominantly white congregations prior to the Civil War, and the second consisted largely of former slaves who separated from the white Baptists after the Civil War. Mainstream congregations are found today in associations such as the National Baptist Convention, USA; the National Baptist Convention of America; the Progressive National Convention; the African Methodist Episcopal church; the African Methodist Episcopal Zion church; the Christian Methodist Episcopal church; and the Second Cumberland Presbyterian Church in the United States. Although many of the congregations in these organizations include working-class and lower-class members, their leadership and orientation are generally middle-class. These bodies constitute the "mainline" or "mainstream" churches in the African American community in that their orientation is toward the black middle class and they have achieved both social legitimacy and stability, but they experience a sectarian tension with the larger society.

Messianic-Nationalist Sects

Messianic-nationalism is a variant of African American nationalism that combines religious belief with the ultimate objective of achieving some degree of political, social, cultural, and/or economic autonomy. Sects of this type are generally founded by charismatic individuals regarded by their followers as messiahs or "messengers" of God, if not God in human form, who will deliver blacks from the oppressive yoke of white dominance. In many cases, the death of the messiah precipitates an internal leadership crisis, often followed by a splintering process within the group. Central to the ideology of the messianic-nationalist sect is the repudiation of "Negro" identity as an oppressive white creation and the substitution of a new ethnic identity predicated on a belief in the unique spiritual importance of black people. Rhetorically, at least, messianic-nationalist sects reject both mainstream goals and values. Additional core features of messianic-nationalism include:

(1) belief in a glorious black past and subsequent "fall" from grace;

(2) vocal opposition to and criticism of American society and whites in general;

(3) anticipation of divine retribution against the white oppressors;

(4) assertion of black sovereignty through the development of various rituals and symbols, such as national flags, anthems, and dress, and a separatist economic base as well as, plus at least in some cases, an interest in territorial separation or emigrationism; and

(5) chiliastic and messianic expectations of a new golden age for black people.

In its own way, each messianic-nationalist sect includes the pivotal features listed above. In one group emigration may be stressed while in another it may play but a minor role in group ideology. Generally, these sects turn to Islam, Judaism, Christianity, or even a combination of all three traditions for their beliefs and rituals. It must be stressed, however, that whatever their outward difference, the majority of messianic-nationalist sects are strikingly similar. Of the four types in our typology, they constitute the most radical protest to and departure from the institutions and conventions of the larger society.

The adoption of an Israelite identity as one form of messianic-nationalism seemed inevitable in that African Americans have historically compared their plight in American society to that of the biblical Hebrews in the Egypt of the pharaohs. Congregations calling themselves "black Jews" appeared about 1915 in Washington, Philadelphia, New York, and smaller cities, although there is evidence of such groups even earlier.

The best-known messianic-nationalist sects, however, are those that adopt an Islamic orientation. The first of the black Islamic or Muslim sects was the Moorish Science Temple founded by Noble Drew Ali in Newark around 1913. The process of Islamization in the black community was in large part continued with the emergence in the early 1930s of the Nation of Islam, first under the leadership of W. D. Fard and later of Elijah Muhammad. The rapid growth of the Nation of Islam, in large part accelerated by the dynamic inspiration of Malcolm X during the 1960s, did not check schismatic tendencies, which led to the appearance of numerous splinter black Muslim sects, including the Ahmadiyya Moslem movement of Chicago, the Hanafis of Washington, D.C., and the Ansaru Allah community of Brooklyn.

The last major wing of the messianic-nationalist movement remained within the Christian fold but modified certain Christian beliefs in its efforts to create a more satisfying black identity. The most noteworthy of these groups is the African Orthodox church, which grew out of Marcus Garvey's massive Universal Negro Improvement Association under the tutelage of George Alexander McGuire, a former Episcopalian clergyman. This assemblage urged blacks to forget the image of a white God and instead worship a black Madonna and a black Christ. A similar orientation developed in Albert B. Cleage's Shrine of the Black Madonna, headquartered in Detroit. Cleage, a minister in the United Church of Christ, attracted considerable attention in the 1960s with his pronouncements that Jesus was a black revolutionary who came to free people of color from white oppression (Harding 1969).

Conversionist Sects

Conversionist sects characteristically adopt an expressive strategy of social action, emphasizing the importance of various behavioral patterns—such as shouting, ecstatic dancing, and glossolalia—as outward manifestations of "holiness" or "sanctification." Wilson notes the following about the conversionist sect: "Its reaction towards the outside world is to suggest the latter is corrupted because man is corrupt. This type of sect takes no interest in programs of social reform or in the political solution of social problems and may even be actively hostile towards them" (Wilson 1969: 364). Conversionist sects tend to be "otherworldly" and apolitical in orientation and rely upon the willingness of the individual to undergo a process of conversion as the meaningful way to affect social transformation. It is this emphasis on personal change, rather than promotion of religious conversion per se, that is the hallmark of these groups. As defined by the conversionist sects, living a life of holiness requires adherence to a puritanical morality and avoidance of the carnal activities, such as drinking, smoking, dancing, gambling, theatergoing, and illicit sex. The focus of the conversionist sect is the worship service as well as the revival meeting.

Next to the established sects, the conversionist sects, which consist primarily of a multitude of small Baptist, Holiness, and Pentecostal organizations and congregations, appear to be the largest religious type in the black community. Many of the congregations, particularly of the "storefront" type, that are found in great numbers in the commercial districts of black neighborhoods are examples of the conversionist sect. A few of the many black Holiness and Pentecostal organizations include associations such as the Church of God in Christ, Church of Christ (Holiness) USA, Christ's Sanctified Holy Church (Holiness), the Apostolic Church of Jesus Christ, the Pentecostal Assemblies of the World, and the House of Prayer for All People (Simpson 1978: 259). In addition, one finds a countless number of Holiness and Pentecostal congregations in the African American community that have no formal affiliations with larger associations.

The Holiness movement, which emerged during the period following the Civil War, was not specifically aimed at black Americans (Washington 1973: 60). On the other hand, despite the close alliance between some of its adherents and the Ku Klux Klan, the Holiness movement did occasionally bring poor whites and blacks together in interracial revivals. Some blacks also established Holiness sects. One of these, the Church of God in Christ, later became a Pentecostal group after its founder was influenced by the Azusa Street Revival, which started in Los Angeles in 1905, and is presently the largest of the Holiness/Pentecostal groups in the black community (Simpson 1978: 259–60). In contrast to the Holiness movement, the Pentecostal movement emphasized one form of ecstatic behavior over all others as a mark of sanctification, namely speaking in tongues, or glossolalia.

Wilson (1969: 372) notes that conversionist sects, if they manage to survive and grow, are prone to a process of "denominalization." Some of the larger conversionist groups, particularly the Church of God in Christ, are being transformed into established sects with a more temporal view of the world and the possibilities for social change. On the whole, however, the great majority of conversionist groups in the black community continue to provide their adherents with an escapist response to the problems of racism and social inequality.

Thaumaturgical Sects

Thaumaturgical sects maintain that the most direct way to achieve socially desired ends—such as financial prosperity, prestige, love, and health—is by engaging in various magico-religious rituals or by acquiring esoteric knowledge that provides individuals with spiritual power over themselves and others. "These sects define themselves in relation to the wider society by affirming that normal reality and causation can be suspended for the benefit of special and personal dispensations. They resist acceptance of the physical process of aging and death and come together to affirm a special exception from everyday realities which assures each individual and his loved ones of perpetual well-being in the next world. For the present, they procure immediate advantages by accomplishing miracles" (Wilson 1969: 368). Thaumaturgical sects tend to hold the individual responsible for his or her present condition and stress the need to develop a positive frame of mind while at the same time overcoming negative attitudes. Thaumaturgical groups generally accept the cultural patterns, values, and beliefs of the larger society but attempt to change the means for obtaining the "good life." Because of their individualistic orientation, such groups are largely apolitical and express little interest in social reform. Members of thaumaturgical sects view themselves as open-minded and are very amenable to religious syncretism.

Of these four types, the thaumaturgical sect has been the most neglected by scholars, despite their prevalence in the African American community. Most commonly representative of this type are those groups that refer to themselves as "Spiritual" churches (Baer 1984). Various scholars, including Hurston (1931), Mays and Nicholson (1933), Jones (1939), Fauset (1971), Drake and Cayton (1945), Frazier (1974), and Washington (1973), refer to these groups as "Spiritualist," but the term "Spiritualist" was contracted to "Spiritual" in most of these groups around the 1930s and 1940s. The Spiritual movement in the black community blends elements from American Spiritualism, Roman Catholicism, black Protestantism, and Voodoo (or at least its diluted form generally termed "hoodoo") and various other religious traditions.

The historical development of the Spiritual movement remains obscure, but it seems to have emerged in various large cities, particularly Chicago, New Orleans, and Detroit, in the 1910s. As was also true of many of the conversionist and messianic-nationalist sects, the growth of the Spiritual churches was in large part related to the migration of African Americans from the rural South to the cities of both the North and the South. Most Spiritual churches are quite small and are situated in storefronts and converted dwelling buildings, but some are housed in impressive edifices and cater to relatively affluent working-class and professional people. Most Spiritual churches maintain at least a loose affiliation with a larger association. Prior to the death in 1979 of its charismatic leader, Clarence Cobbs, the largest of these many associations, the Metropolitan Spiritual Churches of Christ, Incorporated, may have had as many as 125 congregations (Melton 1978, vol. 2: 106).

One of the newest and perhaps the best known of the black thaumaturgical sects is the United Church and Science of Living Institute founded in 1966 by the Rev. Frederik Eikerenkoetter II (better known as "Rev. Ike"). Rev. Ike teaches that the lack of money is the root of all evil and urges his followers to rid themselves of attitudes of deferred rewards in an afterlife and to start believing in their own abilities of acquiring a slice of the "American Dream" (Gallatin 1979). Lesser-known thaumaturgical sects among black Americans include groups such as the Antioch Association of Metaphysical Science, established in 1932 by Dr. Lewis Johnson in Detroit, and the Embassy of the Gheez Americans headquartered in Long Eddy, New York (Melton 1978, vol. 2: 243).

Although Spiritual churches, due to their highly syncretistic nature, exhibit many of the features found in other black religious groups, their emphasis on the manipulation of one's present condition through the use of various magico-religious rituals and the acquisition of esoteric knowledge differentiates them from the latter. The Spiritual religion concerns itself with the concrete problems of its adherents and clients by attempting to provide them with the spiritual means to acquire finances, success in locating employment, love, or the improvement of a strained relationship. In contrast to the common but probably exaggerated view that African American religion is "otherworldly," Spiritual people are concerned primarily with discovering solutions to their difficulties in the here and now.

The next four chapters will examine in further detail the development, the social organization, the beliefs, the ritual events, and the role of the various religious groups representing each of these four sectarian categories.

III

Mainstream Churches

When, in 1953, the prominent African American sociologist E. Franklin Frazier was invited to give the Frazer Lecture in Social Anthropology at the University of Liverpool, he chose the evolution of religion among African Americans as his topic. The published version of the lecture, *The Negro Church in America*, is one of a series of books with similar titles, including W. E. B. Du Bois's *The Negro Church in America*, Carter G. Woodson's *The History of the Negro Church*, and Benjamin E. Mays and Joseph W. Nicholson's *The Negro's Church*. These and more recent books share the tendency to use the term "black church" to refer to the mainstream churches in the African American community, as if these religious bodies subsumed the totality of religious affiliation and practice of African Americans and as if there were a single church organization that embodied the religious life of this diverse population. Both of these common understandings of African American religion are misguided.

Even at the level of the mainstream or dominant churches in the African American community, a fascinating level of diversity abounds. There is not one African American church structure; there are in fact seven different independent denominations controlled and almost exclusively populated by African American members: (1) the National Baptist Convention, USA; (2) the National Baptist Convention of America; (3) the Progressive National Baptist Convention; (4) the African Methodist Episcopal (AME) church; (5) the African Methodist Episcopal Zion (AMEZ) church; (6) the Christian (formerly Colored) Methodist Episcopal (CME) church; and (7) the Second Cumberland Presbyterian Church in the United States. In addition, many predominantly African American congregations are affiliated with white-controlled mainstream denominations such as the Episcopalian, Presbyterian, Congregationalist, United Methodist, and Roman Catholic churches. Because of their more formal and established character, higher social status, and representation in the minds of many people as the essence of African American religion, we begin our typologic examination with these African American and white-controlled mainstream churches. This chapter focuses on four issues:

(1)   the internal polity and complex organizational structure of the mainstream African American denominations,

(2)   the social structure and formal ritual practices of black Baptist and Methodist congregations,

(3)   the juxtaposition of activism and accommodation in the mainstream denominations, and

(4)   the social status and activist orientation of African Americans in white-dominated religious organizations.

The purpose of this chapter is to give a detailed and, to a degree, historical examination of the inner workings of these religious groups that by far hold the largest number of African American members and have made fundamental contributions to the life and character of all African American communities.

The Polity of African American Mainstream Denominations

To date, no scholars have conducted comprehensive studies of specific African American mainstream churches at the denominational level, although a few scholars have carried out ethnographies on congregations affiliated with black mainstream denominations (see Mukenge 1983 and Beck 1989). In their recent book, Lincoln and Mimiya (1990) devote separate chapters to the history and polity of the black Baptists and of the black Methodists. Furthermore, they explore various dimensions of black mainstream churches in rural as well as urban areas. Our discussion of the politico-religious organization of black mainstream churches covers in an abbreviated form some of the material covered in their book.

The National Baptist Denominations

The denominational history of the black Baptists during the twentieth century can be summarized as one of organizational growth, tension between centralization and decentralization, fission, and sporadic reunion. A nationwide black Baptist denomination, namely the National Baptist Convention, USA, Incorporated, coalesced as early as 1895 in Atlanta, despite the strong emphasis among black Baptists upon the autonomy of local congregations, district conventions, state conventions, and the sometimes sharp political differences between southern and northern clergy. At birth, this denomination became the most powerful black religious group in the land.

Fissioning within this new denomination started even before the close of the nineteenth century, however. When the new National Baptist Convention met in September 1897 in Boston, debate revolved around three major issues: "(1) the advisability of the removal of the Foreign Mission Board from Richmond to Louisville; (2) the use of American Baptist literature and cooperation with white Baptists in general; and (3) the primacy of foreign missions as a greater emphasis for the convention" (Fitts 1985: 85). In countering the demand of the "separatist" leaders that the convention sever its ties with white-controlled Baptist societies based in the North, especially the Publication Society, the "cooperativists" attacked the weak convention's foreign mission program (Washington 1986: 187–96). Most of the cooperativists were from the South Atlantic region—Maryland; Washington, D.C.; Virginia; Florida; and especially North Carolina—and "did work for the northern societies to supplement their incomes" (Washington 1986: 194).

Due to their failure to thwart the separatists, the cooperativists formed the Lott Carey Foreign Missionary Society on December 16, 1897, at the Shiloh Baptist Church in Washington, D.C. This organization was renamed "the Lott Carey Baptist Home and Foreign Mission Board" in 1903. The Lott Carey Convention became in 1905 the First District Convention of the National Baptist Convention, USA This arrangement, which applied primarily to the foreign mission program, collapsed due to a crisis over the operation of the National Baptist Publishing Board.

The crisis, culminating in the formation of a second black Baptist denomination, had its roots in the debate between the separatists and the cooperativists on the appropriate publishing mechanism for the new National Baptist Convention, USA Rev. R. H. Boyd, a separatist from Texas, proposed at the St. Louis convention in 1896 a resolution recommending the establishment of a "printing committee" independent of the American Baptist Publishing Society. Contrary to the wishes of the cooperativists, the convention established the committee, later called the Publishing Board, under the jurisdiction of the Home Missions Board. Boyd, a successful businessman and banker, served as the corresponding secretary of both boards.

He incorporated the Publishing Board in Tennessee as a separate legal entity apart from the Convention. There was no formal objection to this move at the time. Over the years the enterprise grew substantially, and in nine years it had grossed nearly two-and-a-half million dollars. Reverend Boyd built a new

building for the Publishing Board [in Nashville] on land by himself, and he
also copyrighted all of the Board's materials in his own name. In other words,
while he made reports to the annual Convention meetings, he clearly viewed
the Publishing Board as the property over himself and the Tennessee Corpora-
tion. (Hamilton 1972: 154)

The 1905 convention in Chicago ruled that the Home Mission Board and the Publishing Board should operate as separate entities with their own corresponding secretaries. Boyd's refusal to comply with the convention's instructions resulted in a decade-long debate as to the legal ownership and control of the Publishing Board. Finally, a major confrontation erupted at the annual convention in Chicago in 1915 when the National Baptist Convention, USA, drew up a new charter that defined the various boards as constituent units under its jurisdiction. Boyd refused a request that he open the books of the Publishing Board to the convention's auditor. At an ensuing court trial, Judge Smith of Chicago referred to Boyd and his followers as the "rump" convention and overturned an injunction that they had taken out against offices of the National Baptist Convention, USA Nevertheless, the Boyd faction was able to use the National Publishing Board as the springboard for forming the National Baptist Convention of America, Unincorporated, on September 9, 1915, at the Salem Baptist Church in Chicago. Conversely, the National Baptist Convention, USA, had to establish an entirely new publishing operation. As Joseph J. Washington, Jr. (1960: 53), notes, this "slip into two groups with identical ecclesiastical nomenclature and social motivation can be accounted for in large measure by external socio-economic pressures." Lacking an ability to significantly change the oppressive social structure of the larger society, the National Baptists channeled their frustration into internal struggles and disputes. Would-be leaders often seize minor issues and use them to fuel a continual pattern of personal promotion and group fragmentation.

After 1915, several attempts were made to reunite the two National Baptist conventions. On March 19, 1918, in Memphis, a joint "peace commission" consisting of representatives from the National Baptist Convention, USA; the National Baptist Convention, Unincorporated; and the Southern Baptist Convention unanimously proposed a merger of the two National Baptist conventions (Jordan 1930: 138–40). Members of the National Baptist Convention, USA, referred to the National Baptist Convention of America as the "Unincorporated Convention," but in reality the former was not incorporated until the early 1930s. Between 1924 and the 1940s, the National Baptist Convention of America and the Lott Carey Convention operated a cooperative foreign mission program. An aborted attempt at tripartite merger among the three Baptist conventions was followed by "a period of decline in both the Lott Carey Convention and the National Baptist Convention of America. Each of these two conventions was unable to raise enough money to pool together for a viable foreign mission program commensurate with the needs of the conventions" (Fitts 1985: 95, 97). Eventually, the National Baptist Convention of America organized its own Foreign Mission Board with mission stations in Africa, Haiti, Jamaica, and Panama. The "Magnificent Men and Women of Troas" program, which raised several million dollars from black Baptist leaders during the 1940s, rejuvenated the previously declining Lott Carey Baptist Foreign Mission Convention.

Tenure as a restricted term of office has at various times prompted contention among National Baptists. In the case of the National Baptist Convention, USA, all national officers theoretically are elected for a period of one year at the annual convention (Jackson 1980: 216–18). Nominations for offices, including the president and chairs of the corporate boards, are called for from the floor on the second day of the convention. Delegates generally return top officers to their former positions routinely, often without an opposing candidate on the slate. In most instances, the president of the national organization is merely reinstated for yet another year of leadership. Presidents are invariably pastors of affluent Baptist congregations and continue in this capacity during their term of office while most of the day-to-day administrative affairs are conducted by the secretaries of the constituent boards and departments of the denomination. The president theoretically receives advice from the Board of Directors, which consists of a hundred members representing all of the state conventions.

In reality, Joseph Washington, Jr. (1960: 68), contends that the National Baptists "are committed to one-man rule on every level." Historically, the autocratic control of the presidency has been challenged on several occasions in the National Baptist Convention USA At the 1925 convention, a small group unsuccessfully attempted to limit the length of officers' terms (Jackson 1980: 151). A constitutional amendment restricting the president's tenure to no more than four consecutive years was ratified at the 1952 convention (Jackson 1980: 333–38). The new policy came into dispute after Joseph H. Jackson was elected president in 1953. Jackson, the pastor of the prestigious Olivet Baptist Church of Chicago, had served as the secretary of the Foreign Mission Board from 1934 to 1941 under the presidency of L. K. Williams and as a regional vice-president from 1947 to 1953 under the presidency of J. V. Jemison (Jackson 1980: 222). Given his influential position, he was able to convince the Board of Directors to vote by a majority of thirty-seven to eleven in 1955 to recommend to the national organization that the tenure clause be revoked. After the 1957 convention in Louisville reelected Jackson to a fifth term by a vote of approximately five thousand to sixteen, a disenchanted group of ministers filed a suit in federal court in Washington, D.C., in early 1958. They charged that, according to the convention's bylaws, Jackson illegally occupied the office of presidency.

> *The plaintiffs, ten ministers from various parts of the country supported by affidavits and petitions from hundreds of others, charged that they had been denied access to the platform, that the floor microphones had been disconnected, that they had no opportunity to place anyone in nomination, and that when Reverend Jackson made his ruling on the invalidity of the 1952 amendment, there were shouts and screaming, the organ played, banners were paraded and people knocked aside. Before the demonstration had subsided, a motion was made and carried to suspend the rules and reelect Jackson.* (Hamilton 1972: 169)

Nevertheless, the federal judge ruled that the 1952 tenure amendment was unconstitutional since it was adopted a day after the stipulated two-day limit on the proposal of new amendments. On the surface it appears that the process of reelecting officers is relatively democratic, but Washington (1960: 69) asserts that the "power of Dr. Jackson [was] so entrenched that he [was] able to maintain his strangle hold on the Convention year after year through the simple declaration that challenging him would be tantamount to breaking up the convention."

A second drive to oust Jackson related more to his accommodationism than tenure per se. In 1956 various Baptist ministers, including C. K. Steele of Florida and T. J. Jemison of Baton Rouge, participated in a symposium entitled "National Baptists Facing Integration—Shall Gradualism Be Applied" (Fitts 1985: 100). Jackson presented Martin Luther King, Jr., to the audience and was in turn congratulated by King for his support of the bus boycott movement, but King's unequivocal denunciation of gradualism at the symposium alienated Jackson. As early as his presidential address to the 1957 convention, Jackson stated that blacks should focus on the development of their own resources rather than spending all of their efforts on civil rights reforms (Paris 1978: 38–9). As a strong proponent of "law and order" and Americanism, he opposed mass protest actions such as marches and demonstrations.

The anti-Jackson forces, supported by various prominent civil rights ministers (e.g., Martin Luther King, Jr., and Ralph D. Abernathy), supported Rev. Taylor for the presidency of the National Baptist Convention, USA, at the 1960 convention in Philadelphia. The anti-Jackson faction announced that it planned to lobby in Washington for civil rights legislation and to work closely with civil rights organizations, such as the NAACP, the Urban League, and the Southern Christian Leadership Conference.

> *On September 8, 1960, the Convention's nominating committee, consisting of forty state presidents, had unanimously recommended reelection of Reverend Jackson for his eighth term. This led to a thunderous uproar of protests from the Taylor forces which lasted more than forty-five minutes. During the commotion, the chair ruled that the report of the nominating committee was declared adopted and that this amounted to the reelection of Jackson. The mass uproar continued, and the Taylor forces demanded a state-by-state vote. The Convention officials declared the meeting adjourned and issued a statement later that Jackson had been reelected.* (Hamilton 1972: 162)

The rivalry between the two factions erupted into fistfights on the floor of the 1961 convention in Kansas City, Missouri, in which a minister died from injuries to his head upon falling from the platform. As a result of a suit filed by the pro-Taylor group, the election of the president was overseen by Rev. D. A. Home, a court appointee, and by tellers representing the opposing factions (Fitts 1985: 101–3). Jackson won the election by 2,732 votes to Taylor's 1,519 votes (Jackson 1980: 479). Because of his involvement in the anti-Jackson campaign, Martin Luther King, Jr., was removed from the vice-presidency-at-large of the convention's Congress of Christian Education. The anti-Jackson forces regrouped by establishing a Volunteer Committee for the Formation of a new National Baptist Convention. Twenty-three ministers met at the Zion Baptist Church in Cincinnati on May 14–15, 1961, and formulated the basic structure for the Progressive National Baptist Convention of America, Incorporated. The third of the major black Baptist denominations adopted a tenure rule "whereby after the first officers served four years, all succeeding officers were to serve a maximum of two years" (Wheeler 1973: 317).

Each of the National Baptist conventions is divided into state conventions and district associations. National Baptists at both levels "still divide and multiply over national convention affiliation and local leadership positions"; furthermore, it is "not uncommon to have multiple state conventions and districts within the same state or associational tract" (McCall 1973: 265). State conventions conduct annual meetings, at which time funds are appropriated from the various member congregations for foreign and domestic missions, ministers' pensions, and Baptists colleges, seminaries, and schools. Each district association also holds an annual meeting of preaching, fundraising, and reports from various boards and departments.

In keeping with Baptist congregationalism, each church may choose which supra-local bodies it wishes to affiliate with. Similarly, although the national convention publishes its own literature (e.g., hymnals, Sunday school study guides, missionary tracts, training manuals), each congregation has the option of adopting whatever materials it desires. Congregations also hire their own ministers and manage their own fiscal and legal affairs.

As table 5 indicates, the National Baptist conventions consist of various boards and other auxiliary organizations. The National Baptist Convention, USA, supports five colleges and the American Baptist Theological Seminary in Nashville, Tennessee. Since, in reality, the white-controlled Southern Baptist Convention has contributed most of the funds since the opening of the seminary in 1924, it retains one-third of the seats on the board. As recently as 1977, in keeping with the old patronage system, "the Southern Baptist Convention established a scholarship program to provide support for 100 church vocation students from the National Baptist churches" (Fitts 1985: 196–207).

The Black Methodist Denominations

By the time the first national black Baptist denomination was formed in 1895, the black Methodist denominations, as we saw in chapter 1, were well in place. In part the earlier development of denominational structures among black Methodists was related to the episcopal policy that they had inherited from the Methodist Episcopal church, and indirectly from the Anglican church. Most instances of fissioning (e.g., the African Union church, the First Colored Methodist Protestant church, the Union American Methodist Episcopal church, the Free Christian Zion Church of Christ) from the African Methodist Episcopal and African Methodist Episcopal Zion churches occurred during the nineteenth century. As in other black religious groups, fissioning within black Methodist denominations frequently takes place at the congregational level. Many of Chicago's AME churches, for example, were founded by "dissident parishioners" from Quinn Chapel (est. 1847), the oldest AME congregation in the city, and Bethel Church in Chicago (Spear 1967: 91).

Some instances of fusion occurred among African Methodists during the late nineteenth century as well. The 1872 general conference of the AME church granted organic reunion to the former schismatic Independent Methodist Episcopal church, and in 1884 the conference did the same for the British Methodist Episcopal church, which had separated from the parent church in 1856 (Shockley and Haynes 1964: 540). Merger attempts between the AME and the AMEZ churches in 1846, 1864, 1868, 1884, 1888, and 1892 proved less successful (Smith 1922: 370). The AMEZ church, at its 1900 general conference, explored the possibility of merger

Table 5

Boards and Auxiliaries of the National Baptist Conventions

National Baptist Convention, USA	National Baptist Convention of America	Progressive National Baptist Convention
Home Mission Board	Home Mission Board	Home Mission Board
Foreign Mission Board	Foreign Mission Board	Baptist Foreign Mission Burea
Education Board	Educational Board	Department of Christian Education
Congress of Christian Education		Congress of Christian Education
	Evangelism Board	Evangelical Board
Sunday School Publishing Board		
Women's Auxiliary Convention	Senior Women's Missionary, Auxiliary #1	Women's Auxiliary
	Senior Women's Missionary, Auxiliary #2	
	Junior Mission Auxiliary	
Laymen's Movement	National Baptist Brotherhood	
Baptist Training Union Board	Baptist Training Union	
	Benevolent Commission	
	National Baptist Youth Convention	
	National Ushers Auxiliary	

with the Colored Methodist Episcopal church (Walls 1974: 471–75). In 1908 the bishops of the AME, AMEZ, and CME churches formed what eventually came to be called the Tri-Federation Council. The council adopted a declaration favoring tripartite union at its second meeting in 1911 and appointed in 1918 a commission that developed "The Birmingham Plan of Organic Union." Although the plan was overwhelmingly approved by the general conferences of the AME and AMEZ churches, it was decisively defeated by the general conference of the CME church. Despite the defeat of the tripartite plan, representatives of the AME and AMEZ churches continued to discuss the possibility of organic merger until the Great Depression. The Tri-Council of Bishops was revived in the spring of 1965, but periodic negotiations to date have not produced any serious merger plans. As of 1986, the AME Zion church reportedly has been involved in merger negotiations with the CME church (Shriver 1989: 101).

Just as has been true of the National Baptists, the black Methodist denominations have had a history of ecclesiastical autocracy. Two disenchanted ministers at the general conference of 1928 proposed a resolution intended to mitigate this pattern within the AME church by requiring the transfer of all bishops who had served two consecutive quadrenniums in a district. As Singleton (1952: 162–63) observes, "Little episcopal principalities had been built up, and the common expression was my district. . . In some instances a brother minister was not permitted to make a motion unless he first told the Presiding Bishop in private what it was." A. J. Carey, the host of the conference and one of the bishops threatened by the resolution, took advantage of his position as a city police commissioner and invited the police band and detectives to be on hand in order to impress the delegates with his power. According to Reverdy C. Ransom (1950: 267), "During our deliberations, policemen scattered through the building and 'frisked' some of the delegates to see if they carried a gun. Detectives in plain clothes sat or stood at the steps leading to the platform where the Bishops resided." Despite this show of force, the conference passed the resolution by a vote of 641 to 263 (Singleton 1952: 167). As part of the broader effort to check the power of the bishops, the conference also passed a resolution giving equal representation to laymen. At least until possibly recently, this strategy did not result in a serious challenge to episcopal autocracy. "The laymen were picked by the Ministers, probably at the behest of Bishop, and there was hardly any deviation from established customary procedures. To get elected, a layman had to be one who would not rock the boat. In the early years of the lay movement, it was really an addition of numbers rather than an addition of various points of view. Within recent years, this situation has changed" (Gregg 1980: 302).

Like the parent Methodist Episcopal church, the three major divisions of black Methodism are organized into general, annual, and quarterly conferences. The general conferences, which meet quadrennially in different cities around the country, act as the supreme governing bodies of their respective denominations. Like lower-order conferences, they consist of both clergy and laity. General conferences establish regulations of church governance, define the authority and duties of bishops and ministers, and elect bishops and denominational officers. Annual conferences assign presiding elders, pastors, and ministers to their respective jurisdictions, ordain ministers, deacons, and elders, and receive general reports from presiding elders, pastors, organizations, and committees. Presiding elders conduct quarterly conferences at each of the congregations within their district. In addition to the quarterly conference, presiding elders in the AMEZ church hold district conferences each year (Walls 1974: 106–7).

The AME church is divided into eighteen "episcopal districts" spread across the United States, Africa, Canada, and the Caribbean. The first thirteen of these are made up of regional (e.g., New England, Puget Sound), state, substate (e.g., Central Arkansas, Chicago) conferences as well as separate conferences for Canada, Bermuda, and the Bahamas. District 16 consists of the remaining conferences in the Caribbean, and Districts 14, 15, 17, and 18 consist of conferences in various African nations. The AMEZ church consists of twelve "episcopal areas," all of which have their headquarters in the United States. The Christian Methodist Episcopal church, which was called "the Colored Methodist Episcopal church" prior to 1954, has ten annual conferences, nine of which were formed at the time of its establishment in 1870. By the 1950s, this denomination had moved beyond its rural, southern roots to the Northern and Western regions of the country (Lakey 1996:538).

Differences exist among the polities of the three major black Methodist churches, but the general conference of the AME church exemplifies the centralized structure of these denominational bodies. A church publication states that the "AME Church operates as top-down organization, with ultimate decision-making capability resting with the General Conference in most legislative, executive and judicial matters" (African Methodist Episcopal Church 1984: 9). The general conference consists of clerical and lay delegates elected from each of the annual conferences. The Board of Trustees administers church properties and financial affairs. The Judicial Council hears "final appeals from any adverse decision by, for example, a bishop, commission, group or pastor, affecting any church member or body" (African Methodist Episcopal Church 1984: 8). The Council of Bishops functions "as an executive body which implements and enforces the decisions of the General Board.

The General Board makes budgetary changes and new appropriations or expenditures between General Conferences" (African Methodist Episcopal Church 1984: 8). Various standing commissions (e.g., Church Extension/Worship and Evangelism, Higher Education, Social Action) and departments (e.g., Department of Finance, Sunday School Union, Women's Missionary Society) administer the policies and programs established by the General Board.

In addition to the domestic and foreign evangelical activities, the black Methodist denominations operate universities, four-year colleges, junior colleges, seminaries, and other educational institutions. AME schools include Wilberforce University in Ohio (an institution at which W. E. B. Du Bois taught for a brief time), Allen University in South Carolina, and Morris Brown College in Atlanta. While the AMEZ church approaches the AME church in total membership, Livingston College in North Carolina constitutes its sole four-year college. The CME church operates Lane College in Tennessee; Texas College in Tyler, Texas; Miles College in Alabama; and Phillips School of Theology at the Interdenominational Theological Center in Atlanta. Apparently in the hopes of attracting funds to bolster their minimal budgets, many of the denominational schools have placed large numbers of individuals on their boards and confer numerous honorary degrees. For example, in 1958 Edward Waters College in Jacksonville, Florida, had some five hundred members on its board, and Daniel Payne College in Birmingham granted twenty-four honorary degrees the previous year (Hamilton 1972: 106–7).

Several sects, most of which emerged as splits from the two African Methodist denominations, continue to function on the periphery of black Methodism. The Reformed Methodist Union Episcopal church, which reported seventeen churches and some thirty-eight hundred members in 1976, was formed in 1885 by disenchanted AME members "who withdrew after a dispute concerning the election of ministerial delegates to the annual Conference" (Melton 1978, vol. 1: 191). The Reformed Zion Union Apostolic church, which reported in 1965 some sixteen thousand members in fifty churches, resulted from a Holiness movement within the AMEZ church. Several ministers from AME, AMEZ, CME, and Baptist churches objected to the system of "overhead connectional taxation" in their respective denominations (Shockley and Hay 1964: 579).

The most notable of the black Methodist sects are the African Union Methodist Protestant (AUMP) church and the Union American Methodist Episcopal (UAME) church. Baldwin (1983: 4–5) argues that the Union movement, which began when Peter Spencer and some forty other blacks left the predominantly white Asbury Methodist Episcopal Church in Wilmington, Delaware, to protest discriminatory policies and practices, constituted the "first completely separate and independent body of African Methodists to assume connectional form in America." Whereas the AME church did not incorporate until 1815, the Union Church of Africans incorporated in Wilmington in 1805. This body split into the African Union and Union American Methodist Episcopal churches in 1851. The former merged with an AME schismatic group called the First Colored Methodist church in 1906. The AUMP church reportedly had thirty-six congregations, and the UAME church fifty-four. The two sects conduct joint founder's-day celebrations and occasionally discuss the possibility of union (Baldwin 1983: 314).

The Black Baptist Congregation

Black Baptist congregations range from large "prestige" churches, such as Abyssinian Baptist Church in Harlem and Olivet Baptist Church on Chicago's South Side, to humble storefronts in the business districts of urban ghettos. As Joseph Washington, Jr. (1960: 75), observes, "It is widely held that the Abyssinian church represents the pinnacle of independent Negro fold religion." In keeping with the spirit of the Harlem Renaissance, Adam Clayton Powell, Sr., moved his historic congregation from its site in the Tenderloin section in midtown Manhattan to the African American Mecca. During the 1920s, Abyssinian operated over fifty organizations, a night school, a weekly lyceum, a nursing home, a Red Cross unit, an employment office, and recreational facilities. In response to economic hardships suffered by blacks during the Depression, the church developed "by far the most extensive relief activities" of any of the Harlem congregations and participated in various protest activities (Kinney 1979: 140). Olivet, the oldest black Baptist congregation in Chicago, had some thirty-one hundred members on its rolls in 1910 and grew to a membership of ten to twelve thousand by the early 1920s (Fisher 1922). Pastor Lacey Kirk Williams "satisfie[d] the intellectual elite and electrifie[d] the washer women in one" (Fisher 1922: 89) and made Olivet a community center that included an employment bureau, a kindergarten, a nursery, and a welfare program.

At the other end of the continuum of black Baptist congregations, one finds storefronts such as the Mt. Carmel Baptist Church in Cleveland's East Side ghetto, which grew out of the disagreements that members of the Alabama Club at the Triedstone Baptist Church had in 1937 with their newly installed pastor (Blackwell 1949: 47–71). Mt. Carmel, which appears to have had a loose affiliation with the National Baptist Convention, USA, consisted primarily of a tiny group of middle-aged poor people who, contrary to the prevailing image of storefront congregations, exhibited very little emotional exuberance and expression.

Most Baptist congregations lie somewhere along the continuum between the prestige churches, such as Abyssinian and Olivet, and the storefronts, such as Mt. Carmel. Mukenge's (1983) ethnography of the North Richmond Baptist Church is the only extensive published account of a black Baptist congregation, but several relatively extensive case studies of black Baptist congregations exist in the form of unpublished theses and dissertations (Fisher 1922; Montgomery 1937; Campbell 1951; Simpson 1970; Jemison 1972). Drawing upon most of these sources, we will present an overview of the black Baptist congregation in its urban setting.

Social Composition of the Membership

First Church (pseudonym) in Nashville, Tennessee, is an excellent example of a prestige Baptist congregation in the African American community. In the early 1970s, its 538 members included "ten ministers, two funeral directors, eleven physicians including the president of a medical college, the president of a university, the president emeritus of a university, the president of a Baptist theological seminary, four dentists, three lawyers, and two druggists" (Jemison 1972: 53). Forty-one percent of the respondents earned over $20,000 a year, and 68 percent owned their homes. Second Church (pseudonym) in Nashville, while not as prestigious as First Church, would still be considered a "respectable" congregation in the African American community. Its generally older membership of 260 included "two ministers, two funeral directors and one physician" and a large number of school teachers (Jemison 1972: 47). A random sample of members revealed that only 16 percent of them had ten or fewer years of formal education, 34 percent had at least completed high school and attended college, and 50 percent had earned either a bachelor's or master's degree (Jemison 1972: 54). The modal family income ranged between $8,000 and $12,000 a year, and 75 percent of the respondents owned their homes.

As with any voluntary association, there is a tendency for the social composition of a church to shift over time in age, gender, and/or socioeconomic status. A transition in age composition occurred at the Reed Street Baptist Church in Atlanta during the 1930s as a result of the pastor's frequent condemnations of the young people's social activities. In response, many of them left the congregation to join Allen Temple Methodist Church, and Reed Street seemed "destined to become a church of stagnant elders" (Montgomery 1937: 50).

An example of a transition in congregational class composition occurred over several decades at the Amity Baptist Church—historically one of the older and more prominent black Baptist congregations in Atlanta. Amity emerged as one of literally a thousand independent African American Baptist congregations that sprang up throughout the South during Reconstruction. Its initial membership consisted of artisans, house servants, and agricultural laborers (Campbell: 1951: 27). Some of the unskilled workers left the church because of the dominance of the artisans during its formative years (1866–69), when it held services in an old boxcar. In 1869 the congregation decided to construct a church building, which was completed the following year on the west side of the city. Since the remaining unskilled workers felt that they were not adequately represented on the deacon board, thirty-eight of them decided to sever ties with Amity and establish their own church in the northeastern section of the city (Campbell 1951: 40–41). A second schism followed shortly thereafter when another group established a congregation in southwest Atlanta. Despite this fragmentation, Amity's rapid growth prompted a move to a new structure in 1873, which upon completion in 1875 had a seating capacity of two thousand.

By the period 1900–1928, many of the children of the artisans and domestics had graduated from college and become professionals. As such, they constituted the "rising group" in the church and occasionally came in conflict with the pastor, the artisans, and the unskilled workers (Campbell 1951: 63). During this period, more of the unskilled workers drifted away from Amity. In 1928 some of the deacons who were cooks and butlers left the church. Shortly thereafter, the pastors reconstituted the deacon board by replacing those from the working-class group with representatives from the expanding professional sector. In response, from 1929 to 1949 many of the by-now retired artisans and unskilled workers either withdrew from the congregation or became sporadic churchgoers. Amity clearly completed its gentrification process by becoming a "church for college presidents, professors, doctors, lawyers, school supervisors, public school teachers, bankers and businessmen" (Campbell 1951: 3).

Politico-Religious Organization

Regardless of their size and denominational affiliation, African American congregations tend to exhibit elaborate political-religious structures with a multiplicity of offices and boards, auxiliaries, or committees. The pastor, at least in theory and generally in practice, plays the most important role in the congregation, especially in urban areas. Indeed, as Harvey (1997: 173) observes, "Preachers with talent and charisma could also wield immense authority in local communities, leading to the charge that the black Baptist polity tolerated and encourage 'one-man rule.'"

If the congregation has one or more assistant or associate ministers, one of them may as a matter of course be designated as the new pastor. In many instances, however, ministers from within and/or outside the congregation will apply for the vacant position. A steady stream of candidates will inundate the congregation's pulpit in order to prove their rhetorical prowess and leadership skills. Congregations will often choose acting pastors to serve for interim periods, either until they have proven their mettle or until alternative candidates are tapped to fill positions on a permanent basis. Selection of a new pastor from a slate of candidates may stimulate considerable debate and even sufficient conflict to split the congregation.

A tremendous array of additional support personnel, boards, auxiliaries, committees, and choirs assist the pastor in the operation of the various religious, social, and community outreach activities of the congregation. Large congregations have one or more assistant pastors or ministers. Due to his busy schedule, Olivet's Rev. Williams was assisted by six or seven ministers, including three or four ministerial students from the University of Chicago (Fisher 1922: 91). In addition to the pastor and the assistant pastor, moderate-sized or large congregations may have a number of other salaried personnel, such as an office secretary, a director of youth programs, a choir director, an organist, and a custodian. In many instances, especially in the smaller congregations, such positions may be carried out on a voluntary and part-time basis.

The deacons and the trustees, along with the pastor, commonly function as the executive body of Baptist congregations. According to Harvey (1997: 175), "Tensions between pastors, deacons, and parishioners split many churches." The deacons and/or trustees generally serve as a nominating committee in the selection of a new pastor. In theory and sometimes in practice, they also constitute the lay power base of the congregation that acts as a check upon the pastor's authority, especially in situations in which the pastor is deemed to be arbitrary and dictatorial. In many instances, however, the pastor may control the boards by virtue of pastoral discretion to select their members. For example, the deacon board at Amity Baptist Church granted Rev. James Cooke, who pastored the congregation from the 1880s until his death in 1944, the power to handle all church monies. As a consequence, the financial committee existed mainly as a nominal entity. Furthermore, the "deacon board gave him the power to appoint new committees without consulting the board, and the power to ordain anyone as a deacon" (Campbell 1951: 62).

It is important to note that not all of the auxiliaries are fully functioning organizations and that the responsibilities of some duplicate or overlap others. Some members may belong to several auxiliaries whereas others do not belong to any. While encouraging women to become involved in ecclesiastical politics, Higginbotham (1993: 195) argues that the women's convention movement within the National Baptist churches emphasized a "politics of respectability" which historically sought to instill middle-class values and behavioral patterns in African American women and their families. At Ol' Zion Baptist church in rural Florida, the church mother constitutes the most prestigious female role (Brown 1994: 178). This status, however, is generally conferred on women only after years of devoted service to the congregation, generally around age seventy. While women in Zion can become deaconesses by virtue of marriage to a "man of God," men can be elected to the deacon board as a result of being married to "insider" women. Based upon her observations at Ol' Zion, anthropologist Audrey Lawson Brown (1994: 182) asserts that women "actively or passively support their own exclusion from formal religious leadership." Virtually anyone, however, who desires to contribute in at least a supportive capacity to an auxiliary may do so. In contrast to males who monopolize the ministerial as well as deacons' and trustees' boards, females play leading roles in most of the congregational organizations, including the various choirs. Because of their high visibility and colorful robes, choirs serve as recruitment tools, particularly of young people. Furthermore, they help appease members dissatisfied with other aspects of the congregation.

Sunday Morning Worship Service

Anthropologist Walter Pitts (1993: 28) observes that African American Baptist religious services exhibit considerable variation in terms of ritual behavior, depending largely upon the socioeconomic composition of the congregation. Although St. John Progressive Baptist Church in Austin, Texas, exemplifies many of the characteristics of the prototypical "black folk church," its middle-class members generally refrain from "shouting" or falling into trance at Sunday morning services (Pitts 1993: 29). Sociologist Robert Simpson (1970) focuses on the "religious sentiment" expressed in services at the Eternal Hope Missionary Baptist (EHMB) Church in St. Louis. Simpson (1970: 1) notes that EHMB is "located within a lower-class residential areas of the St. Louis ghetto," but unfortunately he fails to provide details about the size and social characteristics of its membership. At any rate, EHMB appears to be a medium-sized congregation with a relatively busy schedule of events that, in addition to the Sunday morning worship service, includes: a Sunday school; practice sessions for six choirs; weekday prayer sessions; meetings for church officers, youth groups, and Boy Scouts; special church "teas"; dinners; and occasional weddings and funerals.

Simpson divides the Sunday morning service at EHMB, formally sched-uled to begin at 9:30, into eleven worship events: (1) the devotional, (2) the processional, (3) the meditation, (4) the benevolent offering, (5) the courtesy period, (6) the sick announcements, (7) the musical interlude, (8) the sermon, (9) the invitation, (10) the regular offering, and (11) the benediction. This general structure is repeated in literally thousands of black Baptist churches on Sunday mornings throughout the country, although the exact sequence and tone of ritual events vary from congregation to congregation.

As is the case in most black churches, it is likely that most services at EHMB begin somewhat later than the formally scheduled time. In fact, Sunday morning services in most black churches begin one to two hours later than they do at EHMB. Furthermore, many, if not most, worshippers at EHMB and other African American churches are not present for the start of the services. Ushers escort them to their seats at designated junctures in the service. Singing of hymns by one or several of the choirs as well as the congregation occurs at various points throughout the service and often marks a transition between worship events.

During the devotional, several deacons begin the service from the area immediately below the pulpit by engaging the congregation in the singing of a hymn. A deacon reads from the Bible, and another deacon follows by thanking God for seeing his people through yet another week. As the con-gregation awaits the processional, some people chat with those near them. In the processional, the choirs, officers of the church (although not the pastor), and perhaps visiting religious dignitaries enter the sanctuary. "After the musi-cians have played once through the processional song the two lines move in unison with a halting half-step through the narthex doors and down the two center aisles. At the front of the sanctuary they flair out to the sides so that each line may enter the chancel area and choir loft from opposite sides" (Simpson 1970: 43).

As its members bow their heads and clasp their palms, signaling the beginning of the meditation, the choir slowly and deliberately sings the Lord's Prayer. Most of the congregants reverently listen, but a few sing along. Subsequently, a deacon reads a psalm a phrase at a time as the con-gregation repeats after him in the call-and-response pattern. As the choir sings, two ushers proceed down each aisle with wicker baskets and collect loose change for a fund for needy members. Following the benevolent offer-ing, an usher asks all visitors to rise for the courtesy ritual so that he can welcome them to EHMB. Next a woman reads the sick announcements and urges the congregation to visit or write to those on the list.

While music has served as a supportive element thus far, the musical interlude consists of a series of songs sung by the chorus or its soloists. The intensity of the musical performance often induces various members to "shout" or go into an ecstatic trance in which they may dance in place or run up and down the aisle. As a general rule, the pastor enters the chancel toward the end of the musical interlude. Before beginning his sermon or "message," he may comment on the musical performance, subdue the ecstatic performance of the "shouter," or ask the congregation to join in the singing of a hymn.

> *Once the sermon is under way, it customarily follows a three or four stage pattern. The first stage, consisting of a number of informal remarks or even a short homily, is followed by an expository stage; it rather abruptly begins with a reading from the Bible which reputedly sets the "text" or topic for the remainder of the sermon. The beginning of the third stage is signaled by rather sudden changes in the preacher's demeanor and delivery of the sermon, from straight formal discourse to a combination and dramatic performance. A fourth stage of brief concluding remarks occurs with less frequency than the other three.* (Simpson 1970: 70)

The pastor's sermon may touch on a wide variety of themes, including human relationships, relationships between people and God the Father or Jesus, the nature of the supernatural, the vulnerability of humans to evil, and strategies to pursue in a "world of trouble." The pastor brings the sermon to an abrupt halt by "opening the doors of the church," a gesture of invitation to newcomers to join the church or to backsliders to rejoin the fold.

As the choir prepares to sing during the invitation, the deacons "arrange folding chairs at the front of the chancel so as to seat the persons seeking membership facing the audience" (Simpson 1970: 104). In most instances, no one comes forward to join the church, and the deacons matter-of-factly remove the chairs while the choir sings. On those occasions when someone comes forward, the church secretary records pertinent information about the candidate. The pastor generally queries the candidate about his or her motives for wishing to join the church and may request that he or she state these to the congregation. The congregation invariably accepts the candidate by a voice vote and comes forward to shake hands with the new member.

The regular collection generally is one of the most elaborate ritual events during Sunday morning services in black churches, and its format varies greatly from congregation to congregation. At EHMB "tithers" first drop their envelopes with money in a special box in the front of the sanctuary.

Afterwards, the ushers bring their contributions to the collection tables and systematically guide the congregants, one block of pews at a time, to bring their contributions to the tables. "After the money has been collected, there follows another period of multi-focused activities—announcements, reports of lay persons who have attended conferences, introduction of visitors, appeals for further money to supplement a 'special collection,' and short homilies by the Pastor. During this period functionaries at the collecting tables count the receipts for the day" (Simpson 1970: 107). After the money is counted, the pastor or an ordained assistant may say the benediction; the choir may sing it, or the congregation may repeat it, phrase by phrase, as the pastor leads them.

Although, as Lewis (1955: 148) observes, "a large portion of the time, energy, and inventiveness invested in religious or church matters is devoted to money raising"; this topic has received relatively little attention in the literature on African American religion. Since financial solvency is an absolute requirement for the continued existence of any congregation, it is not surprising that a mundane affair such as the gathering of funds would be transformed into an elaborate sacred event. Individuals who contribute the largest amount of money inevitable gain status and prestige within the encapsulated world of the religious group. Apparently the ability to contribute handsomely is an especially important route for achieving such a position, despite the existence of alternatives in African American churches for obtaining high rank.

As a general rule, the financial burden for maintaining a church falls upon a minority of members. For example, of some 650 members belonging to the Reed Street Baptist Church in the 1930s, slightly over 200 were regular contributors. "That is, in times of financial strain, where . . . tons of coal are needed, or where a lack of dues in the treasury prevented representation at some leading convention, when some business negotiation is delinquent, the chairman of the deacon board, the most outstanding member in the church, usually lends the money" (Montgomery 1937: 64).

The techniques for gathering funds vary considerably from one congregation to another. In their study of the seven historic black denominations, Lincoln and Mamiya (1990: 254–55) report that, out of a total samples of 2,150 congregations (1,531 urban and 619 rural), 85.4 percent raised funds through offertory collections, 54.9 percent through a pledge system, 46.3 percent through special fund-raising drives, and 74.8 percent through other means—such as church dinners, church sales, musical events, and fashion shows. A minority of churches reported earning income from investments (15.6 percent), church-operated businesses (6.9 percent), and properties (13.5 percent) (Lincoln and Mamiya 1990: 255–56). Urban churches were much more likely to derive income from these sources than were rural churches.

Many congregations levy monthly dues on their members. The Reed Street Baptist Church devised a "unit system" whereby unit leaders visited members in their homes to collect monthly dues of one dollar (Montgomery 1937: 65). The Mt. Carmel Baptist Church, a storefront congregation in Cleveland, assessed men one dollar per month, and women fifty cents per month. In reality, few, if any, formal mechanisms ensure that members will pay their church dues.

Linkages with Local Congregations and Other Religious Bodies

Almost all black Baptist congregations maintain some level of contact with other churches in the local community and religious organizations at the district, state, and national levels.

First Church in Nashville is unique in that it maintains ties with three denominations. While it is officially affiliated with the white-controlled American Baptist church, it also contributes funds for missionary activities sponsored by both the National Baptist Convention, USA, and the Progressive National Baptist Convention (Jemison 1972). Like Second Church, which is affiliated with the National Baptist Convention, USA, First Church belongs to the Stones River District Association and the State Baptist Missionary and Educational Convention. In keeping with its active involvement in the civil rights movement (Martin Luther King, Jr., spoke there in 1957), First Church also belongs to the Southern Christian Leadership Conference and serves as the headquarters of the local branch.

The African American Methodist Congregation

Like black Baptist congregations, black Methodist congregations affiliated with black-controlled denominations range from large "prestige" churches to humble storefronts. Gilkes (1995: 180) reports that the AME church in particular has been experiencing an explosion of megachurches, such as Bethel AME in Baltimore, Ward AME in Los Angeles, Allen AME in Queens, and Ebenezer AME in Fort Washington, Maryland. Historically, however, black Methodist congregations have tended to cater to a somewhat more affluent clientele than Baptist congregations. In contrast to the less fundamentalist AME churches, during the Great Migration to Detroit and other parts of Michigan "the Baptists attracted the poor and the newcomers from the South. One indication of the wealth of the members was that in 1897 the Michigan African Methodists were able to support parsonages for fifteen of their twenty churches, whereas the black Baptists could furnish only two parsonages for their twenty-one churches in the state" (Kartzman 1973: 143). Quinn Chapel, Chicago's AME counterpart of Olivet Baptist Church, "did not grow as rapidly" as its rival and "soon gained a reputation as a 'swank' church, not for the common herd'" (Spear 1967: 178). At the other end of the status continuum are the storefront congregations. While some Methodist storefronts have existed historically and even continue to exist, their numbers are far fewer than for the Baptists. Nelson (1996, 1997) conducted an ethnography of Eastside AME Chapel in Charleston, South Carolina—a congregation that tends to cater to working-class people in the surrounding neighborhood. The two other AME congregations in the Eastside tend to cater to a somewhat higher-status clientele. At any rate, it is important to note that some black Baptist congregations attract members of higher socioeconomic status than many black Methodist congregations.

To date, Beck's (1989) ethnography of Mother Bethel constitutes the only detailed treatment of a black Methodist congregation. Mother Bethel appears to be similar to many other black Methodist congregations throughout the country, despite its fame and relatively large membership. Consequently, by drawing upon Beck's excellent ethnography, we will present an overview of Mother Bethel's social composition, politico-religious organization, and worship activities. Mother Bethel is among the twenty largest congregations in the AME church and is the second largest of the fifty AME congregations in the Philadelphia metropolitan area. Yet compared to some of the large black Baptist congregations, its membership of 1,381 adults and 250 children, of whom approximately 600 are active, is not especially large. "The average attendance at the Sunday worship service varies from 550 on the first Sunday of the month to 350 on the last Sunday of the month" (Beck 1989: 22). Mother Bethel is located on the southwestern edge of Society Hill, an area which in recent decades has undergone considerable gentrification. Fewer than 50 of its members are drawn from its immediate neighborhood; most of them reside instead in west and north Philadelphia and in New Jersey.

Social Composition of Mother Bethel's Membership

Unlike the relatively homogeneous congregation consisting of "the best of the great laboring class" that Du Bois (1967: 203–4) found just before the turn of the century, the socioeconomic composition of Mother Bethel became quite heterogeneous during the twentieth century due to several waves of African American migrants from the South Atlantic states. "Mother Bethel is currently a community with a widely dispersed residence pattern, an income range of welfare recipients (under $3,000 annually) to approximately $35,000 annually, occupational range from unskilled workers to professionals, and an educational range from completion of only the third grade to the Ph.D. level" (Beck 1989: 67). The average family income is about $7,000 per year. As is characteristic of many African American mainstream congregations, the existence of two occupational categories, namely the "professionals" and the "domestic and personal service" workers, has been "the source of much tension between groups within Mother Bethel, contemporarily and historically" (Beck 1989: 77). As we will see in greater detail later, Mother Bethel is in large measure governed by a male gerontocracy (somewhat in keeping with an average membership age of fifty-five to sixty), despite the fact that female members outnumber male members by three to one (Beck 1989: 22).

Political-Religious Organization of Mother Bethel

The episcopal polity of the black Methodist denominations places the selection of pastors in the hands of the bishop of the district in which the congregation is located, a notable contrast to black Baptist congregations, who select their own pastors. Members of a particular congregation may petition the bishop for a different pastor, but in theory he may disregard their request. Conversely, the tendency to rotate a minister's assignment periodically means that most black Methodist pastors do not enjoy the tenure that many of their Baptist counterparts do.

Due to unique historical events that resulted in the formation of a corporation in 1807 making Mother Bethel independent of the pastor (who at the time was supplied by St. George's Methodist Episcopal Church), the president of its Trustee Board serves as the president of the corporation, whereas the pastor in all other AME congregations is the president of the Trustee Board. As a consequence, if the members of Mother Bethel become dissatisfied with the pastor, "they can, through the independence of the corporation, create such discomfort for the pastor that his request for transfer is inevitable" (Beck 1989: 133). Failure by the bishop of the First District to recognize the wishes of Mother Bethel could lead to the possibility of secession, as apparently occurred briefly in 1910.

> *More recently, the Connection [denomination or assemblage of A.M.E. congregations] encountered the independence of the Corporation at its full force. According to a member's recollection, the Connection wanted to move Mother Bethel to a Broad Street location, in order to profit from the sale of the Society Hill property just prior to the beginning of redevelopment. The attempt to consummate the transfer failed immediately. As the member stated, "The Connection did not realize the power of the trustees." (Beck 1989: 139)*

As in other African American churches, the successful pastor at Mother Bethel must be an individual who is charismatic both in the pulpit and in his ability to serve as a mediator and counselor for "problems ranging from internal political disputes to financial, medical and marital difficulties" (Beck 1989: 186), despite his paradoxical status within a congregation that historically has resisted charisma.

Of the organizations within Mother Bethel, the Trustee and Steward boards are the most important. In theory the trustees are responsible for temporal affairs and the stewards for spiritual ones, but in reality their respective roles overlap considerably. Although the AME church ordains female ministers, the vast majority of its pastors are males. Male domination over positions of authority is further exemplified by the composition of Mother Bethel's Trustee and Steward boards. The former consists of fifteen men and four women, the latter of eight men and two women. The present head of the Steward Board is a female, but the head of Trustee Board and the corporation has always been a male. Another relatively prestigious organization at Mother Bethel, the Usher Board, is an exclusively male unit whereas the Women's Missionary Society, the nurses, and several other organizations and auxiliaries are all-female units. Exclusively or predominantly female organizations tend to carry out the fund-raising activities of the congregation.

The Sunday Morning Worship Service at Mother Bethel

In its basic outline, the Sunday morning worship service at Mother Bethel resembles those conducted at Eternal Hope Missionary Church and many other black churches. Nevertheless, the African Methodist tradition makes the worship service at Mother Bethel considerably more liturgical than in other black congregations. Table 6 represents a composite of ritual events that Beck observed in several services.

In contrast to most black Baptist, Holiness, Pentecostal, and Spiritual churches, black Methodist churches have a reputation for being relatively sedate. Indeed, in several visits that Baer made to Sunday morning services at two AME congregations with relatively high percentages of middle-class members in the Little Rock area, there were no incidents of "shouting" or ecstatic behavior. While the words of the pastor or visiting preachers were occasionally punctuated by expressions such as "Amen" or "Hallelujah," the tone of the services was, according one informant, "high Methodist." Despite the image of black Methodist services as being relatively subdued, shouting does occur in at least some, if not many, black Methodist congregations, including ones in urban areas.

Table 6

Composite of the Sunday-Morning Worship Service at Mother Bethel

Ritual Event	Description
Organ Prelude	Organ is played after pastor and his assistants take their seats.
Processional	Cathedral Choir enters sanctuary.
Call to Worship	The pastor leads the congregation in liturgical prayer.
Doxology and Hymn of Dedication	The congregation sings hymns of praise and dedication to God.
Morning Prayer	An evangelist, male or female, delivers a contemporaneous prayer.
Decalogue	An evangelist reads the Ten Commandments, followed by congregational singing of the Gloria Patri.
Selection by the Gospel Chorus	Many congregants clap and sing along with the Chorus.
Announcements	A woman announces the organizational meetings, requests for special prayers, and expressions of gratitude for assistance.
Selection by the Cathedral Choir	
Anthem	The congregation sings the church anthem.
Welcome to Visitors	A hostess or host welcomes visitors.
Pastor's Announcements	The pastor announces events and discusses community and church affairs.
Pastor's Prayer	The pastor acknowledges the trials of the congregation.
Offertory	The ushers pass the collection plates while many members bring their pledges and offerings to a collection area in the front.
Hymn of Preparation	The congregation sings in preparation for the sermon.
Sermon	
Invitation	The pastor invites prospective members to join the church.
Consecration	The pastor consecrates the sacramental elements.
General Confession	The congregation confesses its collective sins.
Liturgical Prayers	The congregation recites the First and Second Collects, the Prayer of Humiliation, and the Prayer of Consecration.
Communion	The pastor and his assistants distribute the sacramental elements to the congregation.
Closing Hymns and Prayers	The congregation recites the Apostles' Creed and sings two closing hymns, followed by the pastor's benediction.

SOURCE: Adapted from Beck (1989).

Apparently due to its heterogeneous socioeconomic composition and the southern roots of many of its older members, Mother Bethel constitutes a case in point. A hundred-year-old woman, who left Mother Bethel at the age of twelve to join an Episcopalian church, reported that "there was no shouting and no ecstatic reaction of any other kind at Mother Bethel when she was there. According to her, shouting started at Mother Bethel when the Southern migrants arrived" (Beck 1989: 211). At any rate, shouting is an integral component of worship services at Mother Bethel and is likely to occur during certain ritual events, such as the pastoral prayer, the sermon, and spirited selection by one of the choirs. "Although there are many members who express a disdain for the 'shouters,' all present seem to be more fully drawn into the communal experience when shouting occurs, intensifying the spiritual presence in the event" (Beck 1989: 118).

Protest and Accommodation in African American Mainstream Denominations

We noted in the previous chapter that the mainstream denominations or established sects are committed, at least in theory, to a program of social reforms that aim to integrate African Americans into the larger society. This section focuses on a discussion of social activism in black mainstream churches at three levels, that of: (1) the clergy, (2) the local congregation, and (3) the denomination itself. We argue that elements of protest at each of these levels provide a limited critique of social arrangements in that they fail to examine the relationship between race and class in America society. We apply the notion of hegemony to an examination of black mainstream churches and argue that, by and large, even in instances in which black religious leaders, congregations, or denominations engage in social activism, their protest is framed in such a way that the basic structure of American capitalism remains unchallenged. While these religiously inspired protest efforts express vehement opposition to racism, they generally ignore the intricate relationship between racism and capitalism, implicitly (and often explicitly) accepting dominant values and goals such as material success, individual achievement, personal responsibility for failure, economic competition, and social inequality. As a consequence, African American mainstream churches tend to inadvertently function as agencies of ideological hegemony that legitimize the existing social system.

Social Activism in African American Mainstream Churches

Clerical Level

Individual ministers belonging to African American mainstream denominations have varied widely in the extent of their social activism, ranging from those who were ultra-accommodationists to those who were militant reformers and even occasionally socialists or radicals of one shade or other. Thus, Reverdy Ransom, an AME bishop, was an outspoken Christian Socialist who established Institutional Church and Settlement House in Chicago in 1900—a congregation devoted to a wide variety of social outreach programs, including a nursery, kindergarten, cooking and sewing classes, manual training classes, an employment agency, and social clubs (Morris 1990). W. E. B. Du Bois referred to Ransom's experiment as the "most advanced step in the direction of making the church exist for the people rather than the people for the church" (quoted in Sernett 1997: 131). George Washington Woodbey, a black Baptist preacher, served as a delegate to the Socialist party conventions of 1904 and 1908 (Foner 1983). George Frazier Miller, the rector of the St. Augustine Protestant Episcopal Church in Brooklyn, regarded Jesus as a revolutionary messiah and ran for Congress on the Socialist Party ticket in 1918 (Taylor 1994: 122). J. C. Austin, the pastor of the Pilgrim Baptist Church in Chicago, transformed his congregation into a welfare, education, health care, job training and placement center, and viewed capitalism as a flawed system (Burkett 1994: 138-39). His critical posture, however, probably served as an impediment in his repeated bids for the presidency of the National Baptist Convention, USA. Some black mainstream ministers, including Adam Clayton Powell, Jr., worked for social reform in the ghetto alongside Communist party–sponsored organizations during the 1930s and the 1940s (Naison 1983). In contrast to such clerical activists, one finds black ministers, such as Thomas E. Fuller, a prominent Baptist pastor, who urged compliance when Jim Crow street cars were legally instituted in Memphis in 1905 and "advocated separatism governed by the Golden Rule as the way to solve the present racial troubles" (Tucker 1975: 62). Indeed, accommodative patterns among black preachers took on their most explicit manifestations under the rigid system of southern caste etiquette due to the likelihood of violent repercussions when African Americans publicly objected to the status quo. Although some black preachers in New Orleans occasionally expressed indignation against white society, most of them urged their members to accept their subordinate status (Davis 1940: 47). Various mainstream ministers discouraged blacks from joining labor unions and argued that capitalism would serve as an important source of employment for black workers. Indeed, some black mainstream ministers along with the Urban League urged black workers to function as punctual and industrial workers. Some African American ministers in Pittsburgh were the recipients of contributions from industrialists and were even permitted to conduct services on company premises (Sernett 1997: 145). Most black mainstream ministers remained silent when African radicals such as W. E. B. Du Bois and Paul Robeson became victims of anti-Communist political purges during the 1950s.

While Hamilton (1972), Childs (1980), and Lincoln and Mamiya (1990) comment at length on the political role of African American ministers, there remains a paucity of quantitative studies on this topic. Four of these studies (Broom 1966; Johnstone 1971; Shaw 1973; Turner 1973) create typologies of black ministers. Table 7 lists the mainstream types represented in each of these studies. Broad generalizations derived from a comparison of these four studies concerning the political role of the minister in black congregations and particularly in black mainstream denominations must be made with caution for several reasons.

The studies vary in the way their respective samples were drawn. Johnstone (1971: 276) is the most systematic in that he collected his data from completed interviews with fifty-nine out of seventy-five ministers who comprised a "25 percent random sample of all [black] clergymen in Detroit" based on telephone listings. Given that countless numbers of unconventional congregations in urban areas are not listed in telephone directories, his sample in all likelihood draws primarily from the mainstream congregations. Such sampling bias is actually desirable in that this section focuses on African American mainstream churches. A similar bias exists in Shaw's sample, which was drawn from an apparently non-random sample of twenty-six pastors of what the researcher terms "mainline" congregations (AME, CME, and Baptists of various conventions) and four pastors of Seventh Day Adventist congregations. Broom's non-random sample from a West Coast city includes pastors of ten "established" Baptist, one Methodist, four "storefront" Baptist, one Church of Christ, and ten Holiness or Pentecostal congregations. Initially, Turner's study was based on a non-random sample of eighty-five ministers affiliated with several unspecified religious bodies.

Despite these limitations, these studies suggest that both the moderates and the traditionalists substantially outnumber the social activists. The numerical minority of the social activists is offset in part, however, by the generally larger size of their congregations. In his study, Johnstone (1971: 279) found that "the average number of adult members served by the militants is 752. For moderates it is 308, and for traditionalists 213." Turner's

Table 7

Quantitative Studies of Black Ministers' Political Attitudes
Percentage in Each Category in Various Studies

General Categories of Ministers	Broom (1966)	Johnstone (1971)	Shaw (1973)	Turner (1973)
Social Activist	19.2 (Liberal)	22 (Militant)	14 (Social activist)	13 (Involved in civil rights)
Moderate	34.6 (Moderate)	27 (Moderate)	7 (Synthesist)[a] 50 (Pastor-Administration)	25 (Moderately involved)
Traditionalist	46.1 (Conservative)	53 (Traditionalist)	28 (Pulpit minister)	62 (Uninvolved)

NOTE: [a] The synthesist views the roles of social activist, pastor-administrator, and pulpit minister as complementary and consequently adopts each specific role as the situation demands.

study demonstrates a strong association between degree of civil rights involvement and a minister's educational level—a statistic suggesting that clergy leading larger mainstream churches are more likely to be politically active than ministers of smaller and more sectarian congregations.

The authors of these four studies interpret their roughly similar findings in different ways. For example, whereas Johnstone (1971: 285) argues that "we can see in the [black] clergy as a total category or group no significant or sustaining leadership for continuing civil rights agitations," Turner (1973: 95) concludes that, "[e]ven though the 'Uncle Toms' outnumber the 'abolitionists,' an impressive minority of activist black clergy has been crucial to the civil rights movement." While it is obvious that many black ministers historically have been involved in social activism of one sort or another, it is also important to consider whether clerical activists are sustained in their endeavors by their own congregation or denomination.

The black minister's status as the formal leader of the congregation has received far more consideration than the role of the flock in controlling the nature and scope of the pastor's activities. As Du Bois (1967: 206) observes, however, in reality the typical black preacher is "a shrewd manager, a respectable man, a good talker, a pleasant companion who ultimately must abide by the moral standards established by his congregation." This observation applies especially to Baptist preachers who are appointed and retained at the sufferance of the church's trustee board.

Hamilton (1972: 261) argues that "the strong methods of attentiveness to strictly religious matters still prevails in many black churches." Conversely, clerical activists may be followed by at least some of their parishioners, ignored by others, and even reprimanded by still others for allegedly overstepping pastoral bounds. By and large, civic and political activities are considered personal matters that a minister can choose to engage in. Hamilton's contention about the relationship between black ministers and their congregations is supported by case studies of three pastors conducted by anthropologist John Brown Childs (1980).

The three ministers in Childs's study are relatively active in a variety of community affairs in Buffalo. Rev. Cooke pastors a Progressive National Baptist congregation which began as a storefront church in 1927 and draws its members from many parts of the city. Although it cuts across class lines, the congregation includes a substantial number of middle-class blacks, making it a "prestige church" in the black community. Rev. Cooke does not make secular demands of his members, nor does he receive direct assistance in his community activities from the congregation as a whole. In fact, roughly a quarter of the congregation and a third of the deacons feel that he devotes an excessive amount of time in community activities, despite his being by no means a radical but rather a cautious proponent of black capitalism. Rev. Simon, the pastor of a somewhat less affluent Baptist church serving its immediate neighborhood, purposely compartmentalizes community endeavors from spiritual affairs. His congregation does not play an active, unified part in his community endeavors. Finally, Rev. Wheeler, the pastor of an AMEZ congregation, often participates in protest demonstrations and assisted the Buffalo branch of the NAACP in a boycott of a food chain. While he publicly identifies himself as a minister, he does not speak on behalf of his congregation.

Like the two other ministers, he does not make political statements as a spokesman for his church. Rather, he speaks for the community organizations of which he is a member. Similarly, the support that Rev. Wheeler receives from the church is largely indirect. The congregation and the trustees for the

---

most part support his political activity but do not play an active role in back-
ing that activity. . . . Some members of the congregation have expressed dis-
approval of his secular activity. . . . His ability to assume the duties of the
church and to balance the time spent there with his community work appears
to satisfy the expectations of many in his congregation. (Childs 1980: 105–6)

Childs's study suggests that, as Morris (1984: 21–22) notes, congregations are "not ideal as the decision-making center of a mass movement in
that they are too numerous and preoccupied with too many other functions
unrelated to protest." Conversely, recent survey data gathered by Lincoln
and Mamiya (1990: 225) indicate that the vast majority of a sample of 1,894
members belonging to the seven major historic black denominations (which
includes COGIC) approve of clergypeople participating in protest marches
on civil right issues (91.0 percent) and churches speaking out on sociopolitical issues (91.6 percent).

[C]ivil rights militancy as a dependent variable has a very strong relationship
denominational affiliation (eta = .28828). Although there is not much vari-
ation between the other denominations, COGIC still shows the exception. All
the other six black mainline denominations show a rate of approval with the
90 percent range, while COGIC has a 78 percent positive response. Again,
this may be an indication of COGIC's focus on religious experience, and it also
reflects a somewhat lower educational background for most of its clergy.
(Lincoln and Mamiya 1990: 224)

Based upon this evidence, it appears that a congregation may function as
a local organizational and resource base which supports a larger protest
movement in situations where a clerical activist and a nucleus of activist
members are present. As MacAdam (1982: 129) observes in his analysis of the
development of the black protest movement, "in the case of most church-
related campaigns, it was not so much that movement participants were
recruited from among the ranks of active churchgoers as it was a case of
church membership itself being redefined to include movement participation
as a primary requisite of the role." In essence, the relative autonomy of the
congregation allowed a pastor and his members the option of supporting or
not supporting a protest event, which in turn may have been initiated by a
regional or national organization, such as the NAACP, the Congress of
Racial Equality, the Student Nonviolent Coordination Committee, or the
Southern Christian Leadership Conference.

In the aftermath of the civil rights and black power movements of the
1960s, most African American mainstream congregations have come to
serve an increasingly marginal role in mobilizing protest activities. Instead,

they have tended to retreat into a wide variety of social outreach, self-help, and economic development programs. As Green (1997: 84) observes, "Since 1970, in the wake of the eroding welfare state and too the diminishing influence of secular institutions in the black community, the historic institution has been prompted to action" by turning to a policy of "corporatism" in their search for concrete solutions to local social and economic problems. Based upon a nationwide study of church-related social outreach activities, Billingsley (1999: 95) and his research team found that "Methodist churches (77 percent) are more likely than are Baptist churches (65 percent) or Pentecostal churches (60 percent) to conduct community outreach programs." In the case of black Baptist congregations, the research team found that churches in the Progressive National Baptist Convention are more likely to be engaged in community outreach programs than are churches in other Baptist conventions. Altogether 79 percent of the churches in the Progressive National Convention involved themselves in community efforts, compared with 67 percent of churches in the National Baptist Convention USA Inc., 64 percent in the National Baptist Convention of America, and 52 percent of churches in other Baptist conventions (Billingsley 1999: 96).

African American mainstream churches have turned much of their attention to various housing programs. For example, the Abyssinian Baptist Church in Harlem operates the Abyssinian Development Corporation which has created a $9 million, 100-unit apartment building for senior citizens named Abyssinian Towers as well as additional housing units (Billingsley 1999: 149). Allen AME church in Queens operates various business enterprises, including an 800 unit, $11 million residential complex for senior citizens (Green 1997: 87). Some congregations have organized themselves into community development consortia that seek to collectively rejuvenate deteriorating ghetto areas. For example, the Harlem Churches for Community Development consists of 42 churches, most of them mainstream, as well as two black Islamic mosques (Green 1997: 90). Black mainstream congregations have also developed family-support programs (including ones that provide food and clothing to needy people), and youth programs that seek to address drug addiction and violence. For example, St. Paul's Christian Methodist Church in Savannah runs a food distribution program that feeds over 500 families every month as well as a drug abuse rehabilitation program (Harper 1999: 105). Conversely, as many African American mainstream congregations have experienced the exodus of their more affluent members to suburban areas, they seek to protect their commuting members and their premises from external dangers with security fences, alarm systems, guard dogs, and even armed guards (Franklin 1997: 59).

In one arena of social intervention, in particular, African American churches have had an ongoing moral struggle: how to respond to the AIDS epidemic? The conflicted reactions that have appeared have been conditioned by central theological principles. For most African American ministers, "extramarital sex is fornication, homosexuality is an abomination, drug abuse is a crime against the laws of God and man, and people with AIDS contacted it through sin" (Perrow and Guillen 1990: 100). As a consequence, especially in the early years of the epidemic, various observers noted considerable church resistance to acknowledging HIV as an issue in the African American church (Friedman et al. 1987). At the end of the first decade of the epidemic, Brown (1990: 6) pointed out, "On many occasions in the past, the black church has been a significant and highly visible force for social change. When it comes to HIV disease, however, the response of the black church has generally been silence and lack of support for prevention efforts" (See also Harrison 1992). Indeed, as Brown (1990: 60) notes, there have been some African American religious leaders who "have characterized the HIV epidemic as God's response to sinful behavior." Over time, however, the reluctance of many African American congregations to "'own' the AIDS epidemic, to acknowledge the devastating toll it is taking" (Dalton 1989: 205) among African Americans has come under increasing challenge. As people of color in the United States have been hardest hit by the epidemic and have the highest rate of HIV/AIDS infection, it has become increasingly difficult to assert that AIDS is not a major issue in the African American community (Singer and Weeks 1996). Additionally, theological opposition to offering care and comfort to people with HIV/AIDS on the grounds that AIDS is a punishment from God has been challenged by various ministers and church leaders. For example, Dr. Calvin Morris, a Howard University Professor of Divinity, has argued, "We have to struggle with that kind of theology because we know if that was the case, if sinful folk got their just deserts, most white folk have been dead for a long time" (quoted in Perrow and Guillen 1990: 100). Consequently, many church leaders have embraced the idea that the African American church should "reject the behavior that we know spreads AIDS" while at the same time "stretch out the hand of redemptive love to the person" who is infected (Gilkes 1990: 61). In this light, HIV support and prevention efforts have launched by various African American churches and church-supported groups (Kirkwood 1992; Billingsley 1999). For example, a project in New York City called Balm in Gilead has sponsored the Black Church National Day of Prayer for the Healing of AIDS and the Black Church National Education and Leadership Training Conference on HIV/AIDS (Cohen

1997). In addition, new African American religious organizations, like Unity Fellowship, have emerged with the specific mission of overcoming moral condemnation focused on sexual minorities and others at risk for HIV infection. In sum, as West (1990) maintains, AIDS has pulled African American churches in two opposing directions, with those congregations that embrace a social conservative theology in which "morality" is primary avoiding involvement with AIDS care giving and moral liberal congregations providing services and care to African Americans with HIV/AIDS as an expression of Christian love.

Denominational Level

African American mainstream churches have tended to eschew direct political involvement at the denominational level. Gregg (1993: 69) captures the tension between protest and accommodation within black Methodist denominations in his assertion that African Methodist theology exhibits two "apparently contradictory strands," namely an emphasis on "conservative Methodist forms of worship" and a "liberal, sometimes radical, political philosophy." In a somewhat different vein, the same tension exists within the various National Baptist denominations. At any rate, occasionally certain black mainstream denominations have passed resolutions on racial and other social issues. The National Baptist Convention, USA, passed in 1924 a resolution supporting the Dyer Anti-Lynching Bill and in 1941 issued a "Resolution on Abuse of Colored Soldiers" (Fitts 1985: 145–268). "In 1949, the AME Zion Church sent appeals to Franklin D. Roosevelt asking for continuation of the Federal Fair Employment Practice Commission. The church supported Truman, Eisenhower, Kennedy, and Johnson through public support of civil rights actions by the federal government" (Childs 1980: 34). In 1984 the National Baptist Convention, USA, the National Baptist Convention of America, and the Church of God in Christ, which seems to be exhibiting signs of mainstreaming (e.g., de-emphasis on ecstatic behavior, a growing pattern of middle-class leadership, increasing secularization), endorsed Jesse Jackson's presidential candidacy (Marable 1985: 272). For the most part, however, the African American mainstream denominations have refrained from either making public statements on social issues, endorsing political candidates, or lending financial or even moral support to political movements. While the black mainstream denominations "have regularly appointed committees to report on the state of the nation, and in spite of the fact that each of the [church] boards has offered its own respective analysis of the race problems in voluminous reports, the denominations have never instituted boards or departments on racial justice" (Paris 1985: 93). Furthermore, they either rejected or officially ignored the Black Power movement of the late 1960s and "refused to take official notice of the National Committee of Negro Churchmen (later known as the National Conference of Black Churchmen and recently renamed the National Conference of Black Christians) which attempted to provide a Christian rationale for the movement" (Paris 1985: 120). Conversely, the denominations have allowed, at least in theory, members and church officials to speak and act on their political convictions.

Political involvement on the part of the African American mainstream denominations usually focuses on internal affairs rather than social concerns in the larger society. Some have likened Baptist conventions and Methodist conferences to political assemblies (Woodson 1945: 299). Fission rather than fusion characterizes denominational politics. Attempts to achieve organic merger of the black Methodist denominations have repeatedly failed. The National Baptist Convention of America and the Progressive National Baptist Convention both originated as schisms from the National Baptist Convention, USA The earlier split appears to have been related primarily to a strictly internal power struggle over control of the publishing board, but the more recent rift involved a group of clerical activists who opposed the accommodationist posture of Joseph H. Jackson on civil rights matters. Like the other African American mainstream denominations, the Progressive Baptist Convention also has generally restricted its political involvement to moral persuasion and public statements, despite good intentions to work with various protest organizations.

The emphasis on congregational autonomy, irrespective of Joseph H. Jackson's accommodationism, may provide for a wider range of latitude than the episcopal structure of the African Methodists. As a result of operating, between 1900 and 1904, the Institutional Church and Settlement House, which was based on a philosophy of Social Gospel outreach, R. R. Wright and Reverdy Ransom were forced by the AME hierarchy to resign their positions as co-ministers of this innovative Chicago congregation (Fullinwider 1969: 36). In contrast, despite his decision to commit his life to the socialist movement, George Washington Woodbey was invited to serve as the pastor of Mount Zion Church in San Diego (Foner 1983: 7). As Joseph Washington, Jr. (1964: 76), observes, it appears that a decentralized structure contributes to the emergence of "a higher percentage of real leaders in the Negro community, varying in integrity and quality, among the Baptists than among the Methodists. . . . With the exception of the rare Methodist minister of a large and influential congregation who is able to act according to the dictates of his conscience, Methodist ministers are dictated to by the presiding elder (district superintendent) and the bishop, who are dedicated to one thing—the Methodist system."

The primary agenda of the African American mainstream churches at the denominational level is ecclesiastical politics rather than the politics of liberation. The organizational structure of the mainstream denominations, however, does allow ministers, lay members, and constituent congregations a certain flexibility in choosing whether to participate in social activism. Religious movements often emerge as forms of popular rebellion against the domination of ruling classes, but those movements that escape annihilation or suppression as a result of becoming churches or denominations invariably mollify their critique of the larger society. Conversely, such mollification can inspire the emergence of new militant sects, such as Louis Farrakhan's variant of the Nation of Islam. As institutionalized religions, churches constitute one of the many arenas for the transmission of hegemonic ideology. In their role as hegemonic institutions, most black mainstream churches legitimize social arrangements in America society by participating in reformist political activities rather than in radical or revolutionary ones.

This was not always the case. Indeed, it would be fair to say that modern black politics is rooted in the protest activities of black ministers during the nineteenth century. Particularly in the antebellum North, representatives of African American churches were involved in abolitionist and proto-nationalist movements. Conversely, although hundreds of black Methodist and Baptist preachers participated in electoral politics during Reconstruction, the routine activities of the church and the struggle for its survival in the face of meager funds and white hostility prevented greater attention to vital social issues of the day. With the reinstitution of black codes throughout the South around the turn of the century, political activism diminished. Politics, in short, for many years became church politics only.

According to Wilmore, the "deradicalization" of the black "mainline churches," which accompanied their tremendous institutional growth as a result of the Great Migration of the black masses, continued until the middle of the twentieth century.

> *During the 1920s and 1930s most black churches retained a basically rural orientation and retreated into enclaves of moralistic, revivalistic Christianity by which they tried to fend off the encroaching gloom and pathology of the ghetto. As far as challenging white society, or seeking to mobilize the community against poverty and oppression, most churches were too otherworldly, apathetic, or caught up in institutional maintenance to deal with such issues, even in the good years following the Second World War. The large, social action–oriented, institutional church was always the exception rather than the rule, although it must be acknowledged that they sometimes set the pace for entire neighborhoods or sections of a city.* (Wilmore 1983a: 161)

Although most black churches stood on the sidelines of the events that followed the Supreme Court school desegregation decision of 1954, many black mainstream ministers and congregations joined the black protest movement. Needless to say, Dr. Martin Luther King, Jr., a young middle-class Baptist minister with an affinity for the social gospel and Gandhian nonviolence, became a pivotal figure in—and, with his assassination, the most poignant symbol of—that movement for the African American community and internationally. According to Morris (1984: 77–99), King's Southern Christian Leadership Conference served as "the decentralized political arm of the black church" in the hard-fought struggle for civil rights. King called his view of the Christian social ideal the "Beloved Community"–a term that he learned while a doctoral student at the Boston University School of Theology during 1951–55. Cartwright (1993: xli) asserts that King believed that the "Beloved Community" would gradually emerge as the by-product of the practice of nonviolence and the realization of wider and wider degrees of social cooperation. King drew inspiration for his social activist posture from his father, Martin Luther King, Sr., who served for many years as the pastor of the Ebenezer Baptist Church in Atlanta, as well as Howard Thurman, a black southern-born minister who had met Gandhi while traveling in India. Moses (1997) contends that King gained an understanding of the intricate structural relationship between race and class in American society by drawing upon the work of both A. Philip Randolph, an African American socialist and labor organizer, and Ralph J. Bunche. Bunche instilled in him an awareness of the global nature of the color line —one rooted in imperialism as an international expression of capitalism. Although King rejected the manner in which Marxian theory had been applied in Communist regimes, he admitted to having found inspiration in Marx's writings in late 1949 and admired Marx's passion for social justice.

Even with their involvement in the civil rights movement, the majority of activist ministers and their congregations in the civil rights movement did not define racism as a bulwark of modern capitalism that justifies the super-exploitation of nonwhites through the creation of a split-labor market, fragments the working class in its struggle against the corporate class, and perpetuates thereby an exploitative economic system. As Marable (1983: 169) observes, "King and other Black ministers succeeded in their efforts to achieve democratic reforms within the capitalist democratic system, but were unable to alleviate the suffering of the Black masses caused by institutional racism and capitalism." The corporate class, in its alliance with the state, used tokenism and co-optation to divide and weaken the black protest movement and facilitated the development of a new black political-professional-entrepreneurial class to protect business interests in the central city while ensuring political stability in the black community (Hill 1980). While striking down some of the most injurious expressions of American apartheid and benefiting thereby all oppressed minorities as well as the U.S. working class generally, in the long run most civil rights advances probably disproportionately benefited the black middle class and the tiny black capitalist sector. While the numerical size of these latter groups increased as a result of the civil rights victories and despite the fact that the movement shook up white complacency and complicity in the most degrading expressions of racial domination, the civil rights movement may have had the unintended effect of enhancing polarization within the class structure of the African American community. In the case of African Methodists, as Gregg (1993: 81) so astutely observes, they "tended to protest against their exclusion from American society, not against the society itself."

In its historical role as "the first member of the black professional class, the black elite," the black minister "is torn with conflicting loyalties, sometimes drawn to his people, sometimes drawn to the 'foreign' rulers" (Allen 1969: 12). Even when pulled toward social activism, activist preachers find compelling forces aligned against them, especially if their social critique broadens to include fundamental issues. King's shift from reformism to a critique of American capitalism and foreign policy, for example, very like hastened the end of his life.

> *King's final years provide some parallels with the last months of the major Black nationalist of the 1960s, Malcolm X. Like the former Muslim minister, King had begun to reevaluate the goals of the Black struggle from the simple demand for civil rights to the pursuit of "human rights." . . . By 1967 King was actively leading the U.S. peace movement, addressing rallies and proposing details for U.S. disengagement from Vietnam. He became more concerned about the profound similarity between the oppressed material conditions of the unemployed, and proposed a "Poor People's March" on Washington, D.C. in October, 1967. . . . On April 4, 1968, King was assassinated while assisting 1,375 Black sanitation workers in Local 1733 of the American Federation of State, County, and Municipal Employees. The middle class reformer had become a militant proponent of peace, economic democracy, and Black working class interests.* (Marable 1983: 209–10)

The majority of black ministers in both the African American mainstream denominations and the white-controlled denominations failed to follow King's lead. Most black clerical activists, including notables such as Leon Sullivan in Philadelphia and Jesse Jackson in Chicago, continued to believe that the black masses eventually could make substantial socioeconomic gains by working within the confines of electoral politics and the capitalist economy. As Lincoln and Mamiya (1990: 214) observe, "the politics of black churches have largely been reformist in nature; there have been very few examples of support for revolution."

Ecumenical Level

Some forms of political involvement on the part of African American ministers and congregations have occurred at the ecumenical level. This has included involvement in white-controlled ecumenical organizations, including the Federal Council of Churches, the World Council of Churches, the National Council of Churches, and the Consultation on Church Union (Sawyer 1994: 1). Unfortunately, African Americans have often experienced difficulty obtaining serious consideration of their concerns within the context of such bodies. For example, the World Council of Churches responded to a report drafted by African American proponents of Black Theology entitled "Toward a Common Experience to Faith: A Black North American Perspective" with "disinterested silence" (Sawyer 1994: 5–6). As a result of such forms of indifference among their colleagues in white-controlled ecumenical organizations, African American religious leaders have created an array of black-controlled ecumenical bodies. Sawyer (1994) delineates four stages of African American ecumenical organizations: (1) the Fraternal Council of Negro Churches (FCNC); (2) the Southern Christian Leadership Conference (SCLC); (3) the Black Theology movement, the National Conference of Black Christians NCNC), and the National Black Evangelical Association; and (4) the Partners in Ecumenism situated within the National Council of Churches and the Congress of National Black Churches.

Reverdy C. Ransom created in 1934 the Fraternal Council of Negro Churches (FCNC), a body that included representatives from the National Baptist Convention, USA; the National Baptist Convention of America; the AME church; the AME Zion church; the CME church; the Union African Methodist Episcopal church; the Methodist Episcopal church, the Congregational church; and the Community Center Churches. The FCNC passed a series of resolutions on various social issues between the 1930s and 1950s (Sawyer 1994: 23) before it formally dissolved.

The Southern Christian Leadership Conference emerged during the civil rights era and constitutes the foremost and most effective of the various black-controlled ecumenical organizations. It functions, according to Fairclough (1993: 190), as a "fluctuating number of affiliated organizations that were grouped together by state." Most of its some 100 chapters have been located in the South. As its foremost leader, Martin Luther King, Jr., relied heavily upon the work of a cadre of professional organizers who mobilized local congregations and civic organizations in the civil rights effort. The SCLC's annual conventions and board tended to rubber-stamp King's recommendations. Conversely, King delegated authority and often made decisions with input from advisors within and outside the organization. Many black mainstream ministers in Birmingham and elsewhere in the South felt that the SCLC should not be meddling in local racial politics (Fairclough 1993: 193). Many SCLC leaders distanced themselves from King when toward the end of his life he became a vocal critic of United States military involvement in Southeast Asia. Since then, the SCLC has tended to adopt more progressive positions on international issues, including critiques of human rights violations in Central America, South Africa, the Middle East, Haiti, and Ethiopia (Sawyer 1994: 43). It also has served as a staunch supporter of affirmative action policies, black colleges, and housing and employment programs for African Americans (Sawyer 1994: 63).

The third stage of black ecumenism emerged in the throes of the civil rights movement. We defer a more detailed discussion of the Black Theology movement to our concluding chapter. At the organizational level, the National Conference of Black Christians (est. 1968) and Partners in Ecumenism functioned as the organizational embodiment of Black Theology and as sites of "sometimes anguished discussions regarding whether black members and ministers in predominantly white denominations could justify remaining there" (Sawyer 1994: 68). In contrast, the National Black Evangelical Association (est. 1963) emerged as a result of the failure of white-controlled evangelical organizations, including the National Association of Evangelicals, to address issues of concern to African American evangelicals. It has tended to downplay economic issues.

The Congress of National Black Churches (est. 1978) sought to unify the major African American denominations into a federation similar in purpose to the former Fraternal Council of Negro Churches. It obtained grants from the United States Department of Justice to conduct a national anti-drug campaign. Sawyer (1994: 173) asserts that CNBC has functioned with a "male-dominated, hierarchical model and within the context of the capitalist economic system."

In sum, at various critical junctures in American history, certain black religious leaders, congregations, and even denominations and ecumenical organizations have participated in the struggle against racism and other social injustices. Nevertheless, the African American mainstream churches, especially at the denominational level, have remained for the most part at the periphery of this struggle. A limited number of existing case studies suggests that in general their role is primarily an expressive one. In his study of a black Baptist congregation in the Pruitt Igoe section of St. Louis, Robert Simpson (1970) emphasizes the cathartic role of religion, particularly as it is exemplified in various ecstatic rituals, in assisting the down-and-out in their search for meaning and community. These findings support our contention that black mainstream churches often function as hegemonic institutions that legitimize existing structures and social relations by inadvertently providing them with an aura of inevitability. Ironically, while obviously providing certain needed housing improvements, the recent black mainstream church predilection for corporatism conforms more to the economic policies of African American academic conservatives such as Thomas Sowell at Harvard University, Glen Lowry at Boston University, and Shelby Steele at San Jose State University (Green 1997: 91).

African Americans in White-Controlled Religious Organizations

While about 90 percent of churchgoing African Americans belong to black-controlled religious organizations, the remaining 10 percent or so belong to white-controlled religious bodies. Of the latter, most are affiliated with predominantly black congregations. Writing in the 1950s, Pope (1957: 106) observed, "Even those [blacks] who belonged to predominantly white denominations were largely segregated at the level of the local congregation, though their representatives might have some contact with white Christians in synods or state conferences . . . and generally did at the level of their national churches." Today most Blacks belonging to white-controlled religious organizations fall into one of three categories: (1) "old elites" or members of the old black middle class who tend to belong to the white-controlled mainstream denominations; (2) "new elites" or members of the new black middle class who also belong to white-controlled mainstream denominations or join more unconventional religious bodies, such as Christian Science, Baha'i, Nichiren Buddhism, Unity, or Mormonism; and (3) working-class and lower-class blacks who belong to white-controlled sects, such as the Jehovah's Witnesses or Seventh-Day Adventists.

Frazier (1974: 83–84) maintains that the "ambiguous position" of middle-class blacks in American society prompted many of them to join the Presbyterian, Congregationalist, and Episcopalian churches, and, in recent decades, Catholic churches.

Some middle-class Negroes in their seeking to find escape from the Negro identification have gone from the Catholic church to the Christian Science church and then to the Bahaist church. Moreover there is a tendency among middle-class Negroes to be attracted to Moral Rearmament hoping that they would find a group in which they would lose completely their identification as Negroes and escape from their feelings of inferiority and insecurity. A small intellectual fringe among middle-class Negroes have affiliated with the Unitarian church. (Frazier 1974: 84)

Some middle-class African Americans maintain "dual church affiliation" —membership in a white-controlled religious body for purposes of prestige along with membership in a National Baptist or African Methodist congregation for professional or business reasons (Frazier 1974: 84). In their survey of 475 congregations in Bronzeville, Drake and Cayton (1945: 633) report that 27 of them are affiliated with white-controlled religious organizations. Based upon data drawn primarily for the period of 1942–44, Loescher made the following observation: "Probably 8,300,000 of the 14,000,000 Negroes in the United States belong to some Christian church. Approximately 8,000,000 are Protestants and 300,000 are Roman Catholics. Of this 8,000,000 approximately 7,500,000 are in separate Negro denominations. The remaining 500,000 are members of Negro churches in predominantly white denominations" (Loescher 1971: 76).

Of the white-controlled denominations affiliated with the Federal Council of Churches in the 1950s, 330,600 African Americans belonged to the Methodist church; 60,326 to the Protestant Episcopal church; 60,000 to the Disciples of Christ; 45,000 to the Northern Baptist church; 40,581 to the Presbyterian Church, USA; 19,374 to the Congregational Christian church; 3,132 to the Presbyterian Church, U.S.; 1,774 to the United Lutheran church; and 1,166 to the United Presbyterian church (Loescher 1971: 52). While precise statistics are unavailable, African Americans in white-controlled denominations belong primarily to predominantly black congregations. Pope (1957: 107) estimates "that less than 2 percent of the white congregations had [black] members at the end of World War II and probably considerably less than one percent of the Negroes in American Protestantism were included in white congregations." In contrast to the nineteenth century, interracial churches with more than a few African Americans have been a rarity during the twentieth century, even in racially mixed neighborhoods. Even the Unitarian Universalist church, which along with the Society of Friends is the most liberal among the white-controlled mainstream denominations, reportedly had only some 1,500 black members out of a total membership of approximately 180,000 and only 12 black ministers out of 1,034 fellowshiped ministers in 1968 (Morrison-Reed 1984: ix), although most, if not all of them, are probably scattered about in predominantly white congregations.

Ironically, the Southern Baptist Convention, a long-time bastion of white supremacy, has been attracting a growing number of middle-class blacks in recent years. The Community Baptist Church of Santa Rosa, California, sometime in the 1950s became the first black congregation in the Southern Baptist Convention (Fitts 1985: 305–6). The Southern Baptist Convention now claims to have "approximately 200,000 black Southern Baptists in more than 500 predominantly black churches and an additional 50,000 in predominantly white churches" (Fitts 1985: 308). In the aftermath of the civil rights movement, Southern Baptists became more willing to tolerate blacks within their ranks.

Black Episcopalians

Given that the Society of the Propagation of the Gospel had a mandate to convert blacks and Native Americans to Christianity, the majority of black Christians in North America during the eighteenth century were probably Anglicans or Episcopalians. The fact that many of the slaveowners were Episcopalians meant that their slaves were often at least nominal Episcopalians. Nonetheless, the Episcopalian church's general indifference to African Americans both before and after the Civil War prompted Du Bois (1903b: 139) to assert that it ". . . has probably done less for black people than any other aggregation of Christians." Black Episcopalians generally have been marked as "Black Bourgeoisie" par excellence.

As noted in chapter 1, after Richard Allen and Absalom Jones left St. George's Methodist Church in Philadelphia, Jones went on to head up St. Thomas African Episcopal Church (Bennett 1974), the first black Episcopal parish in the United States. Jones was ordained a deacon in 1795 and a priest in 1804. Additional black Episcopalian parishes emerged in coastal cities of first the North and later the South during the next several decades. In 1819 former black members of Trinity Church in New York City established St. Philip's Church, the second-oldest black Episcopalian parish in the United States (Bennett 1974: 236). Black parishes in the North experienced a tremendous struggle in their efforts to gain full admission into their dioceses with the right to vote at church conventions. Unlike the Methodists and the Presbyterians, the Episcopal church did not split into North-South branches over the slavery issue. Although the vast majority of black Episcopalians resided in the South prior to the Civil War, most of those who had been slaves shifted their affiliation not only to the African Methodist

Episcopal, African Methodist Episcopal Zion, and the Colored Methodist Episcopal churches but also to the Baptist churches (Bennett 1974: 239). In addition to serving as a vehicle of social mobility for certain segments of the black middle class, the ranks of black Episcopalians increased due to the immigration of large numbers of Anglicans from the West Indies during the first half of the twentieth century. Bennett (1974: 433) reports that the some 100,000 black Episcopalians constitute about 3.5 percent of the nearly 3.5 million Episcopalians in the United States. The vast majority of black Episcopalians belong to over 220 exclusively black parishes and missions.

In contrast to the white Methodist and Presbyterian churches, the Episcopal church rejected the racial missionary district plan by adopting the suffragan bishop plan at its 1907 general convention. Initially whites served as suffragan bishops over missionary work among African Americans, but finally in 1910 two blacks were appointed suffragan bishops (Bennett 1974: 241). Alexander Crummell (1819–98), the most influential black Episcopal priest of his day and the founder of St. Luke's Episcopal Church in Washington, D.C., established in 1883 the Conference of Churchworkers among Colored People, the first black caucus in the Episcopal church. Black Episcopalian priests established the Union of black Episcopalians in 1968 and persuaded their church to form the Absalom Jones Theological Institute at the Interdenominational Theological Center in 1972 in Atlanta.

Black Presbyterians

The Presbyterian antipathy toward religious emotionalism is generally regarded to have been a significant barrier to recruitment of African Americans during the Second Great Awakening. On the Presbyterian treatment of slavery, Wilmore (1983b: 62) observes, "No church was more high-sounding and profound in its Biblical analysis of slavery and did less about it." Nonetheless, some blacks were introduced to Presbyterianism while working as slaves in the homes of their white Presbyterian slave-masters. Furthermore, free blacks in the North established Presbyterian congregations, who often found it difficult to support an educated ministry due to the poverty of their members (Murray 1966: 45). In addition to prestige, the educational opportunities associated with membership in the Presbyterian church attracted some blacks to its ranks.

> *The First African Presbyterian Church of Philadelphia prided itself in sponsoring a day school that was strongly supported by white Presbyterians. . . . The earliest Black Presbyterian missionary, John Chavis, organized a*

school for both whites and Blacks in North Carolina, despite laws throughout the South in 1831 that prohibited anyone from teaching slaves to read and write. Almost all Black Presbyterian pastors augmented their salaries by teaching. Relatively few Blacks in the North and only a small proportion of the estimated seventy thousand slaves owned by Presbyterians in the South answered the call to discipleship, but those who did may well have come into the church as much for educational and social advancement as for any other reason. (Wilmore 1983b: 64–65)

The Southern-based Cumberland Presbyterian Church created the Colored Cumberland Presbyterian Church in 1869 (Dvorak 1991: 149).

Despite the fact that black Presbyterian ministers regularly experienced discrimination at meetings of their presbyteries, they served as the most active and vocal leaders in the abolition and civil rights movement of the antebellum period. In attempting to deal with the racist practices of their own churches, four distinguished black Presbyterian pastors established in 1893 the Afro-Presbyterian Council, which in 1947 was renamed the Council of the North and West (Wilmore 1983b: 69). These bodies served black Presbyterians in the North since black Presbyterians in the South belonged to black presbyteries and synods. Black Presbyterians organized into new caucuses in 1963 with the creation of the Concerned Presbyterians group and in 1968 with the creation of the black Presbyterians United.

Black United Methodists

Prior to 1939, the Methodist Episcopal church was composed of five regional jurisdictions and a Central Jurisdiction, which consisted primarily of the various black annual conferences and the black mission conferences (King 1969). The Plan of Union of 1939 merged the Methodist Episcopal church, the Methodist Episcopal Church, South, and the Methodist Protestant church. A constitutional amendment passed in 1958 paved the way for the replacement of the Central Jurisdiction by permitting individual congregations or annual conferences to affiliate themselves with a regional annual conference or jurisdiction (Norwood 1974: 413). In responding to pressure from civil rights activists within the Methodist church, the general conference of 1964 ruled that the Central Jurisdiction should be abolished by 1968 and that its constituent units affiliate with the various regional jurisdictions. A black caucus within the new United Methodist church was formally organized in 1968 at the First National Conference of Negro Methodists in Cincinnati (Norwood 1974: 433).

Black Catholics

The first black Catholics in what became the United States consisted of slaves and free blacks in Gracia Real de Santa Teresa de Mose, a settlement established north of St. Augustine in 1783 (Davis 1993: 30). Los Angeles was initially inhabited by people of black and Indian ancestry and Spanish California was largely "Afro-Catholic in its racial heritage, Hispanic in its culture, and Catholic in its faith" (Davis 1993:33). In terms of the original thirteen American colonies, blacks constituted approximately 20 out of every 100 Catholics in colonial Maryland (Davis 1993:35). In keeping with the African American proclivity for mutual aid societies, black Catholics formed the Society of the Holy Family in 1843. African American Catholic mutual aid societies existed in Baltimore and New Orleans. The estimated 100,000 black Catholics in the South in 1860 were largely concentrated in five regions: (1) Maryland, with some spill-over in Virginia; (2) western Kentucky, in the vicinity of Bardstown; (3) the low country of South Carolina, especially around Charleston; (4) Florida; and (5) the Gulf Coast, particularly in the vicinity of New Orleans (Miller 1980: 38). Washington, D.C., contained many African Americans because of its proximity to St. Mary's, Charles, and Calvert counties in Maryland (Davis 1993:90). The first order of black nuns was established in Baltimore in 1829. The second order of black nuns emerged in New Orleans. Southern Catholic bishops generally supported slavery. Bishop John England of Charleston, South Carolina, defended slavery in a series of eighteen letters published between 1840 and 1841, despite the fact that Pope Gregory XVI had condemned the slave trade in 1839. He contended that the Bible, church councils, or canon law had never proscribed slavery. In contrast to American Catholics, European Catholics exhibited a greater tendency to condemn slavery. Following the Civil War, many of these black Catholics rejected the religion of their slavemasters or were unable to practice it because of the lack of facilities (Feagin 1968: 247). Unlike various Protestant churches, including white-controlled ones, the American Catholic church did not make a concerted effort to evangelize freedpeople to its ranks. The European-based Mill Hill Fathers (or Josephites in the American context) arrived in Baltimore in 1871 in order to proselytize to African Americans. Perhaps in response to the number of black Catholics, in 1875 the church appointed James Augustine Healy the first African American bishop in American history and the second bishop of Portland, Maine (Davis 1993: 149–150). Indeed, the three Healy brothers were the first black Catholic priests in the United States. David Rudd, a former slave, organized a series of Black Catholic Lay Congresses that were held between 1889 and 1894. The Congress movement called for more Catholic schools for blacks, demanded the admission of blacks into labor unions, urged the establishment of industrial schools for blacks, and opposed housing discrimination against blacks (Davis 1991: 259). It appears to have collapsed due to opposition on the part of the Catholic hierarchy which viewed it as an affront to its authority.

Following in the spirit of the Congress movement, Thomas Wyatt Turner, a biology professor at Howard University, played a pivotal role in the creation of the Committee for the Advancement of Colored Catholics in 1916 (Davis 1993: 218). The Committee was reorganized as the Federated Colored Catholics in 1924 which functioned as an early Catholic civil rights organization. Unfortunately, the latter collapsed due to internal factionalism.

Catholicism in the South essentially functioned as a "Jim Crow church, with parishes, schools, church societies, seminaries, and even Catholic universities usually segregated" (McGreevy 1996: 8). Indeed, as McDonough (1993: 80) so poignantly observes, "Southern Catholicism has both accommodated to and rejected various forms of Protestant organization and thought." The Divine Word Fathers established the first seminary for black priests in 1920 in Mississippi. West Indian immigrants came to constitute a significant portion of African American Catholics in Northern cities such as New York and Boston (McGreevy 1996:29). In 1909, over thirty African American men created the Knights of Peter Claver, a fraternal organization that spread throughout much of the South but that also gradually spread to the North (Davis 1993: 236).

The Vatican was bothered by the paucity of African American clergy and reports of racial discrimination within the church, but did little to counter these patterns. Some liberal Catholics began to define segregation as a sin and formed the National Catholic Conference for Interracial Justice in 1958, an organization that included thirty-six Catholic Interracial Councils (McGreevy 1996: 71). Some Catholics participated in the civil rights movement, including the march on Selma, Alabama, in March 1965.

African Americans, particularly upwardly mobile ones, began to join the Catholic church in growing numbers after World War II. According to Lincoln and Mamiya (1990: 159), "Since 1985 black Roman Catholics have grown from 880,000 to close to 2 million members, with the gains coming largely from Caribbean immigrants and upwardly mobile African Americans seeking parochial educational alternatives to urban public school systems." The National Survey of Religious Identification (NSRI) conducted by the Graduate School of the City University of New York in 1990 that 5 percent of American Catholics are blacks, "a figure that is higher than previously supposed and that represents 9% of the total U.S. black population" (Kosmin and Lachman 1993: 127). Kosmin and Lachman (1993: 127) report that African American Catholics constitute a "significant proportion of the Catholic community in their historical enclaves of Louisiana (15%) and Maryland (13%)." Raboteau (1983: 37) reported the presence of 270 black priests, 700 black nuns, and 7 black bishops in the United States during the early 1980s. The period of 1968–70 saw the formation of the Black Catholic Clergy Caucus, the National Black Sisters Conference, the Black Lay Caucus, and the National Office of Black Catholics.

Anthropologist Gary McDonogh (1993) conducted a detailed ethnohistorical and ethnographic study of African American Catholics in Savannah. The city has three black parishes, namely St. Benedict the Moor, St. Anthony's, and the Most Pure Heart of Mary. Whereas St. Benedict's (est. 1889), the oldest of the black parishes, tends to cater to primarily middle-class people, St. Mary's draws its parishioners from different neighborhoods and social classes. The priests and nuns who have served the city's black parishes and schools have been almost exclusively white. The Catholic hierarchy closed the black parish schools in Savannah between 1968 and 1977 in its effort to conform to the spirit of racial integration promoted by the civil rights movement.

Despite an effort to create inner-city interparochial schools, these schools became as "much as 70 percent, including Protestants seeking what they perceive a better, more disciplined education for their children" (McDonogh 1993: 98). Lay catechists have come to assume a pivotal role in the formation of an African American Catholic identity. Savannah's black Catholic parishes have incorporated various African American religious practices, including Gospel music, walking to the altar in order to deposit the offering a basket, and holding of hands during recitation of the Our Father (McDonogh 1993: 316–18).

In contrast to black Protestants who have severed their ties with their white-controlled denominations, black Catholics have not been prone to schismatic tendencies. An exception, however, is George Augustus Stallings Jr., the founder of the African American Congregation. He made a request to Cardinal James Hickey of Washington, D.C., that he be permitted to establish an African American rite that would have an independent liturgy and socio-religious structure comparable to Eastern Rite Catholics. After this request was denied, Stallings established a new congregation called the Imani Temple and was consecrated a bishop on May 12, 1990, by the prelate of the American Independent Orthodox Church. Bruce Greening, one of Stalling's colleagues, went on to form the Independent African American Catholic Rite.

Blacks in White-Controlled Sects

Most blacks affiliated with white-controlled religious organizations belong to mainstream denominations. While reliable statistics are unavailable, however, a fair number of working-class and lower-class blacks also belong to white-controlled sects. For example, an increasing number of middle-class blacks have been joining the Mormon church in recent years (White and White 1992; Embry 1994; Embry and Jacobson 1995). While a small number of blacks belonged to the Mormon church during the period when it had an official ban on blacks entering its lay priesthood, the lifting of the ban apparently has encouraged some blacks to join what remains an overwhelmingly white religious organizations, at least within the United States (White and White 1980; Mauss 1981; White and White 1995). Small black Churches of Christ appeared throughout the South after World War II. Reportedly there are now some 1,200 such congregations (Conkin 1997:40). While these congregations are nominally independent, as are all Church of Christ congregations, in reality they operate "under a [white-controlled] system of spiritual and financial paternalism" (Harrell 1971: 43). The Church of God of Prophecy was probably the largest racially integrated religious body in the South from 1945 to the mid-1960s in that it did not segregate blacks into a satellite organization (Harrell 1971: 94–95). Although local congregations generally are predominantly white or black, state and international assemblies have been integrated throughout the sect's history.

The Jehovah's Witnesses appear to have a larger percentage of black members than any other white-controlled religious organization. According to Cooper (1974: 705), "Estimates of this membership in the early 1960s ran from 20% to 30% of the total Witnesses in the U.S. . . . In the Witnesses' circuit assemblies in North and West Philadelphia during the research period, each of which included more than 2,200 persons, 99% of the audience were Negroes, figures well above the 70% Negro population in North Philadelphia and 60% in West Philadelphia." Although the members of the black Jehovah's Witnesses congregation in North Philadelphia studied by Cooper (1974: 711) believed that they belonged to the only organization in the world that does not practice racial discrimination, no blacks appeared to belong to the higher echelons of the society's hierarchy. In a similar vein, Jim Jones appointed mostly whites as associate ministers in his apocalyptic People's Temple, which had an estimated 70–80 percent black membership (Richardson 1980: 242).

Even some imported sectarian groups have been able to attract a notable African American following. One is the Japanese-based Nichiren Shoshu Buddhist sect. Noted for its "loud, monotonous chanting of 'Nanna-nyohorenge-kyo' (Devotion to the Wondrous Law of Lotus Sutra)" (Oh 1973: 169), this often flamboyant conversionist sect traces its origin to a thirteenth-century Buddhist revitalization movement led by an inspired monk who took the name Nichiren (Sun Lotus). The sect became an increasingly important religious and political force in Japan after World War II and formed an integral part of the postwar religious boom that seized the Japanese population (Babbie 1966). Recruitment in the United States began in the 1960s, initially on the West Coast. In the early 1970s, Oh (1973) found that 55 percent of the seven hundred Americans who answered his questionnaire were white while 9 percent were African American. In recent years, the sect has attracted a growing number of African Americans around the country, especially among middle-class individuals. For example, in a church rally and training session that took place at Trenton State University in New Jersey in 1987, the authors noted that a large percentage of the three hundred to four hundred participants was black.

Protest and Accommodation among Blacks in White-Controlled Mainstream Denominations

One might surmise that blacks belonging to white-controlled mainstream denominations historically have been and continue to be more accommodative toward the larger society than members of black mainstream denominations. After all, the latter belong to organizations that emerged out of religiously inspired protest movements to racism. Conversely, one might conclude that black members of white-controlled mainstream denominations, in large part because of their overwhelmingly middle-class status and their rejection of participation in the most significant self-controlled institution among African Americans, have internalized individualistic bourgeois values that run contrary to black communal objectives. Paradoxically, however, various scholars have argued that black congregations and/or black members affiliated with white-controlled mainstream denominations have tended to be more militant than their counterparts among the black Baptist and Methodist denominations. Meier (1966: 222), for one, asserts that "by and large it was among the more elite Presbyterian, Congregational, and Episcopal churches of the Northern and border states that the protest point of view found its strength" during the period 1880–1915, whereas the Baptist and Methodist churches with mass support tended to be more conservatively inclined. Based upon his examination of black politics in Chicago, Wilson (1960: 128) similarly observes that the "educated, upper-class ministers of the socially preferred denominations—the Congregationalists, the

Presbyterians, the Episcopalians—together with the 'better' Baptist and Methodist ministers form the group from which civic leaders are drawn," whereas "even among the larger churches, many of which claim to have over ten thousand members, support for race causes is spotty." A case in point is Milton A. Galamison, the pastor of the Siloam Presbyterian Church, an avowed socialist who praised Fidel Castro, served as the president of the NAACP branch, and earned a "reputation as one of the most militant civil rights activists in Brooklyn" (Taylor 1994: 128) as result of his involvement in the school integration effort in New York City. In a somewhat similar vein, Father Paul M. Washington (1994) provided space at his Episcopal Church of the Advocate in North Philadelphia for meetings of Black Power advocates, the Black Panther Party, the Black Economic Development Conference, and numerous other progressive groups.

In his classic statistical study of civil rights militancy among church-going blacks, partially summarized in table 8, Gary Marx made the following observations. "[I]t can be seen that those belonging to sects are the least likely to be militant; they are followed by those in predominantly Negro denominations. Ironically, those individuals in largely white denominations (Episcopalian, Presbyterian, United Church of Christ, and Roman Catholic) are those most likely to be militant, in spite of the perhaps greater civil rights activism of the Negro denominations. This pattern emerged even when social class was held constant" (G. Marx 1967: 67).

Table 8

Proportion Militant, by Denomination

Denomination	% Militant	(No.)
Episcopalian	46	(24)
United Church of Christ	42	(12)
Presbyterian	40	(25)
Catholic	40	(109)
Methodist	34	(142)
Baptist	32	(658)
Sects and cults	20	(106)

SOURCE: Adapted from G. Marx (1967).

Unfortunately, no additional detailed studies have been conducted on the sociopolitical attitudes of black members of white-controlled Protestant mainstream denominations. Conversely, in large part because the Catholic church now has more black members than any other white-controlled religious organization in the United States, several such studies have been conducted on black Catholics (Alston, Alston, and Warrick 1971; Collins 1971; Nelsen and Dickson 1972; Hunt and Hunt 1975, 1976, and 1977). While black Catholics overall probably do not exhibit a higher socioeconomic status than black Episcopalians, Presbyterians, and Congregationalists, these studies demonstrate that they do exhibit a higher socioeconomic status than blacks belonging to the black mainstream denominations. Furthermore, black Catholics generally exhibit a higher secular orientation than members of black mainstream denominations (Hunt and Hunt 1975).

In a reexamination of Gary Marx's data on religiously inspired civil rights militancy, Hunt and Hunt (1977) argue that Marx failed to differentiate between "conventional militancy" and "corporate militancy." Whereas the items used to measure "conventional militancy" focus upon "structural awareness" of racial inequality in American society, those items from Marx's data measuring what Hunt and Hunt term "corporate militancy" focus upon the advocacy of collective forms of protest. "In sum, the impression of a new level of militancy on the part of black Catholics rests on their sophistication regarding racism, an aspect of secular orientation related primarily, it would seem, to high status and assimilation. In contrast, on those dimensions of militancy which are more clearly associated with the civil rights movement—black pride and collective protest—black Catholics remain "nonmilitant" and differentiated from other blacks" (Hunt and Hunt 1977: 832).

In assessing research on the sociopolitical attitudes of black Catholics, Peck (1982) suggests that Catholicism may have played a more accommodative role in African American history than has black Protestantism. Indeed, perhaps much the same could be said for Episcopalianism, Presbyterianism, Congregationalism, and even United Methodism relative to black Protestantism.

IV

$\mathcal{M}$essianic-$\mathcal{N}$ationalist Sects

$\mathcal{T}$he first sectarian type in our typology is the "messianic-nationalist." In significant ways, this type stands alone among African American religious groups. As contrasted with the conversionist and most thaumaturgical sects, to be examined in the next two chapters, a distinctive characteristic of messianic-nationalist sects is their committed separatist and overtly militant stance. Indeed, their militancy not infrequently brings them into sharp conflict with other sectarian and mainstream organizations. Central to the vitalizing core of these groups is a fundamental critique of the place and treatment of people of African heritage in American society. Implied in this critique and often expressed outright is a rejection of the accommodationist features found in other African American religious organizations.

As such, messianic-nationalist sects have both religious and political features. They are as much concerned with African American or even Pan-African identity as with achieving spiritual salvation or serving the Lord. In some groups, in fact, political traits seem to have even greater prominence than commonly understood religious practices. Indeed, the defining attribute of these sects is their creative blending of diverse forms of intervention and retribution with the nationalist ideal of achieving autonomy and political or even territorial sovereignty for African Americans. This potentially volatile admixture can be found in an array of sects in the black community, especially the black Islamic and Judaic groups whose emergence and nature has so puzzled outside observers. Given the political tensions between Arabs and Israeli Jews, lumping black Muslims and black Jews into a common pool might appear reckless. In fact, these sects share both a heritage and a basic belief structure, articulated through somewhat differing religious symbol systems.

While variously expressed as black Islam, black Judaism, Yorubaism, Abyssinianism, or even militant Christianity, messianic-nationalism represents a religious counterhegemonic tradition that rejects the label "Negro" as an oppressive white invention and seeks to replace it with a more satisfying self-definition based on a belief in the unparalleled spiritual and historic significance of African Americans. Conversion to a messianic-nationalist sect, consequently, commonly involves acceptance of a new personal identity, often celebrated through the adoption of a new name, as well as changes in dress, diet, and other life patterns. A generally shared belief of messianic-nationalist sects is that, far from being a people without history or national homeland, African Americans are descendants of patriarchs and princes while whites are the temporarily powerful offspring of a barbarous, deviant, or otherwise tarnished branch of divine creation. To messianic-nationalists, black history can only be understood if it is recognized that African Americans are the chosen people, selected by God to pass through a period of agonizing ignominy on the road to spiritual as well as material grandeur.

As a distinct brand of black sectarianism, messianic-nationalism can be traced to the Great Migration of African Americans from the rural South to the urban North that occurred early in the twentieth century. However, messianic-nationalism did not appear sui generis with the migration. Important antecedents of this radical politico-religious tradition can be found in the liberation theme that is vital to black folk Christianity and the return-to-Africa efforts of nineteenth-century black nationalists. It is known that black slaves not infrequently likened their lot to the Israelite servitude in Egypt and later exile in Babylon and, as a result, framed their desire for liberation in terms of a latter-day black Moses who would once again lead the children of God to the Promised Land. Unlike white racists who rationalized black subordination as stemming from the Biblical curse placed on Ham, black nationalists redefined the belief in Hamitic descent as evidence of the historic significance of black people. In their view, as Meier (1952: 96) observes, "since Ham was a Negro, it follows that all his descendants were—and that included most of the civilized peoples of the Ancient Near East: Cushites or Ethiopians, Egyptians, Phoenicians, Babylonians, and Assyrians; and even the Hebrews intermarried with the Cushites, so that Jesus is a descendant of Ham, and therefore a Negro." Beginning before but expanding greatly during the Great Migration, certain "black gods of the metropolis" (Fauset 1971) merged the messianic salvation theme in black folk Christianity with nineteenth-century black nationalist ideology (Singer 1992). These prophets established Judaic, Islamic, and Christian strains of messianic-nationalism.

The Development of African American Judaism

The earliest sects to express some form of black Judaism antedate the twentieth century and thus represent "the first sectarian-based brand of black nationalism . . . which was not explicitly Christian" (Landing 1974: 27). While black Jewish sects have never gained the membership of some black Muslim groups, they have, nonetheless, had a significant impact on black messianic-nationalism. Ideas and individuals move freely between black Jewish and other types of messianic-nationalist sects, allowing not only a constant cross-fertilization but a broad sharing of central values and conceptions.

According to Brotz (1970: 1), "As early as 1900, Negro preachers were traveling through the Carolinas preaching the doctrine that the so-called Negroes were really the lost sheep of the House of Israel." The propinquity established between African Americans and immigrant Jews in northern cities also "gave both potential and practicing Black Jews an unusual opportunity to learn Jewish traditions firsthand" (Shapiro 1970: 61).

The existence of a militant, messianic-nationalist brand of black Judaism first gained widespread attention with the Abyssinian affair, which occurred in Chicago during the summer of 1920. R. D. Jonas and Grover Cleveland Redding, who claimed to be Ethiopian, organized the Abyssinian movement, a group intended to fulfill a purported Biblical prophecy that the time had arrived for all African Americans to return to their ancestral homeland, Ethiopia (Spear 1967: 193–94). To publicize this idea, Redding led a parade of the movement's members down East Thirty-fifth Street in Chicago. When, during the parade, he suddenly set an American flag afire, several whites attempted to intervene, leading to a scuffle that left two people dead and a number injured. The "Ethiopian Connection" that Redding discussed at his trial became an important and recurring theme in black Judaism throughout the twentieth century. In the remaining portion of this section, we will discuss the development of two of the earliest black Jewish sects in New York City, various other black Jewish sects, and finally the Black Hebrew Israelite Nation, a sect with branches in both the United States and Israel, which Merrill Singer (1982, 1985, 1988) has studied in depth.

The Church of the Living God, the Pillar Ground of Truth for All Nations

Despite the attention Redding's arrest and execution generated, the Abyssinian movement was not the earliest of the black Jewish sects. The Church of the Living God, the Pillar Ground of Truth for All Nations, may have been organized by F. S. Cherry, a black seaman and railroad worker, as early as the 1880s (Shapiro 1970). Begun in Chattanooga, Tennessee, the sect later moved to Philadelphia, where it attracted a committed following. Cherry taught his followers that God had called him to enlighten the world that the true descendants of the Biblical Hebrews are African Americans. He maintained that both God and Jesus, as well as Adam and Eve, were black, and that whites were the offspring of Gehazi, a servant cursed by the prophet Elisha with skin "as white as snow," while the Caucasian Jew was "an interloper and a fraud" (Fauset 1971: 34). Like many messianic-nationalist sects to follow, Cherry urged economic independence for the black community. After Cherry's death at the age of ninety-five, leadership passed to the prophet's son, Prince Benjamin F. Cherry. Members of the sect deny that Cherry really died, believing instead that he had merely gone to a place "where his people could not see him" and that he "would return in spirit to lead the Church through the person of his son" (Shapiro 1970: 139–40). To affirm the founder's continued connection with the church, a recording of one of his sermons is played every Sabbath.

The Church of God and Saints of Christ

William S. Crowdy, a cook on the Santa Fe Railroad, proclaimed that he was called by God to lead African American people back to their historic religion and identity. After the Civil War and freedom from slavery, he purchased a one-hundred-acre farm in Guthrie, Oklahoma, where he began to have visions in 1893. Shortly following this, he began preaching in the streets of Guthrie and later in other Texas towns as well as on State Street in Chicago (Wynia 1994: 21). In 1896 he established the Church of God and Saints of Christ in Lawrence, Kansas, but moved its national headquarters to Philadelphia in 1900 where he reportedly was joined by some five thousand members (Wynia 1994: 26). Crowdy asserted that blacks were the heirs of the ten lost tribes of Israel, while Caucasian Jews were the offspring of miscegenation with whites.

The Church of God and Saints of Christ developed into a syncretic African American Judaic-Christian sect which emphasizes repentance of sin, baptism by immersion, commemoration of the Last Supper, foot washing, observance of the Ten Commandments, the holy kiss, and prayer (Wynia 1994: 25). It observes the Jewish Sabbath and Passover and other Jewish holidays and claims to be based upon the teachings of the patriarchs, prophets, and apostles of the Old and New Testaments. The sect also has incorporated elements from Prince Hall Masonry, including the use of rosettes, sashes, crowns, belts and swords, bugles, mortar boards, certain greetings, handshakes, and marches (Wynia 1994: 47–48). Crowdy's written sermons are referred to as "epistles." In a sermon delivered in Lawrence in

1903, he "urged the congregation to wage an unrelenting war against oppression and discrimination" (Wynia 1994: 23). Crowdy performed miracles and received prophesies which served as the basis for the sect's beliefs, rituals, and organization. The Church of God and Saints of Christ held four General Assemblies in Lawrence, Emporia (Kansas), and Philadelphia prior to Crowdy's death in 1908. At the first significant organizational meeting on October 10, 1899, representatives from several states and Ontario created a presbytery consisting of northeastern, northwestern, southeastern, and southwestern districts (Wynia 1994: 30–31).

The Church of God and Saints of Christ reportedly has fifty-three tabernacles in the United States, seven in South Africa, and a few in the West Indies (Wynia 1994: 36–38). The majority of congregations are located on the East Coast, including Pennsylvania, New Jersey, New York, Maryland, Massachusetts, Connecticut, Washington, D.C., and Virginia. The sect also has congregations in Chicago, Jacksonville (Florida), Gary, Cincinnati, Detroit, Greensboro (North Carolina), and Atlanta. It split into two factions following Crowdy's death, one of which emerged in South Africa. At the present time, the Church of God and Saints has an eastern and a western district in the United States.

Following Crowdy's death, leadership passed to his handpicked successor, Bishop H. Z. Plummer. The sect has stressed communalism and economic self-sufficiency. Under Plummer's jurisdiction, the Church of God and Saints of Christ relocated its headquarters to Belleville" (an area within Portsmouth, Virginia) in 1917. At the 1,000-acre Belleville headquarters, members live collectively and operate a farm, several cottage industries, a school, and homes for orphans and the elderly. The Church of God and Saints of Christ also operates a 110-acre youth camp in Galestown, Maryland, that serves as a referral and rehabilitation center for youth offenders. Elders assign jobs in the group's businesses to workers, who turn over their incomes to the church in exchange for weekly rations in the commissary. As Shapiro (1970: 117) indicates, "emphasis is placed upon social stability, parental moral responsibility for children, and care for one's own people through social welfare programs."

Black Jewish Sects Based in New York City

In 1899 Leon Richlieu established the Moorish Zionist Temple in Brooklyn. Rabbi Richlieu, as he was called, maintained that he was of Ethiopian origin and that his congregation was composed of black Jews from Palestine and northern Africa. When interviewed in 1964, he claimed that he had been converted to Judaism by three rabbinical authorities and had studied in an orthodox Jewish yeshiva (Berger 1978). Despite its name, this group may have been the first black Jewish congregation that emphasized a Jewish rather than a black nationalist ideology (Dobrin 1975). The sect apparently included white Jewish members (Shapiro 1970); upon his death in 1964, Richlieu was buried in a Jewish cemetery (Berger 1978).

By the end of World War I, at least eight black Jewish sects were active in New York. The leaders of these groups "were all acquainted and in several cases associated with each other from time to time as congregations would rise, split, collapse, and reorganize" (Brotz 1970: 10). One of the more notorious of these leaders, Warren Robinson (or Roberson), a migrant from Norfolk, Virginia, who established the Temple of the Gospel of the Kingdom in New York, ultimately claimed divine status. As part of their initiation to his church, "each prospective member was forced to kneel in front of Robinson and swear that there was no other 'God' in all of creation but him" (New York Amsterdam News, July 1, 1931). Members of the sect, who believed that both Jesus and Robinson embodied the Christ spirit, lived communally, collectively managing several shops and restaurants. Robinson established branch congregations in Atlantic City, Philadelphia, Detroit, Chicago, and Abescon, New Jersey.

Arnold Josiah Ford, a West Indian admirer of Marcus Garvey's nationalist aspirations, forged a brand of black Judaism stripped of the overtly Christian features so prominent in the groups organized by his predecessors and helped to move the idea of African emigration to the center of black Jewish ideology (Brotz 1970: 11). Ford struggled to have Judaism declared the official religion of Garvey's Universal Negro Improvement Association (UNIA). While a "sizable minority of New York Garveyites were Black Jews" (Vincent 1972: 134), the "black Moses" opposed the Judaization of the UNIA. Following involvement in the Moorish Zionist Temple, which reportedly began as an effort by Mordecai Herman to reorganize Leon Richlieu's group (Shapiro 1970), Ford, with the assistance of Samuel Valentine, established the Beth B'nai Abraham congregation. Ford "repudiated all Christian doctrine" (Shapiro 1970: 16) but incorporated some Islamic elements in his congregation's ritual repertoire, including observance of the fast of Ramadan. He actually rejected the term "Jewish," stressing that he was an Ethiopian Hebrew. In keeping with Garveyist sympathies, Ford regarded Africa as "ancient, bright and glorious" (King 1972: 83) and believed that African Americans had an obligation to help awaken Africa to its predestined glory. In his synagogue, he stressed the importance of a return to the motherland and denounced the term "Negro." Due to internal conflicts at Beth B'nai Abraham, in 1930 Ford left New York. Contrary to Brotz's (1970: 12) speculation that Ford may have subsequently surfaced in Detroit as W. D. Fard, founder of the Nation of Islam, there is good evidence that he migrated to Ethiopia (King 1972; Shack 1974). Ford's interest in Islam reflects the intermingling of Jewish and Islamic ideas and practices long characteristic of black messianic-nationalism.

Following Ford's departure, Wentworth Arthur Matthew, the founder of the Commandment Keepers, Holy Church of the Living God, Pillar and Ground of the Truth, emerged as the leading black Jewish figure in Harlem. In 1929 he claimed two thousand followers and by 1968 estimated that his flock had grown to four thousand (Berger 1978). In 1936 Matthew organized the Royal Order of Ethiopian Hebrews, an association which eventually had branches in Brooklyn and Arverne, New York; Philadelphia, Media, Pittsburgh, and Sharon, Pennsylvania; Cincinnati, Youngstown, Warren, and Ferrell, Ohio; Chicago; Cullen, Virginia; Jersey City, New Jersey; and in the West Indies. Indeed, his followers considered him to be the chief rabbi of all black Jews in North America, although rival sects never accepted this designation. In commenting upon Matthew's death at the age of eighty-one on December 4, 1973, Berger (1978: 96) asserts that "the most colorful, photogenic, inventive and written about Black Rabbi on the Black Jewish pulpit left the scene."

The Abeta Hebrew Cultural Center

Unlike New York with Arnold Ford and later Wentworth Matthew, Chicago's black Jews never developed a dominant leader nor an economically and socially stable main congregation. Commonly, groups have been small with participants meeting in members' homes while they struggled to raise sufficient funds to open a storefront synagogue. Many of these sects were short-lived, with frequent splintering and fragmentation. The better-known black Jewish sects in Chicago include the B'nai Zaken congregation, the Congregation of the Aethiopian Hebrews, the Hebrew Cultural Center, and the Royal Order of the Essenes.

Beginning in the mid-1960s a new congregation, the Abeta Hebrew Cultural Center, emerged among Chicago's black Jews. The sect met at Naphtali Israeli's synagogue and was led by several "elders," men in their thirties and forties who had long been affiliated with black Judaism. The Abeta Center emphasized emigration to Africa, arguing that blacks had no meaningful future in the United States, which they regarded as a latter-day Babylon doomed to destruction. Abeta's elders tried to acquire land grants in Africa for an eventual relocation of the sect. In 1968, following several years of intensive recruitment and fund-raising, several hundred members migrated to Liberia, to land acquired for them by an ex-Garveyite who had moved to Africa in 1951. But migration to the African countryside proved to be tough going. Ultimately, the Abeta colony collapsed due to difficulties in cultivating the heavily forested land, susceptibility of members to tropical diseases, and internal conflicts.

While some members returned to the United States, others undertook a second migration, to Israel. The Israeli government responded by giving the sect a number of apartments in the Negev development town of Dimona. Under the prophetship of Ben Ami ben Israel, the group developed a communal lifestyle and an elaborate politico-religious structure. Members regard Ben Ami, a former foundry worker, as the Son of God and Prince of Peace. While the Abeta sect has survived and grown over the past twenty years to several thousand members in Israel, with branches in several African and American cities, it has not been able to resolve its conflicts over its legal status with the Israeli government. Ethan Michaeli, a journalist reports that: "In October 1990, Illinois state legislators brokered an agreement with the Israeli government that settled—albeit temporarily—the Hebrew Israelites' legal status in Israel. They are now permitted to hold jobs and receive access to social services and housing. Members of the group reclaimed their American citizenship and received support from the American government that allowed them to build a school and expand housing" (Michaeli 2000: 74). Nonetheless, in migrating to Israel, the Abeta sect, now known as the Black Hebrew Israelite Nation, has partially fulfilled the emigrationist vision long vibrant within black messianic-nationalism, a theme always more central to the black Judaic expression of this counterhegemonic tradition than to other variants.

The Development of African American Islam

While no definite connection can be made between twentieth-century black Islam and slaves from Islamic areas in Africa, as Monroe Berger observes, "It is quite possible that some of the various American Muslim groups of the past half century or so had their roots in these vestiges, and that the tradition was handed down in a weak chain from generation to generation" (quoted in Melton, vol. 2: 339). Furthermore, Allen posits that black Hebrewism contributed at least four aspects to African American Islam during its formative stages in the 1920s and 1930s:

> First of all, the enjoining of Christian and Judaic elements in Black Hebrew-ism provided a rough paradigm for the merging of Christianity and Islam in the world views of both the Moorish Science Temple of America and the Nation of Islam. Second, in naming Judaism as the original religion to which people of

African descent had purportedly turned their backs. Black Hebrews of more orthodox mien for the first time brought a sense of the "concrete"—if that is the appropriate term—to the African-American incorporation of Hebrew destiny invoked in Deuteronomy 28. Third, Black Hebrews broadened the field of possibilities regarding the territorial origin of African Americans from a historically grounded West and Central Africa to a mythical North Africa and Palestine. And last, while the notion of black economic self-sufficiency hardly originated with Black Hebrews, their particular embrace of the doctrine of economic uplift, in combination with the previously noted characteristics, may certainly have inspired the MTSA and the NOI along similar lines. (Allen 1998: 174–75)

Of the several black Islamic sects in the United States, the Nation of Islam, which originally carried the official name of the Lost-Found Nation of Islam in the Wilderness of North America, has attracted the greatest number of members over the years. Some founding members were involved in an earlier Muslim sect called the Moorish Science Temple.

The Moorish Science Temple

Timothy Drew, a migrant from North Carolina, established, with the assistance of a Dr. Suliman, the first African American Islamic or Muslim organization, called the Caanite Temple, in Newark in 1913. Little is known about Drew's past, other than that in his late twenties he began to preach a homespun version of Islam to fellow migrants. According to Moorish Science legend, Drew claimed that he visited North Africa, where he received a commission by the king of either Egypt or Morocco to teach Islam to African Americans. Upon his return, some followers assert, he met with the president of the United States to receive a "charter" for his work (Essien-Udom 1962). Noble Drew Ali taught his followers that they were not "Negroes, Colored Folks, Black People, or Ethiopians, because these names were given by slaveholders, in 1779 and lasted until 1865, during the time of slavery," However, he asserted, this "is a new era of time now, and all men must proclaim their free national name to be recognized by the government in which they live and the nations of the earth, this is the reason why Allah the Great God of the Universe ordained Noble Drew Ali, the prophet, to redeem the people from their sinful ways" (quoted in Bontemps and Conroy 1966: 205–6). The prophet maintained that African Americans are "the descendants of the ancient Moabites who inhabited the North Western and South Western shores of Africa" (quoted in Bontemps and Conroy 1966: 206) before being brought to the New World as slaves. In spite of their suffering, the Moors or Asiatics are the descendants of a proud nation with a royal history and a glorious future. Following the coming destruction of white people, the Moors will establish "a world in which love, truth, peace, freedom, and justice will flourish" (Fauset 1971: 48). Drew bolstered the new Asiatic identity of his eager followers with a rich array of national symbols, including a national flag (a star within a crescent on a field of red), a distinctive garb (red fezzes and long beards), a sacred book (a self-composed "Koran"), and membership cards (which identified holders as Muslims "under the Divine Laws of the Holy Koran of Mecca, Love, Truth, Peace, Freedom, and Justice"). The Moors also abstained from meat, eggs, alcohol, and tobacco.

Drew blended together elements from Islam, Christianity, Freemasonry, Theosophy, and pan-Africanism in his creation of a syncretic religious system (Turner 1997: 91–92). In 1927, he published a short book called the *Holy Koran*, also called *Circle Seven Koran*, which went through several versions and drew upon the Quran, the *Aquarian Gospels of Jesus Christ*, and *Unto Thee I Grant* (a Rosicrucian tract). DeCaro (1996: 19) asserts that the *Holy Koran* also drew upon a Tibetan writing entitled *Infinite Wisdom*. Drew established a number of small businesses where his followers could work (Essien-Udom 1962: 47). At any rate, as Turner (1997: 96) observes, "Drew Ali attempted to invert the religious values of American culture by presenting Christianity as an inferior European religion which had been surpassed by Islam, the 'true religion' of African Americans."

By 1916, the Caanite Temple had split into two factions, the Holy Moabite Temple of the World which remained in Newark and the Moorish Science Temple of America which remained loyal to Drew Ali and relocated its headquarters to Chicago.

From Newark, the Moorish Science Temple spread to Chicago, Pittsburgh, Detroit, Philadelphia, and a number of other northern cities. In Chicago, a stronghold of the sect, Drew reportedly attracted as many as ten thousand followers (Carlisle 1975; Bontempts and Conroy 1966). In 1929 Drew Ali began to delegate more power to his subordinates, who reportedly tried to "exploit the members by selling herbs, magic charms, and literature on the movement to the extent that some of them became wealthy" (Marsh 1984: 48). A power struggle led to the death of Sheik Claude Greene and the subsequent arrest of Drew Ali, even though he was not in Chicago at the time of the murder. Drew Ali died a few weeks after being released on bond. One theory posits that he died from injuries inflicted by the police during his imprisonment and another that he was killed by Greene's followers. The council of governors of the sect elected C. Kirkman Bey, Ali's former secretary, to the position of Grand Sheik. John Givens-El, Ali's former chauffeur, claimed that he was the reincarnation of Drew and assumed leadership over a contending faction.

After Drew's death, the Moorish Science Temple split into numerous factions. The FBI capitalized upon factionalism within the Moorish Science movement by infiltrating its temples during the 1940s, but continued its program of systematic harassment into the 1970s (Turner 1997: 107–8). The two principal Moorish Science sects at the present time are the Moorish Science Temple of America and the Moorish Science Temple Divine and National Movement of North America. The former group "seems to have peaked in the 1940s, at which time it had active centers across the Midwest and Northeast and into the South (Richmond, Virginia, and Chattanooga, Tennessee)" (Murphy, Melton, and Ward 1993: 507). In 1981, it moved its headquarters to the Baltimore/Washington, D.C., area, but it also operates a small center in Chicago. The latter group has its headquarters in Baltimore. According to Lincoln (1962: 53), "Many present-day Moors believe that Noble Drew Ali is reincarnate in their present leaders, and the Holy Koran of the Moorish Holy Temple of Science continues to be the sacred book of the various sects."

Grand sheiks serve as leaders of temples. They are assisted by ministers, elders, and stewards. Moorish Americans pray in the direction of Mecca three times a day—at sunrise, noon, and sunset. They observe Friday as their holy day and celebrate Noble Drew Ali's birthday on January 8, New Year's on January 15, Flag Day in August, and Christmas. Only some Moors celebrate Ramadan. They abstain from meat, eggs, alcohol, and tobacco. Moors are urged not to serve in the military. The Moorish movement has, over the course of its history, published several newspapers, including the *Moorish Guide National Edition* (est. 1928), the *Moorish Review* (est. sometime in the 1950s), and the *Moorish Science Monitor* (McCloud 1995: 56). The movement has been involved in various social outreach programs, including feeding the poor and operating drug and alcohol recovery programs.

The Nation of Islam

The exact origin of the Nation of Islam remains clouded in mystery, as does the character of the sect's founder. Some theories maintain that the sect's founder, Wallace D. Fard, was either of Syrian and Caribbean background or of some other Asian extraction (DeCaro 1998: ix). Clegg II (1997: 20) asserts that police records indicate that he was born in either New Zealand or Portland, Oregon, on February 21, 1891, to either Hawaiian or British and Polynesian parents. Based upon his examination of FBI files, Evanzz (1999: 400) asserts he was the son of Zared Fard, a New Zealander whose parents were Muslims from the region of India that eventually became Pakistan, and that he illegally entered the United States from Canada around

1913. The FBI records report that Fard settled in Portland, Oregon, where he married Pearl Allen, later operated a restaurant in Los Angeles, was arrested for violating the federal prohibition law in his restaurant, and made his way to Chicago where he worked as a salesperson (Evanzz 1999: 400–407). Using the alias of David Ford, he joined the Moorish Science Temple and rose to the status of Sheik over the Chicago temple (Evanzz 1999: 67). He was an unsuccessful contender for leadership of the group following the death of Drew Ali and moved to Detroit in 1930 where he renamed himself Wallace D. Fard. Fard canvassed the Paradise Valley neighborhood as a door-to-door peddler of silk scarfs and other handicrafts. He established the Allah Temple of Islam and produced a volume called *Secret Rituals of the Long-Found Nation of Islam* (Evanzz 1999: 70). Fard fell upon hard times when one of his followers, Robert Karriem, performed a human sacrifice as a result of his interpretation of several passages from *Secret Rituals* as a call for such an undertaking (Evanzz 1999: 84–92). In effort to clear his organization's name, Fard reconstituted the Allah Temple as the Nation of Islam. Soon after his appearance, Fard's followers regarded him as "the messiah who had come to lead the so-called Negro into the millennium which was to follow the Battle of Armageddon" (Lincoln 1973: xxvi). According to Bontemps and Conroy (1966), the Nation of Islam attracted some eight thousand members during its first four years.

After his imprisonment in Chicago, Fard reportedly traveled around the country and returned to visit his followers in Chicago one last time in order to bid them farewell in February 1934 (DeCaro 1999:20). In June 1934 he was reported missing and never again made another public appearance. According to Lee, "Many groups attempted to take advantage of the Nation's instability at this Time to infiltrate and win its followers. Among them were the American Communist Party, the Japanese (under Major Takahashi), and an Ethiopian (Wyxzewizard S. E. Challouchliczilczese). None was successful, but their combined effect weakened the movement" (Lee 1996: 24). The mantle of leadership fell upon Elijah Poole, a migrant from Georgia and former member of both the Garvey movement and the Moorish Science Temple. He taught that Fard had been Allah and not a mere prophet and referred to himself as the "Messenger of Allah." This teaching led to a split in the sect, prompting Elijah Muhammad and his faction to relocate their headquarters to Chicago, which became the center of the Nation of Islam's future activities. He spent time recruiting new members in Milwaukee, Madison, and Washington, D.C., where he established a temple in 1939 (DeCaro 1999: 36). Elijah served a sentence for sedition in the federal prison in Milan, Michigan, from July 1943 to August 1946 (DeCaro 1999: 37).

Like other messianic-nationalist sects, the Nation of Islam under Elijah Muhammad asserted that black people were intentionally kept ignorant "of their origins, history, true names, [and] religion" (Lincoln 1973: 71). Furthermore, Elijah Muhammad taught his followers that blacks were the original inhabitants of the earth, and it was not until six thousand years ago that a black scientist named Yakub created the white race. But with the War of Armageddon, to be fought in the "wilderness of North America," whites will be returned to dust and ashes. This cataclysm was to have occurred in 1914, but blacks were given a "grace period" to enable them to learn of their true identity as Muslims of the Tribe of Shabazz. Inexorably, this prophecy was to have been fulfilled by the year 2000.

Until the millennium, blacks are counseled to abide by a puritanical moral and behavioral code that includes a ban on the consumption of pork, tobacco, coffee, alcohol, and certain additional foods, such as cornbread, reminiscent of the southern black diet. The Muslims also emphasize patriarchal households and traditional gender roles.

Elijah Muhammad was not reserved in his critique of white people. In his numerous speeches and newspaper articles, he regularly attempted to demonstrate the shortcomings of whites as part of a campaign to bolster African American pride and self-confidence. In his speeches, he asserted that white athletes were notoriously poor competitors against black athletes; nor should one wonder at the wholesale atrocities committed by "civilized" whites. Only the white man could herd millions of his followers into the gas chambers, set off atomic bombs, and run special trains to a lynching at which the women and children are served cokes and ice cream (Lincoln 1962: 77).

In order to be saved, Elijah taught that blacks must discard their "slave names" and refrain from the evil practices of the whites. Elijah, moreover, rejected any efforts to reform white-dominated American society. Instead, Muslims should prepare themselves for the day of judgment which would occur sometime before the year 2000. When this comes, a Black Nation governing under the guidance of Allah will emerge and the "chosen" will inherit the power of the earth.

The Nation of Islam also stressed economic independence from white people, as well as the creation of a separate nation for blacks consisting of several southern states. Although the black Muslims eventually backed away from many of their less conventional beliefs, economic self-sufficiency through entrepreneurial activities remains a core of the sect. Lincoln (1973: 97) refers to them as "the most potent organized economic force in the black community."

The Black Power movement of the late 1960s and early 1970s prompted many young poor blacks to join the Nation of Islam. The conversion to Islam of Muhammad Ali (the former Cassius Clay), one of the most prominent and popular world-heavyweight boxing champions since World War II, drew much attention to the Nation of Islam. Malcolm X, the charismatic black Muslim minister of the Harlem temple, developed national and ultimately international recognition as a fiery orator and uncompromising black leader, prior to his disaffection from the Nation and subsequent assassination. Under his influence, the Nation grew from a small sect with some 15 temples in the early 1950s to a growing phenomenon with 50 temples in 22 states and Washington, D.C., by 1959 (Gardell 1996: 73). Elijah Muhammad, who remained the central leader of the Nation until his death in 1975, achieved widespread respect in the black community because of the sect's social and economic achievements and its bold critique of white society. Elijah owned two mansions, one in Chicago and the other in Phoenix where he spent much of his later years due to chronic asthma. He had access to a fleet of luxury cars and a private jet (Gardell 1996: 74). He also reportedly purchased at least five other properties in the Phoenix area and a large house in Cuernavaca, Mexico, and amassed over $3.25 million, despite the fact that he denounced "robbers" who exploited African Americans (Perry 1991: 224). At his 1974 Saviour's Day address, Elijah wore a jewel-studded fez reportedly priced at $150,000 (Clegg II 1997: 254).

Yet, of the thousands of blacks exposed to or even converted to the Nation of Islam, "few remain[ed] for any length of time" (Essien-Udom 1962: 83). Howard (1972), who followed nineteen West Coast recruits through their conversion and incorporation into the Nation, found that about 20 percent had become disaffected by the end of his study. In addition to individual disenchantment, internal conflicts and power struggles have been numerous. As Howard (1972: 254) observes, "the organization has no effective mechanism for handling grievances among the rank and file." Some of the apostates went on to form their own Muslim sects, giving rise to a number of competing factions and leaders.

Among the various sects that broke away from the Nation of Islam was a group that came to be called the Harafi Moslems. The group was founded by Harrass Abdul Khaalis in the mid-1960s in New York. Born Ernest Timothy McGee in Gary, Indiana, in 1922, Khaalis was raised a Catholic. Following service in the U.S. Army, he worked in New York nightclubs as a professional musician. During this period, he befriended a Pakistani Moslem named Tasibur Rahman, who taught him about Islam. After Malcolm left the Nation of Islam, Khaalis followed and joined an orthodox Sunni Moslem congregation prior to forming the Harafis. In his group, Khaalis preached an orthodox brand of Islam and openly criticized Elijah Muhammad for killing Malcolm X and for distorting Islam. The most prominent member of the Harafis was former basketball star Kareem Abdul Jabbar. In 1973 several men broke into the Washington, D.C., headquarters of the Harafis and killed seven members of the group, including five children. Five men with ties to the Nation of Islam were convicted of the murders, but Elijah Muhammad vociferously denied that the Nation of Islam was involved. In 1977 Khaalis and several followers took over three buildings in Washington, D.C., and held 134 persons hostage for several hours to protest the failure of the government to try high-ranking members of the Nation of Islam for the murders.

Despite its fissiparousness, the Nation of Islam under the leadership of Elijah Muhammad and later the charismatic rhetoric of Malcolm X achieved, as C. Eric Lincoln (1984: 163) observes, for the first time in American history, "a pronounced public awareness of a religion called Islam."

Temples and mosques sprang up in a hundred cities where none had existed before. Suddenly there was a visible, exotic religious presence in the form of a hundred thousand Black Muslims—conspicuous in their frequent rallies and turnouts, and in their grocery stores and restaurants and bakeries and other small businesses. The clean-shaven, young Muslims hawking their newspapers on the streets, celebrating their rituals in the prisons, debating their beliefs in the media gave to the religion of Islam a projection and a prominence undreamed of in Christian North America. . . . And it was frequently argued in the black community that the Black Muslims had done more to exemplify black pride and dignity, and foster group unity, than some of the more respectable middle-class organizations. (Lincoln 1984: 163)

The unconventional stance of the Nation of Islam vis-à-vis orthodox Islam and the American society in general, however, shifted drastically following the death of Elijah Muhammad on February 25, 1975. Wallace D. Muhammad, one of Elijah's sons, gained the helm of the Nation, despite previous episodic bouts of conflict with his father and a brief period of apostasy from the Nation. Under Wallace's leadership, the Nation was renamed as "the World Community of al-Islam in the West" in 1976 and "the American Muslim Mission" in 1980. In addition to permitting whites to join the group, Wallace came to refer to African Americans as "Bilalians" since Bilal Ibn Rabash, an Ethiopian who had been brought to Arabia as a slave, served as the first muessin or caller to prayer in Medina. He reportedly claimed as late as 1990 to have been in contact with W. D. Fard, the founder of the

Nation of Islam (Evanzz 1999: 408). The American Muslim Mission now exhibits a belief system akin to orthodox Sunni Islam. Wallace reinterpreted key elements underpinning his father's mythological doctrines: ministers of Islam are now called "imams"; temples are called "masjids"; the fast of Ramadan has been rescheduled to coincide with the lunar calendar used by orthodox Muslims; and female members wear simple ankle-length dresses rather than military-style garments.

In fact, some of these changes were begun by Elijah Muhammad shortly before his death. In his February 1974 Saviour's Day address, Elijah told twenty-five thousand of his followers, "Honor and respect those whites who honor and respect you. Stop putting the blame on the slave owner. You have only yourself to blame" (quoted in Reynolds 1976: 38). As early as 1965, the Nation of Islam began admitting non-black Puerto Rican members in New York and Cincinnati. Some moderation, especially on racial issues, was reportedly urged by Libyan government officials who provided the Nation with a $3 million interest-free loan in the early 1970s.

As is characteristic of successful religions once they make accommodation to religious orthodoxy and the larger society, the World Community of al-Islam in the West spawned a revitalized Nation of Islam under the leadership of Louis Farrakhan in 1978. He was born on May 11, 1933, and served as the minister of the Harlem temple after Malcolm's exodus from the Nation in 1964. Wallace D. Muhammad, however, relieved Farrakhan of this status by designating the Nation's international representative with a base in Chicago and renaming the Harlem temple the Malcolm Shabazz Temple No. 7 (Clegg II 1997: 281). In keeping with Elijah Muhammad's teachings, Farrakhan teaches that W. D. Fard was Allah incarnate, that blacks are the original human beings, and that whites are devils. His program includes the same demands for the liberation of all black people found in every issue of *Muhammad Speaks*. For example, reflecting the core of messianic-nationalist ideology, Farrakhan stated in his 1985 speech to fifteen thousand in Los Angeles: "I have a problem with Jews and it is not because I am hateful of Jewish people, not at all. But I have a problem because I am declaring to the world that they are not the chosen people of God. I am declaring to the world that you, the black people of America and the Western hemisphere [are the chosen people]" (Cummings 1985: 10).

The reconstituted Nation of Islam created the Muslim Political Action Committee in Washington, D.C., in the 1980s (Turner 1997: 230). Farrakhan visited Libya in 1986, thereby defying the Reagan administration's ban on travel to that country. He referred to the creation of Israel as an outlaw act and called Judaism a "dirty" or "gutter" religion in a late June 1984 radio broadcast (Gardell 1996: 254). Farrakhan supported Jesse Jackson's presidential bid in 1984 and also served as the key organizer of the 1995 Million Man March—the "greatest black manifestation thus far in U.S. history" (Gardell 1996: 5). He exhibits authoritarian beliefs in that he favors a corporate economy backed up by an authoritarian state, espouses traditional gender relations, and opposes abortion and homosexuality. Farrakhan has expressed admiration for the Saudi judicial system, rejects the American welfare system, demands the creation of a separate state for African Americans, and has maintained close ties with the hip-hop movement. In early 1996, he toured twenty nations, and conferred with many African and Asian heads of state, expressed solidarity with Saddam Hussein of Iraq, and conferred with the Nigerian military regime that had three months earlier hung writer Ken Saro-Wiwa and eight other human rights activists (Marable 1997: 170).

The Ansaru Allah Community

Among the more noticeable Islamized sects to surface in the ghetto since World War II is the Ansaru Allah Community of the Bedford-Stuyvesant district in Brooklyn, New York. The visibility of this group stems from the long white robes and turbans or pillbox hats worn by men and the veils worn by women. Ansara members emerged as a common sight on the street corners of New York during the 1970s as vendors of scented oils and incense. A man who assumed the imposing title of Al Hajj Imam Isa Abd'Allah Muhammad Al Mahdi established the Ansaru Allah Community in 1967. Ansars regard the imam as the great-grandson of Al Imam Muhammad Ahmad Al Mahdi, who led the jihad (or holy war) against the British in the Sudan during the 1880s (Moses 1982: 191).

According to one of the sect's recruitment tracts, Allah made the first man, Adam, from the "rich black soil of the Sudan." The Biblical Israelites, Christ, and Muhammad, therefore, were black. The group traces its own line of descent and the descent of other African Americans from the Nubians of the Sudan to Abraham of the Old Testament. Between 1969 and 1974, the Ansars were called "the Nubian Islamic Hebrews." The presence of an Islamized Hebraic group like the Ansars exemplifies the shared roots of the various messianic-nationalist sects.

While not entirely shedding it Islamic predilections, during the 1990s the Nubian Islaamic Hebrews transformed themselves into the Holy Tabernacle Ministries—a group with a more distinctly Judaic cast (O'Connor 2000). Under the leadership of its founder, the sect shed its distinctive Islamic garb for initially Jewish dress and, after 1994, secular American dress and began to observe the Shabbat, the Fast of Gedaliahg, Pesach, Sukkot,

Rosh Hashanah, and Yom Kippur. Over its history, the Holy Tabernacle Ministries has drawn upon "three prophetic traditions, Judaism, Christianity, and Islam" (O'Connor 2000: 118).

African American Christian Nationalism

While Marcus Garvey's UNIA was not a religious organization per se, he incorporated many religious rituals and beliefs into his movement—prompting Randall Burkett (1978) to refer to it as a "Black civil religion." Garvey, who was sometimes referred to as the "Black Moses," insisted that if blacks were created in God's image, then God must in some sense also be black. He was not the first black nationalist to imply that God was black. AME Bishop Henry McNeal Turner, an emigrationist, began to popularize the same message in the 1890s.

During his period of membership in the UNIA, George Alexander McGuire, an ordained Episcopalian priest from the West Indies, formed the African Orthodox church. McGuire was born on the Caribbean island of Antigua in 1866. He studied theology at a small seminary in St. Thomas prior to moving to the United States in 1894. The next year he was confirmed in the Protestant Episcopal church and ordained a priest in 1897. In this capacity he served Episcopal congregations in several states in the South, Midwest, and Northeast. From 1905 to 1909, he was archdeacon for colored work in the Diocese of Arkansas. In 1913 McGuire returned to Antigua as a parish rector. During this period, he became actively involved in supporting striking sugar-cane workers (Rushing 1972).

Soon after McGuire's return to the United States in 1918, he was appointed by Garvey as the chaplain-general of and a spokesperson for the UNIA. In this capacity, he produced the Universal Negro Ritual and the Universal Negro Catechism, although these two creations were never used extensively in the UNIA (Burkett 1978: 76). Convinced of the need for an independent black nationalist church, McGuire established a congregation called the Independent Episcopal Church of the Good Shepherd on November 9, 1919, in New York, and began to win black clergy and laity to the group. He attempted to affiliate his congregation with the Reformed Episcopal church, an Episcopal splinter group, but in April 1920 incorporated the Independent church, which he regarded as "transitional, as a stepping stone to the 'coming African or Ethiopian Church,' which would be an ecumenical (though, of course, racial) institution capable of allowing for a diversity of specific worship patterns but which it was hoped would reduce some of the destructive competitiveness amongst the various Black denominations"

(Burkett 1978: 92–93). Following his establishment of the African Ortho-dox church, he was consecrated a bishop on September 28, 1921, in Chi-cago, by Bishops Joseph Vilatte and Carl Nybladh of the American Catholic church and the Russian Orthodox church, respectively.

McGuire urged blacks to forget the false image of a white God and instead venerate a black Madonna and a black Christ. At the 1924 conven-tion of UNIA, he reportedly called for "an international day when all the negroes of the world should tear the pictures of a white Madonna and a white Christ out of their homes and make a bonfire of them" (quoted in Rushing 1972: 39). Despite McGuire's hopes, Garvey refused to accept the African Orthodox church as an official religious arm of the UNIA—a posi-tion that contributed to the eventual split between these two men. It is pos-sible that Garvey did not embrace the African Orthodox church in part because he did not want to alienate the many black Jewish members of UNIA in New York. In the United States, the African Orthodox church found its greatest appeal among West Indians who felt disenfranchised within the structure of the Protestant Episcopal church but wished to retain many of the ritual dimensions of their Anglican heritage. "The Church soon spread to the West Indies, where it never had much success, and to Cuba where it had a little more, and from the start it had a parish in Nova Scotia. But its greatest strength was in the cities of the Eastern Seaboard, in New York, in Miami, and to a lesser extent in Philadelphia, Boston, and Chicago. Perhaps at its height it had twenty thousand adherents, perhaps more" (White 1978: 169).

After McGuire's death in 1934, the African Orthodox church frag-mented into at least four groups (White 1978: 171). The two largest fac-tions reunited in 1964 under the primateship of Archbishop Gladstone St. Clair Nurse. The reunited body has eleven congregations in New York City, two in the Boston area, and one each in Chicago, Philadelphia, Miami, and Sydney, Nova Scotia.

Laura Adorkor Kofey established a black Christian nationalist sect inde-pendent of the African Orthodox church (Newman 1996). She had been involved in the Detroit branch of the UNIA but alienated fellow Garveyites when she asserted that she was responsible for the commutation of Garvey's sentence in late 1927. Kofey went on to form the African Universal Church (which appears to have been legally incorporated in Jacksonville, Florida) and referred to herself as the "Warrior Mother of Africa's Warriors of the Most High God." In addition to Jacksonville, her church had branches in Miami, St. Petersburg, Tampa, Mobile, Belforest-Daphne City (Alabama), Atlanta, and New York City (Newman 1996: 115). Although the sect has undergone a decline, several relatively independent congregations continue to exist, including one in Liberia. According to Newman (1996: 117), the African Universal Church has evolved into "a cult of Laura Kofey, who became 'Mother Kofi,' the 'Patron Saint for African-American Relations,' and who motto was 'I'll Take Care of Mine.'"

Since the 1960s, black Christian nationalism has taken its most manifest expression within the context of the Black Theology movement. Because of its implications as a counterhegemonic movement and because of its supra-denominational implications, we have postponed a more extended discussion of Black Theology for the concluding chapter of this book. At the organizational level, Albert Cleage, one of the principal proponents of Black Theology and a former United Church of Christ minister, in 1972 formed the Black Christian Nationalist church. Cleage, who renamed himself Jaramogi Abebe Agyeman, ordained several ministers who have congregations, referred to as Shrines of Black Madonna, in Detroit and several other midwestern cities. He asserts that Jesus Christ was a black revolutionary leader and that blacks are God's "chosen people." In his book, *Black Christian Nationalism*, Cleage begins with the Black Christian Nationalist Creed, which reads, in part:

> *I Believe that Jesus, the Black Messiah, was a revolutionary leader, sent by God to rebuild the Black Nation, Israel and to liberate Black people from powerlessness and from the oppression, brutality, and exploitation of the white gentile world. I believe that the revolutionary spirit of God, embodied in the Black Messiah, is born anew in each generation and that Black Christian Nationalists constitute the living remnant of God's Chosen People in this day, and are charged by Him with the responsibility for the Liberation of the Black People.* (Cleage 1972: 230)

Politico-Religious Organization in Black Messianic-Nationalist Sects

Messianic-nationalist sects, at least in their initial stages, tend to have a centralized, theocratic politico-religious organization. Prophet Cherry, the founder of the Church of the Living God, served as final arbiter of religious beliefs and appointed all of the sect's elders, deacons, deaconesses, and secretaries (Fauset 1971: 33). In the Moorish Science Temple, The prophet (reincarnated) is the final authority. Nothing whatever can be done in any of the branches without his prior knowledge and assent; any command or instruction from must be obeyed summarily. The leader of each branch temple is known as Grand Sheik or Governor" (Fauset 1971: 44).

In their later stages of development, as we will see in the American Muslim Mission, messianic-nationalist sects may undergo a process of routinization of charisma in which the leader presides over a denominational-like bureaucratic structure.

The first part of this section focuses on the politico-religious organization of two black Jewish sects, one that aspires to emigrate to Israel, namely, the Adet Beyt Moshe community, and one that already has established communities in Israel, the Original Hebrew Israelite Nation. The latter part of this section compares the politico-religious organization of the Nation of Islam under Elijah Muhammad and that of the American Muslim Mission, the reconstituted Nation, under Wallace D. Muhammad.

Black American Hebrews in the United States and Israel

While members of Adet Beyt Moshe sect, which is based in Ellwood, New Jersey, and Philadelphia, ultimately aim to return to their homeland in Israel; in the meantime their rural community located between Philadelphia and Atlantic City serves as a place of preparation for the planned exodus to the Promised Land. The Adet Beyt Moshe sect, which was legally incorporated in 1951, emerged as a schism from the Israelite Bible School (Gelman 1965: 100). When anthropologist Martin Gelman (1965) conducted an ethnographic study of the group, it had some thirty-seven members belonging to nine families residing at its community and an additional fifty-two members residing in Philadelphia. Rabbi Abel Respes served as the sole leader of the tiny Adet Moshe congregation, but the rabbi's oldest son occupied the position of heir apparent. All buildings, residences, and facilities are held in mutual trust and by corporate agreement. A board of directors elected by the community administers the corporate enterprise. Rabbi Respes served as the board president and held majority vote in the case of a tie. According to Gelman (1965: 31), "no issue with which the President disagrees has as yet come to the floor of the Board of Directors." Adult members work at outside jobs, mainly in Philadelphia. Each income-producing member pays a general tithe into a special community fund designed to subsidize the members' health and welfare expenses as well as maintenance expenses.

In contrast to the many messianic-nationalist sects that aspire to return to their mythological homeland, as we noted earlier, the Original Hebrew Israelite Nation, which emerged in Chicago during the early 1960s, actually emigrated to Israel, following an unsuccessful settlement in Liberia. While the Original Hebrew Nation continues to have congregations in the United

States, the sect's main contingent resides in a string of Israeli towns in the barren Negev Desert. The black Hebrew politico-religious organization functions as a highly centralized structure with Ben Ami as its undisputed leader. The black Hebrews regard him as the Son of God and the heralded Messiah who will reign over a worldwide Kingdom of God following a war of Armageddon. They believe that their Nation constitutes an embryonic kernel from which this kingdom shall blossom.

Like many sectarian leaders, Ben Ami is known to his followers as "Father" (Abba in Hebrew), in addition to his other titles. He is treated with utmost reverence, and his picture adorns at least one wall in every Nation apartment. When he enters a room, everyone immediately stands and, should he pass by a group of "Saints," as followers are called, the men bow and the women curtsy. Despite overcrowding in the apartments rented by the Nation, the sect maintains two private homes, one in Jerusalem and another in Arad, largely for Ben Ami's private use.

Beneath Ben Ami in the leadership hierarchy are twelve nesim (princes; singular: nasi) or angels who, together with the leader, constitute the Holy Council, the unelected, unquestioned ruling body of the black Hebrew community. The nesim are believed to be the reincarnation of Christ's twelve apostles, and each is seen as personifying one of the "divine attributes" of God. At the time the group was studied by Singer in the late 1970s, only one of the nesim worked at a job outside the black Hebrew community; the rest worked full-time on Nation activities. Four of the nesim were not living in Israel during Singer's fieldwork. One of them was stationed in Ghana, another in Liberia, and the other two were in the United States. The other nine nesim were distributed among three Israeli towns in which the black Hebrews resided, six in Dimona, two in Arad, and one in Mitzpe Ramon.

Three nesim formed the Universal Priesthood set up by Ben Ami during a period of internal discord in 1971–72. These three were Ben Ami—the high priest, the old priest, or priest of agriculture, and the young priest or prince of humility. In contrast to some other black Jewish sects, the black Hebrews do not use the term rabbi to refer to their religious leaders. In their work, the priests are assisted by a group of young men called aspiring priests. The wives of the nesim are titled nesiot (princesses; singular: nesia) and are expected to set a "divine example" for other women of the Nation.

Subordinate to the Holy Council are ten sarim (ministers; singular: sar), many of whom serve as the heads of various government-style ministries. Nine ministries meet the basic requirements of group members, such as food, clothing, shelter, transportation, and entertainment; a tenth ministry provides Divine Music. All of the ministers are males; the two women who head ministries, Divine Health and Divine Food Services, are not accorded this title. All adult members of the community are assigned positions within one or more of the ministries.

Together the nesim and sarim make up what the black Hebrews call their Divine Government. As Kanter (1972: 117) suggests, the hierarchy of authority in societies like the black Hebrews seems to limit "members' access to the ultimate wielder of power in the community and thus enhance the sense of awe surrounding the demands and dictums of the system." While the Saints admit that their projects are sometimes less than perfect, all imperfections are seen as stemming from the shortcomings of the members and not from Ben Ami's leadership.

Adult members who are not in the Divine Government are organized into the Brother and Sisterhoods. Entrance into these groups occurs at age seventeen but can vary depending on the leaders' evaluation of an individual's spiritual progress. Even within the Brother and Sisterhoods there exists a ranking system differentiating members on the basis of spiritual progress or in terms of obedience and dedication to community norms and decisions of group leaders. The more advanced are called "senior brothers and sisters" and are looked upon with deference by junior members.

Polygamy appears to function in the Nation as both a status marker and a reward for spiritual mobility. Whereas only about 20 percent of the men in the Nation have taken plural wives, by 1978 about 70 percent of the nesim had entered "divine marriage." Of those Saints who have more than one wife, only one individual who is not a nasi had more than two wives. By contrast, three nesim had three wives each and two had four wives. About ten senior brothers had plural wives, but junior brothers were monogamous or unmarried.

All production and distribution in the Nation follows the ideal of "from each according to his abilities, to each according to his needs." On payday, all men working outside the group bring their checks to the minister of Divine Economics, who in turn distributes money on a preestablished plan according to need. The minister holds back money to pay the rent and utility bills for all the apartments rented by the community. The funds furnished to each of the families or individuals living together in an apartment are pooled together to provide for the entire household. Although many Saints have obtained jobs outside the community, the Nation operates a number of enterprises, including a leather shop, an appliance repair shop, and a jewelry-making shop.

The Black Muslim Politico-Religious Organization under and after Elijah Muhammad

Within the Nation of Islam, the Honorable Elijah Muhammad, often referred to as "the Messenger," served as the administrator of a system of theoretically independent temples. The Chicago Temple constituted the Nation's national headquarters and the Messenger's home temple, and in a sense the Mecca of the sect. Chicago served as the site for the celebration of Savior's Day, a national reunion commemorating the birth of W. D. Fard and featuring Elijah Muhammad as the main speaker. While temples were said to be equal, some were "more important than others because of their numerical strength and ability to contribute financially toward the general welfare of the Nation" (Essien-Udom 1962: 161). Elijah Muhammad appointed all of the temple ministers and national officers and attempted to reign in ministers and temples that asserted their independence.

Elijah Muhammad was revered by his followers. When he walked into a room, all Muslims would stand to express their respect. His style of leadership is summarized by his son and heir, Wallace Muhammad, as two-sided. If other people were subservient to his wishes, Elijah Muhammad was warm and loving. However, according to Wallace, "Whenever his authority was challenged, he became the Messenger of God. You couldn't bargain with him even in the family. He won't budge, not one fraction of an inch" (Quoted in Gallagher 1977: 4).

The supreme captains acted as the highest-ranking officers of the Nation and were responsible only to Elijah Muhammad. The male supreme captain commanded the captains of the temple men's organizations known as "the Fruits of Islam." The female supreme captain oversaw all of the captains of the temple women's organizations, known as "the Moslem Girls' Training and General Civilization Class." Regional ministers and captains oversaw the three geographical areas (southern, western, and eastern) of the Nation (Muhammad 1980: 90).

The national secretary was responsible for the legal and business affairs of the Nation and collected the weekly and monthly reports of the temple secretaries. A national director of schools and a governing board oversaw the University of Islam, the Nation's parochial school system based in each temple. Elijah Muhammad selected editors of *Muhammad Speaks*, the official newspaper of the Nation.

Beyond its religious structure, the Nation of Islam became a relatively prosperous economic organization.

> *Under Elijah Muhammad's leadership, the organization managed to acquire 15,000 acres of farmland in several states, thousands of head of cattle*

and sheep, poultry and dairy farms, warehouses and cold storage facilities, The
Muhammad Speaks newspaper, tractor-trailer fleets, aircraft, The Guaranty
Bank and Trust Company, apartmental complexes, and wholesale and retail
businesses throughout America. The Nation of Islam also managed to organize
over seventy-six Muhammad Mosques of Islam in the United States and abroad
in Bermuda, Jamaica, Trinidad, Central America, England, Ghana, and the
U.S. Virgin Islands. The Nation of Islam estimated that its business enterprises
were valued at over $85,000,000 by the late 1970s. (Marsh 1984: 91)

This accumulation of businesses, properties, and other assets is probably unparalleled by any other African American religious group in U.S. history. The ability of the Nation to be successful in this realm sharpened the
appeal of the group to the African American masses. Although the general
public was somewhat astonished that Wallace D. Muhammad became his
father's successor despite his low profile, only members of the "Royal Family" were eligible for this position. According to Muslim folklore, W. D.
Fard told Elijah that his seventh child would be a son and his eventual successor (Marsh 1984: 92). In his major reorganization of the Nation into the
World Community of Islam in the West and later the American Muslim
Mission, Wallace D. Muhammad dismantled the Fruit of Islam—the elite
security force affiliated with each temple. Ministers were renamed imams
and temples were renamed masjids or mosques.

On September 12, 1978, Wallace D. Muhammad resigned, at least officially, as administrative leader of the World Community of Islam in the West
to become an evangelist or ambassador-at-large who would speak on behalf
of the organization nationally and internationally. The Council of Imams
meets biannually in various cities to solve internal problems and plan the
general direction of the Mission. "Each member has equal power nationally,
but total power in his respective region; each Imam serves a one-year term"
(Marsh 1984: 100). State imams within each region function to "lessen the
problems that arise because of limited communication for masjids geographically located long distances from the central point of the organization"
(Muhammad 1980: 108). The Muslim Women's Development Class director and the National Steering Committee coordinate the educational, social
welfare, and domestic activities of the Mission.

Wallace D. Muhammad also separated the religious and the economic
operations of the organization by liquidating more than six million dollars
in long-term debts and tax obligations, selling the group's less profitable
enterprises, and leasing farms and other properties to Muslims and non-
Muslims (Marsh 1984: 96). Fiscal aspects of the organization are now managed by the Department of Finance. This unit is responsible for accounting,

payroll, budgets, and fiscal policy (Jones 1983). At the local level, decisions are made by the local mosque steering committee, which is composed of several subcommittees, including the censure board for cultural development, the public information committee, the ways and means committee, the sick committee, and the fairness committee.

The African American Messianic-Nationalist Congregation

As in the case of other black religious groups, messianic-nationalist congregations form the primary locus of the religious and social life of their membership. While historically messianic-nationalist congregations have catered primarily to poor and working-class blacks, some of them, particularly within the American Muslim Mission, appear to be catering to professional and middle-class individuals and families. In terms of politico-religious organization and ritual content, messianic-nationalist congregations range from those that resemble black Baptist, Holiness, and Pentecostal congregations to those that have devised distinctly Judaic, Islamic, or syncretic forms.

Social Composition of Messianic-Nationalist Congregations

Despite the existence of several intensive studies of certain messianic-nationalist sects, relatively little systematic data have been collected on their social composition. In his classic study of the black Muslims, Lincoln (1962: 48) maintains that "The main appeal of all black nationalist movements . . . is to the Negro lower class." It is generally well known that the Nation of Islam found many converts among poor and working-class black prisoners. In the early 1970s, John Howard (1972) conducted in-depth interviews with nineteen recruits to the Nation of Islam in California to better understand the type of person attracted to the group. Fourteen of these individuals joined the Nation because of its aggressive black nationalism. They varied in age between twenty-four and forty-six and in education from a few years of grade school to four years of college. Nine had previously been engaged in criminal or marginally legal activities. None had either a stable marital or employment history. As one explained, "I saw I was nowhere and had no way of getting anywhere" (quoted in Howard 1972: 247). The other five respondents were attracted to the Nation because of its emphasis on hard work and rigid personal morality. They all came from self-help–oriented or upwardly mobile families. Generally, they expressed middle-class values but viewed the established black petite bourgeoisie with disdain. In the interviews, they expressed the importance of achievement and personal accomplishment.

Members of the Adet Beyt Moshe congregation "vary in their endeavor as laborers, domestics, craftsmen, clerks, typists, and general factory workers" (Gelman 1965: 30). In a sample of 101 black Hebrews in Israel, Singer found that

> *the largest bloc of members who were queried about their pre-conversion occupation stated that they were employed in either skilled or unskilled labor. But, there are a number of teachers, small business owners, and white collar workers among the Saints. Interestingly, seven of the respondents were employed as musicians or stage performers in their pre-conversion days (and most of these continue to fill this role in the Nation). It appears that the Black Hebrew "message" has traveled widely in black musical circles in the American Mid-West.* (Singer 1979: 224–25)

Similarly, Harras Abdul Khaalis, founder of the Harafi Moslems, told a reporter that at the time he became a Muslim "a lot of musicians were looking around trying to find an identity" (Chicago Tribune 1977: 17). The founder of the Ansaru Allah Islamic sect, Isa Abd'Allah Muhammad, also is a musician.

Mamiya (1982) maintains that a "growing class split between the two factions of the schism in the Muslim-Bilalian movement" has occurred, with the American Muslim Mission tending to be increasingly middle class in its composition and orientation and Farrakhan's reconstituted Nation of Islam tending to cater to lower-class blacks. However, describing the parking lot outside a Farrakhan speech in Los Angeles, a New York Times reporter noted, "The cars . . . Chevrolets and Toyotas, Mercedes-Benzes and BMWs, family sedans and clunkers, represented the whole spectrum of . . . incomes and lifestyles" (Cummings 1985: 10). Notably, even prior to Elijah Muhammad's death, the old Nation of Islam began to make appeals to the black middle-class (Essien-Udom 1962: 297–98).

The Politico-Religious Organization of Messianic-Nationalist Congregations

The politico-religious organization of some messianic-nationalist congregations bears resemblance to that found in many black Christian groups. For example, Prophet Cherry, the leader of the Church of the Living God, appointed male and female preachers as well as "deacons, deaconesses, and secretaries, . . . to supervise the routine affairs of the church, to watch its finances, to assist in visiting the sick and similar functions" (Fauset 1971: 33). While the leader of each Moorish Science temple was referred to by the regal title of "Grand Sheik" or "Governor," other officers were simply referred to as elders and stewards (Fauset 1971: 44).

Conversely, the Nation of Islam constructed a politico-religious structure at both the sect-wide and the congregational levels that clearly distinguished it from black Christian groups, especially those of the Baptist, Methodist, and Sanctified forms. Under Elijah Muhammad, only members of the Fruit of Islam and the Moslem Girls' Training and General Civilization were eligible to become temple officers (Essien-Udom 1962: 162–65). Ministers and captains served as the principal officers of the temple. They were assisted by male or female secretaries. Each temple had two treasurers, one who was in charge of the general income and expenditures and the other who distributed funds for assistance to the sick and needy and for funerals. A business manager supervised the economic enterprises of the temple. Each temple had a male and female investigator who assessed the material needs of the members and investigated disputes and attempted to mediate or refer them to the appropriate officers. Junior captains supervised the youth organizations for boys and girls in the temples.

As noted, each temple had a male organization called the Fruits of Islam which functioned to "enforce discipline within the ranks and, particularly, to protect them against assaults or external threats of violence" (Essien-Udom 1962: 167). While the Fruits of Islam did not arm its members with weapons or advocate militaristic aims per se, it exhibited some features of military organization in its ranking system and discipline as well as in its emphasis on martial arts training. In addition to social control duties, FOI members organized entertainment for temple social activities.

The Moslem Girls' Training and General Civilization Class (MGT-GCC) was organized along the same lines as the FOI and functioned to impart domestic skills to Muslim females. The organization required all females over thirteen to report for a weight check twice a month. Both the FOI and the MGT-GCC had sick and poor committees to care for needy members of the temple.

Under the national University of Islam system, many temples operated elementary and secondary schools. The first black Muslim school was established in Detroit in 1932 and the second in Chicago in 1934 (Essien-Udom 1962: 253). Except for kindergarten and first grade, Muslim boys and girls attended sexually segregated classes. Instruction in Arabic occurred from the fourth grade through high school. Many temples offered adult education courses in writing, reading, arithmetic, and Arabic.

Each masjid or mosque ratified the resident imam by a majority show of hands. "Masjid participants must attend the masjid at least four days a month if they are to be recognized as active members and participate in nominations, voting or running for masjid committee/board offices" (Muhammad

1980: 106). Wallace D. Muhammad disbanded the FOI and the MGT-GCC and established a masjid committee system consisting of nine committees, each with an elected chairperson, to administer various masjid problems.

> *Many Universities of Islam were closed in late 1975 by the Director of Education because of inadequate school plants, inefficient administrative supervision and unqualified teaching staff. However, in isolated geographical locations, there are surviving masjid schools. Wallace D. Muhammad replaced the name of Muhammad Universities of Islam in 1976 with the Clara Muhammad Elementary and Secondary Schools in memory of his mother, Sister Clara Muhammad.* (Muhammad 1980: 127)

Ritual Activities in Messianic-Nationalist Congregations

Services in messianic-nationalist congregations range from those that preserve many traditional African American ritual practices to those that attempt to replicate as closely as possible those found in orthodox Jewish synagogues or Islamic temples. Except for the avoidance of pork, Landes (1967: 178) characterizes group rituals in the Temple of the Gospel of the Kingdom of God, a Hebraic group, as tending to "'holy roller,' with the usual 'shouting,' ecstasy, fainting, and revelations." Although the Church of the Living God does not observe Christmas or Easter, it performs baptism and observes Passover as its only traditional Jewish festival. Fauset (1971: 36) describes services in this sect as exhibiting a "quasi-holiness" character, although its members frown upon excessive emotional behavior, particularly speaking in tongues. The Church of God and Saints also observes various Christian rituals, including baptism, consecration of the bread and water as the body and blood of Christ, and foot washing. This sect incorporated various Jewish customs as well, such as circumcision, the Jewish calendar, observance of Saturday as the Sabbath, and the celebration of Passover, including smearing animal blood on the outside of homes in celebration of God's method for differentiating Jewish from Egyptian homes in the Book of Exodus.

While religious services take place in the various towns within which members of the Original Hebrew Israelite Nation reside, Dimona, which had about 470 members in the late 1970s, serves as the center of black Hebrew ceremonial life. Regular black Hebrew gatherings include weekly Sabbath services, Saturday talks by Ben Ami, group concerts, brother and sisterhood meetings, sports events, dance performances, plays, parties, food sales, holiday convocations, craft displays, weddings, and classes in group ideology. Concerts and sports events in particular bring members from all three towns together and serve as community-wide rites of group intensification. Black

Hebrew religious services retain various aspects of traditional African American Christianity. The Sabbath service usually consists of an opening prayer, followed by a sermon on group values and beliefs, gospel music, and a closing prayer praising Ben Ami and asking for his divine assistance in achieving group goals. Typically, the Saints shout ken (yes), hallelujah, or other comments after each of the speaker's sentences. Other worship services, which are either based on the holidays listed in Leviticus or are inventions of the sect, also follow this general pattern. Traditional Jewish holidays not listed in Leviticus, such as Chanukah or Rosh Hashanah, are not celebrated. Instead, the black Hebrews commemorate a number of important dates in their own history, such as the exodus from the United States (called the New World Passover) or the inauguration of the Divine Government (called Guidelines of the Kingdom of God Revealed). The black Hebrews issue their own printed calendar citing the holy days of the sect; it is found in all Nation apartments.

Religious services in the Nation of Islam focused on a lengthy lecture in which the minister outlined many of the sect's central beliefs. According to Essien-Udom (1962: 232), "There is virtually no religious ceremony or ritual at Temple meetings except the prayers said at the opening and closing of meetings and perhaps a verse or two read by the minister from the Koran or from the Bible during the course of the lecture." Services in large part served as a mechanism for recruiting people into the Nation. Whites were denied access to the temple, and blacks had to undergo a registration conducted by the temple secretary and a frisking conducted by members of the Fruit of Islam. Males and females sat separately. Black Muslims did not engage in congregational singing and were discouraged from exhibiting any emotional behavior. After prayers, the minister saluted the congregation by saying, "As-Salaam-Alaikum" ("Peace be unto you"), to which the congregation responded, "Wa-el-Alaikum" ("And unto you be peace").

Muslim lectures generally lasted for two or three hours. Unlike the traditional Christian sermon, the minister attempted "every week to present the entire gamut of Muhammad's teachings" and was "interrupted only by the changing of the guard" (Lincoln 1962: 118–19). The minister nearly always began his lecture by writing several Arabic phrases on a blackboard. The lecture by the temple minister or distinguished guest speaker was occasionally punctuated by hand clapping or ovation, but shouting and call-and-response behavior was strictly forbidden.

In addition to the regular Sunday service, the Nation held services on Wednesday and Friday nights following the same general order (Essien-Udom 1962: 245). Unity Parties conducted on Tuesday evenings provided a relatively informal atmosphere permitting Muslims and non-Muslims to mingle. The temple FOI, MGT-GCC, and PTA sponsored various entertainment events on feast days, such as poetry recitations, musical performances, plays, and "fire-eating" demonstrations.

Although the observation of the month of Ramadan in the Islamic world varies annually due to the 350-day Islamic calendar, black Muslims observed Ramadan in the month of December to keep from celebrating Christmas. "The day before the fast began, a great Pre-Ramadan feast for the entire temple membership was prepared by the MGT. The day after the fast was ended, a great Post-Ramadan feast was held in which the whole temple participated. During the Ramadan fast, black Muslims over 12 years old took no food or drink between dawn and dark for those 30 days" (Muhammad 1980: 93).

Wallace Muhammad shifted the time for the observance of Ramadan to conform with the orthodox Islamic calendar and replaced Savior's Day with Survival Day, which is observed at regional centers rather than in Chicago. Every fourth Sunday of the month, he addresses the American Muslim Mission community through a closed radio system. Other Mission collective activities include a weekly Friday Jumah group prayer, regular Sunday lectures delivered by the resident imam, and celebration of the Prophet Mohammed's birthday, the Hijra or New Year commemorating the Prophet's flight from Mecca to Medina, the Day of the Ascension commemorating the Prophet's Ascension into Paradise, New World Patriotism Day on July 1 to demonstrate Muslim pride in American citizenship, and July 4 as American Independence Day and the reputed day of W. D. Fard's arrival in the African American community (Muhammad 1980: 111).

Protest and Accommodation in Messianic-Nationalist Sects

In the course of its hundred-year history, messianic-nationalism has had a seesaw development. At times, messianic-nationalists have achieved great prominence in the African American community as outspoken religious critics of the larger American society. These periods of heightened popularity and visibility commonly have been followed by years of decline, fragmentation, and accommodation. Far from a random occurrence or inexplicable pattern, the oscillation in the social significance of messianic-nationalism reflects the changing relationship of African Americans to capitalism in the United States. During periods of rapid economic change, when black workers are shifted away from traditional occupations into new areas of production or into unemployment, and the black community as a result is disrupted to the point that established social patterns become obsolete, messianic-nationalism tends to be ascendant. The reestablishment of social stability, however marred by enduring patterns of racism and economic exploitation, ushers in a period of messianic-nationalist quiescence. During the latter times, messianic-nationalism does not disappear. Rather, a less militant, more accommodationist orientation emerges, while more marginal, less-committed members fall away in search of more conventional or more individualistic religious or secular alternatives in the black community.

At the ideological level, messianic-nationalist sects provide the most vehement religious critique of racism emanating from the African American experience. As we have seen, they often transpose the white racist interpretation of blacks as a cursed race into one in which they constitute the first and most select human beings. Conversely, whites are portrayed as diabolic beings working in opposition to the will of God. Elijah Muhammad, for example, taught his followers that whites are "blue-eyed devils" of low physical and moral stamina.

Except for a few black Christian nationalist sects, such as the African Orthodox church and the Shrines of the Black Madonna, messianic-nationalist sects reject Christianity as a false religion and sometimes see Jesus as a false messiah. Alternately, Jesus is depicted as an African American messiah. Commonly, messianic-nationalists regard Christianity as a simple extension of white racist ideology. Members of the Adet Beyt Moshe congregation, for instance, believe that the New Testament contains folklore, lies, and myths, and that Christianity grew out of European paganism (Gelman 1965: 66–67). In contrast to the traditional Christian conception of the afterlife, this black Jewish sect maintains that heaven and hell are conditions of this life and that its adherents should aim to establish the Kingdom of God on Earth.

Similarly, Elijah Muhammad asserted that Christianity is a "slave religion" keeping blacks in social and spiritual bondage. "The black Christian preacher is the white man's most effective tool for keeping the so-called Negroes pacified and controlled, for he tells convincing lies against nature as well as against God" (Lincoln 1962: 79). In contrast to their uniform critique of racism, messianic-nationalists vary in their assessment of capitalism as an economic system. The Original Hebrew Nation portrays capitalism as an unrighteous system that creates needs rather than fulfilling them. In their classes, the black Hebrews are taught that capitalism is exploitive and oppressive, especially toward people of African heritage. For example, a black Hebrew teacher told one of his classes:

> *We aren't content to get money anymore, We want the land to produce the food.*
> *We always wanted the money instead of the machines which produce things.*
> *The reason Europe is economically powerful is because they rape Africa for its*

*abundant resources. There are few resources in Europe. What they do is extract
everything out of the earth of Africa. . . . In former times Africa was Eden, but
all we got was the crumbs and the man got the stove.* (Singer 1979: 176)

Following the War of Armageddon, the black Hebrews believe, Israel
will be divided into twelve provinces functioning under the principle of
stewardship. To insure fairness and equity, each province will be assigned a
"province economist" and each city a "city economic advisor" by the minister of Divine Economics.

Despite these beliefs, the black Hebrews are not sympathetic toward
post-revolutionary or socialist-oriented societies. Instead, they reprove the
atheism of Marx and see ideologies stemming from his writing as just other
"isms" of the white oppressor. In the words of one black Hebrew teacher,
"Even in socialist countries things ain't distributed justly, except on paper"
(Singer 1979: 176).

As part of their counterhegemonic ideology, the black Hebrews subscribe to a form of anti-modernism that views technological development as
the work of the devil. They regard modern technology, including "scientific" medicine, as part of the devil's effort to complicate what God intended
to be simple. Advanced technology has thrown the world out of its natural
cycles, causing disease, death, and destruction. Prior to World War II, the
black Hebrews maintain, people were kinder to each other, children
respected their parents, and almost everyone believed in God. Despite this
disdain for modern technology, they use many mechanical devices, including automobiles, stoves, refrigerators, radios, recording equipment, sound
amplifiers, and electronic musical instruments. The black Hebrews justify
use of these modern devices on the grounds that at the present time it would
be hard not to use them, but alternative methods are being sought and will
be adopted in the future. Anti-modernism acts as a boundary maintenance
mechanism for preserving the black Hebrew counterculture. While most
people in the world, including their Israeli neighbors, strive for technological advancement, the black Hebrews see themselves as striving for the natural, God-intended route to salvation.

In contrast to the Original Hebrew Israelite Nation as well as the communally oriented Adet Beyt Moshe congregation, Elijah Muhammad
espoused a religious form of black capitalism for the Nation of Islam. He
urged his followers to acquire property and business enterprises and to gain
the necessary skills for them to administer both Nation-owned and privately
owned businesses. Elijah Muhammad was a propertied man himself and
rented apartment buildings to his own followers. He pointed to "the businesses owned and operated by the Chicago Temple as examples of what

Negroes could do 'if only they had enough sense'" (Essien-Udom 1962: 287). Undoubtedly, one of the tensions contributing to the rift that emerged between Elijah Muhammad and Malcolm X was the latter's assertion that capitalism and racism are interrelated, with racism serving to divide the working class and isolate people of color for super-exploitation. According to Malcolm, "the American political, economic and social atmosphere . . . automatically nourishes a racist psychology in the white man" (Malcolm X 1965: 371).

While apparently Wallace D. Muhammad and Malcolm X became close friends and came to share common understandings in their respective views of Islam, Wallace did not adopt Malcolm's growing critique of American foreign policy and capitalism in his reorganization of the Nation into the World Community of Islam in the West and later the American Muslim Mission. The changes initiated by Wallace D. Muhammad appear to have made the group more compatible with the U.S. government and the dominant society. "In February 1979, the WCIW was awarded $22 million (the largest amount ever awarded to a black firm) by the Department of Commerce. The WCIW, in conjunction with American Pouch Foods Company, is producing pre-cooked combat rations for the United States military" (Marsh 1984: 97).

Although Louis Farrakhan, the leader of the reconstituted Nation of Islam, espouses an anti-imperialist stance and criticizes American foreign policy in the Middle East,

> *He proposed a kind of reform capitalism for the Black "family," starting first with production and sale of consumer products like toothpaste and soap— necessities. Using the brand name POWER and a $5 million loan from Libya, he is launching an organization that hopes to capture the $200 million Black American market. . . . To help Blacks acquire land, he suggests buying it from bankrupt Western farmers. Nationalism narrows his perception: he doesn't see this as land grabbing at all, just as an opportunity.* (Doyle and Doyle 1985: 19)

As the preceding discussion reveals, like other black religious groups, messianic-nationalist sects exhibit a complex juxtaposition of protest and accommodation to the larger society. This complex ordering of opposed stances is expressed in the various positions taken by Wentworth Arthur Matthew, the leader of the Commandment Keepers. Over the years, he attempted to gain recognition from the white Jewish community, applying unsuccessfully for membership in the B'nai B'rith in 1941, and for certification by the New York Board of Rabbis in 1952 and 1961. Despite this rejection by the mainstream Jewish community, he came to emphasize accommodation to black Judaism and the larger society as well. In his sermons, he stressed "personal regularity, neatness, conformity with social mores, steady work habits, strict parental supervision to prevent juvenile delinquency, the maintenance of a sedate order of worship without [what he termed] 'niggeritions' such as possession, shouting, or speaking in tongues" (Shapiro 1970: 177). At times, Matthew even questioned the civil rights and the Black Power movements and encouraged allegiance to the U.S. government, including support of the Vietnam War. Conversely, on occasion he admitted there may be a need for a more militant response to racism and discrimination than he usually recommended. Toward the end of his life, he even rejected the idea of gaining recognition from the white Jewish community (*Newsweek*, December 26, 1966).

Messianic-nationalism, as a distinct voice in African American religious life, emerged as a fairly explicit protest movement against racism and social stratification in American society. In his analysis of the Nation of Islam in the United States and the Ras-Tafarians in Jamaica, Watson argues that

> . . . *neither of these movements should be summarily dismissed as ephemeral religious cults. Religion per se is not their major attraction. Both are social protests which move on a semi-religious vehicle, with emphasis on social action geared to transforming their objective life situations. They are nationalistic, and nationalism is political: their foci move from one plane to another—from one based on the quest for religious experience to one grounded in a struggle for readjusting the status systems of their respective societies to accord with an ideal concept of society.* (Watson 1973: 199)

E. U. Essien-Udom (1962), however, who conducted extensive research among the black Muslims, questions the proposition that the Nation of Islam constitutes a political movement. While granting that the Muslim objectives of establishing a black homeland and their image of a post-apocalptic Black Nation were political in theory, he asserts that the Nation in practice was apolitical, as well as nonrevolutionary, because it eschewed any clear-cut political program as well as direct involvement in local or national politics. Instead Muslim chiliasm claimed that the oppressor would be destroyed by Allah or that whites by their own inequities would destroy themselves. Elijah Muhammad taught that the U.S. government was corrupt in the eyes of Allah and would in time be replaced by a utopian Kingdom of Righteous through a process of divine intervention. According to Essien-Udom,

> *The final hope is timeless. It is placed both in the present and the future. For the present, the Muslims become preoccupied with the techniques of attaining the good life in the here and now. This is their "proper" concern. The attainment of black power over the whole world is relegated to the intervention of "Almighty*

Allah" sometime in the future. Theoretically, the Muslims are absolved, as it were, from political schemes or programs intended either for changing the present regime or modifying its institutions. . . . The revolutionary possibilities of the movement are thus mitigated by the ideology of the Nation and by the Muslims' need for achievement and status. The most the Muslims may hope for is work, watchfulness, and prayer. (Essien-Udom 1962: 313–14)

Indeed, Elijah Muhammad encouraged his followers to be thrifty, clean, honest, hardworking, and to abstain from illicit sexual relations, pork, alcohol, nicotine, and narcotics. He admonished Muslims to obey their employers both within and outside the Nation and to abide by the laws of the land, so long as they did not contradict those of the Nation. But contradictions between an oppressed group and the dominant society are unavoidable. Thus both Elijah and Wallace Muhammad went to prison as draft evaders rather than serve in the U.S. military, which they viewed as a violation of their beliefs. Muhammad Ali was stripped of his heavyweight boxing championship for the same reason. During the years that Elijah Muhammad headed the Nation of Islam, temples often were raided by the police, leading to occasional armed confrontations. Yet, unlike more explicitly nonsupplicant political organizations like the Black Panther party, the Nation of Islam never was targeted for complete annihilation. In part, this fact may reflect recognition by agencies of social control of the accommodative potential of messianic-nationalist groups. While leveling considerable criticism at the dominant society, messianic-nationalist sects tend to foster many middle-class values and to channel latent hostility into economic development and self-improvement efforts. At the same time, they provide their adherents with a satisfying identity denied them by the larger society. Ultimately, in their acceptance of the Protestant work ethic and emphasis on a form of black Puritanism, messianic-nationalist sects unwittingly serve as hegemonic agencies of the white-dominated society.

Various scholars have interpreted acceptance of these patterns in Weberian terms as vehicles of social mobility (Benyon 1938; Parenti 1964; Mamiya 1982). While undoubtedly some black Muslims propelled themselves from the lower into the middle class through hard work, frugality, and diligence, there is no definitive data available indicating whether the class transformation of the Nation of Islam occurred primarily as a result of the upward mobility of massive numbers of Muslims or through the recruitment of middle-class blacks to the group. According to Lincoln,

By the time Elijah died in 1975, the Nation of Islam was no longer exclusively a community of the poor and the fallen. With Malcolm X as its chief public

representative, the Nation had attracted a substantial number of college students and a small element of black intellectuals and numerous former Christian ministers. A large number of celebrities of the world of sports and entertainment, clearly influenced by the Nation, became Muslims, even though they tended to affiliate with the more orthodox branches of Islam. (Lincoln 1984: 163)

By the early 1960s, the Nation of Islam had made some significant accommodations with the larger society, including greater acceptance of integrationist leaders in the black community, decreasing emphasis on racial separatism, growing interest in conventional political life, the recognition that some improvement can occur within the American political economy, and the moderation of antiwhite rhetoric (Parenti 1964: 187–91). While Malcolm X played a role in these changes, he found himself increasingly at odds with Elijah Muhammad in his critique of the larger society. Around 1963, Malcolm X began to question more and more the Nation's doctrines and political inactivity. He publicly spoke out against American military intervention in Southeast Asia and the government's lack of commitment toward solving domestic problems. He attempted to obtain permission from Elijah Muhammad to allow members of the Nation of Islam participate in demonstrations and, according to FBI sources, sought to establish links between Muslims and the political left in the larger society (Perry 1991: 212). Following the assassination of President John F. Kennedy, Malcolm commented following a speaking engagement that "I saw it as a case of chickens coming home to roost. I said it was the same thing as had happened with Medgar Evers, with Patrice Lumumba, with Madam Nhu's husband" (Malcolm X 1965: 301). Elijah Muhammad silenced him for ninety days for these remarks and removed Malcolm as the minister of Temple #7 in Harlem in January 1964.

On March 8, 1964, Malcolm announced his departure from the Nation of Islam and his plans to establish his own organization based upon orthodox Islamic principles called the Muslim Mosque Inc., with an associate political body, the Organization of Afro-American Unity. Although his organization did not admit whites, Malcolm expressed a willingness to work with whites against racism and for social justice. His pilgrimage to Mecca in April 1964 convinced him that people of various colors could worship and live in harmony. Malcolm presented a series of lectures at Militant Labor Forum sponsored by the Socialist Workers Party and invited renowned revolutionaries such as Che Guevara to address the Organization of Afro-American Unity (Perry 1991: 277–78, 337). He also began to embrace black Christian ministers involved in the civil rights struggle, including Martin Luther King, Jr., (Perry 1991: 254). On February 21, 1965, an assassin's bullet ended

Malcolm's growing influence in the African American community. Three former members of the Nation of Islam were imprisoned for the death of Malcolm X, although controversy continues as to whether the Nation of Islam itself as well as the Federal Bureau of Investigation played a part in his assassination. The black Muslims, as a significant mass movement, appear to have died with the death of Malcolm X—the charismatic and radical figure who took many of the Nation's "angry young men" with him (Kaplan 1969).

Although Wallace D. Muhammad rehabilitated the status of Malcolm posthumously in the World Community of Islam in the West, he also continued the accommodation with the larger society that his father had initiated. As Lincoln (1984: 164) observes, "In the cult phenomenon, few successors are able to hold intact the disparate forces controlled by a charismatic founder, and Wallace was no exception. The transition of power was neither complete nor fully successful, and while the movement did not shatter upon his succession, as was widely predicted, there was dissatisfaction, disillusionment, and an inevitable erosion of membership." Unfortunately, figures as to how many drifted away from the black Muslim movement or joined the schismatic sect established by Farrakhan are unavailable. Under the leadership of Wallace D. Muhammad, the American Muslim Mission has relaxed admission standards (particularly for whites), de-emphasized black nationalism and separatism, stressed American patriotism (including acceptance of military duty), accentuated the spiritual and subordinated the secular dimensions of group life, increased interfaith cooperation and openness, and ceased overt antiwhite hostility (Jones 1983: 435). Wallace D. Muhammad stressed the need for interracial, intercultural, and interreligious encounters at the World Council of Churches in Chicago in 1977, spoke of Islamic respect for Jesus, and invited Christians to visit the World Community of Islam in the West (Muhammad 1980: 119). He also has urged Muslims to participate as loyal American citizens in the affairs of their local communities, states, and the nation. While Wallace regards racism as the poison of America, he teaches "Muslims that America's great blessing is the freedom to acquire personal wealth, social mobility and move from city to city unhampered" (Muhammad 1980: 123). Like other successful religious organizations, the American Muslim Mission by and large has made peace with the larger society by dropping the counterhegemonic components of its original ideology.

As we have seen in this chapter, the growth of messianic-nationalism, as an angry response to racism and social stratification, was a consequence of the historical and cultural background of African Americans and the nature of their relation with the larger American society. Messianic-nationalism emerged as a counterculture in opposition to mainstream society. Within this counterculture, a set of sectarian doctrines developed concerning the true identity and spiritual standing of black people, along with an embittered rejection of their subservient position in white society.

Despite its often cogent criticisms of the wider social structure, messianic-nationalism has never successfully forged an acceptable alternative for most African Americans. Thus, it has remained, like many movements of social transformation, "segmentary, politically decentralized, and reticulate" (Gerlach and Hine 1970: 388). Conversely, messianic-nationalism has provided succor to some blacks since its emergence and to many during periods of extreme structural imbalance. And consequently, it is during such periods that new black sects have tended to blossom. The Nation of Islam emerged during the 1930s when blacks were in the midst of the Great Depression and movements such as Garvey's Back-to-Africa campaign had failed. Similarly, the appearance of the Abeta Cultural Center or Original Hebrew Israelite Nation in about 1963 was a response to a later period of disequilibrium in the African American community. In short, messianic-nationalism, like other sectarian configurations, is best understood as part and parcel of the complex dialectical response of people of African ancestry to the appeals and injuries of American society. Expressing a profound and at times explicitly political awareness of the contradictions of American life, even the most militant messianic-nationalist organizations have, over time, made a rough peace with society and adopted the trappings of mainstream churches or nonnationalist sectarian types.

V

Conversionist Sects

Conversionist sects exemplify a desire by many African Americans to return to "that old-time religion." They emphasize a profound conversion experience, which Johnson and Watson (1969: xvii) define as "a sudden and a striking 'change of heart,' with an abrupt change in the orientation of attitudes and beliefs" accompanied by "emotional regeneration, typically sudden in its advent and consummation." The black Baptist and Methodist denominations once constituted conversionist sects and still contain congregations that maintain a conversionist posture toward the larger society. Generally, however, most mainstream churches in the African American community have significantly toned down the emotional exuberance of their historical predecessors. In response, an array of conversionist sects, particularly of the Holiness and Pentecostal varieties but also some that wished to retain a more "primitive" form of the Baptist tradition, began to appear during the late nineteenth century in the rural South and, following the turn of the century, in the cities of both the South and the North. These developments apparently prompted Zora Hurston (1981: 103) to assert that "The Sanctified Church is a protest against the high-brow tendency in Negro Protestant congregations as the Negroes gain more education and wealth."

The Development of the Black Holiness-Pentecostal ("Sanctified") Movement

The terms "Holiness" and "Pentecostal" often are used to refer to many conversionist sects, but various scholars attempt to differentiate between them on historical, doctrinal, and sociological grounds. Warburton (1969: 132), who admits that "Both Pentecostal and Holiness groups fall very clearly within Wilson's conversionist type," delineates four distinctions between them. Holiness sects, which drew upon John Wesley's emphasis on a "second blessing" following sudden conversion, view "sanctification" or "holiness" as an inward and subjective experience produced by faith in the Holy Ghost. In contrast, Warburton (1969: 134) asserts that "the doctrine of Entire Sanctification rarely has served to set apart Holiness groups to the extent that glossolalia has in the case of Pentecostals." At the organizational level, Holiness groups tend to be "interdenominational" and often merge whereas Pentecostal sects are more separatist and prone to splinter. As opposed to the relatively subdued tone of Holiness services, Pentecostalism emphasizes "inspirational" outbursts of ecstasy such as shouting, gesticulating, twitching, fainting, rolling on the floor, and especially speaking in tongues. Finally, whereas Pentecostal sects tend to appeal to people from the lowest echelons of society, the Holiness groups cater to those from somewhat higher social strata.

At the ideological level, black Holiness and Pentecostal sects emphasize the notion of "sanctification." "Baptism of the Holy Spirit" constitutes the most overt sign of sanctification and is manifested by shouting, waving one's arms, weeping, running up and down the aisles, leaping, repeatedly calling the name of Jesus, and speaking in tongues. Adopting a phenomenological approach and basing their observations on forty-five visits to an urban Church of God in Christ congregation, Burns and Smith (1978: 201) interpret the Sunday morning services as a "process of Becoming" that "allows for a gradation of contact with the Spirit." The person who has undergone sanctification demonstrates her or his condition through heightened commitment to religious activities and avoidance of the ways of the world.

Warburton's dichotomy may better apply to whites, either predominantly or exclusively, rather than to their black counterparts since he drew his data from fieldwork with two British sects, the Emmanuel Holiness church and the Faith Mission, and publications on white American groups, such as the Church of the Nazarene and the Assemblies of God. Specific black religions refer to themselves as either "Holiness" or "Pentecostal," but the distinction between the two forms is not clear-cut from a social-scientific perspective. As Washington (1973: 67) observes, "Whether they are identified as Holiness or Pentecostal, the roots of these groups are identical." Indeed, within the African American community, there is a strong tendency to lump these two categories together by referring to them as "Sanctified churches." Many of the religious bodies that anthropologist George Eaton Simpson (1978: 255–56) categorizes as "Pentecostal," because they exhibit "Fundamentalism, millennialism, baptism by total immersion, and the 'baptism of the Spirit' evidenced by talking in tongues," employ the terms "Holiness" or "Holy" in their formal names.

The Holiness movement emerged largely as an effort to restore Wesley's doctrine of "entire sanctification" within white Methodism following the Civil War. Initially the Holiness movement, according to Synan (1971: 40), "began as an urban force among the better educated circles" and included "leading figures in the Methodist Church," but its most radical wing attracted primarily Methodists and some Baptists in the rural South and Midwest.

> *Both the holiness and the populist movements were protests against the Eastern "establishment." In the same period that Tom Watson and [William Jennings] Bryan were fulminating against the 'banking interest' of Wall Street and the "monopoly powers" of big business, holiness dissenters were preaching livid sermons against the "autocracy" and "ecclesiastical power" of the Methodist "hierarchy." Whether the populist and holiness revolts were triggered by the exigencies of the panic of 1893 is something for other writers to explore. Nevertheless, it appears that the rise of the holiness denominations after 1894 was a religious revolt which paralleled the political and economic revolt of populism.* (Synan 1971: 53)

Most of the major white Holiness sects developed during the Jim Crow era and, like populism, often exhibited racist sentiments. Nevertheless, some Holiness sects appeared on the periphery of the larger Holiness movement, and occasionally poor whites and blacks broke with the reigning patterns of segregation and joined together for interracial Holiness fellowships. According to Shopshire (1975: 40), the first black Holiness sects emerged in rural areas of the South. The United Holy church (established in 1886 in Method, North Carolina), perhaps the earliest of the black Holiness groups, merged with several other small bodies in 1902 with the assistance of W. H. Fulford, a black elder in the predominantly white Fire-Baptized Holiness church, and later became a full-fledged Pentecostal sect (Turner 1984). In 1889 William Christian established a Holiness sect called the Church of the Living God in Wrightsville, Arkansas, and asserted that the "saints" of the Bible were blacks (Simpson 1978: 259), a messianic-nationalist trait not uncommon among Sanctified sects. While several black Holiness bodies arose out of the AME and AME Zion churches, most emerged as schisms from the Baptist associations and conventions (Shopshire 1975: 51).

C. H. Mason and C. P. Jones started another black Holiness sect in the Mississippi Valley. Mason, who began his ministry in the Mt. Gale Missionary Baptist Church in Preston, Arkansas, and attended Arkansas Baptist College for a few months, underwent sanctification in 1893 and "preached his first sermon in holiness shortly thereafter" (Shopshire 1975: 45). He joined

C. P. Jones, J. A. Jeter, and W. S. Pleasant in conducting a Holiness-style revival in Jackson, Mississippi, in 1895. After being expelled from the Baptist church, Mason and Jones established a congregation in Lexington, Mississippi, which they eventually named the Church of God but renamed shortly thereafter the Church of God in Christ to distinguish it from the white-controlled Church of God (Jones 1975: 147).

The Emergence of African American Pentecostalism

The origins of the Pentecostal movement as opposed to its historical predecessor, the Holiness movement, has been the subject of considerable debate, one shaped in part by white discomfort with the significant African American contribution to the development of Pentecostalism. Some scholars see the roots of Pentecostalism in the Latter Rain revival in 1886 in the mountains of eastern Tennessee and western North Carolina or in the teachings of Benjamin Hardin Irwin, the founder of the Fire-Baptized Holiness church (Clark 1965: 100). Distinguished church historians Winthrop Hudson (1973: 345) and Sydney Ahlstrom (1975: 292) as well as many white Pentecostalists point to developments such as Charles Fox Parham's Bible school in Topeka, Kansas, in 1901 as the genesis of modern Pentecostalism. While indeed Parham's teaching that glossolalia constitutes the only overt evidence of a convert's reception of the Holy Ghost played a significant role in the beginnings of Pentecostalism, the Azusa Street revival of 1906–9 in Los Angeles under the leadership of William J. Seymour, a black Holiness preacher and former student at Parham's Houston Bible school, as Synan (1971: 121) correctly observes, "acted as the catalytic agent that congealed tongue-speaking into a fully defined doctrine." Due to Seymour's role in the Azusa Street revival, Tinney (1978: 213) contends that he was the "father of modern-day Pentecostalism," despite his often being overlooked "by those who are contemptible of his race."

In addition to an interracial audience drawn from the "poorest of the lower classes" (Synan 1971: 107), many prospective converts and curiosity seekers from all over the United States as well as many other countries attended the Azusa Street revival. Some of the "third blessed" returned home to establish Pentecostal groups of their own. G. B. Cashwell, a white Holiness preacher from North Carolina, repressed his racial prejudice and asked Seymour and several of his black assistants to lay hands on his head so that he would be filled with the Holy Ghost. After receiving the Spirit, he spread the Pentecostal gospel to many people, both white and black, in the Southeast. "Elder Sturdevant, a Black preacher, opened the first Pentecostal congregation in New York City at 351 West Fortieth Street" (Synan 1971:

113). In early 1907, Charles H. Mason, J. A. Peter, and D. J. Young also spoke in tongues during their five-week stay at the Azusa Street Mission. After he returned to his headquarters in Memphis, Mason asked an assembly of the Church of God in Christ that the sect become a Pentecostal group —a move that forced his compatriot, C. P. Jones, to form the Church of Christ (Holiness) USA (Cobbins 1966).

The initial interracial character of the Pentecostal movement began to break down in the years following the Azusa Street revival. The Azusa Street Mission, renamed "the Apostolic Faith Gospel Mission," continued to function until sometime after Seymour's death around 1920, despite the withdrawal of whites from it (Tinney 1978: 222). Both before and after 1906, C. H. Mason ordained many white ministers of independent congregations because the Church of God in Christ was one of the few legally incorporated Holiness-Pentecostal bodies in the Mid-South. According to Anderson (1979: 189), "The whites appear to have operated independently, using the name Church of God in Christ (COGIC) with no indication of its connection with the black group, and publishing their own official organ, Word and Witness." In 1914, COGIC-ordained white ministers formed the Assemblies of God in Hot Springs, Arkansas, at a gathering which reportedly was addressed by Bishop Mason. During the 1920s, Parham occasionally preached at gatherings of the Ku Klux Klan and wrote articles for a racist, anti-Semitic, anti-Catholic periodical. Conversely, many white Holiness and Pentecostal bodies instructed their members not to join the Klan, not because of its racial policies but on the grounds that it was a secret organization. The division along racial lines in 1924 of the Pentecostal Assemblies of the World, which initially had "roughly equal numbers of Negroes and whites as both officials and members," formally ended the interracial period in American Pentecostalism (Synan 1971: 221).

While the roots of the black Holiness-Pentecostal movement in the rural South still await detailed examination, Goldsmith's (1985) analysis of the emergence of black Pentecostalism on the Georgia coast provides some clues. As elsewhere, the black Baptist and Methodist missionaries who arrived on the Georgia coast following the Civil War were appalled by the ecstatic rituals practiced by the ex-slaves on the plantations. By the end of the nineteenth century, "the energetic 'shout' had disappeared from the [St. Simons] island's religious worship, and the stately hymns sung by the Baptist nationally were adopted in its place" (Goldsmith 1985: 90). In their evolution from conversionist sects into mainstream denominations, many black churches emulated the somber style of the white middle-class churches, even though members of the former continued to occupy an inferior socioeconomic status.

While St. Simons and the Sea Islands remained backwaters longer than most areas of the rural South did, the growth of the tourist industry in the mid-1920s transformed many tenant farmers and sharecroppers on the Georgia coast into unskilled and semi-skilled laborers. In 1927 Pentecostal evangelists made their first converts on St. Simons Island. The initial converts to "holiness" did not renounce membership in the Baptist churches, but their ministers and fellow congregants objected to their ecstatic outbursts and ultimately forced them out.

> The appearance of Pentecostal "sanctification" on the Georgia coast offered a means of disregarding the dominant socio-economic criteria for measuring success in life. Material measures were jettisoned in favor of a binary distinction between "sinner" and "saint." Those in the former category—including unconverted Baptist brethren—were excluded from the company of the elect, both in the present time and in the coming millennial order. The Baptist faith was consequently regarded as incomplete and insufficient for ultimate salvation." (Goldsmith 1985: 94)

Flourishing beyond its roots in the rural South, the black Holiness-Pentecostal movement has functioned for some time as an urban phenomenon as well. After his split with Jones, Mason located the headquarters of the Church of God in Christ in Memphis, one of the largest cities in the South, and the Azusa Street revival occurred in the rapidly growing metropolis of Los Angeles. Southern-based Holiness and Pentecostal sects established new congregations in the wake of their members' movement to the North. As Sernett (1997: 95) observes, "As a result of the Great Migration the Pentecostal and Holiness movements, which spawned scores of groups other than COGIC and the Church of Christ (Holiness), USA, became important alternatives to the near hegemony of the Baptist and Methodist denominations." Elsewhere, Sanders (1996: 123) has characterized the "Sanctified church tradition" as an "African-American reform Christian reform movement that seeks to bring its standards of worship, personal morality, and sociocultural concern into conformity with principles of holiness and spiritual empowerment." The "mission" that Mother Beck (pseudonym), a member of the Church of God in Christ, formed with the assistance of several women in her home around 1918 served as the beginnings of the Zion Holiness Church (pseudonym) in Pittsburgh's Hill District (Williams 1974: 19). Complying with Mother Beck's request, in 1919 Bishop C. H. Mason sent Elder Baxter (pseudonym) to pastor the new congregation and act as the overseer of Pennsylvania and Delaware.

In addition to the Holiness and Pentecostal evangelists who followed the black migrants to the North, countless numbers of new Sanctified sects appeared in the "Promised Land" alongside the other gods of the black metropolis. In 1917 Bishop R. C. Lawson, who decided to leave both Columbus, Ohio, and the Pentecostal Assemblies of the World at the same time, established the Church of Our Lord Jesus Christ of the Apostolic Faith in Harlem (Shopshire 1975: 95). He and his associates formed a dozen or more branches throughout New York City (Anderson 1979: 132). Unable to find satisfaction in the historic Olivet and Ebenezer Baptist churches on Chicago's South Side, Lucy Smith, following a brief introduction to the Holiness religion in a predominantly white congregation, began to conduct prayer meetings in her home in 1916 (Washington 1973: 66). In her role as "a black puritan preaching holiness," Elder Smith transformed the Church of All Nations into one of the most colorful ministries in Bronzeville (Drake and Cayton 1945: 643).

According to Tinney (1978: 227–28), most of the growth of the black Pentecostal movement occurred "after 1930, when the churches accompanied their members in the migration to the Northern urban centers." We present a brief description of two black Holiness-Pentecostal sects. Unfortunately, lack of evidence and space precludes a detailed discussion of the many groups in the black Holiness-Pentecostal movement.

The Church of God in Christ (COGIC)

From its birth as small sect in the Mississippi Valley, the Church of God in Christ has grown into the largest black Pentecostal body in the country. Upon returning from the Azusa Street revival, C. H. Mason "began holding all-night meetings from 7:30 in the evening until 6:30 the following morning in a small frame church on Wellington, and after five successful weeks, even the white Memphis press took notice" (Tucker 1975: 90). In addition to witnessing, shouting, glossolalia, healings, and exorcisms, visitors to the revival could "examine the collection of misshapen potatoes and crooked roots which the Elder called examples of the 'mystical wonder of God'" (Tucker 1975 : 92). The First General Assembly of COGIC elected Mason to the office of "Chief Overseer" in 1907 and adopted a centralized, pres-byterian polity. Since 1907, COGIC has held annual convocations in Memphis, avoiding the practice characteristic of many black mainstream denominations of rotating the convention site. An active program of evangelism contributed to the rapid growth of COGIC. In 1908, V. M. Baker, a school teacher from Pine Bluff, Arkansas, established COGIC congregations in St. Louis and Kansas City, Missouri.

Elder Mason himself carried the holiness doctrine far beyond the mid-South: in 1907, for example, he traveled to Norfolk, Virginia, holding a three-week revival which planted the seed of Pentecost on the east coast. Thus, when blacks began their migration north during the First World War, Church of God in Christ evangelists would travel with them, preaching holiness, telling the simple stories of the Bible, and offering religious joy and warmth not found in the established northern churches. By 1917 COGIC congregations were organized in Pittsburgh, Philadelphia, and Brooklyn. Evangelists were also in work at Harlem, and in 1935 Elder Fletcher opened a storefront church at 137th and Lenox Avenue, placing Mason's message before the largest urban black population in America. (Tucker 1975: 95)

During the 1910s and 1920s, COGIC evangelists established congregations in Chicago, Detroit, Dallas, Houston, Fort Worth, Los Angeles, and many other American cities. In the 1920s, COGIC expanded its operations to the West Indies, Central America, and West Africa.

In addition to the formation of the Church of Christ (Holiness), USA, as a response to Mason's conversion to Pentecostalism, COGIC has undergone several additional schisms, including some that have not been documented, during its relatively short history. In 1915 sixteen members of the National Baptist Convention, USA, led by J. H. Morris, formed a Pentecostal sect which they called the Church of God in Christ (Melton 1978, vol. 1: 298). In 1921 the sect joined the older COGIC, "but in 1975, as a result of dissensions over a state charter, the group withdrew and became again an independent sect, this time taking the name of the Free Church of God in Christ" (Clark 1965: 119). In August 1927 Bishop S. E. Looper organized the First Unity of God in Cleveland as a schism from COGIC and eventually established branches of the sect in Cincinnati, Columbus, Akron, Chillicothe, and Barberton, Ohio (Blackwell 1949: 208). In 1932 Bishop J. Bowe of Hot Springs, Arkansas, established the Church of God in Christ, Congregational. Church leaders rejected his proposal that COGIC adopt a congregational polity, in which authority is vested in the local church members, rather than an episcopal polity, in which authority is vested primarily in a body of bishops (Melton 1978, vol. 1: 297). When Bowe returned to COGIC in 1945, George Slack became the senior bishop of the sect. In 1971 COGIC, Congregational, headquartered in East St. Louis, Illinois, reportedly had forty-three congregations, including six in Mexico and four in England. Yet another schismatic group was organized by Mother Mozella Cook, a convert to COGIC, as the Sought Out Church of God in Christ and Spiritual House of Prayer in 1947 in Brunswick, Georgia (Melton 1978, vol. 1: 298).

> *[W]hen C. H. Mason . . . died in 1961, his Church of God in Christ split into at least three groups, all claiming to be true successors to the COGIC name and property. These were in litigation for six years before the courts determined that a constitutional convention should be convened in 1968. It was, amidst brandished pistols; and Mason's son-in-law, J. O. Patterson was elected to succeed to the title of presiding bishop. Patterson's lenient attitude toward defecting ministers and congregations eventually led most to return.* (Tinney 1978: 258)

Fourteen COGIC bishops, however, formed the Church of God in Christ, International, in 1969 in Kansas City, Missouri (Melton 1978, vol. 1: 298). Despite separate ecclesiastical bodies, "congregations from both factions continue to fellowship with each other" (Tinney 1978: 250).

COGIC has grown into the largest African American body in the world, claiming to have some 6,500,000 members in 12,816 churches (Mead 1995: 114). Its membership count is probably greatly inflated since it has never conducted a systematic census, but COGIC constitutes, along with the three National Baptist denominations and the three black Methodist denominations, one of the seven largest African American religious organizations in the United States.

The Church of God

The renowned black radio evangelist Elder "Lightfoot" Solomon Michaux established one of the many Holiness or Pentecostal sects, both black and white, that refer to themselves as the "Church of God." Michaux was born on November 7, 1884, in Newport News, Virginia, with "a veil covering his face"—a sign auguring, according to African American folklore, "an exceptional life" (Webb 1981: 13). Michaux was reared a Baptist, but he began to attend St. Timothy Church of Christ after his wife, Mary, converted to the Holiness religion. In 1917 Mary persuaded her husband to construct a frame building to house "Everybody's Mission"—an interracial, nondenominational congregation in Hopewell, Virginia, in which "she could conduct services to her liking" (Webb 1981: 11). Soon Michaux became a licensed and ordained evangelist, and Everybody's Mission was accepted as a branch of the Church of Christ (Holiness), USA He began a three-month revival in September 1919 in Newport News. With a small group of converts, who by and large were "poor, propertyless, and without formal schooling" (Webb 1981: 15), Michaux moved his congregation into a storefront building in late December. In the spring of 1921, after learning that his bishop planned to reassign him to another mission, Elder Michaux seceded from the Church of Christ (Holiness) and organized the Church of God. He formed new congregations as many of his followers migrated to the coalfields of northwestern Pennsylvania and northern cities such as Baltimore and Washington, D.C. Michaux also established new congregations following successful revivals in various cities throughout the South and North.

According to Webb (1981: 31–32), Michaux's decision to begin a radio ministry in 1929 fell at "a time when people abandoned futile pursuit of the deceitful Mammon and sought other diversions, such as entertainment." Adopting the theme song "Happy Am I," Michaux's radio broadcast, which combined a call for repentance and the promise of salvation with positive thinking, rapidly grew into a national and even international phenomenon.

> When they released statistics on the program in 1934, CBS officials esti- mated that 25 million Americans tuned in on Saturday nights, a prime time, and that over 2 million listened to the "Happy Am I" program daily. Thou- sands rained fan mail on the evangelist. . . . Hundreds similarly showed appre- ciation for the program by going to Washington to observe a broadcasting session in the new Church of God edifice on Georgia Avenue. They made pilgrimages in heavily laden buses, on trains, and in automobiles. (Webb 1981: 43)

After being accused in 1937 of mishandling fund-raising monies, the "Happy Am I Preacher's" popularity declined even more rapidly than it had arisen. Nonetheless, "Though the radio audience was small, he continued to broad- cast weekly, without cessation, and when he died in 1960, his was said to be the longest uninterrupted radio broadcast in U.S. history" (Webb 1981: 48).

Elder Michaux's following constituted much more of what Stark and Bainbridge (1985: 26–30) term an "audience cult" than a "cult movement." Whereas the latter constitutes a full-blown religious movement with a more-or-less identifiable membership, the former consists of geographically dispersed individuals who learn about the group's activities through media sources. Although Michaux claimed to have millions of followers, the actual membership of the Church of God probably never numbered more than a few thousand (Webb 1981: 130). Like his Depression-era contemporaries Father Divine, Sweet Daddy Grace, and Prophet Jones, all classic examples of Fauset's (1971) "black gods of the metropolis," Michaux maintained a tight rein over his operations and the members of his organization. How- ever, his style did not reflect the "jive" tradition of contemporaries, despite the annual baptisms that he conducted—complete with drama, fireworks, and celebrities. Mary Michaux, in particular, castigated Father Divine and Daddy Grace and expressed antipathy toward Pentecostalists or what she disparagingly termed "tongue people." As Webb (1981: 168) observes, "The Church of God was in the structural mold of the organized Negro church, and Michaux did not measurably move it from that form." In contrast to his worldwide radio audience, Michaux's religious organization encompassed only a string of congregations stretching along the Atlantic seaboard from Virginia to Pennsylvania and New York. Following Michaux's death, the Church of God fell into a bitter legal battle with its founder's family over the remnants of the elder's financial empire.

Politico-Religious Organization in the Black Holiness-Pentecostal Movement

We have alluded to the Holiness and Pentecostal churches in the black community as constituting a "movement." In many ways the wide assortment of black Holiness and Pentecostal groups do conform to the model of movement organization proposed by Gerlach and Hine (1970), despite the fact that members of various Sanctified churches or associations may not view themselves as belonging to a larger movement. These researchers describe movements as being characterized by three primary organizational principles: decentralization, segmentation, and reticulation.

An acephalous (headless) or polycephalous (many-headed) pattern of leadership expresses the decentralized character of social movements. Like the larger Holiness-Pentecostal movement, which Gerlach and Hine (1970) discuss, the black Holiness-Pentecostal movement has no overarching organization to coordinate or define its structural content, beliefs, activities, and membership requirements. Many Sanctified congregations are affiliated with one of many national or regional associations, but others are essentially independent from such ties. No single individual can be identified as the dominant leader of the movement either today or in the past. Instead, the black Holiness-Pentecostal movement encompasses many leaders, each of whom exerts some degree of influence over an association, an informal assemblage of congregations, or an independent congregation. In essence, the black Holiness-Pentecostal movement is a loose network of groups of varying size that view "sanctification" as their common objective. Yet, even at the ideological level, Sanctified churches exhibit considerable variation (Simpson 1978: 258–59). Many black Pentecostal sects, for example, adhere to a unitarian conception of the Godhead as opposed to the traditional trinatarian view. Melton (1978, vol. 1: 224–28, 295–304), who provides a far from exhaustive tabulation of specific Sanctified groups, presents brief descriptions of nine black Holiness associations and nineteen black Pentecostal associations. Tinney (1982: 23) maintains that over 100 separate black Pentecostal organizations exist in the United States. In a compendium on black Holiness-Pentecostal sects, Charles Edwin Jones (1987) lists some 120 separate religious groups. In her recent compendium of African American Holiness-Pentecostal bodies, Dupree (1996) lists 73 "Trinitarian Pentecostal groups," 137 "Apostolic Pentecostal groups," and 106 "evangelical charismatic or neo-Pentecostal groups." Given the numerous small Sanctified associations and independent congregations, probably several hundred black Holiness and Pentecostal groups exist in the African American community.

Segmentation in a movement means that it is "composed of a great variety of localized groups or cells which are essentially independent, but which can combine to form larger configurations or divide to form smaller ones" (Gerlach and Hine 1970: 41). Even more so than the Baptist and Methodist traditions, fission and fusion have characterized the Holiness-Pentecostal movement. Around 1920, the Pentecostal Assemblies of the World spawned the Church of Our Lord Jesus Christ and the Church of the Lord Jesus Christ of the Apostolic Faith (Shopshire 1975: 130). This association, which actually originated as an interracial body in 1914, became a predominantly black one in 1924 when many whites withdrew to form the Pentecostal Church, Inc. (Mead 1975: 211). In the late 1950s, the Pentecostal Assemblies of the World also spawned the Living Witnesses of the Apostolic Faith, Inc., and the Bible Way Churches of Our Lord Jesus Christ World Wide (Shopshire 1975: 130).

A specific Sanctified congregation "may be affiliated with several denominations at different times in its history, or with none at all. Despite the many schisms, there is a camaraderie of spirit, and all come together for fellowship meetings and revivals and conventions" (Tinney 1978: 250). In the case of the Church of God in Christ, which is divided into jurisdictional districts, a specific congregation may choose to affiliate with the jurisdiction of its choice, regardless of geographical considerations. For example, some congregations in Cleveland, in northeastern Ohio, belong to the Southern Ohio Jurisdiction since Ohio is regarded as an "open" state. In an attempt to make jurisdictions correspond more closely to geographical regions, pastors of COGIC congregations in Arkansas have agreed to refrain from switching their jurisdictional affiliations.

The final organizational principle of movements, reticulation, refers to the system by which "cells, or nodes, are tied together, not through any central point, but rather through intersecting sets of personal relationships and other intergroup linkages" (Gerlach and Hine 1970: 55). The linkages between cells or congregations operate at both the personal and organizational levels. Leaders of Sanctified churches often are acquainted with leaders of other congregations in either their vicinity or other parts of the country. These connections may emanate from friendship or kinship ties or mutual membership in an association. Revivals conducted by traveling evangelists also serve to reticulate Sanctified congregations. Thus far, black Holiness and Pentecostal groups have not formed counterparts of white-controlled interdenominational or ecumenical bodies such as the National Holiness Association, the Pentecostal Fellowship of North America, the National Association of Evangelicals, and the Full Gospel Businessman's Fellowship International. While black American Pentecostalists participate in the World Pentecostal Conference along with African and Caribbean churches, even here racism prevails. According to Tinney (1979: 46), "The only black denomination represented on steering committees is COGIC—and that is token representation. Detailing planning is almost exclusively white-controlled, and programming follows suit."

While in theory most Sanctified associations exhibit an episcopal polity in that they are overseen by a senior bishop or a board of bishops, in reality their politico-religious organization tends to combine aspects of the episcopal, presbyterian, and congregational forms. Founders of Sanctified sects typically were charismatic men or women who were revered by their followers. As these founders died, they "were succeeded by their sons (or daughters), or by close associates according to charisma and seniority in the organizations" (Shopshire 1975: 144). The larger Sanctified associations have created boards, assemblies, committees, and councils at national, regional, and even local levels to administer affairs such as Sunday schools, evangelism, publications, education, and pensions. In this regard, their politico-religious organization has begun to resemble that of the black mainstream denominations.

A case in point is the Church of God in Christ—a religious body that continues to exhibit rapid growth. Throughout his tenure as senior bishop, C. H. Mason "held nearly complete authority in matters of doctrine and polity" (Shopshire 1975: 145). In the mid-1950s, Mason created a seven-man Board of Bishops to assist him and to succeed him in the event of his death. After Mason died on November 17, 1961, at the age of ninety-five, the General Assembly elected an additional five men to the Board of Bishops. When the General Assembly elected O. T. Jones to the position of "Senior Bishop," a dispute erupted as to whether so much authority should be concentrated in the hands of one individual, and this led to several years of litigation in Tennessee, Alabama, Texas, and several other states (Patterson, Ross, and Atkins 1969: 77). Eventually the Chancery Court of Memphis, Tennessee, ordered the litigants to resolve their differences at a Constitutional Convention, which met on January 30–February 2, 1968.

The new constitution stipulated that the General Assembly would elect a General Board of Twelve Bishops, including a presiding bishop, for a period of four years. The presiding bishop, as the chief executive officer, in turn selects his first and second assistant presiding bishops from the members of the General Board, appoints all the department heads and national officers, and appoints new bishops. The General Assembly acts as the supreme legislative and judicial authority of COGIC and meets annually during the National Convocation in November as well as in April. Delegates to the General Assembly include members of the General Board, jurisdictional bishops, jurisdictional supervisors of the women's auxiliaries, pastors and ordained elders, and two district missionaries and one lay delegate for each jurisdictional assembly, and foreign delegates (Robinson n.d.: 46). National departments include the Women's Department, the Sunday School Department, the Young People's Department, the Home and Foreign Missions, the Department of Evangelism, the Board of Education, the Board of Publications, and the Department of Public Relations. Each bishop convenes over an annual jurisdictional assembly, and appoints new pastors and ordains elders.

COGIC congregations within the United States are organized into 109 jurisdictions, each of which is presided over by a bishop. Various states (including Colorado, Delaware, and Iowa) and the District of Columbia correspond to the territory of jurisdictions, but many states are divided into two or more jurisdictions. Illinois, for example, consists of six jurisdictions: First, Fifth, Sixth, Northern, Southeast, and Southern. States and the jurisdictions are in turn grouped into nine "apostolic regions" and a mission territory. The First Apostolic Region consists of Tennessee, Alabama, Arkansas, Mississippi, and Louisiana while the Mission Territory consists of Montana, Idaho, Wyoming, North Dakota, and South Dakota. A bishop presides as an "apostolic representative" over each of the apostolic regions. Foreign bishops serve under the supervision of the Department of Missions and the Missionary Bishop. Canada and Mexico are each served by two bishops. The Bahamas, Chile, England and Wales, Haiti, Jamaica, Japan, South Africa, and Panama are each overseen by one bishop.

In contrast to COGIC, which with its rapid growth appears to be evolving into a denomination, the Mt. Calvary Holy Church of America, Inc., has stabilized in its growth and development into what Yinger (1970) terms an "established sect." Bishop Broomfield Johnson formed the Mt. Calvary Holy Church in Boston during the mid-1920s as a schism from the United Holy church. At the time of its founder's death in 1972, church records reported eighty congregations in thirteen states scattered about the

Northwest, Southeast, and Midwest—a figure that Arthur E. Paris, a sociologist who studied the group, suspects was "somewhat exaggerated."

> *There is a "revolving" phenomenon whereby new members simply take the places of others who leave. The size of the church remains roughly the same, although new members are constantly being added. This is also true of entire congregations. At the death of the founder, several churches in Connecticut "pulled out" and went independent, forming their own body. Their loss was offset when one or two formerly independent churches joined the Mt. Calvary body. During the last year of fieldwork . . . (1973), some Washington, D.C., churches severed their ties and became independent; other churches continue, however, to replace those that leave."* (Paris 1982: 36)

Presiding and vice-bishops along with a National Board of Bishops and a National Board of Presbytery serve as the principal authorities of the sect (Paris 1982: 107). State organizations function as abbreviated versions of the national association. Despite an elaborate formal structure, individual congregations exert considerable autonomy over local affairs.

The Sanctified Congregation

In contrast to the paucity of case studies of black Baptist and Methodist congregations, the Sanctified congregation has received a fair amount of attention. Most Sanctified congregations are housed in modest facilities—storefronts, house churches, and apartments in urban areas and simple frame structures in small towns and the countryside—but some (particularly those with relatively prosperous middle-class and working-class members) are situated either in substantial edifices formerly occupied by white congregations or in modern structures. Pentecostal Temple Institutional Church of God in Christ, located on the edge of downtown Memphis, for example, is housed in an ornate modern structure completed in 1981 at the cost of approximately four million dollars (Patterson 1984). Since James Oglethorpe Patterson, the presiding bishop of COGIC, served as the senior pastor of the congregation until his death in December 1989, it was referred to as the "Mother Church" of the organization. As such, Pentecostal Temple Institutional symbolizes the mainstreaming that COGIC is undergoing. The sanctuary, highlighted in royal blue and white colonial furnishings, seats up to 2,500 congregants in cushioned pews and has a choir stand with a seating capacity of 250. The Old Temple now serves as a reception, dining, and cafeteria area. In addition to these facilities, the building complex includes the Rushton M. Henley Memorial Chapel (seating capacity 400), a prayer chapel, a courtyard, twenty-four classrooms, a gymnasium, and an office complex.

The Boston congregations affiliated with the Mt. Calvary Holy Church of America, Inc., are housed in a range of facilities more typical of the black Holiness-Pentecostal movement. Gamma Church is held in "a commercial building, a frame structure about thirty feet deep and fifty wide . . . [which] comfortably holds no more than forty or fifty people. The Alpha church is somewhat larger" (Paris 1982: 39). The Beta church, which serves as the national headquarters of the association, has a sanctuary (seating 200–300) for regular church services, and a facility (seating nearly 1,000) for convocations and revivals.

Social Composition of the Membership

Sanctified churches historically have held their greatest appeal for lower- and working-class blacks. Williams (1974: 48) found that the Zion Holiness Church (pseudonym for a COGIC branch in Pittsburgh) still catered to poor people whose incomes did "not exceed five thousand dollars a year," despite its having been in existence for over fifty years. Most of the sixty-five members belonging to the Harlem Church of God in Christ on St. Simons Island on the Georgia coast are employed in service and manufacturing occupations (Goldsmith 1989: 91). Although the pastor is male, female members outnumber males by about three to one. About 90 to 95 percent of the more active members are consanguinal or affinal relatives belonging to three extended families.

Old members of the Holiness Church of Christ (pseudonym), a storefront in Washington, D.C., took jobs as domestics, cooks, seamstresses, night watchmen, janitors, and unskilled laborers after migrating to the city from the South (Moore 1975: 81–82). While older members clearly remained within the working class, many improved their material standard of living. Mother Edna Johnson, one of the more outstanding "success stories," went from "living in a wood shack in South Carolina and 'chopping cotton,' to living in public housing in Washington and working as a domestic, to owning her own home, two cars, and selling Avon products and hats" (Moore 1975: 82). The young women of the church hold positions as cooks in government buildings, charwomen, secretaries, and clerks; young men are employed as janitors, store cashiers, electricians, painters, and musical performers. Rev. Lewis T. Williams, the pastor and a civil service employee, appears to occupy the best-paying job of all the members. Like many storefront churches, HCC is largely a "family church" in that seventeen out of the twenty-four regular members are either consanguinal or affinal relatives of the Hannibal family. In contrast to the relatively modest socioeconomic composition of most Sanctified congregations, including many in COGIC (see Boggs 1977),

Lincoln and Mamiya argue, "[T]he class situation with the Church of God in Christ is changing rapidly. It is estimated that more than half of COGIC members are now within the coping middle-income strata (largely working-class and some middle-class members). Many of their churches are reflecting the socioeconomic change from storefront to regular church edifices" (Lincoln and Mamiya 1990: 269). Expressing a growing pattern of bourgeoisification in COGIC, the late Bishop Patterson—senior pastor of Pentecostal Temple Institutional—noted in his Sunday morning sermon in April 1987, observed by Baer, that many of his parishioners have been "blessed with nice homes, cars, and diamonds."

Politico-Religious Organization

The politico-religious organization of most Sanctified congregations closely resembles that of black Baptist and Methodist ones. Women in the former, however, sometimes occupy many of the offices monopolized by men in the latter two. Williams (1974: 33–36) identifies four categories of members in the formal organization of Zion Holiness Church: (1) elite members, (2) core members, (3) supportive members, and (4) marginal members. Elite members, including the pastor, the church secretary, the president of the pastor's aide group, the chairperson of the deacon board, and the church treasurer (also a deacon), generally sit within or around the "sacred inner space" during services. Core members, who include the remainder of the deacons, the trustees, the pastor's aide group, the financial captains, the choir, choral members, the missionaries, the ministers, and other officers, pay tithes and participate in most activities of the church. Supportive members generally attend Sunday morning services, annual meetings, and special programs or activities. Marginal members include teenagers, "chronic backsliders," and individuals who exhibit physical, mental, and financial deficiencies. While Sanctified churches in theory emphasize puritanical moral standards for their members, many of them welcome individuals who have a personal history of engaging in behaviors that the larger society judges to be deviant. Of course, it is hoped that the "sinner" will in good time become a "saint."

Although Holiness Church of Christ has several dozen members, its politico-religious organization replicates in abbreviated form that of larger Sanctified congregations. Most of these individuals occupy one or more offices. Like many small congregations, HCC has both a formal leader and an informal leader. Rev. Williams, the pastor, serves in the formal capacity while Mother Johnson, an active member, has achieved the latter status. The pastor's wife commonly serves as the church mother in storefront congregations, but Rev. William's wife is too ill to participate in church affairs.

Rev. Williams appointed Edna Johnson to the honorific position of church mother, but she actually earned it through her diligent involvement in HCC. Rev. Williams and Mother Johnson jointly make most of the decisions for the church. "Since more than half of the regular members of HCC are relatives of Mother Johnson's, and Rev. Williams has no relatives in the church other than a son who comes reluctantly, Rev. Williams is careful not to make decisions or take repeated action that will be disapproved by the church mother" (Moore 1975: 187).

Below the pastor and the church mother, HCC's polity includes five deacons, four trustees, two ministers, five missionaries, ten women working in religious education, two choirs, four clerical offices, and four small auxiliaries. The existence of an elaborate politico-religious organization in such a small congregation like HCC can appear superfluous to the outsider. After all, why would the members of a small group who are well acquainted with one another and often related to one another construct such a hierarchical structure? Such a view, however, overlooks the role these groups play in the lives of their members. HCC and other small religious congregations can, following Victor Turner (1969), be termed "liminal movements" in that they exhibit many of the features—such as homogeneity, equality, absence of property, abolition of rank, total obedience to one or more authority figures—characteristic of the "liminal" phase in Arnold Gennep's *rites de passage*. *Communitas* or an intense feeling of social solidarity characterizes the liminal or intermediate phase in rites of passage and liminal movements. Conversely, liminal movements "have a multitude of offices but a small number of members" (Turner 1969: 192). According to Turner, the hierarchical structure of liminal movements inverts the hierarchical structure of the larger society. In other words, whereas the members of a liminal movement in actuality exist on the margins of society, within the confines of their own universe they create an alternative reality that permits them to see themselves as an elite or superior category.

Women have often compensated for their relative powerlessness cross-culturally by participating in and even sometimes rising to positions of leadership in religious movements. In light of the importance of the ministry as an avenue of social mobility in the African American community, it is obvious why males often attempt to monopolize positions of religious leadership for themselves. Since male ministers in Baptist and Methodist churches rely upon women for the bulk of attendance, financial support, and general church work, they maintain a constant surveillance for any attempts by women to question their subordinate status. Consequently, as Drake and Cayton (1945: 632) observe, "The ban on women pastors in the regular churches has increased the popularity of the Pentecostal, Holiness, and Spiritualist churches where ambitious women may rise to the top."

The Mt. Sinai Holy Church of America, Inc., is an excellent example of the heights many women have attained in the Holiness-Pentecostal movement. Bishop Ida Robinson formed the sect in Philadelphia in 1923, later appointing Elmira Jeffries to serve as "vice-bishop" (Fauset 1971: 13–21). Elder Mary E. Jackson, the national secretary, filled the third most important office in the association during the early 1940s. Although Mt. Sinai Holy Church also has many male officers, women make up a notable portion of its elders and preachers. The Fire Baptized Holiness Church of the Americas and various Church of God sects also ordain women to the ministry. Conversely, while the Church of God in Christ, unlike most Baptist bodies, allows women to preach in the role of evangelist, the offices of bishop and elder are restricted solely to males. To compensate for male dominance in the highest echelons of the politico-religious organization, COGIC encouraged women to establish strong women's departments. Like black Baptist and Methodist churches, COGIC and various other Sanctified bodies have institutionalized the role of church mother. The church mother may be the widow of a pastor or bishop or deacon, delivers sermonettes, may also function as a community activist, and is regarded to function as an "overseer or bishop of women" (Gilkes 1994: 94).

Religious Activities

As in most churches in the black community, Sundays are extremely busy for Sanctified churches, beginning with Sunday school in the early morning and evolving into the Sunday worship service in the late morning and early afternoon. A special program, such as a musical performance or a "tea," may occur in the afternoon. Finally, an evening service of two hours or longer often brings to a close the most sacred day of the week. This round of religious activities may be punctuated by more profane affairs, such as a midday dinner or a picnic. Many Sanctified churches also conduct services on Friday nights as a way of making the transition between the profanity of life in the larger society and the sacredness of the Lord's Day. Midweek activities, such as prayer service, choir rehearsal, and a Bible study class, are not nearly as well attended as those conducted on Sundays. This is not without social significance. According to Williams (1974: 101), Tuesday night services at Zion Holiness Church allow core and elite members to "engage one another without the presence of the marginal and supportive membership or visitors who are usually present during Sunday and Friday services."

The sequence and specific content of ritual events (e.g., testifying, offerings, the sermon, the altar call, hymn singing, etc.) varies among congregations, but the overall structure of Sanctified religious services closely resembles those in black mainstream churches. Other than occasional instances of speaking in tongues and ritual healing, there is little that a National Baptist or an African Methodist would find offensive or unfamiliar in a black Holiness or Pentecostal religious service. Yet some differences would be noticed, such as the Saints being more inclined to clap their hands, stomp their feet, shout, and dance. Similarly, during his youth in Patterson, Georgia, Arnor Davis (1970: 60) was struck by the fact that the local branches of the Church of the Living God, the Pillar and Ground of the Truth, and the First Born Church of the Living God "offered the added attraction of drums, tambourines and other musical instruments not then used in the Baptist or Methodist churches." When Gospel music made its advent in Chicago and other northern cities during the 1920s, it found a ready haven among the Holiness, Pentecostal, and Spiritual churches at a time when most black mainstream churches eschewed this important mode of expression. In time, of course, many of the Baptist and Methodist churches came to appropriate these musical styles as well.

In large measure, the early Sanctified churches attempted to recapture the evangelical fervor that the Baptist and Methodist churches were discarding in their quest for middle-class respectability. Goldsmith describes the impact that the Pentecostal evangelists made on the younger residents of St. Simons Island in the late 1920s:

> *Recruited from the ranks of the Baptists, the initial handful of converts to "holiness" did not originally intend either to renounce their memberships in the Baptist churches or to form a congregation or church of their own. But the Baptists objected to the shouting and dancing of the "saints" in the midst of their otherwise decorous worship service, and the converts were forced out. The objections were far more fundamental than the disruption their style of worship caused; the boisterousness of Pentecostal worship had its roots in a complex of beliefs and behaviors, an ideology which presented a direct challenge to the ideological premises of middle-class religion.* (Goldsmith 1985: 93)

In theory, Pentecostalists place great emphasis on speaking in tongues, but in reality they often treat it as one of many overt manifestations of sanctification. Ethnographic accounts of religious services at the Zion Holiness Church (Williams 1974), the Holiness Church of Christ (Moore 1975), the Mt. Nebo COGIC (Boggs 1977), an urban COGIC congregation (Burns and Smith 1978), the Harlem COGIC on St. Simons Island (Goldsmith 1989), and Baer's observations at several Sanctified churches, including congregations affiliated with the Church of God in Christ in Memphis, Akron (Ohio), Flint (Michigan), North Little Rock (Arkansas), and Dumas (Arkansas) indicate that expressions of glossolalia tend to be sporadic, spontaneous, and individualistic. This pattern stands in marked contrast to many white Pentecostal churches that often expect and actively encourage members of the congregation to speak in tongues either collectively or individually.

In addition to speaking in tongues, Sanctified churches recognize eight other gifts of the Holy Spirit, including interpretation of tongues, teaching, preaching, prophesy, and healing. Faith healing has been an integral component of the Holiness-Pentecostal movement since its beginnings, and healing revivals have often served to bring together its white and black adherents under the same tent or at the same auditorium (Harrell 1975). The emphasis given to healing as a ritual event varies considerably from congregation to congregation. Rev. Williams, the pastor of the Holiness Church of Christ, occasionally lays on hands or touches the head or afflicted part of a person's body during regular religious services (Moore 1975: 153). For the most part, healing rituals occur on special occasions. According to Goldsmith (1985: 96), "Healing itself is talked about more than it is actually practised in the course of a Pentecostal service. Examples of divine intervention in cases of illness, especially those regarded by doctors as intractable, are the preferred topic of testimonies, for they illustrate most potently both divine power's capacity to effect changes in the lives of men and the superiority of divine solutions." Boggs (1977: 42) observed instances of healing rituals at the Mt. Nebo COGIC church involving anointing with holy oil and laying on of hands only at private prayer meetings or when traveling ministers visited the church. Revivals at the Boston branches of the Mt. Calvary Holy Church of America include a prayer and healing ritual after the altar call.

> During the prayer and healing service, people come forward and discuss their particular ills and needs with the minister, who lays hands upon the supplicant while praying over him or her. The prayers may vary, depending on the preacher and the person being prayed over. "O God, we come before you this evening; heal your faithful servant, O God. Rebuke this ill, O Lord; deliver her from the affliction. Heal this backache; make her every whit whole. We ask in Jesus' name. Amen." (Paris 1982)

Other Conversionist Sects in the Black Community

In addition to the Sanctified churches, countless numbers of other religious bodies in the African American community exhibit a conversionist orientation. According to Spear (1967: 176), "Not all of the storefront churches that sprang up during the migration years were Pentecostal. Many called themselves Baptists, although they often closely resembled the Holiness churches in their uninhibited form of worship." Many conversionist groups are "non-denominational" and may even cater to individuals who belong to established Baptist or Methodist churches. Anthropologist Frances Kostarelos conducted an ethnographic study of First Corinthians Missionary Baptist Church (pseudonym)—an "independent" storefront congregation on the West Side of Chicago. First Corinthians grew quickly in the 1950s and 1960s by attracting primarily the "southern relatives of the church's founding members" (Kostarelos 1995: 23). In addition to a Sunday morning service and a Bible class on Tuesday evenings, the congregation conducts a prayer and healing service on Wednesday evenings (Kostarelos 1995: 103–7). While such groups generally are situated in urban areas, they sometimes exist in small towns. Sister Thompson formed such a group, called the "Saints," in Oakboro, a university town in the Piedmont region (Keber 1971). In the late 1960s, most of the Saints were recent migrants from the surrounding countryside who found employment in Oakboro as janitors at the university, a grocery store, and town hall, and as maids in private homes, schools, and businesses. Sister Thompson conducted healing services on Friday nights in the Saints' homes, but she also encouraged her followers to attend the formal churches. Indeed, most of the Saints belonged to the largest black congregation in town.

The Primitive Baptists are the largest of the conversionist Baptist sects in the black community. Strongholds of Primitive Baptists, who are also called "Footwashing Baptists" and "Hardshell Baptists," include Tennessee, Kentucky, Alabama, North Carolina, and Virginia (Sutton 1983: 26). Given their emphasis on the doctrine of predestination, the classic conversion experience in which the "sinner" undergoes a solitary soul-wrenching vision serves as assurance to Primitive Baptists that they indeed are among God's elect. The vision experience must be validated in a public declaration by the convert that he or she has been living in grace. Following a vote of acceptance by members of the congregation, the candidate will be baptized at a nearby pond or stream. In his recent study of the rural congregations affiliated with two Primitive Baptist associations in the North Carolina Piedmont, Sutton (1983: 76) found that some converts no longer undergo the traditional vision experience—a development that reflects "a liberalization of the policy that pertained in the past." Reports on the salience of ecstasy in black Primitive Baptist churches vary. Andrew Watson (1932) reported that shouting, leaping from bench to bench, jumping up and down, screaming, crying, and jerking frequently occurred in the various Primitive Baptist services that he attended in Nashville and two middle-Tennessee towns. Conversely, while shouting and other forms of ecstatic behavior are encouraged in the Primitive congregations that Sutton (1983: 59) attended, he reported that their members "tend to be somewhat more concerned with decorum" than many of the Missionary Baptist congregations in the area. Furthermore, in keeping with their Calvinist theology, Primitive Baptists in the North Carolina Piedmont do not proselytize and reject the belief that humans can achieve perfectibility through "sanctification."

In contrast to the Missionary Baptists and the Methodists, as well as Sanctified sects, black Primitive Baptists in the North Carolina Piedmont eschew the development of an elaborate politico-religious organization (Sutton 1983). They do not pay their preachers, do not organize Sunday schools and church choirs, and tend to avoid involvement in local interdenominational ministerial associations. The offices of elder and deacon are permitted since they are mentioned in the Bible, but a quasi-independent board of trustees administers the congregation's property. Trustees generally have little or nothing to do with the routine affairs of the congregation and sometimes do not even belong to the Primitive Baptist sect. Since most of the Primitive Baptist congregations in the North Carolina Piedmont conduct services only one Sunday of every month, members generally attend services at other Primitive Baptist congregations in their immediate vicinity on other Sundays.

Some Primitive Baptist congregations choose to remain completely autonomous, but most congregations join a regional association. The association functions more as a social unit than an administrative one in that it "actually exists only during the three-day convention, held twice yearly, that [is] attended by official delegates of the constituent churches and by a large number of other members as well" (Sutton 1983: 313). Since the association does not maintain missions, educational programs, or outreach projects, the convention carries out little policy-making and permits much time for fellowship.

> Controversial matters are not generally discussed in the association business meetings, or if discussed are disposed of as quickly as possible. The bitter factionalism that sometimes emerges in the national conferences of some denominations does not commonly occur among Primitive Baptists. There is little interest here, or at the church level for that matter, in legislating new administrative rules, because the New Testament is understood to be the sole charter of the church and obviously in no need of revision. (Sutton 1983: 314)

Apparently not all black Primitive Baptists are as opposed to the process of ecclesiastical bureaucratization as those studied by Sutton. The National Primitive Baptist Convention of the USA, organized in 1907 and headquartered in Huntsville, Alabama, operates Sunday schools and aid societies and even considered a proposal, which was defeated, to begin foreign missionary work in 1967 (Piepkorn 1971: 312).

Other Baptist associations that probably exhibit a strong conversionist posture include the United Free Will Baptist church (organized in 1870 and headquartered in Kingston, North Carolina) and the National Baptist Evangelical Life and Soul Saving Assembly of the USA The latter, which was organized by A. A. Banks in 1970 as an evangelical group within the National Baptist Convention of America, declared its independence in 1936 or 1937 in Birmingham and espouses a "Bible doctrine as announced by the Founder of the Church, Jesus Christ" (Mead 1975: 55). In recent decades, in a manner reminiscent of neo-Pentecostalists in predominantly white mainstream denominations, "Bible believers" in the black mainstream denominations as well as in black congregations affiliated with white-controlled denominations have created state evangelical bodies and the National Black Evangelical Association (Bentley 1975).

Protest and Accommodation in Conversionist Sects

As we have seen, black conversionist sects, especially of the Holiness and Pentecostal varieties, emerged as responses to changes in the American political economy during the decades following the Civil War, but particularly following the turn of the century. As changes in agriculture forced blacks to leave tenant farming, sharecropping, and even independent farming, they often accepted menial jobs as unskilled and semi-skilled laborers and domestics in nearby towns and small cities. In many other instances, however, they migrated to obtain similar occupations in faraway cities in the North or the West or the large urban areas of the South. Following the "culture shock" theory developed by Holt (1940), several social scientists have interpreted the black Holiness-Pentecostal movement as an attempted adjustment to the social disorganization and cultural conflict that many blacks experienced as they became urban dwellers (Jones 1939; Eddy 1952; Harrison 1971; Frazier 1974). According to Melvin Williams (1974: 182), Zion Holiness Church emerged as "one of those social entities created by the stresses and strains of people dislocated from the rural South settling into the urban North." In a similar vein, Paris (1982: 105) argues that the migrations of blacks from the rural South to the industrialized North "provided the soil for Holiness-Pentecostal expansion in the cities."

Testimonies and ecstatic rituals, including shouting and glossolalia, can be understood in this context as providing members with an emotional release from the frustrations and anxieties that social dislocation created in their everyday lives. The sense of shared emotional and spiritual experience produced by these rituals helped to cement a feeling of renewed social connectedness and intersubjectivity. As Harrison (1971: 244) observes, "storefront holiness groups and storefront Baptist groups" create a Durkheimian sense of reborn social identity, personal dignity, and newfound community. Conversionist congregations generally exhibit a familial ethos, in either a real or fictive sense. Furthermore, for many of their adherents, conversionist sects substitute high religious status as "Saints" and God's elect for a relatively humble social standing in the larger society. Whereas in the dominant secular domain, one may be a janitor, unskilled manual laborer, domestic, or an unemployed person, the church creates opportunities for members to serve as elders, deacons, evangelists, missionaries, ushers, nurses, and choir members. In Williams's view (1974), Zion Holiness Church provides its members not only a "refuge from the world" but also a subculture that "allocates social status, differentiated roles, resolves conflicts, gives meaning, order, and style to its members' lives, and provides for social mobility and social rewards within its confines" (Williams 1974: 157).

Beyond their stabilizing and palliative functions, some scholars argue, Holiness-Pentecostal sects serve as a Weberian vehicle of social uplift by instilling socially approved attitudes and behavioral patterns in their members (Johnson 1961; Parsons 1965). Adherence to an ascetic code of conduct, it is argued, motivates individuals to work hard and spend their limited resources prudently. However, Flora (1976: 231) argues that Pentecostals in Colombia exhibit no more entrepreneurial aspirations than Catholics of similar class backgrounds and that "the amount of potential capital accumulation resulting from worldly asceticism practiced by lower class individuals was determined to be negligible to the development process."

More broadly, Robert Mapes Anderson (1979: 224) maintains that Pentecostalism emerged as a response to the transition from competitive to monopoly capitalism during roughly the same period (1890–1925) that populism, labor-capital class conflict, and progressivism appeared in American society. While in theory Pentecostalism rejected "the world," it encouraged its followers to adapt to processes of industrialization and urbanization.

> *Pentecostalism has internalized in its adherents those characteristics and moral values that the society as a whole subscribes to, but only the lower classes are expected to live up to: passivity, obedience, honesty, hard work, thrift, self-denial, and sobriety. In short, Pentecostalism has served the social function of developing the ideal proletariat for urban-industrial capitalism—just as other sectarian movements have. And it has probably succeeded in doing this among those who had the most difficulty in acculturating. Religious crisis experiences*

often involve a reorganization of personality, values, and behaviors that enable someone to adjust better to the imperatives of the situation. That Pentecostals found it necessary to pass through two, three, and sometimes more crisis experiences before they could feel at peace, suggests that, in their case, acculturation to urban-industrial society was acutely painful. (Anderson 1979: 239)

Black Pentecostals commonly exhibit a pattern of "apolitical fatalism" in that they mystify the gradual erosion of control of some rural African Americans over the means of production (Goldsmith 1989). In a similar vein, Paris (1982: 147), based upon his observations among urban congregations, maintains that black Pentecostalism emphasizes "the mediation of an economy of salvation and not the secular political economy."

Unfortunately, no systematic research has been conducted on patterns of social mobility among black Holiness-Pentecostal sects. While in the past virtually all Sanctified congregations catered almost exclusively to black working- and lower-class people, a fair number of them today, especially among those affiliated with the Church of God in Christ, serve a relatively affluent working- and middle-class clientele. Is this shift in social composition of the black Holiness-Pentecostal movement due to strict adherence to the Protestant work ethic, overall socioeconomic improvements among certain black Americans in the wake of the civil rights movement, or recruitment of members from higher social strata? The ethnographic record on Sanctified churches provides only a few hints.

Sidney Harrison Moore (1975: 292–93) asserts that Holiness Church of Christ (HCC) allows rural migrants to adapt to the city "on their own terms" and inculcates in them "the pragmatic values of mainstream American culture, including honesty, hard work, and thriftiness." Older members of HCC have experienced modest improvements in their material standard of living, but they and their children continue to remain, by and large, members of the working class. In other words, their relative position in the American class structure has not appreciably changed. Furthermore, Moore (1975: 246) observes that the "attraction of leadership roles at HCC stems largely from the general inaccessibility of such roles for blacks in the wider society, and particularly so for low income blacks, who make up the congregations of storefront churches." Apparently the shift in the overall socioeconomic status of some Sanctified congregations results more from the recruitment of new members than from social mobility among their original members. In his study of three black Pentecostal congregations in Boston, Paris (1982: 155) found that Alpha Church's relocation to a more affluent neighborhood on the periphery of black settlement "improved its appeal to a 'better' class of potential members," enabling it to shift its overall social composition from "lower-class (lower-lower, middle-lower?)" to "upper-lower class."

Regardless of whether one adopts a Weberian or a Marxian interpretation, it is evident that black Holiness-Pentecostal sects tend to facilitate the adjustment or accommodation of their members to the values and behavioral patterns considered appropriate in a capitalist society. Thus they emphasize the transformation of personal identity as opposed to the larger social order. As Paris (1982: 97) observes, "the salvation of which the [Mt. Calvary] church sees itself as guardian is a personal one to be worked out inside the church itself. The world is taken as a given and is sinful; thus, the call to salvation is a call to men to leave the world and enter the church." While Mt. Calvary members function as workers and consumers in the larger society, most of their primary relationships are within the setting of the church. Furthermore, most members eschew involvement in community affairs and social activism. As a consequence, church membership can be seen as having a politically pacifying effect, contributing to the creation of a more compliant working class. Nevertheless, Mt. Calvary members may exhibit a pattern of "practical politics" when the local congregation itself faces an immediate threat. For example, when the Boston Redevelopment Authority proposed to raze Alpha Church, its members rejected, despite their pastor's advice to the contrary, the agency's offer of monetary compensation (Paris 1982: 133–34). Their opposition, however, emanated not so much from their religious beliefs as the exegeses of survival.

Unlike the reactionary politics of many white Holiness-Pentecostal sects, however, Sanctified sects generally avoid a staunch anti-Communist posture. According to Tinney (1978: 244), black Pentecostals "fear that, not the Soviets, but the American political system may at times represent the demon-possessed political Babylon." Like his Socialist contemporary, Eugene Debs, C. H. Mason was imprisoned for his vocal public opposition to American involvement in World War I. It is important to note, however, that "Mason did recognize the Scriptural injunction to obey those in authority, and gave his endorsement of Liberty Bonds" (Tucker 1975: 97–98). Nonetheless, Mason's pacifism and his appeal among the black masses prompted J. Edgar Hoover to order the FBI to keep the chief apostle of COGIC under close surveillance.

Sanctified sects, as well, exhibit other partially counterhegemonic elements. Goldsmith (1989) maintains that Harlem COGIC and other Holiness-Pentecostal congregations on the Georgia coast reject the middle-class ideology (which embodies a belief in the possibility of upward mobility by means of disciplined work and adherence to a concept of "bureaucratic time") espoused by Baptist churches, even those consisting primarily of working-class members. Similarly, specific black Holiness-Pentecostal ministers and congregations, in fact, have, especially in recent decades, been involved in social protest and reform. According to Tinney (1978: 268), such activities are "difficult to document since the press has never been interested in black Pentecostalism, let alone this particular kind of social Pentecostal activism." Notably the Church of God in Christ provided the headquarters for the sanitation workers' strike, which was punctuated by the assassination of Dr. Martin Luther King, Jr., in Memphis in 1968 (Simpson 1978: 262).

> *Although there is no strong social or political platform from which this pentecostal organization currently acts, a great deal of deference is afforded its presence and potential in the city of Memphis and other larger urban areas. The growing power and influence of the Church of God in Christ in religious, as well as in social and political affairs, is clearly evident. The Presiding Bishop of this body, J. O. Patterson, has been consistently recognized in recent years as one of the most influential Black persons in America.* (Shopshire 1975: 104)

Based upon in-depth interviews with activist Pentecostal pastors in Boston, McRoberts (1999) posits that an increasing number of African American Pentecostal congregations have become more politically and socially engaged due to three factors: (1) the impact of the civil rights and black power movements on a third generation of black Pentecostal ministers, (2) the transition of Pentecostalism from a small sectarian movement into a "major faith community," and (3) the ability of innovative ministers to adapt literalistic and conservative theological premises. Indeed, he asserts that the openness of various black Pentecostal ministers to social activism has made Pentecostalism more palatable to middle-class African Americans (McRoberts 1999: 50).

Pentecostal Institutional Temple, COGIC's mother church, played an instrumental role in the establishment of the Ministers and Christians League, an organization that spearheaded a drive that doubled the number of the black registered voters in Memphis. Sanctified ministers in Washington, D.C., and elsewhere have joined mainstream ministers in campaigning for candidates and distributing political literature (Davis 1970: 78). As for many black mainstream congregations, political candidates often speak at Sanctified services. Black Pentecostals have won seats on city councils and in state legislatures and have been appointed to minor cabinet positions in the executive branch of the federal government (Tinney 1978: 265). Robert L. Harris, a COGIC pastor, became the first black state legislator in Utah history when he defeated a white Mormon candidate. J. O. Patterson, Jr., the son of the late leader of COGIC, is the first African American candidate from Shelby County, Tennessee, to be elected to the Tennessee state senate since Reconstruction (Lincoln and Mamiya 1990: 84). Samuel Jackson, a COGIC member, served as an assistant secretary of the Housing and Urban Development during the 1970s. COGIC Bishop F. D. Washington, who regards a strict conversionist stance toward the world as a "mental block," established a job training center and low-income housing project (Hollenweger 1974: 17). Al Sharpton, a controversial and flamboyant COGIC minister based in Brooklyn, made an unsuccessful bid for the U.S. Senate in 1992 (Taylor 1994: 229). He had had links with the New Alliance Party, has blamed "capitalist Zionists" for the socioeconomic problems faced by African Americans, and has embraced Louis Farrakhan. Such examples of social activism on the part of Sanctified ministers and congregations have prompted Sanders (1996: 140) to argue that, theological speaking, that Sanctified people can be best characterized as "liberal literalists" "because the exilic experience of being black in a racist society prevents them to follow uncritically conservative, fundamentalist readings fostered by descendants who used the Bible to justify slavery."

Some Sanctified ministers have been involved in Leon Sullivan's OIC, the NAACP, Operation PUSH, and, during the 1970s, children's breakfast programs sponsored by the Black Panthers (Tinney 1978: 252). Arthur Brazier and several other black Pentecostals created the Woodlawn Organization, a self-determination program for low-income blacks in Chicago. Following the organizing principles developed by Saul Alinsky, the group has organized rent strikes, reported flagrant practices by slum landlords to the media, established control stations for consumers who feel that they have been cheated in stores, attempted to upgrade neighborhood schools, and formed two youth organizations dedicated to the eradication of violence in the Woodlawn neighborhood (Hollenweger 1974: 14–15).

Luther P. Gerlach conducted research on the House of Deliverance (pseudonym), a midwestern inner-city Pentecostal congregation consisting of some thirty black and five white core members. "The church was founded as a branch of a national Negro Pentecostal denomination but by 1956 became essentially autonomous under the aggressive leadership of its founding minister and his wife" (Gerlach 1970: 127). Drawing upon the patronship of white "supporting" members, many of them middle class, the pastor was able to obtain money, goods, and services for operating his church and job referrals for migrants from Mississippi. Although, prior to late 1969, the pastor "had overtly been very conservative on civil rights issues and had opposed militant Black Power," later he became a staunch proponent of "black pride" and black-white social reform endeavors. He also developed into an articulate opponent of environmental pollution and pointed out that blacks in particular suffer from pollution since many of them reside in the vicinity of industrial facilities.

In short, Sanctified sects and other black conversionist groups, such as the Primitive Baptists and countless independent Baptist storefronts scattered throughout urban America, exhibit the complex and vacillating juxtaposition of protest and accommodation characteristic of African American religion. Most notable in this regard is the lack of a rigid and unvarying stance toward either the meek acceptance of the status quo or the spiritual rejection of interest in this-worldly activism. Rather, over time, groups have evolved changing postures and concerns. Certainly historically and to a large extent today, most conversionist sects have been highly accommodative in that they emphasize otherworldly orientation and focus upon personal as opposed to social transformation. At the same time, they have exhibited a passive form of resistance in their rejection of mainstream values and aspirations. As Diane J. Austin (1981: 242) observes, "Religious forms among the poor and oppressed inevitably will have radical implications. To the extent that believers live in and thereby represent their social situation, their religion will pass a moral judgment on that situation." Yet, as Austin discovered among Jamaican Pentecostalists, such movements rarely, if ever, become vehicles of revolutionary change. According to Goldsmith,

> *Millenialism may not be the pressing business of the Harlem [COGIC] Church, but it is the linch-pin of its ideological structure. Events of an individual's life are ultimately meaningful to the extent that they determine his status in the coming of the new order, that is, whether he will be among the saved or the unsaved. . . . Pentecostal millennialism . . . is an alternative that insists that there is nothing inevitable about the status quo, that in fact what is inevitable is an eventual overturning of present injustices and the establishment of a harmonious new order.* (Goldsmith 1989: 218)

As the discussion in this chapter suggests, conversionist sects tend toward the accommodationist pole—and more so as they undergo processes of embourgeoisement with the attraction of wealthier members. At best, as we see in some black Holiness-Pentecostal groups in the United States, they adopt a reformist strategy, much like the better-established sects (or mainstream denominations within the context of the African American community). Conversionist sects struggle to make a bad situation better without daring to risk small gain by openly challenging the oppressive structures of society. In this sense, they also serve as hegemonic institutions which, while calling into question its racist dimensions, accept the overall structure of capitalist society. Ironically, the larger and more affluent Sanctified congregations, such as Pentecostal Temple Institutional in Memphis, reflect a growing shift within the black Holiness-Pentecostal movement away from traditional concerns with spiritual salvation to an acceptance of bourgeois values of temporal success and material acquisition. In this transition, the Church of God in Christ has come full circle from its origin as a protest against the loss of folk-oriented "old time religion" in the African American community. In contrast to the increasingly reformist elements in COGIC and some other Sanctified groups, the vast majority of African American conversionist sects remain apolitical in their posture toward the larger society.

VI

Thaumaturgical Sects

*T*haumaturgical sects emphasize the reordering of one's present health or social condition through magico-religious rituals and esoteric knowledge. In their celebration of individual efficacy they contrast most sharply with the critical and collectivist orientation of the messianic-nationalist sects; with their embrace of material gain as public indicator of spiritual advance, they invert the conversionist disdain for worldly accumulation and display; finally, these sects eschew the reformist stance of the mainstream denominations. In these ways, and in their interest in the occult, the thaumaturgical sects are unique. Yet, as we shall see, these special qualities are blended with others that are shared by other types of African American sects. Because their uniqueness is constrained, the thaumaturgical sects remain a clear expression of the African American experience.

The first part of this chapter focuses on the largest group of thaumaturgical sects, namely Spiritual churches. This will be followed by a discussion of varieties of thaumaturgical expression, such as Reverend Ike's United Church of the Living Institute in New York City and Reverend Johnie Colemon's Christ Universal Temple in Chicago.

Characteristically, thaumaturgical sects unabashedly emphasize the acquisition of the "good life" along with its worldly pleasures. Even when other-worldly dimensions are present, they generally are overshadowed by more temporal concerns. Since conventional avenues of achieving success and economic prosperity are not readily open to their adherents, African American thaumaturgical sects promise that such benefits may be obtained through the performance of special rituals and positive thinking. In short, these sects concern themselves with the concrete problems of their adherents or clients by providing them with alleged spiritual means for acquiring needed finances, employment, health, mental tranquility, love, or the reconciliation of a strained social relationship. In fact, the leaders of thaumaturgical sects often argue that heaven and hell are states of the human mind—the former being a product of a positive attitude and the latter of negative thinking.

The Black Spiritual Movement

Because all religious groups claim to deal with spiritual matters, the term "Spiritual" as a term of reference to a specific category may appear be problematic. Yet, just as members of other religious bodies call themselves Baptists, Methodists, Pentecostals, or Muslims, members of certain religious groups in the African American community refer to themselves as "Spiritual." Furthermore, they often include the term "Spiritual" in the title of their congregation (e.g., St. Dymphna Spiritual Kingdom of God) or association (e.g., Universal Ancient Ethiopian Spiritual Church of Christ). In addition to their thaumaturgical orientation, a characteristic that somewhat distinguishes Spiritual sects from many other religious groups in the black community is their rampant syncretism. The Spiritual movement essentially combines elements from Spiritualism, black Protestantism, Roman Catholicism, and Voodoo or hoodoo, but also exhibits a considerable amount of heterogeneity, including at the congregational level. Furthermore, specific congregations or associations may add elements from New Thought, Islam, Judaism, Ethiopianism, and astrology to this basic ensemble.

Thus, the Spiritual movement cannot be viewed simply as a black counterpart of white Spiritualism. Rather, African Americans adapted Spiritualism to their own experience. As a result, much of the social structure and ritual content of Spiritual churches closely resembles those of other religious groups in the black community. Furthermore, Spiritual people in southern Louisiana, many of whom probably were reared as Catholics, added many elements from Catholicism and, at a somewhat more subtle level, Voodoo. Over time, Spiritual churches in other parts of the country adopted these elements as well.

Spiritual people generally admit that their churches have incorporated aspects of the Baptist, Sanctified, Catholic, and even New Thought traditions, but they usually deny vehemently any association with Voodoo or hoodoo. Rather than recognizing that Voodoo constitutes a viable Caribbean religious system focused on communication with and appeasement of the spiritual realm, they accept the general stereotype of Voodoo as witchcraft or sorcery. Yet, based on her research as a participant-observer of "hoodoo" in New Orleans, Zora Hurston (1931: 318–19) argued that "spiritualism" often provided a protective screen for the "hoodoo doctor" and his or her congregation. Like Voodoo and hoodoo, the Spiritual religion places a strong emphasis on "mysteries" and "secrets": a set of magico-religious techniques and beliefs that are intended to arm an individual with "power" over his or her destiny and fortune (Metraux 1972: 84). Voodoo in the United States, contrary to both popular and scholarly thinking, has not so much disappeared as it has become transformed, at both a group level and an individual level. Voodoo degenerated from a religious system to a strictly magical system—that is, it became part, perhaps the larger part, of hoodoo. In its diluted form, Voodoo continues to thrive discreetly and quietly as part of the underside of African American culture. At the collective or group level, it has essentially been transformed into a component of the Spiritual movement but is surreptitiously reappearing in certain areas, such as New York and Miami, which have undergone an influx of Haitian immigrants. (See Brown's [1991] ethnographic account of a "Vodou" priestess and her temple in Brooklyn.) At least one African American Spiritual congregation acknowledges the presence of Voodoo elements in the Spiritual religion, namely the Voodoo Spiritual Temple in New Orleans, which was established by Miriam Williams and Oswan Charmani (Pinn 1998: 44). Williams refers to the "temple's orientation as one of 'Afrocentric American Voodoo'" (Pinn 1998: 47).

The Development of the Black Spiritual Movement

The origins of the Spiritual movement remain obscure, but it appears to have emerged in various large cities of both the North and the South—particularly Chicago, New Orleans, New York, Detroit, and Kansas City—during the first quarter of the twentieth century. Various African Americans were attracted to Spiritualism, perhaps in part because its doctrines were favorable to equality and liberalism, as well as the concept of spirit possession in African religions. Paschal Beverly Randolph, who had both European and African ancestry and was born in New York in 1825, became a renowned Spiritualist trance speaker during the 1850s (Deveney 1997). He later became associated with Rosicrucianism and Theosophy and taught middle-class women about his concepts of true sexuality. Early black Spiritual churches appear to have resembled both ritually and doctrinally many of the predominantly white Spiritualist churches of the period, but the former adapted themselves to the African American religious experience by incorporating aspects of black Protestantism. In New Orleans, but also elsewhere, black Spiritualist churches liberally borrowed from Roman Catholicism as well.

The earliest evidence of predominantly black Spiritualist churches comes from Chicago—a city that remains the foremost center of the black Spiritual movement. According to Spear (1967: 96), several "Spiritualist" churches were established in Chicago's black community during the first decade of the century. On August 28, 1915, the Chicago Defender advertised services at the Church of the Redemption, a black Spiritualist congregation on State Street. Mother Leafy Anderson, a black Spiritualist who was destined to play an instrumental role in the development of the Spiritual religion in New Orleans, established the Eternal Life Christian Spiritualist Church in Chicago in 1913 (Kaslow 1981: 61). Sometime prior to 1915, the Lake City Spiritualist Church began to attract poor blacks, particularly southern migrants who had recently arrived in Cleveland (Kusmer 1976: 96). If indeed black Spiritual churches started in Chicago, their appearance in New Orleans appears to have been vital in determining their present content. Despite the strong opposition in the South to American Spiritualism, it nevertheless spread to cities such as Memphis, Macon, Charleston, and New Orleans (Nelson 1969). Spiritualism found an appeal among certain southern blacks, perhaps partly due to its liberal views on racial issues as well as its compatibility with African religions. "A stronghold of Spiritualism in the south seems to have been New Orleans, where many circles were held not only by the white but also by the coloured population, and many coloured persons were found among the mediums. Dr. Barthet who became a leading spiritualist in the city was known to have experimented with animal magnetism in the early eighteen-forties, and Dr. Valmour, a free creole, attained great celebrity as a healing medium" (Nelson 1969: 16–17).

The institutionalization of black Spiritualism as a church movement in New Orleans appears to have awaited the arrival of Mother Leafy Anderson from Chicago sometime between 1918 and 1921. Mother Anderson established the Eternal Life Spiritualist Church in the Crescent City and attracted not only blacks but some poor whites. She reportedly purchased a three-story building at 2719 Amelia Street and received messages from several spirit guides, including Black Hawk, Father Jones from Chicago, White Hawk, and the Virgin Mother (Berry 1995: 61–62). Her services were accompanied by "six piece swing band that played hymns in jazz time and style" (Berry 1995: 62). She trained several women, who established congregations of their own in New Orleans, and eventually she became the overseer of an association that included congregations in New Orleans, Chicago, Little Rock, Memphis, Pensacola, Biloxi, Houston, and some smaller cities (Kaslow and Jacobs 1981). Although Mother Anderson detested Voodoo, other Spiritualist churches in New Orleans, including some that were outgrowths of her own, were among the first to incorporate elements of Voodoo as well as Catholicism. Mother Anderson passed away in 1927, but in dreams and visions "she still appears to the women who carry on her work and gives instructions as to her wishes" (Tallant 1946: 174).

Mother Catherine Seals in 1922 established one of the earliest and most renowned Spiritual churches in New Orleans (New Orleans City Guide 1938: 199). Her Temple of the Innocent Blood incorporated many ritualistic aspects of Catholicism, such as the use of the sign of the cross, votive candles, holy pictures, elaborate altars and statues of the saints. Other Spiritual temples established during the early 1920s included Mother C. J. Hyde's St. James Temple of the Christian Faith, Mother L. Crosier's Church of the Helping Hand and Spiritual Faith, and Mother E. Keller's St. James Temple of Christian Faith No. 2. Prior to turning to the Spiritual religion and becoming a disciple of Mother Hyde, Mother Keller claimed that she "received training in Voodooism from a Mohammedan prince in New York, met some of the greatest Voodoo doctors in the country, and became well versed in this mysterious art" (New Orleans City Guide 1938: 208). Women established many of the early Spiritual groups in New Orleans, but Bishop Thomas B. Watson, a school teacher and a graduate of Xavier University, formed a small association called the Spiritualist Church of the Southwest (Saxon, Dreyer, and Tallant 1945: 407). Another male leader was Father Daniel Dupont, who established St. Michael's Church No. 9 in 1932. His sister, Mother Kate Francis, started St. Michael's Church No. 1 (New Orleans City Guide 1938: 208–11).

Anthropologists Andrew J. Kaslow and Claude Jacobs (1981) found that Spiritual churches continue to thrive in the locale where the Spiritual movement received much of its early impetus. In a very real sense the Crescent City continues to serve as the "soul" of the Spiritual movement, despite the fact that Chicago and Detroit have more Spiritual congregations. They report that Spiritual churches consisted of almost 100 congregations out of the estimated 600 African American congregations in New Orleans in the 1930s (Jacobs and Kaslow 1991: 43).

Like many other sects in the African American community, the Spiritual movement underwent a tremendous growth due to the Great Migration, especially in northern but also in southern cities. In 1923, Father George W. Hurley, a contemporary of Father Divine and also a self-proclaimed god, established the Universal Hagar's Spiritual Church in Detroit (Baer 1984: 82–109). On September 22, 1925, in Kansas City, Missouri, Bishop William F. Taylor and Elder Leviticus L. Boswell established the Metropolitan Spiritual Church of Christ, which became the mother church of the largest of the black Spiritual associations. Drake and Cayton (1945) note that the Spiritual movement flourished in Bronzeville, the black section of Chicago, during the period between the world wars. "In 1928 there were seventeen Spiritualist storefronts in Bronzeville; by 1938 there were 51 Spiritualist churches, including one congregation of over 2,000 members. In 1928 one church in twenty was Spiritualist; in 1938, one in ten" (Drake and Cayton 1945: 642). Reid (1926) notes the presence of Spiritualism in Harlem by the 1920s. In 1931 Addie M. Battie established the Mt. Zion Trinity Spiritual Church in Cleveland (Blackwell 1949: 72).

Sometime during the 1920s, Sister Moore established the Redeeming Christian Spiritualist Church, the first black Spiritual church in Nashville, Tennessee (Lockley 1936). A man who belonged to this congregation told Baer that Sister Moore broke away from the St. Louis association with which her church was affiliated and renamed it "the House of Redemption Spiritual Church." As a result of a power struggle between the pastor and her assistant ministers, the congregation disbanded sometime in the late 1930s. Bishop Wilma Stewart established St. Joseph's Spiritualist Church (later called "St. Joseph's Spiritual Church") sometime in the 1940s. St. Joseph's, which was affiliated with an association headquartered in Cincinnati, appears to have been the largest Spiritual congregation in Nashville during the 1940s and 1950s, with a membership of over three hundred. When Bishop Stewart died sometime in the 1960s, her husband pastored the church and renamed it "St. Michael's Spiritual Church." Apparently he lacked his wife's charisma, because the congregation rapidly declined, prompting him to close it and move to Michigan. The oldest of the eleven Spiritual congregations that Baer (1984: 30–42) found in Nashville was organized during the 1930s and 1940s. Rev. Mary Arnold (pseudonym) established in 1976 St. Cecilia's Divine Healing Church No. 2 (pseudonym), the newest and by far the largest Spiritual church in Nashville. She also pastors St. Cecilia's Divine Healing Church No.1 in Cleveland and oversees an association that includes churches in Indianapolis and Philadelphia. Rev. Arnold claims that her Nashville church has about five hundred members, including some "associate members" who continue to maintain ties with other congregations.

Brief sketches of two Spiritual associations illustrate the diversity of development within the Spiritual movement. The first, the Metropolitan Churches of Christ, is significant because it probably is the largest of the Spiritual associations and includes overseas congregations. The second, the Mt. Zion Spiritual Temple, characterizes certain Spiritual associations that are organized into "kingdoms."

THE METROPOLITAN SPIRITUAL CHURCHES OF CHRIST, INCORPORATED

Bishop William G. Taylor, a former Colored Methodist minister, and Elder Leviticus L. Boswell, a former Church of God in Christ minister, established the mother congregation of the Metropolitan Spiritual Churches of Christ in Kansas City, Missouri, on September 22, 1925. According to Tyms (1938:

112–14), by 1937 the group had grown to thirteen congregations nationwide. These included the national headquarters in Kansas City, two congregations in Chicago, one in Gary, two in St. Louis, one in East St. Louis (Illinois), one in Detroit, one in Tulsa, one in Oklahoma City, one in Omaha, and two in Los Angeles. In 1942, the Metropolitan Spiritual Churches of Christ merged with the Divine Spiritual Churches of the Southwest, based in New Orleans under the leadership of Bishop Thomas B. Watson, to form the United Metropolitan Spiritual Churches of Christ.

About the same time, a succession crisis occurred in the new organization following the death of Bishop Taylor. One version of the events indicates that, prior to his departure for California in 1942 for a period of rest due to health problems, Taylor arranged for his own funeral, placed Boswell in charge of the mother church, the Metropolitan Spiritual Church in Kansas City, and appointed Rev. Clarence Cobbs his successor. Cobbs, who had started the First Church of Deliverance on Chicago's South Side in 1929, apparently now regarded Chicago as the national headquarters. With Taylor's death,

> *The Southwest organization had saved the considerable assets of Metropolitan (estimated at between one and two million dollars) from reverting to the family of the late Bishop Taylor. . . . Metropolitan had no bona fide charter, unlike Southwest, and thus entered the merger for somewhat opportunistic reasons. Bishop Watson quickly assumed a somewhat autocratic rule of the United organization, leading to a split only three years later, after he unilaterally called a conference in New Orleans without consulting the national executive board. Two groups emerged as a result: the United Metropolitan, under Watson, and the Metropolitan under Cobbs and the Kansas City people* (Kaslow and Jacobs 1981: 100)

The United Metropolitan group experienced yet another schism in 1951, resulting in the establishment of the Israel Universal Spiritual Churches of Christ, with Bishop E. J. Johnson as its head. The original Metropolitan group prospered under the astute leadership of Cobbs, affectionately called "Preacher" by his followers. Cobbs started his church in the home of his mother Luella Williams with nine members (First Church of Deliverance 1979: 1). As its size grew, the First Church of Deliverance expanded a storefront at 4155 South State Street and joined the Metropolitan Spiritual Churches of Christ in August 1929. The rapid growth of its congregation prompted its acquisition of larger quarters in October 1930 at 4633 South State Street, and yet again in June 1933 at 4315 South Wabash Avenue. According to Drake and Cayton (1945: 645), although the First Church of Deliverance, "like other Spiritualist churches, is still considered lower-class by the 'dicties,' it was rising in status during the late Thirties, and had begun to attract middle-class members." The six-foot, slender Cobbs came to symbolize the gods of the black metropolis with his dapper mannerisms and love of the "good life."

> *The Reverend Cobb* [sic] *wears clothes of the latest cut, drives a flashy car, uses slang, and is considered a good sport. Such a preacher appeals to the younger lower-class people and to the "sporting world"—he's regular. To the older people he offers the usual Spiritualist wares—advice in time of trouble, "healing," and good-luck charms—as well as a chance for self-expression in a highly organized congregation. . . .*
>
> *The Reverend Cobb's* [sic] *power in the lower-class world has been demonstrated on several occasions. Once he gave a candlelight service at the White Sox ball park, charged for candles, and attracted almost 3,000 visitors on a cold, rainy night. At another time, after he had been accused of some delinquency, he held a vindication service at a downtown auditorium and drew a crowd of nearly 10,000 persons.* (Drake and Cayton 1945: 645–46)

After a fire destroyed the Wabash Avenue facility in 1945, the First Church of Deliverance built a modern, flat-roofed sanctuary with a seating capacity of 1,200 on the same site. The congregation opened a community/day-care center in 1956, erected a convalescent home in 1970 and a "Children's Church" in 1977 (First Church of Deliverance 1979: 4–6).

Figures on the number of congregations and members in the Metropolitan Spiritual Churches of Christ vary widely. Ebony (October 1960: 69) reported that the organization had some 80 congregations and an estimated 100,000 members (these figures were probably highly inflated). Melton (1978, vol. 2: 106) indicated that in 1968 the group had 125 congregations and some 10,000 members. The book marking the fiftieth anniversary of the First Church of Deliverance reports that the Metropolitan association had 65 congregations, including three in Africa (First Church of Deliverance 1979: 3).

Since Cobbs's death shortly following this event, the size of the Metropolitan Spiritual Churches of Christ has declined somewhat (Baer 1988). While the exact sequence of events is not clear, Cobbs's death, like that of Bishop Taylor, sparked a succession crisis in the association. Many pastors pulled their congregations out, and some established their own associations. Rev. James Anderson, the founder of the Redeeming Church of Christ in Chicago, formed the United Evangelical Churches of Christ, and "Father" Hays, the pastor of the Cosmopolitan Spiritual Church in Chicago, also formed his own association. Lucius Hall, the director of radio broadcast programs at the First Church of Deliverance, established an association called the First Church of Love and Faith. In May 1986, Rev. Hall told Baer that his organization had grown to about 25 congregations during the first six years of its existence.

Dr. Logan Kearse, the founder of the Cornerstone Church of Christ (formerly a congregation affiliated with the National Baptist Convention, USA), in Baltimore, became the head of the Metropolitan Spiritual Churches of Christ. At one point, two prominent trustees of the First Church of Deliverance filed an unsuccessful lawsuit to sever it from the Metropolitan association. Given the tensions that exist between Dr. Kearse and various pastors in the Chicago area, church leaders proposed that the national headquarters be moved to a more "neutral" site, namely Indianapolis.

According to Melton (1978, vol. 2: 106), the Metropolitan Spiritual Churches of Christ draw elements from Christian Science and Pentecostalism and emphasize a "foursquare gospel" consisting of preaching, teaching, healing, and prophecy. Baer's visits to congregations affiliated with the association in Indianapolis, Detroit, Kansas City, Baltimore, and Chicago indicate that it is a reflection par excellence of the Spiritual movement, adding elements of Spiritualism, Catholicism, black Protestantism, voodooism or hoodoo, astrology, and probably other religious traditions to those mentioned by Melton.

THE MT. ZION SPIRITUAL TEMPLE

King Louis H. Narcisse, D.D., who reportedly died several years ago, was one of the most colorful of the Spiritual leaders. In 1943 he established the Mt. Zion Spiritual Temple, which was incorporated in 1945. King Narcisse maintained his "International Headquarters" in Oakland, California, and his "East Coast Headquarters" in Detroit. In addition to these two temples, the association has seven other congregations, including a second temple in Detroit and temples in Sacramento, Richmond (California), Houston, Orlando, New York City, and Washington, D.C.

Baer met King Narcisse, a tall stately man who appeared to be in his sixties, in 1979 at the King Narcisse Michigan State Memorial Temple in Detroit. He was chauffeured in a shiny black Cadillac limousine with his title and name inscribed upon the door. As he entered the sanctuary midway into the Sunday morning service, two attendants rolled a white carpet down the center aisle and the congregants stood to greet their majestic leader. His regal attire included a golden toga, a cape with a white surplice, a white crown with glitter and a golden tassel, eight rings on his fingers, and a ring in his left ear. During the remainder of the service, except when he was preaching and conducting various rituals, King Narcisse sat on a throne in the front, occasionally sipping a beverage from a golden goblet.

For those occasions when King Narcisse could not be with his flock in Detroit, a large picture of "His Grace" faced the congregation. Below the picture was a sign reading:

GOD IS GREAT AND GREATLY PLEASED TO BE PRAISED IN THE SOVEREIGN STATE OF MICHIGAN IN THE KINGDOM OF "HIS GRACE KING" LOUIS H. NARCISSE, DD WHERE "ITS's [SIC] NICE TO BE NICE, AND REAL NICE TO LET OTHERS KNOW THAT WE ARE NICE."

Ironically, in contrast to the massive sanctuary with its elaborate altar and chandeliers, the presence of only some thirty congregants at the service suggested that the Kingdom of Louis H. Narcisse had seen better days.

The Politico-Religious Organization of the Spiritual Movement

Even more so than the black Holiness-Pentecostal movement, the black Spiritual movement manifests the three organizational principles of decentralization, segmentation, and reticulation (Gerlach and Hine 1970). Like Spiritualism in the larger society, the black Spiritual movement has no central organization that defines dogma, ritual, and social structure. Many Spiritual congregations belong to a regional or national association, but some choose to function without such formal ties. In many instances, the formal leader of a Spiritual association exhibits a clear pattern of dominance over its local congregations, as was the case when Rev. Clarence Cobbs was president of the Metropolitan Spiritual Churches of Christ.

In other cases, the formal head of an association may be closer to a "first among equals" relationship with the various pastors of affiliated congregations. This appears to be the case for the Greater Universal Spiritual Unity Union. Despite Baer's observation of activities and interviewing individual members of two affiliated congregations in Nashville, he never heard any specific reference to a "Supreme Bishop," by either a name or title. In fact, he learned who the formal leader of the association was only by reading a copy of its manual. The primary role of the Spiritual association appears to be one of providing local congregations with a sense of legitimacy and a social network. The association charters member churches and ordains ministers, elders, and other religious functionaries.

Associations sometimes try to impose certain rules, policies, and even dogmas upon their constituent congregations, but for the most part they fail to exert effective control. Instead, like many other movements, the Spiritual sects are characterized by an "ideology of personal access to power" (Gerlach and Hine 1970: 42–43). In principle, anyone who is touched by the Spirit can claim direct personal access to knowledge, truth, and authority. Although associations may attempt to place constraints on such claims by requiring individuals exhibiting a "gift" to undergo some process of legitimization, the latter may easily thwart such efforts, either by establishing their own congregations and associations or by realigning themselves with some other Spiritual group. Since the Spirit is believed to be the ultimate arbiter of the authenticity of any person's claim, the control of the association over those under its organizational umbrella tends to be minimal.

Leaders of Spiritual churches are reticulated with leaders of other Spiritual congregation, not only in their own association but in other associations. Such a linkage can be illustrated by the friendship between Bishop F. Jones (pseudonym), the pastor of the Temple of Spiritual Truth in Nashville (pseudonym) and Reverend Brown (pseudonym), the pastor of the United House of the Redeemer (pseudonym) in Indianapolis. After the two pastors became acquainted, Bishop Jones invited Reverend Brown to preach at a revival at the Temple of Spiritual Truth. After the revival, Reverend Brown reciprocated by inviting Bishop Jones and his congregation to visit his church in Indianapolis. The exchange of visits between the two churches occurred despite their affiliation with different associations. Reverend Brown urged Bishop Jones to shift the Temple of Spiritual Truth to the association that the United House of the Redeemer belonged to. The invitation suggests the potential for such a shift as a result of reticulation, regardless of whether Bishop Jones eventually accepted it.

In effect, the decentralized, segmentary, and reticulate dimensions of the Spiritual movement allow a kaleidoscopic pattern of fusion, fission, and recombination. There seems to be a constant jockeying for position among constituent parts not only at the associational level, as we have seen in the case of the Metropolitan Spiritual Churches of Christ, but at the congregational level as well. Reverend F. Jones of the Temple of Spiritual Truth in Nashville noted that one of his elders had discussed the possibility of "jumping out" and starting her own congregation for years, but he felt that she did not have the "stuff" to carry it out. Ironically, although he seemed to resent her desire to strike out on her own, he himself had established his congregation as a result of a schism from another Spiritual church in Nashville. Rev. Jones's term for launching a new group, "jumping out," reflects linguistic diffusion from girls' jump rope, which has long been extremely popular in the African American community.

Various sources present partial tabulations of other black denominations or associations but unfortunately almost completely fail to list Spiritual bodies (Mead 1975; Ploski and Marr 1976; Melton 1978, vols. 1 and 2). In his extensive *Encyclopedia of American Religions*, Melton lists only two black Spiritual or

Spiritualist associations: the Metropolitan Spiritual Churches of Christ and the National Colored Spiritualist Association of Churches. The latter emerged in 1922 as a schism on the part of blacks who belonged to the predominantly white National Spiritualist Association of Churches. The National Colored Spiritualist Association reportedly follows the doctrines and rituals of its parent organization, maintains its national headquarters in Detroit, and has congregations in Detroit, Chicago, Columbus (Ohio), Miami, Charleston (South Carolina), Phoenix, and St. Petersburg. For the most part, Baer had to rely upon personal contacts during his fieldwork among Spiritual churches in various parts of the country in developing the limited tabulation of black Spiritual associations in table 9.

Table 9

Partial List of Spiritual Associations

Association	Headquarters
National Colored Spiritualist Association of Churches (est. 1922)	Detroit
Universal Hagar's Spiritual Church (est. 1923)	Detroit
Metropolitan Spiritual Church of Christ (est. 1925)	Indianapolis
Spiritual Israel Church and Its Army	Detroit
Greater Universal Spiritual Unity Union	St. Louis
Temples of the Living God	Memphis
Universal Orthodox Christian Spiritual Faith and Churches (est. 1932)	
Universal Ancient Ethiopian Spiritual Church of Christ	Cincinnati
Mt. Zion Spiritual Temple (est. 1943)	Oakland
St. Mary's National Congress of Churches (est. 1947)	Kansas City
Israel Universal Spiritual Churches of Christ (est. 1951)	New Orleans
Alabama Spiritual Conference	Gaston, Alabama
Temple of Israel	Atlanta
Holiness Science Churches	Cleveland
Rock of Faith Spiritual Church in the South	North Little Rock, Arkansas
Universal Christian Association	Indianapolis
First Spiritual Churches of Truth	Chicago
Redeeming Church of Christ	Chicago

Sources: Kaslow and Jacobs (1981), Baer (1984), Jones and Matthews (1977).

Many of the associations listed in table 9 are "national" organizations in the sense that their congregations are dispersed throughout the country. Nevertheless, even an "international" organization such as the Metropolitan

Spiritual Churches of Christ tends to have a regional quality in that its congregations are heavily concentrated in northern Illinois, northern Indiana, southern Michigan, and the New York City metropolitan area. Most Spiritual associations probably serve as a loose social network for congregations in a particular region or even state. For example, the Rock of Faith Spiritual Church in the South consists of three or four congregations in Arkansas. Bishop Augusta Harris, overseer of the association and pastor of the Damascus Spiritual Church in North Little Rock, adhered to the organizational principle of reticulation by maintaining informal ties with several "sister" churches in the state that are not affiliated with her organization. In her younger years, she frequently visited Spiritual congregations in other states, especially in Chicago.

The Spiritual Congregation

Even more so than their Sanctified counterparts, Spiritual congregations tend to be housed in storefronts, apartments, house churches, and simple frame church structures. Spiritual churches are primarily located in relatively large urban areas; some are found in small cities; very few appear to be situated in rural areas. Like messianic-nationalist groups, the black Spiritual movement remains an almost exclusively urban phenomenon. Although most Spiritual congregations are housed in modest quarters, some of them, particularly those that cut across socioeconomic lines, are housed in impressive edifices that can accommodate several hundred, if not a few thousand, people. The latter include the Metropolitan Spiritual Church of Christ in Kansas City, the First Church of Deliverance in Chicago, the Alpha Church in Memphis, and the Alpha and Omega Spiritual Church in Detroit. In contrast to certain Holiness-Pentecostal groups, especially the Church of God in Christ, which continue to enjoy a pattern of growth, most Spiritual congregations at best find themselves in a holding position in membership numbers, and many appear to have been in a state of stagnation or gradual decline since the 1940s and 1950s. Conversely, some young, well-educated Spiritual ministers are attempting to revitalize their congregations by appealing to the tastes of young blacks as well as somewhat older blacks who have achieved some degree of social mobility.

Social Composition of the Membership

Spiritual churches have found their greatest following among lower- and working-class African Americans. Drake and Cayton (1945: 670) found that members of Spiritual (as well as Holiness) churches in Chicago's Bronzeville were "marked down 'low-status.'" In her study of Redeeming Christian Spiritualist Church in Nashville, Lockley (1936: 37) found that "This small group represents a variety of occupations which include cooks, maids, nurses, laundresses, dressmakers, chauffeurs, peddlers, and pressers. More than half of the group are unemployed at present." Out of the fifty individuals (all adults except for one adolescent) who regularly attended services at the Temple of Israel Spiritualist in Atlanta, which was established by Bishop Juanita White Henderson as a schism from the Progressive Spiritualist Training School, sociologist Robert Kenyon (1949: 29) classified twenty-nine as domestics, ten as unskilled workers, five as unemployed workers, and six as professionals. Females heavily outnumbered males by a ratio of forty-three to seven. Of the twenty-three "official" members on the church roles, only two were males.

Kaslow and Jacobs (1981) conducted a comparative survey of the social composition of two Spiritual congregations in New Orleans. King David Universal Spiritual Church of Christ (pseudonym) is one of the older Spiritual congregations in the city. In contrast, Helping Hand Spiritual Church of Christ (pseudonym) was established around 1979. In keeping with the respective ages of these congregations, "At King David S. C., 51.5% of the members are over fifty years of age; at Helping Hand 50.0% of the members are in their twenties, and none is over fifty years old" (Kaslow and Jacobs 1981: 83). Sex ratios in the two congregations are almost identical. Of the thirty-three adult "core and elite members" in King David, twenty-two (66.67 percent) are female and eleven (33.33 percent) are male. Eleven (68.75 percent) of the sixteen "core and elite members" in Helping Hand are female; five (31.25 percent) are male (Kaslow and Jacobs 1981: 80). All of the core and elite members in King David, except for a retired school teacher and an unemployed women, hold or are retired from working-class occupations (e.g., printer, domestic, taxi driver, hospital attendant). Whereas most of the adult core and elite members of King David work or had worked in semi-skilled and unskilled occupations, all of their generally younger counterparts, in Helping Hand, except for a law student, are employed in skilled working-class positions. Whereas only 33.3 percent of the members of King David had been reared in the Spiritual tradition, 75 percent of those in Helping Hand are products of it. Kaslow and Jacobs (1981: 79) contend that Helping Hand Spiritual Church of Christ "gives some indication of the future of some of the Spiritual churches."

Larger congregations (numbering in the hundreds) are less homogeneous and tend to cut across socioeconomic lines. As noted earlier, Drake and Cayton (1945) found that some middle-class blacks were being attracted to the First Church of Deliverance in Chicago as early as the late 1930s. In a similar vein, St. Cecilia's Divine Healing Church No. 2 in Nashville and the

United House of the Redeemer in Indianapolis attract some lower middle-class and even professional blacks. Both congregations also count a few whites within their ranks.

Despite the presence of some whites in the larger Spiritual congregations, the great majority of Spiritual congregations are exclusively black, except for places like New York where some Puerto Ricans and other Hispanics have joined them or where African Americans have joined predominantly Hispanic Spiritualist groups (Singer and Borrero 1984). In the past, however, Spiritual churches in certain cities were more racially integrated than they presently are. According to Kaslow and Jacobs (1981: 98), Spiritual churches in New Orleans during "the twenties and thirties were frequently interracial congregations which included a large number of Italian American members, a surprising phenomenon considering the intensely segregationist climate of the era." Lockley (1936) found that a fair number of whites attended Redeeming Christian Spiritual Church in Nashville, although apparently most of them were not formal members and may have come primarily to obtain "messages" from the Spirit. The church had a more racially integrated composition during its inception in the 1920s, but white members, probably as a result of external pressure placed upon them for violating the caste etiquette of the South, established their own Spiritualist congregation and affiliated themselves with the Independent Spiritualist Association of the USA (Lockley 1936: 29).

Organization of the Local Spiritual Congregation

Although the Spiritual movement has drawn its rituals and beliefs from a variety of religious traditions, the politico-religious organization of many Spiritual congregations in large measure resembles that of many black Protestant congregations. The long list of church organizations and auxiliaries at the First Church of Deliverance includes: the Trustee Board, the Lady Trustee Board, the Ministers Board, the Medium Board, the Acolytes, the Spiritual Union, the Sunday School Board, the Usher Board, the Senior Nurses Board, the Men's Group, the Women's Department, the Group Captains Club, the Christian Service Guild, the Community Enrichment Center, the Rev. Mattie B. Thornton (Cobbs's assistant pastor for many years) Memorial Group, the Luela Williams (Cobbs's mother) Memorial Group, the Rev. C. H. Cobbs Volunteer Group, and several choirs (First Church of Deliverance, 1979). The Children's Church, opened in 1977, in part replicates the organization of the First Church of Deliverance and serves as a training ground for future leaders of the parent body.

Most Spiritual congregations are considerably smaller than the First Church of Deliverance, but they also exhibit a similarly elaborate politico-religious structure. Offices or positions at the Temple of Spiritual Truth (pseudonym) in Nashville include pastor, assistant pastor, elders, deacons, deaconesses, missionaries, ushers and junior ushers, nurses, choir members, a secretary, and a treasurer. Despite the fact that the Temple of Spiritual Truth is a small storefront congregation, both its pastor and assistant pastor carry the title of "Bishop." Some Spiritual sects grant more regal titles to their leaders. Offices in the Mt. Zion Spiritual Temple, Inc., which was formed by King Louis H. Narcisse, D.D., in Oakland, California, in 1943, include those of Reverend Princes, Reverend Princesses, Princes, Princesses, Reverend Ladies, Prophets, Reverend Mothers, Grand Duchesses, Ministers, and Junior Ministers. Nonetheless, it should be noted that many Spiritual people contend that religious leaders who are into "kingdoms" are attempting to deify themselves.

In keeping with their thaumaturgical orientation, most Spiritual churches maintain the status or office of "medium," "spiritual advisor," "prophet," or "messenger." Mediums possess the gift of prophecy—that is, the ability to "read" people or tell them about their past, present, and future (Baer 1981). Pastors of Spiritual congregations almost always are mediums, but one or more of the prominent members of the congregation may also be mediums. Some Spiritual groups, such as the Universal Hagar's Spiritual Church and Spiritual Israel Church and Its Army, have established auxiliaries for mediums. Mediums give "messages" in special religious services, referred to as "prophecy and healing," "bless," or "deliverance" services. They also give messages in private consultations, often to individuals who do not belong to a Spiritual church. For the most part, mediums focus upon a wide variety of problems of living, ranging from finding a job or spouse to removing a spell or hex.

Based on her observations of four Spiritualist groups, Haywood (1983: 165) concludes, "Though it fails to address the problem of women's empowerment in any explicit way (i.e., ideologically), Spiritualism nonetheless accepts women's legitimate role as religious authorities without question and encourages some empowerment of women through its modification of the conventional identity of women." Of the fifty active Spiritual congregations that Kaslow and Jacobs (1981: 33) identified in New Orleans, "Approximately three-fourths of the pastors are women." Furthermore, "Many of the converts from the Church of God in Christ (Pentecostal) to the Spiritual church stated that they were stifled in their churches, and were seeking greater avenues of expression and authority" (Kaslow and Jacobs 1981: 33).

Baer's own data also indicate that the black Spiritual movement provides an alternative for ambitious women who are barred from the upper echelons of the politico-religious hierarchy of Baptist and, to a lesser extent, Methodist churches, the messianic-nationalist sects, and some conversionist sects, including the Church of God in Christ. Of the forty Spiritual churches that he visited in various cities, eighteen had female pastors. Six of the eleven Spiritual churches in Nashville had female pastors during the period of Baer's fieldwork in that city.

At St. Cecilia's Divine Healing Church No. 2 in Nashville, Rev. Mary Arnold's husband serves as the assistant pastor, and although there are many males among the ministers and deacons, they appear to assume a position subordinate to the female ministers and assistants. Conversely, while many organizations in the Metropolitan Spiritual Churches of Christ have female pastors, the First Church of Deliverance always has exhibited a pattern of male dominance. In selecting Mattye B. Thornton (known as the "Little Missionary") as his assistant pastor in 1929, Cobbs established a model emulated by many other male pastors in the association whereby the pastor is male and the assistant pastor female. Male dominance at the First Church of Deliverance is shown by the fact that in 1979 the Trustee Board consisted of fifty-two men while there were twelve Lady Trustees (First Church of Deliverance 1979: 6). Nonetheless, women often have rebelled when male clerics have attempted to assert dominance over them. When Thomas Watson, the senior bishop of the Spiritualist Church of the Southwest, "decided that women should no longer be bishops, and demoted Jr. Bishop Johnson to 'Reverend Mother Superior,' she formed shortly there-after the Everlasting Gospel Eternal Life Christian Spiritual Churches of Christ" (Kaslow and Jacobs 1981: 99).

Religious Activities

Much of the Spiritual services closely resembles the practices of many Holiness, Pentecostal, and the more exuberant Baptist churches. In fact, this is because the syncretic nature of the Spiritual movement leads the Spiritual churches to include rituals from other religious traditions in their services. Although some Spiritual people today recognize a historical connection between their religion and mainstream Spiritualism, many of them view the latter in a cautious, even disparaging manner, perhaps in part because they do not wish to be regarded as a "cult." Many groups contracted the term "Spiritualist" to "Spiritual" during the 1930s and 1940s to separate themselves from the white-dominated Spiritualist groups. During Baer's visit to the First Church of Deliverance in May 1986, for example, a member showed him a photograph of the dedication of the church building at 4315 Wabash Avenue on June 18, 1933. The photograph, which included Elder Boswell and Reverend Cobbs, was captioned "First Church of Deliverance Spiritualist," reflecting an earlier period in the use of group labels. Some Spiritual people, it bears mentioning, remain more receptive toward the Spiritualist movement in the larger society. For example, the manual of the Greater Universal Spiritual Unity Union states that "Spiritualism is a science, a philosophy and a religion of continuous life."

The seance, once a defining feature of Spiritual groups, including the Metropolitan Spiritual Churches of Christ (Tyms 1938: 117), is only a minor aspect of the contemporary black Spiritual movement. Many Spiritual congregations, however, place a great deal of emphasis on a message session conducted as part of a religious service, either on Sunday evenings or during the week. Like mainstream Spiritualism, the black Spiritual movement stresses therapeutic activities (Fishman 1979; Good and Good 1980; Baer 1981; Jacobs 1990). Individual spiritual advising, counseling, and the healing of physical ailments are integral parts of both movements. Many Spiritual people, like white Spiritualists, subscribe to the notion of reincarnation or the belief that spirits occupy a series of human bodies. Some Spiritual churches in New Orleans even have statues of black Hawk and conduct rituals of veneration and propitiation to this important Native American Spiritualist spirit guide.

It is difficult to determine whether Catholic elements in the Spiritual movement were derived directly from Roman Catholicism or indirectly from Voodooism. The sanctuaries of many Spiritual churches, particularly in southern Louisiana but also elsewhere, more closely resemble those of Catholic churches than of the Protestant groups that black Americans have traditionally been associated with. Spiritual churches make use of many Catholic accoutrements, including crucifixes; statues of Jesus Christ, the Blessed Virgin, and the saints; incense burners; and holy pictures. Spiritual people often engage in routine Catholic rituals such as making the sign of the cross, genuflecting while passing before the altar, and burning incense and candles. For the most part, such rituals are interspersed with activities more typical of black Protestant services, such as testifying, hymn singing, shouting, and the long sermon. Baer has never seen or heard of anything resembling the Catholic mass occurring in a Spiritual congregation. As Raboteau (1978: 272) observes, "the formal structure of the Catholic Mass, with each gesture and genuflection governed by rubric, did not allow the bodily participation and ecstatic behavior so common to Protestant services and so reminiscent of African patterns of dance and possession."

Rituals celebrating the various Catholic saints are quite important in many Spiritual churches. The names of many Spiritual churches incorporate the name of a saint. The burning of candles as well as incense is an integral part of the devotional activities conducted by Spiritual people in their churches and homes. As in Catholicism, the saints are considered intermediaries between an individual and God or the Spirit. Whereas most Spiritual churches emphasize possession by the Holy Spirit, those in New Orleans also recognize possession by a wide array of "spirit guides," including "deceased relatives, individuals from the Old or New Testament, or other figures in the group's hagiography" (Jacobs 1989: 47). The "spirit guide" Black Hawk in particular has achieved preeminence among Spiritual churches in New Orleans.

Both Voodoo and the Spiritual movement emphasize "mysteries" and "secrets." Bishop F. Jones of the Temple of Spiritual Truth told Baer that the Lord gives people "secrets" in order to help them with their problems and gives Spiritual leaders "special secrets" because others seek their advice and assistance. Some Spiritual people use floor washes, perfume oils, special soaps, powders, roots, and herbs. Despite the ambivalence expressed by some Spiritual people toward such articles, Reverend Brown of the United House of the Redeemer testified to the efficacy of many of them. Many Spiritual churches in New Orleans during the 1940s bore the name of St. Expedite, a Voodoo saint who can be appealed to when things must be done in a hurry.

Although Spiritual churches engage in a variety of ritual practices shared with many black Baptist, Methodist, and Sanctified groups, their emphasis on public prophecy is one of the characteristics that distinguish their religious services. Prophesying or the delivery of messages from the Spirit generally happens within the context of a "bless service," "deliverance service" or "prophecy service." In most cases a bless service is much like the Sunday morning service, except that the prophecy session will be substituted for the sermon. During the session, the prophet, who may be the pastor, one of the mediums in the congregation, or a traveling medium, relates various aspects of the present, past, and future of selected individuals in the congregation. In most small Spiritual churches, the prophet delivers the messages from the pulpit or front portion of the sanctuary; in a larger church, he or she may move up and down the aisles, selecting recipients for messages.

Bless services conducted by prophets from distant cities often attract large numbers of people, not only from the Spiritual congregation hosting the prophet but also from other Spiritual churches in the vicinity. Members of the religious groups or individuals who are not regular churchgoers often also attend such events.

The flavor of the bless service can be conveyed through a brief description of one such an event in June 1979 at St. Cecilia's Divine Healing Church No. 2 (witnessed by Baer). The event was advertised in a Nashville newspaper as a "healing and prophecy." Rev. Arnold, the pastor of the church, was born in Mississippi, belonged to the African Orthodox church during her youth in Pittsburgh, and moved to Cleveland in 1949 to establish St. Cecilia's Divine Healing Church No. 1, which became one of the largest Spiritual churches in that city. At the age of eight, she realized that she had the gift of prophecy but feared that people would regard her as a "fortune teller." Years later, the Lord "put" her into a coma, during which time He told her that she had a mission to prophecy and heal. Because she continued to disregard the Spirit's wishes, He had to " put her down" a second time before she embarked upon her ministry. Unlike most Spiritual pastors, Rev. Arnold is able to support herself in a comfortable manner from her salary as pastor of the Cleveland church, her spiritual advising, and "love offerings."

Two male deacons initiate the service, eventually attended by about two hundred people. After several hymns, Rev. Arnold's closest confidant at the church, a woman appearing to be in her late fifties, complains, "We are singing like we don't care." The band picks up its tempo and a young woman begins to play a tambourine. Around 7:50 P.M., Rev. Arnold, a moderately heavy woman with olive skin and facial features revealing her African-Indian ancestry, enters the sanctuary dressed in a long purple dress, a white hat that tightly fits her head, and tinted glasses. When she is ready to minister the blessings of the Spirit, she ambles down the center aisle to greet those who are to receive messages and healings. The musical instruments and the congregational singing make it difficult to hear what she says to people. She gently strokes the back of a woman. She tells another woman not to worry, hugs her tightly, and quickly pulls her hand away from the woman's body. Rev. Arnold tells a third woman, "Don't change your mind. . . . The Devil tried to make you say something which you had no business saying. Thank God you held your peace." When she instructs a fourth woman to stand, the woman goes into a trance. Rev. Arnold tells yet another woman, "You are happy now because you know me." As she touches this woman's hand, the woman screams "Oh" several times. Later, she hugs a middle-aged man and kids him about something. Then Rev. Arnold instructs a young white man to stand, tells him something about his visit to her due to an illness, and embraces and kisses him.

After several more prophecies and healings, Rev. Arnold urges the congregation to attend the next Sunday morning service, which will be conducted by her husband. She informs them that she will not return to Nashville until the fifth Sunday in July and counsels them to "see how long it will be without seeing me. I am going home tomorrow." Toward the end of the service, she states that she wants "everyone to give $25, $100, $200 or whatever" in the offering.

Other Thaumaturgical Sects

While Spiritual groups constitute the principal representatives of the thaumaturgical sect, at least several other religious groups in the black community fit into this category. In 1932 Dr. Lewis Johnson established a New Thought group in Detroit called the Antioch Association of Metaphysical Science, which by 1965 had six congregations and served a predominantly black membership (Melton 1978, vol. 2: 243). Another metaphysical group catering primarily to blacks is the Embassy of Gheez Americans headed by Empress Mysikiitta Fa Sennato, who operates the Mt. Helion Sanctuary at Long Eddy, New York. The empress, who claims to have come from the sun in a spaceship and to have occupied a body upon her arrival, aims to gather members of the ancient Gheez-Nation, or the Hamites, into a unified people who "will become the leaven in lifting all of humanity" (Melton 1978, vol. 2: 243).

The best known of all the thaumaturgical sects in the African American community is Reverend Ike's United Church and Science of Living Institute. Rev. Ike's organization is headquartered in the former Loew's United Palace Theater at Broadway and 175th Street in Manhattan. In his unpublished dissertation on the sect, Martin V. Gallatin (1979) delineates four phases in Rev. Ike's ministry:

(1) the conversionist period from 1958 to 1968,

(2) the transitional period from 1969 to 1972 during which Rev. Ike began to adopt a New Thought perspective,

(3) the gnostic period from 1972 to 1976 during which New Thought became an institutionalized dimension of the group, and

(4) the consolidation of the group after 1976 during which Rev. Ike rediscovered Jesus but essentially continued to operate with a strong New Thought orientation.

Frederick J. Eikerenkoetter II, better known as "Rev. Ike," was born around 1935 in Ridgeland, South Carolina, and was reared in the Holiness-Pentecostal tradition. After purportedly obtaining a bachelor's degree in theology and completing a tour of duty in the U.S. Air Force, Rev. Ike opened the United Church of Jesus Christ For All People in the late 1950s in his hometown. In the mid-1960s he moved his church to Boston and later to the Sunset Theater in Harlem and in 1969 purchased the five-thousand-seat abandoned theater in Washington Heights as the base of operation for his new United church. He later returned the administrative arm of his operations to Boston.

In his early ministry, Rev. Ike preached a literal interpretation of the Bible, the importance of speaking in tongues, the imminence of the Second Coming of Jesus Christ, the traditional concepts of heaven and hell, and an ascetic morality. Feeling that he sounded "just like another Holy Roller" (quoted in Gallatin 1979: 5), Rev. Ike began to discard much of his conversionist posture and to adopt a thaumaturgical one around 1968. Gallatin (1979: 194–209) identifies eight basic premises that Rev. Ike adopted over the next few years:

(1)   the notion that salvation must be achieved in the here-and-now,

(2)   positive-thinking,

(3)   the notion that God dwells in everyone,

(4)   the notion that thoughts govern behavior,

(5)   the belief that healing emanates from individual desire,

(6)   a rejection of the Devil as a tangible entity,

(7)   an approval of monetary and material acquisitiveness, and

(8)   a rejection of the traditional Christian doctrine of sin.

In keeping with his ideological shift to Mind Science, Rev. Ike ceased wearing pink suits and other loud outfits, sometimes including a cape, and began wearing more reserved attire, including three-piece business suits, as obvious symbols of his newly acquired philosophy of worldly success and prosperity. Rev. Ike frequently states, "the lack of money is the root of all evil" (quoted in Gallatin 1979: 109), and often his sermons and literature refer to public figures, such as Henry Ford, Colonel Sanders, and Tom Bradley, who achieved fame and fortune.

Rev. Ike asserts that donations to his church are an integral part of his "Blessing Plan," which will ensure health, prosperity, and success for his followers. Snook provides the following description of Rev. Ike's style in the early 1970s:

> Ike expects to applaud the success of his people and to see them rejoice in his prosperity. He laughs and jokes with the congregation, and the "testifying" he encourages is a series of recitations of how following his leadership paid off in material success and attendant happiness. . . . It is a nonpolitical message; Ike's advertising states that "people of all races, religions and those with no religion are welcome.". . . In his talk to the congregation, the preacher emphasizes that they have no black power among them, only green power (Snook 1973: 86).

In addition, he provides his followers with three principal techniques for implementing his ideology: visualization, affirmation, and meditation. Visualization involves closing one's eyes and creating a mental image of the object of one's desires. In Rev. Ike's words, in affirmation, "whatever you add to 'I AM,' this is what you become. This is what you 'buy'" (quoted in Gallatin 1979: 123). Meditation allows one to mentally focus in a relaxed, positive manner upon one's ambitions and desires. Rev. Ike operates a nationwide television and his services "are broadcast over eighty-nine radio and twenty-one television stations primarily in the eastern United States and Hawaii" (Payne 1991: 124). On May 1973, he lectured in the psychiatry department at Harvard Medical School; in January 1975, at the University of Alabama; in November 1975 at the Atlanta University Center; and in 1977 at Rice University (Murphy, Melton, and Ward 1993: 247). He claimed in 1982 that more than seven million people received his quarterly magazine and that more than seventy million had order the red prayer cloths that he distributed at no cost.

Although not as well known as Rev. Ike, Rev. Johnie Colemon of Chicago also preaches the gospel of material prosperity. Colemon, a former Chicago school teacher who recovered from an "incurable disease" in the early 1950s, was introduced to the Unity faith by her mother and later established Christ Universal Temple in 1958 (Samuels 1981: 53–60). Her church initially functioned as a study group but moved to a site on the western edge of the relatively affluent Chatham section of the South Side in 1963. In 1973 Christ Universal Temple moved into a facility consisting of two buildings with a closed-circuit television system in order to accommodate multiple religious services. Colemon preaches Holy Materialism, positive thinking, and Practical Christianity. She serves as the overseer of the Universal Foundation for Better Living, an association of reportedly one hundred congregations that formerly belonged to the Unity School of Christianity (a New Thought organization) headquartered in Lee's Summit, Missouri (Jones and Matthews 1977: 243). Christ Universal is affiliated with the International New Thought Alliance. Smaller versions of Rev. Ike's and Johnie Colemon's congregations exist here and there through the black ghettoes of America, offering their adherents thaumaturgical solutions to their plight, or in some cases validating their recently achieved affluence.

The migration of many Haitian Americans and African-Cubans to the United States in recent decades has resulted in the growth of *vodun* or *Voodoo* and *santeria*, both highly syncretic religions with thaumaturgical dimensions, in large urban areas, especially Miami and New York but also Chicago, Los Angeles, Oakland, St. Louis, and San Francisco (Brandon 1983; Laguerre 1984; Davis 1987; Murphy 1988; Brown 1991). With the migration of adherents to smaller cities, these groups have also appeared in outlying areas (Singer and Garcia 1989). Temples and congregations associated with these two Caribbean religions tend to be situated in apartments and houses, making them inconspicuous to the general public. The reportedly one hundred or more botanicas scattered about the five boroughs of New York City and Bergen County in New Jersey serve as the most public manifestation of both

Afro-Cuban *santeria*, which focuses on the veneration of the *orishas* and *santos* (the African gods), and Puerto Rican *espiritismo* (Singer and Borrero 1984; Murphy 1988). Haitian Americans, African Cubans, African Americans, and Puerto Ricans worship together at African-Caribbean rituals and seem to be engaged in a complex process of cross-fertilization with more established black sects, particularly Spiritual groups. Singer observed African American as well as Jamaican clients at the Puerto Rican *centro de espiritismo* that he studied in Hartford, Connecticut, between 1982 and 1985.

One group of African Americans is attempting to perpetuate Yoruba culture and religion (referred to as *orisha voudou*) at the community of Oyotunju Village in Sheldon, South Carolina. Walter Serge, who adopted the name Oba (King) Afuntola, founded Oyotunju in 1969 or 1970, practices African divination, and wears regal robes in his role as the community's high priest (Cohen 1972: 213; Davis 1987). After becoming an Obatala priest in Cuba in 1959, he established a temple on 125th Street in Harlem and formed an alliance during the 1960s with the Republic of New Africa, a black nationalist organization.

> *Today, 80 people live on the nine-acre, tree-filled settlement of African-style huts, temples, and shrines. The inhabitants, most of them from the North, wear African clothing. Their children scuttle among free-roaming chickens and goats and attend their own state-approved school. Members of the royal family bear three small knife scars on their forehead, distinguishing them from others in the village, whose markings are on their cheeks. Some villagers spend their days inside the compound, doing chores, conducting visitors' tours, or giving spiritual advice. Others work outside and return each evening. Each morning at 7, the beating of a communal drum signals the start of a new day.* (Davis 1987: 84)

Unfortunately, with the exception of the groups discussed thus far, there is a paucity of data on the profusion of thaumaturgical sects in the African American community. Most such groups remain obscure unless they undergo tremendous growth or come into conflict with an agency of the government.

Black Thaumaturgical Bodies and Cult/Sect Theory

We have avoided the term "cult" in referring to a variety of unconventional black religious groups because of the strong negative connotations associated with this label. In the mass media and in popular awareness, the term has been used to refer to small groups under the powerful sway of dominant, often exploitive, leaders. Implied in the use of this term commonly is the idea that followers have undergone sensory or nutritional deprivation or in some way been psychologically manipulated to the point that they are no longer fully capable of exercising free will. For the most part, within the sociology of religion the term has been used in a quite different sense without suggestion of a loss of personal agency among group members. Drawing on this social-science tradition and in an effort to resolve terminological inconsistencies in the literature, Rodney Stark and William Sims Bainbridge (1985) have developed a framework for categorizing varying types of emergent religious groups. While recognizing that both "sects" and "cults" are "deviant religious bodies . . . in a state of relatively high tension with their surrounding socio-cultural environment," like many other social scientists, Stark and Bainbridge differentiate between them as major categories. In their view, a sect is a schismatic movement which "must have been found by persons who left another religious body for the purpose of founding the sect" (Stark and Bainbridge 1985: 25–26). In contrast, cults "are deviant religious movements that remain within a nondeviant religious tradition," such as Christianity or Judaism (Stark and Bainbridge 1985: 26).

If we momentarily accept Stark and Bainbridge's dichotomy, the Spiritual movement and certain other thaumaturgical groups could be termed "cults," in that they emerged as new religious traditions rather than as schisms from previously existing religious bodies. In syncretizing elements borrowed from other religions with a set of new religious conceptions and rituals, the black Spiritual movement developed through a combined process of *"cultural imposition"* and *"cultural innovation"* (Stark and Bainbridge 1985: 25; emphasis in original). Of course, once a cult comes into being, as Stark and Bainbridge (1985: 26) recognize and as we have seen in the Spiritual movement, internal schisms or sects frequently appear. Also, once the Spiritual tradition began, individuals did leave other religious traditions for the purpose of starting (or converting existing groups into) Spiritual congregations.

Within their framework, Stark and Bainbridge (1985: 26–30) identify three degrees of cultic organization: (1) audience cults, (2) client cults, and (3) cult movements. Audience cults are groups only in a loose sense with leaders communicating with followers primarily by way of magazines, books, newspapers, radio, and television. Client cults entail a relationship between a teacher, consultant, or therapist and a client or student who seeks esoteric knowledge or spiritual power. Cult movements are full-blown religions with distinct organizations, discrete rituals and doctrines, and behavioral expectations, although in many instances these are very loosely defined.

Thaumaturgical bodies in the African American community operate at one or more of these degrees of cultic organization. In keeping with our earlier decision to eschew the now-tainted label "cult," we refer instead to "audience sects," "client sects," and "sect movements." Most Spiritual churches function as both "sect movements" and "client sects" in that they simultaneously serve two more-or-less discrete clienteles: (1) actual members of congregations and (2) free-floating individuals who seek the services of a prophet, advisor, or medium, sometimes by visiting a Spiritual church for a bless service or prophecy session but more often through private counseling. The latter category includes members of other black religious groups, people not affiliated with any specific religious group, and even some whites, Hispanics, and other non-African Americans.

In reality, some if not many Spiritual churches started out as "client sects." In his study of black churches in Chicago, Robert Lee Sutherland (1930: 38) found seventeen "Spiritualist" churches and an additional twenty-eight "Spiritualists" who functioned as free-lance mediums and advisors. The latter conducted seances on weeknights, for which those in attendance were expected to pay a fee or make a donation, but also offered private consultations or readings at other times. Some of these establishments advertised themselves as "science and development" schools. According to Sutherland (1930: 39), "those who seek to give dignity to their work, change the letters on windows to read 'Spiritualist Church.'" Somewhat later, "more than a hundred individuals not affiliated with a church were operating as spiritual advisors and readers in Bronzeville on the eve of the war. Many of these persons had merely erected an altar in a front room of a house, and hung out a sign" (Drake and Cayton 1945: 643).

Stark and Bainbridge (1985: 35) assert, "Client cults usually do not serve a low status market, if for no other reason than they charge for their services." In fact, while Stark and Bainbridge present no evidence for their claim, they maintain that Spiritualists draw on middle- and upper-class clients. Some relatively affluent blacks as well as whites seek out the services of prophets and advisors, but Baer's (1981) intensive interviews with eight Spiritual mediums in Nashville as well as his more casual interviews and conversation with other Spiritual mediums indicate that the majority of their clients are lower-class individuals. Most clients of Voodoo doctors, rootworkers, and independent Spiritualists in the African American community also are lower-class individuals (Baer 1982). Inadequate financial resources do not necessarily prevent working- and lower-class individuals from seeking out the services of a Spiritualist or Spiritual advisor, especially if they are convinced that their investment will result in a blessing.

Although some Spiritual churches have radio broadcasts and a few have sporadic television broadcasts, none appears to function as a full-fledged "audience sect." In contrast, Rev. Ike's United church operates much more as an "audience sect" than a "sect movement." Rev. Ike maintains contact with the great majority of his followers through his biweekly Action Magazine, radio broadcasts, and periodic television broadcasts. He claims that he has some 1.5 million followers—a figure apparently based upon his extensive mailing list which repeats many of the names on it (Gallatin 1979: 245). As a result of the transformation of his church from a conversionist sect movement to a thaumaturgical audience sect, Rev. Ike greatly increased its financial holdings. The IRS reported that the United church had an income over $6,500,000 in 1972—a figure that Rev. Ike himself boasted represented only a fraction of his organization's annual income.

The United church constitutes a sect movement in only the most rudimentary sense. Rev. Ike has not attempted to establish branches of his church outside Manhattan and has not created any formal membership requirements. Indeed, since Sunday services begin promptly at 3 P.M., many followers attend morning services at other churches. Those who attend services at the United church are "largely poor, Black, female, middle-aged and Southern in origin" (Gallatin 1979: 131). Since Rev. Ike generally preaches at the United church on only two Sundays of the month, four associate ministers conduct services in his absence. About 2,000 are in attendance when Rev. Ike is not preaching although many more than this attend when he is present. Gallatin (1979: 135–38) identifies six categories of followers who attend the United church:

(1) the "inner circle" consisting of functionaries such as devotional leaders, Sunday school teachers, choir members, nurses, ushers, and missionaries;

(2) "true believers" who attend United church exclusively but do not occupy a church office;

(3) the "dedicated" who rarely miss a service but also attend other churches;

(4) "seekers" who come for a blessing or healing;

(5) the "holiness people" who are "members of pentecostal churches who occasionally attend his services despite their theological differences with him"; and

(6) the "occasional attendee" who attends only when Rev. Ike is preaching.

A seventh category consists of "the disenchanted," previous followers who objected to the ideological changes that Rev. Ike introduced. Based upon his attendance at the United church for more than two years, Gallatin (1979: 139) presents the following rough breakdown of followers in each category: the inner circle, 125; the true believers, 500; the dedicated, 1,300; the seekers, 1,500; the holiness people, 1,000; and the occasional attendees, 100.

Rev. Ike maintains a pronounced social distance between himself and his followers, despite his exemplifying the "cult of personality" in the tradition of the "gods of the Black metropolis." Unlike most Spiritual pastors, he does not deliver messages or "readings," either publicly or privately. As Gallatin (1979: 245) observes, "while he has a large following, his church currently offers little assistance of a personal character to its membership. At this time, adherents attend United Church to hear a sermon and feel good and go to pentecostal churches to take care of their religious need." As a consequence, Gallatin (1979: 139) regards Rev. Ike's ministry as a "supplementary religion" for the majority of his followers. Spiritual churches also function as a supplementary religion for many people, though more as client sects than as audience sects.

On balance, Stark and Bainbridge's typology has only the roughest fit with the complex reality of African American religious life. The origin of new groups frequently is a combination of schism and new creation; groups do not easily fit into a single one of their "cultic" subtypes, and more compelling differences between groups are lost in the application of their framework. Needless to say, the construction of typologies is always difficult and usually guilty of the "violence of abstraction." As the next chapter indicates, we are quite aware of the limitations in our own scheme, although we are convinced it provides a useful roadmark to the tangled thicket of African American religion.

Protest and Accommodation in Thaumaturgical Sects

Despite functional similarities between thaumaturgical sects and black Protestant groups, the emphasis on the manipulation of one's present condition through the use of magico-religious practices distinguishes the former from the latter. Magical practices designed to control everyday affairs are found in all walks of life, but particularly among the poor. The acquisition of the "good life" and the "American Dream" (or at least a larger slice of it) are central concerns of Spiritual people and members and clients of other thaumaturgical sects. People resort to magical ritual in order to obtain supernatural power. Anthropologists have long pointed out that people commonly resort to magic when they feel anxious about their inability to contend with powerful external forces. As Robert Murphy (1979: 180) observes, magic usually enhances a sense of self-assurance and "produces the illusion that people are masters of their fate, controllers of their environment and not its pawns."

In attempting to manipulate their fate, Spiritual people burn candles, pray before an image of Jesus or the Virgin Mary or one of the saints, use a wide variety of occult articles, and seek messages from prophets in bless services or private consultations. Spiritual churches also conduct special services, often referred to as "demonstrations," during which thaumaturgical techniques for obtaining spiritual power or a blessing are revealed. Some Spiritual leaders have developed elaborate metaphysical systems which they combine with other aspects of the Spiritual religion. The pastor of Unity Fellowship (pseudonym), for instance, in Nashville places great emphasis on the power of positive thinking and prescribes various rituals intended to raise the level of one's "consciousness."

Leaders of other thaumaturgical sects also prescribe various rituals or dispense articles intended to create prosperity, love, and health. In October of 1972, Rev. Ike held a mortgage-burning celebration at which one of his assistants presented a "cancelled mortgage instrument" to the faithful. In keeping with his frequently repeated claim that "you can't loose with the stuff I use," Rev. Ike provides his followers with items such as the "money hook" and the "special miracle prayer card," all for a small donation.

Although the majority of Spiritual people are poor, others—especially some who belong to the larger congregations—appear to be stably employed working-class or middle-class individuals. The appeal of the Spiritual religion for the latter is not entirely clear and requires further investigation. According to E. Franklin Frazier (1974: 84–85), members of the "new Negro class" or upwardly mobile blacks are often fascinated by "'spiritual' and 'psychic' phenomena." Perhaps part of the appeal of the Spiritual religion for certain upwardly mobile blacks is that its "positive-thinking" ideology serves to validate and sanction their achievements in the face of continued poverty among many of their contemporaries. It appears that some African Americans were attracted to certain large Spiritual congregations in recent decades—a period during which a significant number of blacks acquired well-paying white-collar and blue-collar jobs. The phenomenal growth of St. Cecilia's Divine Healing Church No. 2 in Nashville and the United House of the Redeemer in Indianapolis probably reflects this pattern. In both congregations, the more successful members are quickly singled out and held up as living testimonies to the efficacy of the Spiritual faith and are quickly promoted to positions of leadership and respect.

The appeal of thaumaturgical rituals prompts many individuals who are not regular members of Spiritual groups to attend prophecy or bless services or to visit Spiritual prophets and advisors for private consultations. In his elaborate discussion of Haitian Voodoo, Alfred Metraux (1972: 25) argues that it is a "practical and utilitarian religion which cares more for earthly than for heavenly goings-on." In a similar vein, the Spiritual religion concerns itself with the concrete problems and needs of its adherents and clients. Like many other African American religions in other parts of the New World, including *shango* in Trinidad and *batuque* in Brazil, the Spiritual movement provides blacks in the United States with a theology for existence and survival (Simpson 1978; Leacock and Leacock 1975). It is a pragmatic religion with a strong temporal orientation in that it emphasizes the acquisition of health, love, economic prosperity, and interpersonal power.

However, while the Spiritual religion provides an important coping mechanism for a certain segment of the black community, it also exhibits a profoundly accommodative dimension in that it unwittingly encourages its adherents and clients to accept existing socioeconomic arrangements. This pattern manifests itself in the type of advice that Spiritual pastors, elders, and mediums give in sermons, sermonettes, prophecy sessions, and private consultations: to a considerable degree, it appears that the counseling provided in these settings focuses on individualistic concerns and does not call for social-structural changes. This is not to say that Spiritual leaders never make note of the need for social cohesiveness among members of their congregations and associations or within the black community as a whole. Spiritual churches also provide members with a sense of social identity and elaborate mutual support networks. For the most part, however, the Spiritual movement focuses upon private concerns by providing people with certain thaumaturgical rituals that are a designed to help them overcome everyday problems. In essence, Spiritual pastors, elders, and mediums promise their followers improvement in their lives if they engage in various magico-religious rituals, develop a positive attitude, and overcome negative thoughts.

The advice that Spiritual leaders and other thaumaturgical spokespersons, such as Rev. Ike, impart to their followers tends to focus on individualistic concerns. Life in modern America, particularly in large cities, is characterized by increasing privatization, or what John Wilson (1978: 358–59) terms "individuation." The positive-thinking approach, whether expressed in a secular voice, as by Dale Carnegie, or in a religious form, as by Norman Vincent Peale, appeals to many Americans. The emphasis on positive thinking in the thaumaturgical sects in the black community is a black version of its counterpart in the larger society. In both cases, the American cultural emphasis on individual achievement and personal responsibility for success is the underlying drive.

This approach to problem solving tends to deny "political conflict by stressing the importance of the individual over society, the insignificance of social arrangement and plans, and the irrelevance of group conflict beside the paramount importance of the individual" (Wilson 1978: 356). In this sense, the approach of Spiritual prophets and advisors resembles that of conventional psychotherapists, who often urge their clients to muster the psychic resources necessary to adjust to the demands of society. In doing so, they inadvertently engage in a process of "blaming the victim." Instead of pointing out how social and economic forces may be at the root of many of their followers' and clients' problems, this approach holds the individual solely responsible for his or her failures.

In this way, the Spiritual movement and other thaumaturgical sects function as hegemonic vehicles by which the poor and other working-class African Americans come to accept or at least avoid openly challenging existing social relations. The "cult of private life," which is championed by such agencies of socialization as the family, the schools, the media, advertisers, social workers, and psychotherapists, also is promoted by thaumaturgical sects. From the privatization perspective,

> *the source, if not the cause, of mental disorders is invariably traced to the client himself and/or his friends and relations. Society-at-large does not, and cannot, figure significantly in these treatments, although the collective ill-effects of living day-to-day in advanced industrial society have been repeatedly demonstrated. Thus psychology, counseling, and allied techniques further privatize the individual, leading her or him to search for exclusively existential solutions, more sophisticated avoidance mechanisms, and tried and true adjustment techniques. Marcuse's remark about "shrinks" being so-called because they shrink minds to manageable proportions is appropriate as social problems are telescoped into personal ones.* (Greisman and Mayers 1977: 61–62)

Although many blacks, like other social groups on the lower rungs of the American class system, are quite aware of the contradiction between the ideal definition of reality and the starkness of their owns lives, they often are unable—in large part because of the hegemony of mainstream beliefs, values, and attitudes—to unambiguously locate the source of their discontent. The individualistic orientation of American culture is rooted so deeply that most people are unable to fully recognize the extent to which larger social forces shape their destinies. And realization is achieved—as in groups like the Black Panther party or other politicized individuals and groups in the African American community—that the combined effect of social control, co-optation, and ideological hegemony can wear down and limit the vitality of collectivist understandings and initiatives. Not infrequently, as a result, even those who have embraced a social-structural explanation of African American suffering return ultimately to a religious orientation and the safety, solace, and community connectedness it can offer.

Unlike messianic-nationalist sects, most thaumaturgical sects in the African American community tend not to identify external enemies or oppressors, and their members often fault themselves for their miseries. Like many other working-class people, Spiritual people and followers of figures such as Rev. Ike, as Parkin (1971: 90) observes, "generate a meaning which is of purely parochial significance, representing a design for living based upon localized social knowledge and face-to-face relationships" and fail to adopt a "macro-social view of the reward structure and some *understanding of the systematic* nature of inequality" (emphasis in original). In like manner, thaumaturgical sects deflect attention from the social and economic roots of the problems of their members and clients and thus conform to the Marxian notion of religion as an opiate or a device that leads the downtrodden to accept their plight.

Without a doubt, to view Spiritual churches and possibly other thaumaturgical sects only in this light does injustice to their dualistic nature, which includes some elements of social protest. Although these elements are not as pronounced as the accommodative ones, Spiritual leaders occasionally offer critiques of the racial and class dimensions of American society in their sermons or sermonettes. For the most part, however, social protest in Spiritual churches assumes more subtle forms. In his discussion of the belief in Indian spirits among the Spiritual people of New Orleans, Kaslow (1981: 64) alludes to their symbolic meaning: "Black Hawk is regarded as a warrior who can cause justice to be done, and his intercession is frequently sought in court cases, or in seeking the release of loved ones from prison. The role of the Indian as an opponent of white domination is an expression of protest against status inferiority in the larger society." Protest also is manifested in the widespread belief among Spiritual people that heaven and hell exist in the here and now. Members of Spiritual churches often pride themselves in their rejection of what they disparagingly call "pie-in-the-sky religion." The refusal to wait for one's reward in some nebulous afterlife suggests some degree of non-acceptance of existing social conditions, but it may be argued that the means that members of Spiritual churches use in attempting to attain heaven on earth are in large part accommodative.

Also, Spiritual people reject certain conventional notions of how to achieve success—namely, abiding to the Protestant work ethic. As is generally true of the poor, most Spiritual people work hard to make ends meet. Furthermore, because of the hegemonic influence of mainstream values, they value the prestige symbols of the American Dream. Lower-class African Americans share in the cultural goals of the larger society, especially in an era of mass education and communication, and their behavioral deviation from the alleged means of obtaining these objectives cannot be simply attributed to what some refer to as the "culture of poverty" (Lewis 1966). As Charles A. Valentine (1968) observes, the values and aspirations of the poor, who generally have been enculturated into the dominant society, are very similar to those of middle-class people but become modified in response to the situational stresses that the former experience in everyday life. Since many African Americans are denied access to opportunities for social mobility, Spiritual people often reject mainstream platitudes about the Protestant work ethic that function to legitimize patterns of racial and class inequality. It is not that members of thaumaturgical sects do not see any merit in work but rather that they recognize that financial success is dependent on more capricious factors. In that these factors are at best ambiguously defined, adherents of thaumaturgical sects attempt to cope with their marginal position in American society by resorting to magico-religious rituals and a positive attitude.

VII

Social Transformations in African American Religions

Religious groups are not static; like other cultural forms, they undergo a constant process of transformation as they adjust or respond to forces both in their larger social and cultural milieu and within themselves. Underlying the metamorphic potential of religious formations is the critical role religion plays in engaging the world of experience in light of human need for coherence, social relationship, and meaning. Religion represents, among other things, a species-specific mechanism for responding to social, environmental, and even biological stressors. Changes in the external or internal context of a religious group are likely to produce changes in belief and ritual as people mobilize their religious resources to restabilize themselves. The trajectory of change, unavoidably, is conditioned by prior experience, the nature of the stressor, and the available pool of cultural elements that can be expropriated. These are the factors that energize the religious syncretism of diverse sects and denominations in the African American community.

Indeed, these groups richly exemplify such processes of transformation. Unfortunately, any typology freezes or oversimplifies the social dynamism of religious organizations, and we, of course, recognize the potential of this flaw in our classification system. As Bryan Wilson (1969: 362) observes, "Sects are not easily marshalled into a few dichotomies." The mixed or transitional type eludes easy classification because it prominently exhibits characteristics of two or even more ideal categories. The mere fact that sects evolve over time due to both external and internal pressures creates the possibility of mixed or transitional forms.

In this chapter, we first discuss two excellent examples of the "mixed type," namely Father Divine's Peace Mission movement and "Sweet Daddy"

Grace's United House of Prayer for All People. We then discuss a model that attempts to illustrate processes of socio-religious development within African American religion.

The Father Divine Movement as a "Mixed Type"

Father Divine's Peace Mission is one of the most studied groups in the African American religious experience (Hoshor 1936; Parker 1937; Cantril and Sherif 1938; Harris 1971; Burnham 1979; Weisbrot 1983; Watts 1992). Perhaps more than any other religious figure, Father Divine embodied the tradition of the "black gods of the metropolis." His Peace Mission is one of the most elusive to classify in the multiplicity of religious groups in the African American community. This sect incorporated, to a greater or lesser extent, aspects of all of the four categories in our typology of African American sectarianism in the United States, at least during its zenith in the 1930s.

While various writers have situated the birthplace of Father Divine, who was christened George Baker, in Savannah, Mineola (Long Island), and Providence, Watts (1992) provides archival evidence that he was born in Rockville (Maryland), where his mother reared him in the Jerusalem Methodist Church. After his arrival in Baltimore in 1889, he worked as a gardener and jack-leg preacher. In the course of his new-found ministry, he met Samuel Morris, who referred to himself as Father Jehovia, and St. John the Divine Hickerson in 1906. Both Morris and Hickerson taught that God dwells within the individual—a notion common to New Thought. Baker viewed himself as a harbinger of Morris and referred to himself as "the Messenger." Whereas Morris was the incarnation of God the Father, Baker was the incarnation of God the Son. He reportedly attended the Azusa Street revival in Los Angeles. Baker's exposure to various religious traditions prompted him to develop a new syncretic religion that "blended New Thought with Methodism, a little Catholicism, Pentecostalism, and African American storefront theology" (Watts 1992: 30). In 1912, both Hickerson and Baker broke with Morris and established their own ministries.

Baker left Baltimore, served a stint as an itinerant preacher in the southeastern United States, and established a following in Valdosta, Georgia, in 1914. In Valdosta, he simply referred to himself as God. After being arrested for his evangelical activities and being found guilty of insanity by a jury, the judge released him, despite opposition by members of the African American community, and instructed him to leave town. He established a base of operations in Americus, Georgia, but made his way in late 1914 to Harlem where he contacted a former colleague, the Reverend Bishop Saint John the Vine, the founder of the Church of the Living God, the Pillar and Ground of Truth. After converting some of the sect's members to his flock, Baker continued his search for followers in various locations. In 1917, he established a congregation in Brooklyn where he began to conduct his famous communion banquets. Baker and his first wife (Pinninnah) lived communally in a house with his followers, operated a job-placement service for his followers, and administered their earnings. He also began to advocate celibacy among his members on the grounds that sex constitutes a depraved act.

In 1919, Baker and Pinninnah became the first African American residents of Sayville, Long Island, and established a congregation and communal dwelling unit there. Baker signed the deed of sale with the name "Major J. Devine." He placed many of his followers in domestic jobs in surrounding estates, stressed hard work, sobriety, and sexual abstinence, and declared himself the Second Coming of Christ. Although his followers had referred to him as Major Jealous Divine, he began to refer to himself as Father Divine in 1930. He drew busloads of followers to his services, much to the annoyance of local residents who attempted to shut down his congregation. The police raided his services on November 15, 1931, and arrested him and some eighty members. Judge Lewis J. Smith found Father Divine guilty but died suddenly of a heart attack three days after having pronounced sentence. Although he spent thirty-three days in jail, an appellate division of the Supreme Court in Brooklyn reversed the decision. Despite his victory, in 1933, Father Divine moved the headquarters of his sect to Harlem, where he was in great demand. He evangelized up and down the East Coast and established residences along the way. Father Divine created a string of hotels and other businesses (including grocery stores, barber shops, restaurants, apartment buildings, and a coal operation). His sect became legally incorporated as the Peace Mission in 1941, and he moved its headquarters in 1942 to Philadelphia. Hotels formed the economic backbone of the movement and constituted the primary sites of the banquets that drew much publicity. Father Divine's movement emerged largely as a response to the hardships that African Americans experienced during the Great Depression. Unlike most other predominantly black religious groups, the Father Divine movement attracted many white people despite an ideology that portrayed Father Divine as the incarnation of God. As Weisbrot (1983: 108) notes, "The boldness of the Peace Mission's stand on integration is further underscored by the absence of almost any other predominantly black church or cult that deliberately encouraged an interracial membership." The Peace Mission comprised three movements in one: (1) an Eastern section, composed largely, but not exclusively, of poor blacks; (2) a Western section, located primarily in California, that catered to a predominantly white membership (many of whom were middle class); and (3) a foreign section that appealed especially to urban working-class people in Canada, Australia, and Western Europe. Women constituted between 75 and 90 percent of the Peace Mission members (Weisbrot 1983: 60). While Father Divine claimed some 2 million adherents and Hoshor (1936) estimated that the Peace Mission had some two million, Weisbrot (1983: 69) contends that "Divine's strength in New York City was never much more than 1,000. Since over 10 percent of all the Peace Mission centers were in New York City and since Father Divine focused his leadership there, one could place the number of his strongest supporters at about 10,000 as an upper limit." Some 150 to 160 Peace Mission branches were in operation during the Depression and through the early 1940s. The Peace Mission addressed itself primarily to the oppressive situations of blacks in American society and is generally considered to have been an African American movement, but Father Divine tended to choose whites for upper-echelon positions in his organization. His first wife was black, but his second, who succeeded him as leader of the Peace Mission, was white.

Like the mainstream denominations in the American American community, Father Divine was committed to a wide range of social-reform programs. He regarded his movement as a practical program that would provide his followers with health, food, clothing, shelter, and jobs. In addition to establishing schools for both children and adults, Father Divine urged his followers to register and vote in national elections. He supported the Harlem Political Union and in 1936 helped to establish the All People's party, a coalition of eighty-nine Harlem-based organizations that endorsed a small slate of radical candidates, including white communist Vito Marcantonio and black communist and labor organizer Angelo Herndon. The Peace Mission cooperated with the Communist party in Harlem between 1934 and 1936 because Divine viewed it as much more progressive on racial issues than both the Democrats and the Republicans. During the mid-1930s the Peace Mission developed the Righteous Government Platform with fourteen planks, including three concerned with economics, education, and politics, and eight concerned with racial issues.

Despite Father Divine's sponsorship of cooperative ventures and a brief flirtation with the Communist party, he was by no means a revolutionary but rather a reformer committed to working within the framework of the capitalist system. He staunchly advocated the Protestant work ethic, self-support, savings, investments, and the sanctity of private property (Burnham 1979: 50). Further, he pointed to corporate giants such as Henry Ford and Andrew Carnegie as role models for his followers (Weisbrot 1983: 198) and loftily praised the U.S. Constitution and the Declaration of Independence.

Social Transformations

Although the Peace Mission resembled the black mainstream denominations in its emphasis on social reform, it also exhibited some dimensions, at
least in subtle form, or messianic-nationalism. According to Essien-Udom
(1962: 44), Father Divine's "teachings, like those of black nationalists, display
the mood of alienation from the existing society." Father Divine taught that
color is inconsequential, but he held himself up as a living testimony of the
notion that "Black is beautiful." After all, had not God decided to take on the
body of not only a short, squat, bald man but also one who was black? In this,
Father Divine joined with messianic-nationalist sects in their rejection of a
white Christian God. Despite some obvious differences between the Peace
Mission and messianic-nationalism, Weisbrot (1983: 193) argues that "Divine
shared with Garvey some doctrines of racial uplift often associated with black
separatists—indeed, their range of agreement was far broader than either
Garvey or Divine ever acknowledged. . . . They spurred disciples to cultivate
both psychological and financial independence, and they envisioned a society
free of racial oppression." Even more so than the Universal Negro Improvement Association and many of the messianic-nationalist sects, Father Divine
established business cooperatives in the black ghettoes and an agricultural
cooperative, called "Promised Land," in Ulster County, New York. Like the
black Muslims, the Peace Mission engaged in the reform of inmates and
delinquents by emphasizing a program of honesty and self-discipline. While
some former members of Garvey's UNIA joined offshoots of their old movement, the Nation of Islam, or Daddy Grace's House of Prayer, perhaps most
former Garveyites joined the Father Divine movement (Weisbrot 1983: 191).
Elijah Muhammad apparently recognized the inherent rivalry between the
Nation of Islam and Father Divine and told Essien-Udom (1962: 201) that
alienating followers from the Peace Mission was an official policy of the
Nation. Because, unlike most messianic-nationalist sects, Father Divine promoted integration, he was severely criticized by militant nationalists.

Like the conversionist sects, the Peace Mission stressed salvation through
profound change in oneself. Although ecstatic behavior per se was not a central focus as it is in many black Holiness and Pentecostal groups, the elaborate
banquets that Father Divine held were often characterized by dancing, shouting, clapping, testifying, and joyous singing on the part of his followers, black
and white alike (Harris 1971: xxi–xxii). Peace Mission members also were
expected to abide by a strict code of conduct prohibiting alcoholic beverages,
smoking, social dancing, gambling, theatergoing, and most notably, all forms
of sex. Father Divine, in fact, claimed that he maintained a life of total celibacy during his two marriages. Despite the addition of New Thought and
social activism to his religious repertoire after he arrived in New York, he

never surrendered the evangelical fervor that he had apparently acquired as a youth in the Baptist faith in Georgia and later stressed in his itinerant preaching in the South.

Finally, the Peace Mission exhibited and continues to exhibit many aspects of the thaumaturgical sect. The opulence of Father Divine's banquets exuded a magical quality suggesting an unlimited bounty befitting a god. As Weisbrot (1983: 35) observes, "It was a repast without end, for Divine was continually welcoming new guests and blessing new rounds of food and drink. When asked how many he served in a day, Divine promptly replied, 'We feed as many as come. We serve from early morning until midnight.'" In reality, Father Divine carefully orchestrated his banquets in such a way that beverages were served first, followed by starches and some fruits and vegetables, and finally, when his guests had largely filled up on these less expensive foods, climaxed with the arrival of elaborately prepared roasts, ducks, and chickens. Father Divine denied personally curing people of their ailments, but many of his followers believed that his touch or mere presence could heal them.

During the Sayville years Father Divine incorporated ideas from the writings of Robert Coller, Jiddu Krishnamurti, and other New Thought exponents in his religious framework (Weisbrot 1983: 28). He distributed selected New Thought tracts among his followers rather than explicitly stating his own religious premises. Much like the Spiritual churches and Rev. Ike, Father Divine advocated a temporal and instrumental rather than an other-worldly orientation to solving the problems of his followers. He taught that the more conventional churches had used religion to keep the masses of blacks in their downtrodden and miserable condition. According to Harris (1971: 128), the Peace Mission promoted "visualization of the positive" as its philosophical basis.

Apparently because even many African Americans benefited from the improved economic conditions of World War II and due to Father Divine's failing health, the Peace Mission began to undergo a decline during the 1940s. Many of the cooperative businesses were either closed or sharply contracted, and "Promised Land" was shut down during the 1940s (Weisbrot 1983: 212). Father Divine shifted his political stance from radical reformer to reactionary as he engaged in an increasing number of anti-communist and anti-union tirades. By the time the civil rights movement emerged among blacks during the 1950s, the Peace Mission had evolved into an incorporated religious organization exhibiting almost a strictly thaumaturgical orientation to the larger society. Since the death of Father Divine in 1965, the remnants of the group, both in the United States and abroad, have been under the guidance of Mother Divine, a white woman. The Peace Mission still conducts

communion banquets, services, and anniversary celebrations, and even operates some businesses, but it has adopted a much more introversionist posture
than it had during its heyday (Burnham 1979). The May 3, 1980, issue of the
sect's newspaper, The New Day, for example, headlined a sermon given by
Father Divine in 1947.

The Daddy Grace Movement as a "Mixed Type"

Although not as well known as Father Divine, "Sweet Daddy" Grace, the
founder of the United House of Prayer for All People, served as an even more
flamboyant "god of the Black metropolis."

> *Bishop Charles Emmanuel Grace is a man of mixed parentage, said to be Negro*
> *and Portuguese. Bronze of color, and with flowing hair, he does not admit to*
> *being a Negro. Frequently he adopts a patronizing attitude toward his Negro*
> *followers (who in Philadelphia and New York represent nearly 100 percent of*
> *the members) by pointing out to them when he took on earthly form he chose to*
> *lead the Negroes, lowly in state though they are, rather than the members of*
> *some more privileged racial group.* (Fauset 1971: 23)

Daddy Grace was born Marcelino Manoel da Graca on January 25, 1881,
in Brava, Cape Verde Islands, a Portuguese territory in the Atlantic Ocean off
the coast of Mauritania and Senegal in West Africa (Robinson 1974: 213).
Around 1900 he moved to New Bedford, Massachusetts, where he worked as
a short-order cook, salesperson, and grocer. In 1921 Grace established the
United House of Prayer for All People on the Rock of the Apostolic Faith in
Wareham, a suburb of New Bedford (Alland 1981: 347). His congregation
attracted primarily poor blacks, along with some whites.

Responding to the slow growth of the sect in Massachusetts, Grace proselytized in the South, where he attracted a substantial following in cities such
as Charlotte, North Carolina, and Norfolk and Newport News, Virginia.
Additional congregations were added in the North as well. "Grace opened a
church in Brooklyn in 1930 and one in Manhattan in 1938. The first church
in New England during this period was built in 1956. After that congregations were established in Stamford, Hartford, and Bridgeport (all in Connecticut), all cities with substantial black populations. Sometime during this
period Grace also established himself in Detroit, but the sect had little success
in Chicago. A Los Angeles branch was also founded . . ." (Robinson 1974:
214). His sect also had branches in Maryland, Delaware, New Jersey, South
Carolina, and Georgia (Whiting 1952: 52). Grace located the headquarters of
the United House of Prayer for All People in an elegant seventeen-room

mansion on Logan Circle in Washington, D.C. (Robinson 1974). Although Grace claimed over one million members, Alland (1981: 347) maintains that "several thousand is a more likely guess."

The United House of Prayer for All People incorporated aspects of conversionist, messianic-nationalist, and thaumaturgical sects but appears to have eschewed the reformist efforts of the mainstream denominations. In contrast to Father Divine's relatively somber attire, Sweet Daddy Grace attracted attention "with his one-to-three inch fingernails, his shoulder-length hair, his colorful cutaways, and his flashy jewelry" (Robinson 1974: 213). Grace's sect assumed many of the characteristics associated with Pentecostal groups, emphasizing conversion, sanctification, reception of the Holy Ghost by speaking in tongues and "a putting aside of bad habits," including smoking, tobacco chewing, drinking, card playing, gambling, and dancing (Whiting 1952: 62). His followers achieved "joy in the House of the Lord" by dancing, singing, testifying, and shouting for God and their leader (Alland 1962).

Daddy Grace presented himself as a messianic figure who manifested the spirit of God. Some members of the sect believed that Grace was God Incarnate whereas others regarded him as an inspired prophet or intermediary between God and humans (Whiting 1952: 66). While Grace did not assert that he was God, he reportedly told his followers: "Never mind about God. Salvation is by Grace only. . . . Grace has given God a vacation, and since God is on His vacation, don't worry him. . . . If you sin against God, Grace can save you, but if you sin against Grace, God cannot save you" (quoted in Fauset 1971: 26).

In contrast to the founders of messianic-nationalist sects, Grace's assertion that he was a white man probably reinforced feelings of racial inferiority in his followers. However, his physical appearance undoubtedly prompted a sense of racial pride in many of his followers that God had manifested himself in the form of a black man. For the most part, however, Daddy Grace was more of a messiah than a nationalist. His followers shoved money at their messiah and built money trees and money houses with bills pinned onto them in his honor (Robinson 1974: 215). After his death on January 12, 1960, the IRS assessed the net worth of Daddy Grace's estate at the end of 1956 to be $4,081,511.62 (Robinson 1974: 217). His estate reportedly included 111 churches and missions, apartment houses, stores, an eighty-four-room mansion in Los Angeles, a mansion, a twenty-two-acre estate near Havana, and large homes in several cities.

Finally, Grace's sect exhibited several thaumaturgical elements. He claimed to have raised his sister after she had been pronounced dead by a physician (Robinson 1974). As in many Spiritual churches, Daddy Grace's

followers utilized a variety of magico-religious articles, which could be purchased at the canteen of each House of Prayer, to bring them good luck in
this life.

> *Thus Daddy Grace soap will cleanse the body, or reduce fat, or heal, according
> to the individual need. Daddy Grace writing paper will aid the writer in com-
> posing a good letter. Has the follower a cold or tuberculosis? The* Grace Maga-
> zine *will, if placed on your chest, give a complete cure.*
>
> *Similarly there is Daddy Grace tooth paste, transcontinental tea and cof-
> fee, men and women's hair pomade (which ostensibly cancels the taboo against
> beautifying the person), face power, cold water soap, talcum powder, shoe polish,
> lemon cream, cold cream, pine soap, vanishing cream, castille and palmolive
> soap, and even Daddy Grace cookies.* (Fauset 1971: 30)

Walter ("Sweet Daddy Grace") McCullough succeeded Bishop Charles
Emmanuel Grace as the leader of the United House of Prayer for All People
following a series of contested elections within the sect and court actions
(Robinson 1974: 226–28). Bishop McCullough lacks the charisma of the original Daddy Grace, but his organizational skills have prevented the demise of
the sect and resulted in the construction of additional Houses of Prayer,
improvements on old facilities, and the establishment of a ministerial school
in Richmond, Virginia.

The Socio-religious Evolution of African American Sects

New religious sects may undergo one of several developments: extinction,
sectarian maintenance, or denominationalization. Most of the black sects
mentioned in this book constitute relatively successful religious experiments
in that they were or have been in existence for a relatively extended period—
long enough that one or more scholars or journalists have taken note of them.
Whereas many proponents of church-sect theory contend or imply that sects
tend to evolve into churches or denominations, Stark and Bainbridge (1985:
137) argue that "Most sects are, in fact, dead ends. They start small, remain
small, and slowly wither away." In a survey of 417 American sects, they found
that 51 percent of them are declining in size, 18 percent are stable, and 31
percent are growing. Furthermore, only 6 percent of the sects in their sample
exhibit a pattern of rapid change.

While most churchgoing African Americans belong to one of several
Baptist or Methodist denominations, many belong or have belonged to a
plethora of conversionist, messianic-nationalist, and thaumaturgical sects. In
time, a few of these sects may evolve into a sizable religious organization and

even begin to closely resemble the structure, belief system, and posture toward the larger society of the mainstream denominations. As with most sects, however, most black sects remain small and obscure, and many simply disappear. In our own ethnographic research on African American religion, we have come across many black sects, all of them small, that scholars have never even given a footnote in their writings. Scholars have addressed only the tip of the iceberg in describing and chronicling the African American religious experience in the United States. While we do not believe that it is imperative that each and every black religious group that exists or ever existed be identified, even if this were possible, we feel that an appreciation of the diversity of major strains of African American religion is significant for comprehending the range of strategies that black people have devised in dealing with their historically oppressed and inferior socioeconomic status or the "hardness" of their lives in American society. And, given the nature and history of U.S. society, we do not feel it is possible to begin to understand America unless we understand African American experience and forms of struggle and survival over the last four hundred years.

Most sects that do manage to survive undergo a process of socio-religious transformation by which they may evolve from one sectarian type into another. Figure 2 presents a model of the various socio-religious transformations that black religious sects may undergo.

As Raboteau (1986: 541) observes, the thaumaturgical orientation of African religion was manifested in two basic ways: its focus on the acquisition of protection from the gods and its use of protective charms and sacred medicines in order to provide security in everyday life. African religious beliefs and practices continued to flourish in Afro-Christianity among the slaves in three distinct forms: (1) ecstatic trances and spirit possession, (2) belief in witches and malevolent spirits, and (3) and the practices of conjuration and sorcery. Conjure "symbolized the translation of African sacred charms into Afro-American magical medicine" (Raboteau 1986: 548).

Path 1–2 in Figure 2 constitutes the most common developmental trajectory by which the thaumaturgical religion of the slaves became transformed into the conversionist posture of the nineteenth-century independent black Baptist and Methodist churches and finally into the established or reformist stance of the black mainstream denominations, such as the National Baptist Convention, USA, or the African Methodist Episcopal Church. Slave religion emphasized ecstasy, prophesying, healing, and conversion. According to Sobel (1979: 101), the conversionist message of "You must be born again" found in the Afro-Baptist faith provided blacks with a "Sacred Cosmos" by which they could integrate African initiation rituals into Christianity.

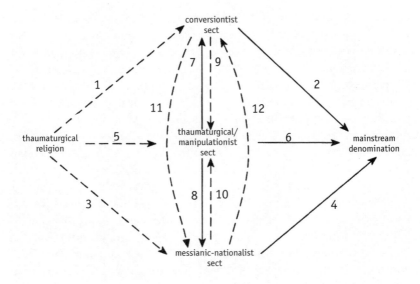

*Fig. 2. Model of the socio-religious transformation
of African American religious groups.*

Following Emancipation, many black Baptist and Methodist congregations, particularly in urban areas, began to adopt a less exuberant worship style
and to model themselves along white middle-class patterns of worship. Bishop
Payne believed that the African Methodist Episcopal Church should have
educated ministers and "dignified" services and advocated strict adherence to
the worship outline in the AME Discipline (Walker 1982: 23). He attempted
to introduce choral singing and instrumental music into AME services
(Walker 1982: 141). Rank-and-file black Baptists and Methodists, however,
often resisted clerical efforts to mainstream their churches. For example,
AME members rebelled when middle-class leaders attempted to substitute the
word "American" for "African" in the name of their church (Frazier 1974:
82). Nonetheless, by the twentieth century, many black Baptist and Methodist congregations had become bastions of middle-class respectability, even if
most of their members remained within the working class. Furthermore, in
the process of mainstreaming their religious orientation, many African Americans who achieved middle-class or even upper-class status shifted their affiliation to predominantly white-controlled denominations, such as the
Episcopalian, Presbyterian, and United Metho-dist churches, and, in more

recent years, the Roman Catholic church and even the Southern Baptist Convention, formerly a stanch bastion of white supremacy.

While paths 3 and 5 (fig. 2) are somewhat difficult to trace historically, we have see that the inability of the black mainstream denominations, the formerly conversionist black Baptists and Methodists, to meet the needs of countless poor working-class African Americans during the period of rapid industrialization and urbanization following the turn of the century prompted many of these people to seek salvation in a plethora of new conversionist, messianic-nationalist, and thaumaturgical sects, most of which emerged in the cities and towns of both the North and the South. Many Sanctified, Judaic, Islamic, and Spiritual sects first appeared during the Great Migration, and many others appeared during subsequent periods of massive migration or social disequilibrium. While many of these sects developed a more-or-less stable membership and politico-religious organization, others eventually disintegrated within a generation or two, if not within a few years. While there may be whole groups that evolved along path 3 (fig. 2), it appears this is a road most often traveled by individuals or families, especially during periods of social upheaval in the African American community.

In time, some successful conversionist, messianic-nationalist, and thaumaturgical or manipulationist sects evolve, as portrayed in paths 2, 4, and 6 (fig. 2), into mainstream denominations, or they at least assume many characteristics of mainstream denominations. Among the conversionist sects, the Church of God in Christ is a case in point. The largest messianic-nationalist sect in African American history, the American Muslim Mission, also exhibits tendencies toward mainstreaming, not so much by coming to adopt the belief system of the National Baptists and African Methodists but in its politico-religious organization, promotion of middle-class values, acceptance of American social institutions, avowed patriotism, and emphasis on social reform programs within the context of a capitalist political economy.

Some of the larger thaumaturgical or Spiritual associations (or at least individual congregations within them) tend to emulate the mainstream denominations. In some ways, the United House of the Redeemer (pseudonym) in Indianapolis, St. Cecilia's Divine Healing Church #2 (pseudonym) in Nashville, and the Redeeming Church of Christ in Chicago (Baer 1988) exhibit such a development. These congregations cut across socioeconomic lines and, while they still find their greatest appeal in the lower classes of their respective communities, have attracted some upwardly mobile African Americans. It is possible that some middle-class members of the black mainstream denominations find these churches appealing because they provide them with a certain degree of social recognition that they would not achieve otherwise.

Another strategy for achieving great social respectability adopted by some Spiritual groups involves more clearly separating thaumaturgical and manipulationist responses to the larger society. As defined by Wilson (1969: 367), manipulationist sects are "those which insist on a particular and distinctive knowledge. . . . They frequently proclaim a more spiritualized and ethereal version of the cultural ends of global society but do not reject them." Wilson (1969: 368) asserts that thaumaturgical groups "differ little from manipulationist sects, except that their response to the world is less universalist and more personal." Yet, historically thaumaturgical responses, which draw heavily on magical techniques, tend to precede manipulationist ones (Wilson 1973). In those situations that thaumaturgical movements institutionalize by centralizing control and regulating the training of religious personnel, socialization of the young, and initiation of new members, they evolve in manipulationist movements. As Wilson (1973: 130) observes, "The organization of thaumaturgical practitioners into leagues is a possibility which is open most typically where thaumaturgy is practiced in an urban context, in a society in which other social limitations are conspicuously organized on rational bureaucratic lines, in which rational-legal types of authority structure, role specificity, and rational decision-making models are available models."

Like some other black Spiritual groups, the Metropolitan Spiritual Churches of Christ organization has attempted to disassociate itself from certain aspects of the larger Spiritual movement (e.g., seances and especially Voodoo), but its strong emphasis on New Thought and other esoteric belief systems as well as the generally low socioeconomic status of its adherents prevents it from achieving the mainstream respectability it seeks.

While many of the congregations within Metropolitan or the Spiritual movement as a whole have entered a period of stagnation, some young, relatively well-educated Spiritual ministers are attempting to revitalize the declining congregations that they inherited from elderly or deceased pastors by "streamlining" the Spiritual religion. In essence, this involves discarding many of the traditional thaumaturgical practices (e.g., praying before the statue of a Catholic saint, burning candles, using incense sprays and floor washes) but emphasizing manipulationist practices (e.g., positive thinking, elevating one's consciousness). At the same time, these ministers encourage their members to obtain additional education and vocational skills. Rev. Paul Southerland, the pastor of Redeeming Church of Christ in Chicago, has created a job placement program for his members, many of whom are young, and promotes an "academic program" by bringing in outside speakers. He invited Baer to present in May 1986 two talks on his research on Spiritual churches and to engage in a "dialogue" with his members, many of whom had read Baer's book on the black Spiritual movement (Baer 1984). Rather than emphasizing reliance on the traditional paraphernalia associated with Spiritual churches, he urges his followers to believe in themselves and to think positively.

While it is not clear whether the smaller Spiritual sects are also emulating the patterns of the mainstream denominations, some of them are in the process of modeling themselves after the conversionist sects, as portrayed in path 7 (fig. 2). Such a trend is most apparent in the tendency of some Spiritual churches to include the term "Holiness" (as opposed to "Spiritual") in their formal name and/or to refer to themselves as a "Holiness" group, despite their retaining many beliefs, rituals, and normative patterns of Spiritual sects. Some Spiritual groups have, at least in theory, adopted some or many of the puritanical proscriptions generally found in Sanctified or Holiness-Pentecostalist sects. Conversionist sects commonly are regarded to be more respectable than Spiritual sects in the African American community, despite their tendency to draw heavily from the working and lower classes. Consequently, the adoption of the trappings of the conversionist sects serves as one strategy by which some Spiritual groups attempt to diminish or mitigate the stigma associated with the larger movement of which they are part.

Finally, a few Spiritual sects have embarked upon the trajectory portrayed in path 8 (fig. 2) by adopting various aspects of messianic-nationalism. The Universal Hagar's Spiritual Association, established by George Willie Hurley on September 13, 1923, in Detroit, evolved in the direction of messianic-nationalism. (For a more detailed discussion of the Father Hurley movement, see Baer 1984: 82–109, 139–156.) Sometime around 1933, if not earlier, Father Hurley began to teach his followers that his "carnal flesh" had been "transformed into the flesh of Christ." He also identified himself as the "Black God of this Age" and the "Christ, the God, the Saviour, the Protector of this seven thousand year reign of the Aquarian Age." By the 1920s, if not earlier, Hurley and some early members of the Universal Hagar's Spiritual Church had become members of Garvey's UNIA. At any rate, some of the doctrines that Father Hurley taught bear a strong resemblance to those promulgated by the dynamic leader from Jamaica as well as those of other messianic-nationalist leaders. He maintained that Ethiopians were the first people in the world, the original Hebrew nation, God's chosen ones, the speakers of the original language of Arabic, and the creators of civilization and hieroglyphics. The first religion, according to Hurley, was the Coptic Ethiopian religion. All the Old Testament patriarchs and prophets—including Adam, Abraham, Moses, Solomon, and Daniel—as well as Buddha, Jesus, and the Apostle Paul were Ethiopians in his view.

According to Father Hurley, whereas blacks are the first human beings, whites are the offspring of Cain. He argued that whites forced the Ethiopian people to join their churches and foisted Christianity upon them as a "pie-in-the-sky" religion. In contrast to the seemingly apolitical posture of many Spiritual sects, Father Hurley took unequivocal stands on a number of political issues, particularly the status of blacks in American society. Some of his writings suggest that the Aquarian Age will eventually be one of black denomination. Since Father Hurley's death in 1943, the staunchly nationalist and critical rhetoric of his message has been considerably tempered. While he often denounced the oppression of blacks and the racism of America, the writings and sermons of his successors have been more inspirational and less political. Nevertheless, each issue of the Aquarian Age—the newsletter of the Universal Hagar's Spiritual Church, carries one or more of the articles that Father Hurley wrote, undoubtedly serving as a reminder to his followers that their God, as one prominent member of the sect noted to Baer, was indeed a "very radical man who felt our people were being kept under bondage."

Black sects that follow paths 9 and 10 (fig. 2) appear to be rare. As we saw in chapter 6, Rev. Ike moved his United Church away from being a fairly typical conversionist sect toward becoming a thaumaturgical sect with a strong infusion of manipulationist elements. There appear to be no clear-cut cases of a messianic-nationalist sect developing into a thaumaturgical sect, although some of Noble Drew Ali's lieutenants reportedly engaged in the "sale of herbs, magical charms and potions" (Fauset 1971: 43) and the Ansaru Muslims continue street sales of these items. An example of a conversionist sect evolving into a messianic-nationalist sect (path 11, fig. 2) is the Christ Miracle Healing Center and Church. The group began as a Holiness sect with congregations in Macon, Mississippi, and Chicago. In 1979 the group's leader, the Rev. Francis Thomas, had a vision that Chicago would be destroyed by fire and led her flock to Miracle Valley, Arizona. Named by its founder, A. A. Allen, a white fundamentalist, Miracle Valley presented a less than hospitable reception to the three hundred or so African American members of Thomas's congregation. The intensity of the conflict led group members increasingly to adopt the rhetoric of messianic-nationalists. In a public statement, Rev. Thomas's son asserted: "It seems that we victims of a scandal to be forced to be dehumanized and classes as a (nothing) or else we can kowtow to those would-be slave masters and be caged like animals of captivity" (Quoted in Reinhold 1982). Trained in martial arts and armed with weapons, group members launched armed patrols of the community while continuing to practice divine healing and communal worship. Tensions reached a peak in 1982 in a shoot-out between group members and the police, leaving William Thomas and another group member dead.

Less dramatically, there do not appear to be clear-cut cases of messianic-nationalist sects evolving into conversionist sects (path 12, fig. 2), although this may be a product of limited research rather than an impossible transition. However, as we have seen earlier in this chapter, Father Divine's Peace Mission and Sweet Daddy Grace's group both started out as fairly typical conversionist sects that incorporated some elements of messianic-nationalism.

The foregoing discussion affirms the degree to which the term "African American religion" is misleading in that African Americans have developed not one but a wide array of religious traditions to both capture their spiritual vision and provide succor and direction through the course of four centuries of economic, social, and cultural oppression. Nevertheless, the ready transition of one sectarian type into another, and the common movement of individuals and congregations across sects and sectarian types, suggests that all forms of African American religion share basic elements that give voice to both the underlying essence of black experience as well as the basic aspirations of African people in the "wilderness" of North America.

VIII

African American Religious Healing and Folk Medicine

Religion as a group spiritual activity and healing are intertwined in most sociocultural systems. Despite this fact, most of the literature on African American religion in the United States tends to either neglect or downplay this connection. Nevertheless, it should be no surprise that healing activities are part and parcel of various African American religious groups in the United States. As Fontenot (1994: 82) observes, "for African Americans in rural Louisiana [and elsewhere], syncretic Christian customs, prayer, faith, and the power of the supernatural became the basis for healing rituals." Unfortunately, in contrast to African American religion per se, folk medicine among peoples of the African diaspora in the United States has received relatively little systematic attention. Because of the secretiveness surrounding the activities of many black folk healers and the preference for anonymity expressed by most of their clients, research on African American folk medicine has been uneven, impressionistic, and anecdotal (Fox 1995). Nevertheless, there has been a growing scholarly interest in African American folk medicine and its relationship to religion (Hill 1973; Jackson 1981; Roberson 1985; Raboteau 1986; Csordas 1987; Spector 1996:191–205; Abrums 1999).

The Sociocultural and Historical Contexts of African American Folk Medicine

Like African American religion, black folk medicine emerged within the context of slavery. African peoples sought both the protection of their gods and ancestral spirits and relied upon charms and medicinal plants in dealing with the uncertainties of life and death. They turned to various priests, diviners, mediums, and healers who served as intermediaries between themselves and the supernatural realm. Cross-fertilization occurred in the health beliefs and practices of blacks, whites, and American Indians during the antebellum period in the rural South.

The terms *conjure, rootwork,* and *hoodoo* came to be applied to an elaborate system of health care, magic, divination, herbalism, and witchcraft widespread among African American slaves. There has been considerable debate as to the origin of the term *hoodoo.* While some have argued that *hoodoo* is an adulteration of *voodoo,* others have maintained the former term is traceable to the term *juju* (Haskins 1978: 66). At any rate, since the nineteenth century there has been a tendency for both African Americans and European American scholars to use the two terms interchangeably (Hurston 1931). In this regard, Raboteau (1978: 66) is perhaps correct in his assertion that "[s]ince New Orleans was looked upon as the prestigious center of conjuring, the term 'voodoo' was extended to conjuring and conjurers throughout the United States, regardless of the term's original reference to *vodun,* the syncretic folk religion of the Haitian people." Kuna (1974–75: 276) stresses the importance of making a precise distinction between hoodoo and voodoo, noting that the former term, "although a system of belief and therapy, is not a cult, nor does it engage in cult or group activities or worship." Voodoo, by contrast, is a full-blown ceremonial complex that is widespread in Haiti, was common during the nineteenth century in southern Louisiana (Anderson 1960), and still has adherents in scattered parts of the United States, such as Miami and New York City. For analytical purposes, we follow the distinction that Kuna makes while at the same recognizing that in the minds of many African Americans the two terms are not precisely differentiated.

Raboteau (1986: 548) views *conjure* as the "symbolized translation of African sacred charms into Afro-American magical medicine." In a somewhat similar vein, Crowder argues that "[c]onjure represented a belief system which attempted to explain the unknown or mysterious happenings in life. The conjurer, usually a man but sometimes a woman, was the primary agent in the slave community who functioned to regulate and interpret the supernatural. . . . Any prolonged illness unresponsive to natural and herbal medicine or an unexpected misfortune was determined by the slave community to be 'fixed' by a conjurer" (Crowder 1980: 6–7). Conjure was also referred to as hoodoo or rootwork. Many conjurers were skilled herbalists and adept observers of human relationships.

The slaves and their descendants also drew upon Christianity for comprehending illness and misfortune. They came to regard illness as the result of the will of God, the malevolence of the devil, or the commission of sin. As noted in earlier chapters, the slaves were able to discover elements in Christianity that were consistent with their own aspirations for freedom and experience-

shaped perception of reality. The slaves did not exhibit a simple, rigid acceptance of the whites' cosmology. While heaven indeed might at times be constructed in otherworldly terms, it might also be viewed, depending on the
context, as Africa, Jerusalem, Canada, or some other sought-after earthly sanctuary. Jesus was a knowable helper and healer who approached humans as
imperfect beings rather than as condemned sinners. In their construction of a
theology of hope, the slaves preserved their own sense of identity and dignity
while resisting the psychological trauma of an oppressive social system. While
the Baptist and Methodist churches to which African Americans adhered during both the antebellum and the post–Civil War era expressed criticism of
mediums and diviners, these roles reappeared in the various Holiness/Pente-
costal and Spiritual sects that emerged in the early twentieth century.

In essence, African American folk medicine became a diverse ensemble
drawing upon various cultural traditions. Snow gives the following description of the system of medical beliefs and practices found among African
Americans: "The system is a composite of the classical medicine of an earlier
day, European folklore regarding the natural world, rare African traits, and
selected beliefs derived from modern scientific medicine. The whole is inex-
tricably blended with tenets of fundamentalist Christianity, elements from the
Voodoo religions of the West Indies, and the added spice of sympathetic
magic. . . . It is a coherent medical system and not a ragtag collection of iso-
lated superstitions" (Snow 1974: 83).

Folk practices continue to be a vital part of health-care delivery for
African Americans in both the rural South and the cities of the South and the
North. Many working-class African Americans rely on home remedies, many
of which are religiously oriented, of various sorts as well as an array of folk
practitioners. African American folk medicine combines both naturalistic and
personalistic theories of disease etiology (Snow 1977). Maintaining health
in African American culture commonly is viewed as the "ability to 'keep on
keepin' on'" as well as being a product of the harmony of body, mind, and
spirit (Snow 1993: 73). Blood plays a central role in African American folk
medicine and contributes to illness as a result of being "too high" or "too low"
in volume, "too thick" or "too thin" in consistency, too pure or impure, and
as shooting too high or falling too low in the body (Snow 1993: 99).

Types of African American Folk Healers

As table 10 below indicates, contemporary African American folk healers can
be divided into four main types: (1) independent generalists, (2) independent
specialists, (3) cultic generalists, and (4) cultic specialists (Baer 1982). Healers
may or not affiliate their healing practice with a religious group or congrega-

tion. If a healer operates as an individual or is affiliated with some sort of occult supply store—either as the owner, an employee, or someone who rents office space therein—she or he is referred to simply as an *independent healer.* Conversely, if a healer is affiliated with a religious group and operates a healing practice through it, she or he is referred to as a *cultic healer.* Whereas independent healers function exclusively or almost exclusively in private settings, cultic healers may practice in both public (e.g., at a revival meeting or healing service) and private settings. In some instances, certain individuals may actually function in both capacities with a strong tendency either to compartmentalize or mix the two modes of practice. An excellent example of this compartmentalization is described in Winslow's (1969) case study of Bishop E. E. Everett and his occult store in Philadelphia. Bishop Everett is the pastor of and a healer in the Calvary Spiritual Temple, a congregation affiliated with the Apostolic Church of Christ in God, headquartered in Martinville, Virginia. He is also the proprietor of the Calvary Religious and Occult Store, an enterprise located in a different place than his church shop. Everett sells a wide array of magico-religious articles and gives advice on them to a largely working-class African American and Puerto Rican clientele. Importantly, "many members of his congregation are persons whom he contacted when they came to his store to make purchases or seek spiritual advice" (Winslow 1969: 63).

Table 10

Typology of Black Folk Healers

Affiliation of Healer	Nature of Practice	
	Limited or specialized	General
Independent	"Old Lady herbalist" "granny" midwife neighborhood prophet magic vendor or magic storeowner miscellaneous specialists	conjurer/ rootworker spiritualist eclectic
Cultic	evangelistic faith healer spiritual divine healer	voodoo priest or priestess spiritual prophet/advisor messianic nationalist healer

The central character in African American folk medicine historically has been the *conjurer*, who also goes under a various other labels, including *conjure doctor*, *rootworker*, *hoodoo doctor*, and *hungan*. Whitten (1962: 315–16) describes the conjurer as a "professional diviner, curer, agent finder, and general controller of the occult arts" in the African American community. Elsewhere, Roberts (1989: 65–104) describes the conjurer as an African American folk hero who historically enabled blacks to confront the oppressive conditions of slavery and institutional racism.

Initially conjurers were confined to slave communities on plantations, but as poor rural blacks migrated to cities, they were accompanied by the masters of the occult. During the nineteenth century, New Orleans became known as the voodoo capital of the country (Hurston 1931). Hoodoo as a system of magic, divination, and healing appears to be widespread, although it may be particularly prevalent along the Gulf Coast and, in addition to New Orleans, in certain cities such as Savannah, Biloxi, Baton Rouge, Lafayette, Shreveport, and Houston. Furthermore, hoodoo tends to vary from region to region by adapting itself to the brand of Christianity that African Americans in various locales practice. In southern Louisiana, hoodoo relies upon various religious articles associated with Roman Catholicism, whereas in rural areas of other southern states, such as Florida and Mississippi, such paraphernalia tend to be absent (Brown 1965; Webb 1973; Maduro 1975). Conversely, religious articles associated with Catholicism and/or voodoo are commonly used and prescribed by various other kinds of black folk healers, including those in urban areas such as New York, Chicago, Detroit, Memphis, and Atlanta.

Conjurers reputedly possess one or more traits that distinguish them from ordinary mortals. These include "double-sight," or the ability to see ghosts, being born on Christmas, being a seventh son, or a wide variety of atypical physical traits, including albinism, dwarfism, green eyes, and three birthmarks on the left arm (Bass 1981: 381). Individuals become conjurers in one of the following ways: (1) inheritance of the position, (2) apprenticeship under the tutelage of an established practitioner, and (3) a "calling" from God.

The conjurer's most important functions are to cure persons who have been bewitched—that is, "conjured," "fixed," "crossed," or "hexed"—and to place a direct spell or counterspell upon their clients' enemies. In an early study of conjure based upon a series of papers written by students in the mid-1880s, Herron and Bacon (1981: 366) listed five distinct services that the conjurer rendered to his client: "(1) He must tell him whether he is conjured or not. (2) He must find out who conjured him. (3) He must search for and find the 'trick' and destroy it. (4) He must cure the patient. (5) He will, if the patient wishes, turn back the trick upon the one who made it."

Conjurers also concern themselves with a wide array of other conditions, ranging from somatic ailments to problems of everyday life. Clients seek out conjurers for success in business or financial endeavors, gambling, and the search for gainful employment; resolution of strained social relations with significant others; the search for a spouse; avoidance of the law; a favorable decision in court; control over superordinates, such as a landlord or employer; and discovery of unknown enemies. Furthermore, conjurers are often resorted to as fortunetellers or curers of a wide variety of physical ailments. In attempting to solve their clients' problems, conjurers generally prescribe a variety of items, including perfumes, oils, seeds, powders, roots, pictures of Catholic saints, candles, medals, and readings from the Bible or the Sixth and Seventh Books of Moses.

With the mass migration of African Americans to the cities of both the North and the South, hoodoo or conjure became incorporated and transformed into new forms, such as Spiritualism and commercialism. Cooley (1977: 193) describes the new guise of conjurers as "psychics," "spiritualistic readers," and "prophets" as a move toward respectability and legal protection. Hurston (1931: 319) notes that hoodoo was often closely combined with Spiritualism in New Orleans in order to provide hoodoo doctors a protective cover from legal prosecution. Elsewhere, McCall (1963: 364) maintains that "hoodoo has been assimilated to the bewildering variety of store-front spiritualist churches in its truly religious aspects, leaving a heavy residue of sorcery and fetishism as the remaining native elements."

Despite the fact that many Spiritualists and psychics claim to be ministers, in reality they often function in effect as independent healers who are willing to treat a wide array of problems and concerns. According to Jordan (1979: 39), "Some claim to heal incurable diseases and solve financial problems, while others of inscrutable nature give hot numbers [for purposes of playing at the lottery]." Some Spiritualists reportedly work only with benign spirits or the "loving dead," while others work with malevolent spirits in addition to good ones. Spiritualists may be affiliated in some capacity with an occult supply store or operate on a strictly individual basis. In time, they may convert their practice into a religious congregation, perhaps using some of their clients as the group's core membership. In contrast to conjurers and rootworkers, who make extensive use of roots and herbs in attempting to gain control over the hidden forces of the universe, Spiritualists tend to have limited knowledge of the use of these substances and are more likely to use them in the form of baths and teas. Many Spiritualists advertise in various African American newspapers, magazines, and radio station (Snow 1978), and some engage in dubious and exploitative activities (Snow 1979).

In addition to conjurers and Spiritualists, there are other black independent generalists who defy simple classification. Weidman et al. (1979) refer to such healers as "eclectics," apparently because they incorporate aspects of evangelical faith healing, rootwork, hoodoo, and Spiritualism. Some African American healers, such as those described by Garrison below, have incorporated aspects of the occult revival that emerged in the 1960s and 1970s.

> *In Downtown Newark, near the Campus of Rutgers University, there is a "religious store" that does not share the tradition of the other religious stores. In the window there are, among other things, a live boa constrictor and an ancient Sanskrit text. Inside there is a strange mixture of the products, such as mineral salts, which are prescribed in accordance with astrological signs. This store is owned by a young Black man who calls himself a "guru," and there are two young women, one Black and one White, who provide monthly astrological readings. . . . This type of mystical revival seems to be infrequent among Black inner-city youth, but several Black practitioners of "new" mystic and pseudo-scientific practices of various forms of mind and body healing have been identified in the suburbs where many more White practices of this type have been found.* (Garrison 1979: 48)

INDEPENDENT SPECIALISTS

Probably the best-known independent specialists are herbalists or rootworkers in the strict sense of the word. Herbalists are specialists in the application of medicinal plants and other remedies for common ailments. In her discussion of four famous "voodoo doctors" who resided within a fifty-mile radius of Cottonville (a pseudonym for a Mississippi town), Powdermaker refers to a Mr. T, who explained that although he is considered a conjurer, he really was a herb doctor. "He does not believe in charms or voodoos, nor does he give advice in love or business affairs. He does, however, give certain medicine made from herbs, which if smeared on the body will keep away danger or attract people" (Powdermaker 1967: 294). Mr. Lee, a herbalist in Louisiana, relies upon medicinal plants found in Chatum and Lee counties in North Carolina (Payne-Jackson and Lee 1993: 27). Although herbalists are most common in rural areas, undoubtedly due to the ready availability of medicinal plants, Hall and Bourne (1973: 138–39) mention the presence of three persons, two male and one female, who operate herb shops in the Price neighborhood of Atlanta.

Female neighborhood practitioners, who are closely related to herbalists, often are referred to by terms such as "Old Lady," "granny," or "Mrs. Markus." The Old Lady is essentially a local consultant on common ailments. She does not have office hours or dispense medicine per se but merely advises clients on how to treat ordinary illnesses. Although she occasionally may receive monetary compensation for her services, this neighborhood practitioner is more likely to receive an expression of gratitude or a gift of food. A subtype of the Old Lady is the "granny" midwife, a black woman who works under the informal supervision of a biomedical physician (Dougherty 1982). Commenting on the rural county in North Carolina where they did research on granny midwives, Mongeau, Smith, and Maney (1961: 504) assert that while African American midwifery constituted an "active" but "restless and uncertain" endeavor, particularly because there no longer were apprentice midwives in the area. The decline of granny midwifery is also indicated by the fact that whereas in 1936 in North Carolina, 67.4 percent of all recorded "nonwhite" deliveries and 11.4 percent of all white deliveries were attended by lay midwives, by 1966 the rate for whites had dropped to a small fraction of 1 percent and the "nonwhite" rate to 23.6 percent (Mongeau, Smith, and Maney 1961: 297). More recently, Mathews (1992) interprets the disappearance of the granny midwife role in North Carolina as a consequence of the effects of restrictive legislation that pushed them out of practice. The biomedical establishment and state health agencies discriminated against granny midwives as members of a triple minority, namely poor black women.

An important source of advice for some African Americans in their quest for health, love, economic success, and interpersonal relations is the "magic vendor" (Hall and Bourne 1973). Magic vendors are owners or employees of commercial enterprises that specialize in the sale of occult articles. Although probably most of the small and medium-sized occult stores (often referred as "candle stores") are owned by blacks, many of the large stores are owned by whites, as apparently are the companies that manufacture the articles that are sold in them. Some regular drug stores in ghetto areas also stock a variety of occult items.

CULTIC GENERALISTS

The term cultic generalist refers to Spiritual advisors, Voodoo priests, and black Islamic and Hebraic healers who deal with a variety of illnesses either within the context of religious services or in private consultations. Voodoo priests and priestesses serve as important religious functionaries in temple.

They not only conduct ceremonies in honor of the African gods *(loa)* but also engage in healing, divination, and allegedly—at least occasionally—sorcery. Slaves from the islands of Martinique, Guadeloupe, and Saint Dominique were brought to Louisiana as early as 1716. Although voodoo was probably imported into Louisiana with these slaves, its principal impetus in the region apparently occurred around 1809 when French masters escaping the Haitian revolution brought slaves with them. During the nineteenth century, voodoo meetings—presided over by "queens" and "witch doctors"—catered to slaves, free blacks, and some white women (Reinders 1961: 241). As a result of white anti-voodoo sentiment (borne of the belief that black Haitians used voodoo to defeat the French colonialists) and legal action, beginning about 1820, and surfacing periodically during the nineteenth century, voodoo in New Orleans was forced to go into hiding. Nonetheless, in recent decades voodoo, or *vodun*, has undergone a revitalization in the United States as a result of the migration of Haitians to southern Florida, New York, and other urban areas (K. Brown 1991).

Anthropologist Loudell Snow conducted ethnographic research with Mother D, a voodoo practitioner in a southwestern city. She identifies herself as a *mambo* and claims that she inherited her power from her maternal grandmother (Snow 1973: 277). Mother D holds a ministerial license and a doctor of divinity from the International Universal Church. She maintains a religious healing complex consisting of two stucco buildings in a Mexican American barrio, about a mile from a predominantly African American neighborhood.

> *The larger of the buildings, an old house, contains a store where oils, incenses and religious items may be purchased, a small chapel, and the home of her son, Fred G, and his wife. The chapel is a curious combination of Roman Catholic, African, and zodiacal elements. The altar table holds votive candles, a large portrait of St. Theresa of the Little Flower, the Infant Jesus of Prague, a Pyrex bowel of water, and a large, jointed, wooden snake. Sticks of incense burn in holes in the snake's back. . . . [T]he snake is a symbol of the African serpent God, Damballah Ouedo, of West Africa and Haiti.* (Snow 1978: 89–90)

Mother D conducts regular services on Sunday mornings and Friday evenings.

While most of the members of her congregation are African Americans, most of her clients are Mexican Americans but some are Native Americans or Anglos. Mother D treats her clients in the smaller building. Her examining room contains a hospital bed, a chair, a small table covered with bottles and jars, and statues of the Virgin Mary and various saints. Fred G also has an office where he performs massages, prescribes herbs and other medicinal substances, and gives advice. Mother D reports that most of her clients are suffering from "nervousness." She also treats clients who believe that they have been bewitched and claims that people can bewitch themselves. Mother D maintains that she can cure cancers, tumors, arthritis, and other "natural" illnesses by laying-on of hands. She also provides advice for problems of living and administers herbal teas and massages.

Spiritual prophets or advisors function within the context of the highly syncretic Spiritual movement, which essentially combines elements from American Spiritualism, Roman Catholicism, African American Protestantism, and voodoo as well as other esoteric systems, such as New Thought, Islam, Judaism, and/or astrology (Baer 2001; Jacobs and Kaslow 1991). Spiritual prophets or mediums, many of whom are women, claim to possess a gift from the Spirit which enables them to prophesy and heal (Baer 1981; Jacobs 1990). Although they may treat physical ailments, Spiritual prophets address a wide variety of socioeconomic and psychosocial problems which particularly poor blacks, but also middle-class and non-poor working-class blacks, as well as some whites clients, encounter in everyday life. Spiritual prophets often direct messages concerning the past, present, and future to specific individuals during the course of religious services, particularly ones referred to as "bless services" or "prophesy services." Furthermore, they provide private consultations for their clients. In addition to the "reading" or message from the Spirit, Spiritual prophets say prayers or recite scriptural passages and provide magico-religious rituals or roots and herbs for their clients.

Some, if not most, messianic-nationalist sects, such as the various African American Muslim and Judaic groups, appear to have healers of some sort. Singer (1981) discusses the role of religious healing in the social system of the Original Hebrew Israelite Nation, a group with African American congregations in both the United States and Israel. Unlike many African American Holiness-Pentecostal and Spiritual groups, divine healing among the black Hebrews consists of a fully developed and exclusive set of beliefs about disease causation and a related regimen of treatment procedures. The chief healer or "Rofa" in the Nation's community in Israel at the time of Singer's study was a middle-aged woman who took on this role during the group's interim settlement in Liberia. She is assisted by a staff of "nurses" and trains other divine healers. According to Singer (1981: 218), the "Rofa serves both as a somatic healer and psychotherapist for the Black Hebrew community." While much of her time is devoted to the delivery of infants, she also attends to a variety of physical ailments and listens to the personal problems of members of the community.

Cultic specialists refer to faith healers who tend to focus on emotional disturbances within a religious setting. Both African American Holiness-Pentecostal
("Sanctified") and Spiritual churches have religious healers, often referred to
as "divine healers," who claim to possess the gift of healing, but who may lack
the gift of prophesy. Black divine healers use a variety of techniques, including laying-on of hands, anointing with oil, using blessed water, and applying
prayer cloths to the sick body. African American evangelical faith healers generally are the pastors or prominent members of religious congregations.
Despite the possibility that evangelical faith healers may constitute the largest
single category of folk therapists in African American communities, relatively
little has been written about them. Hall and Bourne (1973: 139) note that
healing in their services generally is used as "a mechanism to underscore some
message of the teaching and as evidence of the validity of their promising
good times on this earth" if that teaching is followed. It appears that the most
commonly employed healing technique used by faith healers is some variation
of laying-on of hands. They also anoint with holy oil and give their clients
prayer cloths and blessed waters. Although it does not appear that most evangelical faith healers do "readings," many offer advice to clients on how to
solve problems of living.

The Persistence and Contradictory Nature of African American Religious Healing and Folk Medicine

Payne-Price (1991: 133) correctly asserts that African American folk medicine
"continues to be a vital component in health care delivery, despite the
advances and availability of modern scientific medicine." Snow (1993: 265–69)
ascribes the persistence of African American folk medicine to the following
factors: (1) the poor treatment of blacks in conventional medical settings, (2)
economic deprivation that often makes quality biomedical care unavailable,
and (3) the search for strategies that offer its adherents with a sense of control
over their lives. Many African Americans, particularly those belonging to the
working class, continue to rely on folk medical remedies and healers who treat
not only physical but also emotional problems stemming from racism and
poverty (Payne-Price 1991). As Watson (1984: 53) argues, "The widespread
development and persistence of traditional medicine among Afro-Americans
and their corresponding underutilization of modern medical practitioners are
largely traceable to the economic poverty, ignorance [better phrased as lack of
access to information], and poor health."

In addition to providing a cheaper form of health care than biomedicine in many instances, African American folk medicine serves as a significant source of cultural identity and pride. In addition to catering to working-class blacks, "root doctors are enjoying increasing popularity among young blacks, middle class blacks, and in urban areas such as Charleston and Savannah" (de Albuquerque 1981: 56). While African American folk medicine continues to exhibit various forms, it has evolved from African-based syncretic religions, such as in voodoo, which existed in southern Louisiana during the nineteenth century; to conjure, rootwork, or hoodoo, as it existed in slave communities and has continued to exist in rural areas of the South; to religious healing practices based primarily in Sanctified (Holiness-Pentecostal) and Spiritual churches; and, most recently, to highly visible religious or psychic healers, such as the Rev. Ike, who promises his adherents "Green Power," and Dionne Warwick, who appears in television commercials advertising the services of the "Psychic Connection"—a capitalistic venture. As Semmes (1996: 79) observes, "Southern, rural, and small town migrants, and others carried health-related magico-religious beliefs with them to large cities, which became important but not dominant variants of traditional healing practices." Another indication of the process of assimilation manifested in African American health practices is the growing interest on the part of some African Americans in various heterodox medical systems, such as naturopathy and chiropractic (Semmes 1996: 89–103).

Like African American religion, with which it is intricately intertwined, African American folk medicine juxtaposes elements of protest and accommodation to the larger society. Historically, whites feared the conjurer whom they regarded as the Devil's secret agent. Brown views conjure as a multivalent force that did more than provide comfort to its clients, even in the wake of Emancipation. "After slavery conjure continued to serve as a subtle counterhegemonic role—at least to the extent that in reported cases it subverted white expectations of black behavior and labor productivity. Conjure was regularly used, moreover, as an effective weapon—it was claimed—to subvert prosecution of blacks in court. It often effectively prevented the prosecutor from 'talking' or prevented the judge from finding or using court 'papers'" (D. Brown 1990: 35).

As we have seen, conjure served as the prototype for other variants of African American religious healing and folk medicine, all of which also juxtapose elements of protest and accommodation. Within the context of the Spiritual movement, prophets and advisors function as folk therapists who are well acquainted with (and communicate a genuine concern about) the problems of their clients. It is possible that the techniques utilized by prophets and advisors affiliated with Spiritual churches enable clients, at least to some extent, to overcome a state of demoralization. A common theme in the Spiritual movement is the notion that one has to think positively and overcome negative modes of thought. Prophets and advisors constantly remind their clients that they must believe in themselves and assert that if they do not, no one else will. Based upon observations among Spiritual churches in New Orleans, Jacobs argues, "The Spiritual churches' ritual, including healing and prophecy, are effective for two reasons. First, worshipers have the opportunity to act out the sacred, thereby linking the temporal to the eternal, and second, they participate in religious celebrations that reflect a feature of the black culture" (Jacobs 1990: 365).

While Jacobs's phenomenological analysis captures the essence of the complex of prophets and advisors in the Spiritual movement, it overlooks its hegemonic components that unwittingly prompt its clients to acquiesce to the status quo in a racist and socially stratified society and over the long run may prevent them from improving their mental health. For the most part, Spiritual prophets and advisors focus on individualistic concerns—a pattern that is in keeping with the increasing privatization, or what Wilson (1978) terms "individuation," that characterizes much of modern life, particularly in urban areas. Consequently, the complex of prophets and advisors has a hegemonic dimension in that it tends to downplay "political conflict by stressing the importance of individual over society" (Wilson 1978: 356). Spiritual advisors inadvertently "blame the victim" by overlooking the social and economic roots of many of their clients' problems. They promise their clients improvements in their lives if they engage in various magico-religious rituals, develop a positive attitude, and overcome negative thoughts.

Like conjure and the complex of prophets and advisors in the Spiritual movements, other variants of African American religious healing and folk medicine, such as Pentecostalism, juxtapose elements of protest and accommodation to the larger society. African American folk medicine in various forms exhibits a pattern of dynamic change and adaptation to conditions both within the black community and the larger society. In many instances, it provides a meaningful, albeit contradictory, alternative to conventional medicine for many blacks and serves a significant vehicle for maintaining a sense of cultural pride.

IX

*P*raise and *P*rotest

African American Religious Music

Praise Him with the sound of the trumpet;
Praise Him with the psaltery and harp.
Praise Him with the timbrel and dance:
Praise Him with stringed instruments and organs.
Praise Him upon the loud cymbals:
Praise Him upon the high sounding cymbals.
Let everything that hath breath praise the Lord.
Praise ye the Lord.

Psalm 150: 3–6 (KJV)

*A*frican American religion and vocal music are as inseparable as lightning and thunder: it's possible to encounter one briefly without the other, but where one goes the other is sure to follow. In the African American community, religion and music have been closely intertwined historically, with spiritual music long serving as a source for the emergence of new forms of African American musical expression and the church as a training ground for numerous secular musicians and vocalists. Often, what African Americans most remember about "church going" as youngsters is the music that filled the air and moved the spirit. Indeed, a great deal of what African American religion accomplishes in terms of personal uplift, spiritual fulfillment, and the experience of collectivity is achieved through the idiom of music (with the sermon and direct experience of the Holy Spirit being the other two major pillars of African American religion). "The spirit will not descend without song," as Baraka (1963: 41) observes, "is an old African dictum that very necessarily was incorporated into Afro-Christian worship." Moreover, as Lincoln and Mamiya (1990: 346) stress, "In the Black Church good preaching and good singing are almost invariably the minimum conditions of a successful ministry." As a result, African American religious music provides a picture window for seeing essential aspects of African American religion, a window through which this chapter seeks to gaze. In this observation, what is most noticeable is the intensely *duplex nature* of African American religious music in all of its forms: at once, this rich and varied musical genre is about the glorious world after and the inglorious world all around us, about the not-so-distant African her-itage and the unique, ever-present, ever-ambiguous, North American experi-ence, about Euro-American and distinctly African American melodic textures and styles, and about individual and social accommodation and resistance. Each of these themes will be explored in this chapter, both within the context of explicitly religious (especially Christian) music and in terms of the religious elements at the core of African American secular music as well.

Twoness: The Melodic Syncretism of African and Euro-American Influences

One of the thorny debates that long characterized the social scientific ethno-musical study of African Americans concerned the degree to which Africa per-sisted as an influence in the cultural heritage of this population. In the realm of music, by the 1930s, emphasis among white scholars was on the centrality of European influences on African American religious singing. In the assess-ment of a number of prominent early writers, including Newman White (1928), Guy Johnson (1930), and George Pullen Jackson (1943), African American religious music (more so than work songs or other secular music) was derived largely from European models. These scholars identified similar-ities in the lyrics, themes, and musical structures of slave spirituals and the religious music of white Methodists and Baptists of the late eighteenth and early nineteenth centuries and concluded that the source of these parallels was in their common European roots.

While noting the similarities described by these early scholars, Levine (1973) and others have effectively refuted the arguments of those who assert a narrow Euro-American provenience for African American spiritual music. In Levine's assessment, to the degree that white evangelical music incorpo-rated complex rhythmic structures, polymeter, percussive qualities, syncopa-tion, and overlapping call-and-response interaction between a leader and chorus, the direction of diffusion was from African American music to white music rather than the reverse. Moreover, while the spirituals of the slaves may have employed biblical references that showed up as well in white religious music (e.g., the Promised Land, Egyptian Bondage), this hardly proves that they carried the same symbolic understanding for their different audiences. A considerable body of anthropological research, in fact, affirms that different social groups can use the same cultural images and symbols but imbue them with quite different meanings (Singer, Davison and Gerdes 1988). At the same time, argues Levine (1973), poorer white audiences may well have looked to the deliverance theme in religious music with the same material immediacy as the slaves, even if this meaning was lost on the wealthier classes in white society. Overall, Levine maintains that the similarities asserted by those who argued for a white derivation of African American religious music were overdrawn, owing in part to the limited collections available for analysis, as well as to the ethnocentric cultural tendency to dismiss the significance of African American creativity, originality, and influence.

Specific African elements retained in the religious music of African Americans include: (1) common use of a call and response structure; (2) considerable melodic ornamentation (as seen in the use of slides, slurs, bends, moans, shouts, and wails); (3) complex rhythmic patterns; (4) percussion styles; and (5) integration of song and dance (Maultsby 1983). As Epstein affirms, "A theory preserved in many . . . reference books that was widely promulgated by prestigious scholars in the 1930's and 1940's can now be laid to rest: that the music of blacks was wholly derived from European models. . . . Further evidence is needed to resolve the questions of the degree of African influence on American music at different times and places, but the theory that European influences account for all the elements in Afro-American music has been refuted" (Epstein 1977: 344).

Contemporary students of African American music have moved beyond the simplistic parameters of the origin debate with an eye toward understanding the processes of syncretism of African and European American sources. Indeed, the very dynamism of African American music, and its capacity to continually generate powerful new musical forms—ones that have significantly shaped the religious and secular music of North American and the world—appears to come from what W. E. B. Du Bois aptly called "twoness": "One ever feels his twoness—an American, a Negro; two souls, two thoughts, two unreconciled strivings; two warring ideals in one dark body whose dogged strength alone keeps it from being torn asunder" (Du Bois 1972: 17). In their music, the slaves reflected this "twoness" by adopting European American hymns and folk songs with their biblical images and characters and "altered them significantly in terms of words, musical structure, and especially performance" (Levine 1973: 103) as part of the process of making them their own. The product, confirms Levine (1973: 103), "was a hybrid with a strong African base."

Two Worlds of African American Religious Music: The Here and Now and the World to Come

Frederick Douglass (1962: 146–47), reflecting on his memories of the music of slavery, recalled the following words of a popular song:

> *We raise de wheat,*
> *Dey gib us de corn;*
> *We bake the bread,*
> *Dey gib us de crust;*
> *We sif de meal,*
> *Dey gib us de huss;*
> *We peal de meat,*
> *Dey gib us de skin;*
> *And dat's de way*
> *Dey take us in;*
> *We skim de pot,*
> *Dey gib us de liquor,*
> *And say dat's good enough for nigger.*

The biting critique of this secular song, an unambiguous precursor of various subsequent African American lyrical forms from the blues to rap, makes evident the inclination of the slaves to use music to give expression to their immediate feelings and experiences as an oppressed population. Did this same pattern hold for the religious music of the slaves and for subsequent generations of African Americans?

Anderson Edwards, who grew up in slavery and was later freed, recalled the following during an interview with researchers from the 1930s Works Progress Administration (Rawick 1977: 6–7):

> *We prayed a lot to be free and the Lord done heered us. We didn't have no song books and the Lord done give us our songs and when we sing them at night it jus whispering so nobody her us. One went like this:*
>
> > *My knee bones am aching,*
> > *My body's rackin' with pain,*
> > *I 'lieve I'm a child of god,*
> > *And this ain't my home,*
> > *'Cause Heaven's my aim.*

The last line of this song could be interpreted to mean that, from the earliest days, African American religious music was focused narrowly on a future spiritual salvation "in Heaven." This was the view of E. Franklin Frazier (1964: 12), who maintained that "Spirituals were essentially religious in sentiment and . . . other-worldly in outlook." However, the detailed focus in the earlier lines of the song on the misery of day-to-day physical experience under slavery suggests a rather different interpretation, namely, that this song expresses the desire of the slaves "for freedom in this world as well as in the next" (Raboteau 1978: 250). Indeed, in the worldview of the slaves, like that of their African progenitors, the separation between these two realities was narrow. For the slaves, as reflected in this song, God was immediate, personal, and concerned, an understanding that has characterized much of African American religious music and belief ever since. The Old Testament figures Daniel, David, Joshua, Jonah, Moses, and Noah who populated the religious music of the slaves "were delivered in *this* world and in ways which struck the imagination of the slaves" (Levine 1973: 121). Thus, it is fair to conclude that the music of the slaves and the religious music of African Americans generally is not other-worldly; rather, it is the nexus that unites the here-and-now with the world-to-come.

Further, as Lincoln and Mamiya (1990: 347) stress, singing in African American churches functions to "transcend or to reduce to insignificance those social, cultural, or economic barriers which separate individuals in their secular interests in order that genuine corporate worship might take place." In other words, one of the "this-world" issues addressed by music is the heterogeneity of all contemporary African American communities. Music, by its power to pull performers and audiences together into a common mood, a common focus, is able to create what Lincoln and Mamiya (1990: 347) refer to as an "ad interim sense of community" that overwhelms social alienation, interpersonal antagonisms, and the sense of isolation so common in modern life. Upon the sense of unity, however temporary, created by African American religious music, the other work of the African American church can proceed.

Praise and Protest: Accommodation and Resistance in African American Religious Music

Related to the "worldly orientation" issue, is that of political stance: is African American religious music primarily accommodative, expressing a religious conservatism that promotes patience and shies away from open rebellion, or is it by nature the melodic voice of resistance of an oppressed people? In responding to this question, Levine (1973: 121) looks to the song "O my Lord Delivered Daniel" for an answer:

> *He delivered Daniel from de lion's den,*
> *Jonah from de belly ob de whale,*
> *And de Hebrew children from de fiery furnace,*
> *And why not every man?*

Based on an examination of hundreds of religious songs, Levine (1973: 121) concluded "there was always a latent and symbolic element of protest in the slave's religious songs which frequently became overt and explicit." Exemplary of the latter is the following variant of "Go Down Moses" that appeared during the Civil War period (cited in Raboteau 1978: 249):

> *Oh! Fader Abraham*
> *Go down into Dixie's land*
> *Tell Jeff Davis*
> *To let my people go.*
> *Down in de house of bondage*
> *Dey have watch and waited long,*
> *De oppressor's heel is heavy,*
> *De oppressor's arm is strong,*
> *Oh, Fader Abraham.*

The political message that found expression in such music was not lost on slave owners, who would punish and imprison slaves for singing songs with explicit political messages about impending freedom (especially if it was implied that the slaves intended to fight for their freedom). Through their spiritual music, the slaves, and the descendants of slaves as well, found ways to intertwine praise and protest, glorification of a fair God and rebuke of the white oppressor.

Sacred Music: Spirituals, Gospel, and Hymns

The emergence of a distinctly African American religious music tradition can be traced to the latter part of the eighteenth century and the early nineteenth century, following evangelical conversion of slaves to Christianity as described in chapter 1. Critical to the introduction of slaves to Christianity were the camp revival meetings of the Second Great Awakening (1770–1815). As Maultsby (1983: 163) remarks, "Music played an important role in creating an emotional atmosphere during camp meetings. The hymns and spiritual songs, which were an integral part of the services, were sung in a manner that resembled the musical practices of slaves. . . . Slaves responded to these familiar performance trends by participating with 'exuberance and excitement.'" As this account implies, religious music was a vital element in the Christianization of the slaves. Without it, this process might have never achieved the enduring impact that it did on the African American population. A white participant at the camp revivals noted: "singing tune after tune, scarce one of which were in our hymn books," but that emerged instead from the "Negro section" of the tent-covered camp grounds (quoted in Maultsby 1983: 164). Repeatedly it was reported that African Americans sang louder and longer than their white counterparts at the revival meetings, often singing long after white revivalists had headed to their family tents for the evening. The lyrics of these camp songs were said to consist of a mixture of lines from established prayers, excerpts from Scripture, and pieces of orthodox hymns, intersected by choruses and other elaborations. The tunes for these songs initially appeared to have been taken from work songs, dance songs, and other secular folk music. For example, a verse of the song "Swing Low, Sweet Chariot," that was published in 1903 (cited in Epstein 1977: 219) included the following clearly secular references:

> *Banjos pickin', jewsharps zoonin',*
> *All de hebbenly ban' a-chunin,*
> *Swing low, sweet charriyut.*
> *Sing en shout bofe night en day,*
> *Stop jus long ernuff to pray,*
> *Swing low, sweet charriyut*

According to Southern (1983: 85), "Spontaneous songs were composed on the spot [during a revival meeting] often started by some excited preacher and developed by the crowds who shouted 'Hallelujah' and similar praise words or phrases between the preacher's lines." The combination of unorthodox lyrics, secular melodies, and the fervor with which they were sung by African American revivalists unnerved some white preachers who condemned the appearance of these distinctly African American "camp-meeting hymns." There was even an effort to eradicate these unapproved songs and replace them with more controlled and "pious" hymns. Needless to say, such efforts failed. Ultimately, a number of different religious genres developed among African Americans, including spirituals, gospel music, and hymns.

Spirituals

Historically, the singing of a distinct spiritual repertoire among African Americans can be traced to the southern plantation "praise house," structures that were built on plantations by some slave owners for the religious worship of slaves following the conversion of most slaves to Christianity. It is not known when the term spiritual was first applied to African American religious songs. It evidently was in common use by the 1860s, as it was applied without definition in *Slave Songs of the United States* by Richard Allen and his co-workers. While the term spiritual had been in use as a label for religious music prior to its application to African American religious songs, once so applied the term was as much defined by the music as the music by the term.

Collectively, African American spirituals are distinguished by their "poetic beauty, . . . emotional intensity, [and] . . . rich imagery" (Levine 1973: 108). Based on an analysis of the lyrics of a rich corpus of spirituals, Levine (1973) found that the most prominent theme is that of the "chosen people." Repeatedly spirituals affirm that African Americans are the "children of God," thereby addressing directly the identity issue for a people forcibly removed from their land, culture, and society and brought as strangers to "a strange land." Moreover, Jesus is depicted as a confidant and close friend, as seen in the informality of the following song:

> *In de mornin' when I rise,*
> *Tell my Jesus huddy ho;*
> *I wash my hand in de mornin' glory,*
> *Tell my Jesus huddy ho.*
> (cited in Raboteau 1978: 259)

In addition to being a friend, Jesus is portrayed as a rescuer:

> *Jesus make de dumb to speak*
> *Jesus make de cripple walk*
> *Jesus give de blind his sight*
> *Jesus do most anything,*
> *Rise poor Lajarush from de tomb.*
> (cited in Raboteau 1978: 260)

Another frequent theme is that of travel, on either a spiritual level (e.g., to heaven) or worldly level (e.g., to a biblical location). In "Jordan's Long Road" (cited in Raboteau 1978: 256) these two planes are merged, exemplifying the unity, as noted above, of these domains in African American religious music:

> *De rough, rocky road what Moses done travel,*
> *I's bound to carry my soul to de Lawd,*
> *It's a mighty rocky road but I mos' done travel,*
> *And I's bound to carry my soul to de Lawd.*

Death is also a common theme, but certainly not a sad one, as it is but the beginning of a desired spiritual journey:

Death is gwinter lay his cold icy hands on me, Lord
Death is gwinter lay his cold icy hands on me . . .
One of dese mornin's it won't be long,
Yo'll look fo' me an' I'll be gone.
(cited in Frazier 1963: 14)

While sometimes peaceful, spirituals are often action-filled. Battling with the devil is a common source of such activity,

The Devil's mad and I'm glad,
He lost the soul he thought he had.
Ole Satan toss a ball at me
O me no weary yet.
Him tink de ball would hit my soul
O me no weary yet.
Ole Satan though he had a mighty aim;
He missed my soul and caught my sins.
Cry Amen, cry Amen, cry Amen to God!
(cited in Levine 1973: 110).

Another common subject is apocalyptic judgment of sinners, as reflected in "Down in the Valley" (cited in Raboteau 1978: 253):

De lightnin' and de flashin' (thrice)
Jesus set poor sinners free
I can't stand the fire (thrice)
Jesus set poor sinners free.
De green tress a-flamin' (thrice)
Jesus set poor sinners free.
Way down in the valley,
Who will rise and go with me?
You've heern talk of Jesus
Who set poor sinners free.

Also important in spirituals is a strong communal sentiment. After death, unification with loved ones will occur—including with those ripped away by the slave master to be sold to another plantation.

When we all meet in heaven,
There is no parting there;
When we all meet in heaven,
There is no parting no more.
(cited in Raboteau 1978: 262–63)

Praise and Protest

While, in the final analysis, spirituals are a joyful and optimistic genre, in that they continually emphasize that a better time will come through the intervention of God and that great happiness is awaiting in heaven, melancholy and sorrow are nonetheless commonly expressed, as seen in well-known songs like "Sometimes I Feel Like a Motherless Child" and "Nobody Knows the Trouble I've Seen" (cited in Raboteau 1978: 259):

> *Nobody knows de trouble I seen*
> *Nobody knows but Jesus*
> *Nobody knows de trouble I've had*
> *Glory hallelu!*

In fact, rapid and jarring shifts from great happiness to dark sadness are not uncommon in Spirituals. However, frank recognition of the suffering borne of slavery notwithstanding, Spirituals are "almost devoid of feelings of depravity or unworthiness, but . . . rather. . . [are] pervaded by a sense of change, transcendence, ultimate justice, and personal worth" (Levine 1973: 118). While to varying degrees spirituals were both accommodative and rebellious, more than anything they were sustaining. Spiritual music was a source of comfort and support, a vehicle for communal bonding, an outlet for venting grief and frustration, and a means of instilling the world with order, moral certainty, and hope. In these ways, under the gravest of circumstances, spirituals sustained an oppressed people and helped to carry them through, with their heads held high in song, to their emancipation, and, when that proved less than what they rightfully hoped it might bring, religious songs remained a continuing source of spiritual nourishment for those in need.

One of the scholarly debates over spirituals concerns the use of "coded messages." Some have maintained that Spirituals and their biblical allusions were actually disguised references to particular places and events of importance to slaves relative to escaping slavery. Several scholars have pointed to Frederick Douglass' statement that "I am bound for the land of Canaan meant something more than our hope of reaching heaven. We meant to reach the North, and the North was our Canaan" (quoted in Levine 1977: 52). Similarly, Southern (1973: 195) maintains that place names like Jerusalem were used as hidden references to specific local rendezvous sites and that singers were "concerned not so much with a journey to Jerusalem as with a trip to the next plantation for a secret religious meeting."

Frazier (1963), among others, discounts this role of Spirituals, even though he admits that some songs may make reference to specific earthly locales that would only be meaningful to the composer and his/her immediate audience. As this admission suggests, little noticed in this debate over content is the issue of context, specifically, who is singing which songs under what conditions to which audiences. In different contexts, in different times and places, it is likely that the same song could have very different meanings and be put to different purposes. This is the nature of folkloric materials. They are inherently malleable and responsive to new situations (Singer 1985). This makes music especially useful for African Americans—a population that has faced more than its share of grave challenges and deadly threats.

Gospel

Gospel music dates to the Great Depression. The term was first used as a label for a distinct form of African American religious music by Thomas A. Dorsey, who has been called the "Father of Gospel Music." The development of gospel was a conscious effort by Dorsey, the son of an itinerant Baptist preacher from rural Georgia. From childhood, Dorsey learned to play religious music on the pump organ and later he played piano in several jazz bands. Just prior to the Depression, he toured with blues singer Ma Rainey as the head of his own musical group, the Wildcats Jazz Band. During this period, Dorsey wrote numerous songs and, under the nickname Georgia Tom, began to develop a reputation as a noted blues performer. But Dorsey never cut his ties to the church nor lost his strong feeling about the power of church music. Nonetheless, he found much Baptist religious music to be rigid, too dependent on European religious music, and out of step with the changing African American urban experience. Beginning in the late 1920s, he started writing in a new style, intended to enliven church services by using folk imagery and melodies from the African American cultural experience.

Dorsey began to promote his gospel sound by seeking opportunities to perform his new songs at Baptist churches in Chicago during Sunday services, but was denied. Some ministers did allow him to perform after the regular service was over, however. Dorsey led a complex life during this period, playing the blues and spending time with jazz musicians on Saturday night, and then getting up the next morning to attend church and listen to church choirs. Like other musicians, Dorsey was deeply impressed by the ability of effective African American ministers to unite religion and entertainment. It was one such preacher, the Rev. W. M. Nix, whose intense half-spoken, half-sung preaching style won Dorsey's commitment to the church (Harris 1992).

In 1930, one of Dorsey's songs, "If You See My Savior," was performed at the National Baptist Convention and received a tremendous response among conventioneers. A year later, he organized the first gospel chorus at the famous Ebenezer Baptist Church as well as the Chicago Gospel Choral Union, Inc. In 1932, he launched the Dorsey House of Music, the first gospel publishing company. Over the years, he composed almost a thousand songs, and published most of them, including a number that became gospel classics, such as "Precious Lord," "Take My Hand, "When I've Done My Best," and "There'll Be Peace in the Valley." In time, several subtypes of gospel groups evolved, including the all-male quartet (often dressed in nicely cut business suits singing a capella) and the female gospel chorus (often dressed in choir robes and accompanied by piano), both of which attracted Dorsey's interest.

Dorsey explained that his goal was "to strike a happy medium for the downtrodden. This music lifted people out of the muck and mire of poverty and loneliness, of being broke, and gave them some kind of hope, anyway. Make it anything than good news, it ceases to be gospel" (quoted in Carter 1999: 54). Gospel songs like "Don't Let Nobody Turn You Around" provided inspiration for the Civil Rights Movement, earning the genre the designation "soul of the movement" from the Rev. Martin Luther King, Jr., Gospel was also a major influence on several secular musical forms in the African American community and beyond, including Rhythm and Blues (R&B), soul, and rock and roll. Ultimately, in addition, it became the singing voice of the church in the African American community, even finding its way into African American Catholic churches (Djedje 1983).

Leading African American singers involved in gospel music included Mahalia Jackson (who merged gospel with the blues), the Original Five Blind Boys, Marion Williams (hailed by many as one of the greatest singers who ever lived), Aretha Franklin, and Kirk Franklin (who merged gospel with rap music). While these singers became nationally known recording artists, as Patterson (1988: 91) notes, gospel "rests on [a] base of extremely active local music making in virtually all communities with a strong black presence." In 1998, gospel records had more than a half-billion dollars in sales, making gospel as much secular success as it was spiritual expression, while confirming Dorsey's hunch that this musical genre had tremendous commercial possibilities. In light of the tendency for new African American musical styles to be adopted (and often taken over by) white performers (who then earned many times more than the African American originators), it is notable that, in her doctoral dissertation "The Black Gospel Music Tradition: Symbol of Ethnicity," Mellonee Burnim (1980) points out that gospel music is the sole existing genre of African American music that is still being produced and performed primarily by and for African Americans. Indeed, both in and out of the church, gospel is seen as the epitome of African American religious music.

One expression of the status of gospel is the emergence of what Lincoln and Mamiya (1990: 363) refer to as "gospel music groupies," African American college students who may not be particularly religious but have a fan-like attachment to gospel music and attend local churches near their college campuses specifically to hear particular gospel choirs. In a sense, this development represents part of the secularization of gospel music, even when it is performed within the context of a church service. The movement of gospel from the church to concert halls and recording studios is further expression of this secularizing trend. As a result of these developments, it has been noted that some types of gospel now "sound more like pop music and jazz" (Lincoln and Mamiya 1990: 363), a development that causes great concern to some clergy and laity in the African American church.

Despite expressions of secularization, gospel music has been an extremely important factor in the evolution of the African American church. The rapid growth of Pentecostalism in the African American community, especially of certain denominations like the Church of God in Christ, has been credited in no small part to the influence of particular gospel performers. The Hawkins Singers, Andre Crouch, and the Clark Sisters, for example, are hailed by Lincoln and Mamiya (1990) for having left a Pentecostal mark on all gospel music wherever it is performed.

Hymns

In 1801, Richard Allen, an AME minister, published *A Collection of Spiritual Songs and Hymns, Selected from Various Authors.* Historically, this was of note because a young African American minister took the bold step of publishing his own hymn book rather than relying on the official Methodist hymnal. The book is also noteworthy because it includes religious folk songs and chorus styles that Allen learned "out in the community" as a circuit preacher. Most importantly, the collection represents an early effort to make church music meaningful to the unique experience of African American parishioners.

Over the years, the various African American Protestant denominations have developed (and sometimes updated) their own hymnody, but the struggle for hymnal relevance continues. Indeed, there is a continual tension in African American churches that finds expression in dissatisfaction with the content of available hymn books. This tension arises from the fact that hymn books tend to be conservative preservers of established musical styles. But secular culture continues to change, including the ideas, sensitivities, and understandings that embody the ethos of secular culture, creating the regular opportunity for an experienced gap between rapidly changing cultural expectations and a slowly changing hymnody. Since the Civil Rights Movement, for example, there has been an effort to bring African American hymn books up to date by deleting songs and references that imply the inferiority of the color black (e.g., "Wash me white as snow"). According to Spencer (1992: 200), based on a review of the history of hymn singing in the African American community, "the black church tends to be held captive by a kind of theological, doctrinal, and social backwardness that works to stifle impetus toward black self-identity and self-determination in the larger social milieu. . . . [This] problem is not simply reflected in the hymnody; to a considerable degree the problem is the hymnody." Spencer advocates updating African American hymn books to keep them in harmony with contemporary (post–Civil Rights Movement) sensitivities and needs, just as Richard Allen did two hundred years ago. As always in African American music, the line between the secular and the spiritual is thin, with influences flowing in both directions.

The Soul of African American Secular Music: Controversial Preachers and Secular Religion

Cornel West and Amiri Baraka, two leading commentators on the African American experience, have both observed that the barrier between secular music and African American religiosity is highly porous. Notes West (1988: 174), the entrenched spiritual impulse in African American culture "direct[s] the Christian religiosity of black church music into the secular spirituality of Afro-American popular music." More broadly, Baraka (Jones 1968: 253) asserts, "The church carries directly over into the secular music, which is really not secular at all." These are striking assertions in light of extensive condemnation of many forms of popular music that have emanated from the pulpit of African American churches and found expression in the sermons and writings of African American theologians. For example, in criticizing the claim made by Richard Wimberly (1989) and Alton Pollard (1989a) that there are significant African American religious themes in the songs of the enigmatic rock musician Prince, an editorial published in the *United Methodist Reporter* argued:

> *Prince, in case you haven't heard, doesn't sing nursery rhymes. By and large, his music, matched by his performance on stage and video, is sexually explicit. It's offensive by nearly any standard of decency, Christian or cultural. . . . [Prince] isn't a preacher. He's a shameless entertainer who sells his music by exploiting the most base human instincts. Furthermore, it's "straining at a gnat" to suggest that Prince's music is worth listening to because something resembling religion is buried in the filth.* (quoted in Spencer 1989: 148)

Still, based on his analysis of Prince's music, Pollard (1989a: 140) maintains that a central theme of all of Prince's work is that in a world of hedonistic indulgence, decay, pollution, and growing anarchy, "there can be no abiding peace, not until the Lord comes." In effect, argues Pollard, Prince represents the most theologically dangerous aspect of this sinful world (e.g., unbridled sexuality) so as to call forth an apocalyptical vision of a better world to come. These startlingly contrasting analyses of Prince's music, interestingly, exemplify the "two worlds" theme of African American religious music, namely, as noted above, in their religious music African Americans have struggled deeply and sought to reconcile the harshness of the corporal world with the glories to come in the spiritual world. In the view of a number of contemporary ethnomusicologists and theomusicologists, African American secular music is no different.

Elements of religious expression have been identified in all secular African American lyrical traditions, including ragtime, the blues, R&B, jazz, soul, and even Rap. Even before these more modern musical forms, religious themes (with primarily African referents until the nineteenth century) probably were evident in the work and recreational songs developed by African Americans from the earliest days of their arrival in North America. It is known that such music flourished among the slaves, despite assertions in the literature that they lacked a secular musical tradition. However, as Southern (1983a) emphasizes, we have relatively few accounts of early African American secular music because slaveholders did not pay much attention to music emanating from the slave quarter and did not bother to record much about it in their diaries, travelogues, or other letters. Some of the secular music of slavery can be grouped into the genre of "work songs." These were sung to make the time pass and to provide a cadence to organize the work effort. Corn songs, for example, were sung by slaves during the picking and shucking of corn (the latter, in addition to its economic value, being an important component of the slave diet in a number of regions). One such song, a traditional call-and-response tune (recorded in Epstein 1977: 188), and similar to a version published in 1841) preserved by a white clergyman's daughter, was composed following an announcement by the minister that slaves would have to work on Sunday. The song laments the hypocrisies of white Christianity, a trait that is common in African American secular music:

Leader:	*'Twas on a blessed Sabbath day.*
Chorus:	*It rain, boy, It rain*
Leader:	*The parson says his prayers in church (chorus)*
Leader:	*He cut the matter short, my friends (chorus)*
Leader:	*Now's the time for planting 'bacco (chorus)*
Leader:	*Come my Negroes get you home (chorus)*
Leader:	*Go draw your plants and set them out (chorus)*
Leader:	*'Twas on a blessed Sabbath Day (chorus)*
Leader:	*Here's a pretty preacher for you (chorus)*

Indeed, slave owners and overseers often encouraged slaves to sing as they worked. As Frederick Douglass, a former slave and leading abolitionist leader recorded (reproduced in Southern 1983b):

Slaves are generally expected to sing as well as to work. A silent slave is not liked by masters and overseers. "Make a noise, make a noise," and "bear a hand," are the words usually addressed to slaves when there is silence among them. This may account for the almost constant singing heard in the southern states. There was generally, more or less singing among the teamsters, as it was one means of letting the overseer know where they were and that they were moving on with the work.

However, as noted, not all music was tolerated by slave owners. In particular, mournful music was restricted, in part so as to insure a faster work pace. In fact, the same songs were sung in different ways in different work settings in accord with the nature of the labor involved. As noted in *Slave Songs in the United States* (Allen, Ware, and Garrison 1967) with reference to "Poor Rosy," for example, which was an especially common work song that lamented various woes and carried the refrain: "Heav'n shall-a be my home," the tempo of the song differed depending on the situation in which it was sung: "On the water, the oars dip 'Poor Rosy' to an even andante; a stout boy and girl at the hominy mill will make the same 'Poor Rosy' fly, to keep up with the whirling stone; and in the evening after the day's work is done, 'Heab'n shall-a be my home' peals up slowly and mournfully from the distant quarters."

Songs also were a common feature of slave coffles, parades of chained slaves marching to a new location (e.g., after being sold) under the watchful eye and cracking whip of slave drivers. Southern (1983a: 158) notes the following example that expresses the common theme of religious redemption:

See these poor souls from Africa
Transported to America:
We are stolen and sold to Georgia, will you go along with me?
We are stolen and sold to Georgia, go sound the jubilee.

See wives and husbands sold apart,
The children's screams!——it breaks my heart;
There's a better day a-coming, will you go along with me?
There's a better day a-coming, go sound the jubilee.

Comparatively little is known about African American secular music in the urban North during the antebellum period. As Epstein (1977: 189) points out, however, "One tantalizing question that needs more attention concerns the use of songs as signals, both in connection with the Underground Railroad and in other affairs kept secret from whites." It would not be surprising to discover that religious elements played a role in this hidden musical tradition. Notably, Harriet Tubman, an escaped slave who became a leading "conductor" on the Underground Railroad, is known to have used music to signal slaves "that their 'Moses' had come after them, and they would begin to make preparations for leaving " (Southern 1983a: 143). For this purpose, Tubman commonly used the following song with unmistakable religious symbolism:

> *Dark and thorny is de pathway*
> *Where de pilgrim makes his ways;*
> *But beyond dis vale of sorrow*
> *Lie de fields of endless days.*
> (recorded in Southern 1983a: 143)

As these examples suggest, while religious elements were not central in all of the African American secular music from the slave era, sacred imagery, values, and symbols were common found expression in the day-to-day folk songs of the slaves as well as among freemen from this period.

After the Civil War, new forms of African American secular music appeared or older slave idioms were reworked to reflect new conditions and experiences. The prison song, for example, developed at this time as former slave owners and their henchmen were quick to arrest and incarcerate African Americans who showed any signs of resisting a return to the old social order of inequality. Although sharecropping replaced slavery, insuring that most former slaves would still be tied to the land, other work opportunities opened up. As the work experiences of African Americans began to change after the war, other new genres, like the railroad songs, lumber camp songs, and landowner songs, appeared. William Wells Brown (in Katz 1969: 107), for example, recorded the following landowner song, which parodied a popular spiritual to express the hope and fears of freedom:

> *Sing yo' praise, bless de lamb,*
> *Getting plenty money;*
> *Cotton's gwine up, 'deed it am,*
> *People, ain't it funny?*
> *Chorus: Rise, shine, give God the glory, glory (repeat)*
> *Don't you thin it's gwine to rain?*
> *Maybe was, a little;*
> *Maybe one ole hurricane*
> *'S bilin' in the kittle!*
> *Repeat chorus*

One important arena of work and recreation that exploded after the war was public entertainment. During the era of bondage, slaves often were called to "the big house" to sing songs, dance, or put on shows to amuse the Master and his family and friends. Through these experiences, as well as during performances in the slave quarter, many African Americans gained experience as amateur performers. Strangely, during the first decades of the 1800s, a group of white theatrical entertainers took to imitating the musical and dance repertoire of slaves (for white audiences) while dressed in blackface (usually charcoal). This self-interested music appropriation, which nonetheless expressed true appreciation of African American music, set in motion a pattern that continues today (e.g., in white rap singers). Known as Ethiopian Minstrelsy, this highly emotional genre created an entertainment (and employment) niche that could be filled by freed slaves. By 1865, a number of organized black minstrel troupes were touring. One such troupe, formed by Charles "Barney" Hicks, an African American performer, was called the Georgia Minstrels (one of several such groups by that name). The troupe, with its thirteen-piece brass band, toured widely (around and outside of the United States) and achieved considerable celebrity. Other groups were smaller, less permanent, and lacked a full band accompaniment, but collectively these groups ushered in the minstrel tradition in African American folk music. The songs that were popular among the minstrels, by African American songwriters like James Bland, Gussie Lord David and Samuel Lucas, were ballads, comedies, and specialty numbers, including religious pieces. Even songs that were not specifically religious in their orientation had African American religious themes. Indeed, many who hurried to hear minstrel bands assumed that they were hearing authentic slave songs rather than formal compositions by identifiable African American songwriters.

James Bland's songs became favorites among both African Americans and whites (many of the latter not realizing that the composer of their favorite songs was African American). One of his songs (of approximately seven hundred), "Carry Me Back to Old Virginny," was adopted as the official state song of Virginia in 1940, although by then it was forgotten that the composer was an African American. The popularity of the minstrel, as well as other forms of stage entertainment, created the foundation for the emergence of many subsequent genres of distinctly African American music. Additionally, in places like New Orleans, aspects of the minstrel have been retained still in the extravagant and clamorous Second Line street parades sponsored by African American social clubs and benevolent societies. These grand musical festivals feature strong religious themes. For example, as noted by Regis, a Second Line tune that was made popular by the Re-Birth Brass Band draws its lyrical inspiration (which is chanted by processional participants) from the book of Exodus (Regis 1999: 494).

Two of the earliest uniquely African American secular music traditions that developed after the Civil War were ragtime and blues. The former, from its first appearance, was tied to the piano, an instrument to which slaves had little access. After Emancipation, and despite their cost, keyboard instruments became popular in African American households. Initial reports of the syncopated rhythms and accompanying dance forms of rag-music came from those who were impressed by the African American performers of this instrumental style (many so poor that their clothes were not much better than rags), who played for tips in inexpensive cafes, saloons, dance halls and honky-tonks in the South and on the eastern seaboard. Ultimately, in the work of composers like Scott Joplin, known as the "King of Ragtime," Thomas Million Turpin, called "the Father of St. Louis Ragtime," and Ferdinand Joseph "Jelly Roll" Morton, the genre outgrew its "lowly" origins and achieved widespread appreciation. In latter years, ragtime became a direct influence on Bebop, "an improvisational music that combined the rhythms of the black church with the music of ragtime and blues" (Roberts 1989: 53). Like many secular musical traditions that were to follow, ragtime was not initially well received by "church-going" African Americans. Eubie Blake, for example, who at the age of six began "raggin" the tunes taught to him by his organ teacher at the Negro Methodist Church, was ordered by his deeply religious mother to "take that ragtime out of [her] house" (quoted in Southern 1971: 325).

Whatever the specific religious influences on rag-music, with the blues the connection is unambiguous. As Southern (1983a: 331) observes, "The dividing line between the blues and some kinds of spirituals cannot always be sharply drawn. Many spirituals convey to listeners the same feeling of rootlessness and mystery as do the blues." Indeed, some musicologists have used terms like "blues-spirituals" or "gospel blues" to classify certain ambiguous tunes, an ambiguity that Spencer (1989: 18) maintains stems from the fact that "the ethos of blues is thoroughly religious" despite the recognized absence of references to Jesus Christ and an unambiguous critique of religious hypocrisy. Thus in Cone's (1972) assessment, blues songs should be viewed as "secular spirituals." The close connection between spirituals and blues music was undoubtedly influenced by the personal histories of some of the leading bluespeople. As Southern (1973: 498) comments, "While some of the successful blues singers learned their art through the traditional apprentice method, most began their careers in church choirs or with traveling gospel groups, and several were offsprings of ministers."

Notably, the first professional blues singer, Gertrude "Ma" Rainey, was a touring minstrel performer when she first encountered folk singing in the plaintive blues style while traveling through Missouri. She was captivated by the heart-wrenching poignancy of loss, abandonment, hard luck, abuse, and grief that characterized the musical form that came to be called the blues (a labeling for which she took credit). By the time that William Christopher Handy, also a minstrel performer, published his first blues composition, "Memphis Blues," in 1912, the blues had become established as a popular musical form in the African American community and beyond. His "St. Louis Blues," published in 1914, drew attention to blues from around the world. The son of a minister, Handy faced stiff opposition from his parents because of his interest in "worldly" music, and they, in fact, made him return his first guitar— which they labeled "a sinful thing"—to the store and use the money to buy a dictionary instead. Over time, Handy published his original music, which, in addition to the blues, included arrangements for spirituals and hymns. Among his collected works is the *Book of Negro Spirituals* published in 1938.

The actual nature of the religious expression in blues is an issue of debate. Striking an uncompromising tone, Garon (1975: 135–36) asserts:

> *The blues critique, emphatically materialist, is directed not against heavenly abstractions (God, Jesus, the Holy Ghost) but against the hypocrisy and pretension of the pompous self-appointed "representatives" of God on earth. Nothing would be more false, however, than to suggest that the blues is therefore not opposed to religion as such, but only to this or that organized religious institution, or (still worse) to suggest that the blues itself is some sort of "secular religion." . . . On the contrary, [the blues] is wholeheartedly on the side of Evil. The "Devil's music" [as the blues has been called by some fundamentalists] is the denunciation of everything religious stands for and the glorification of everything religious condemns.*

In response, Jon Michael Spencer (1989: 17) claims that at the heart and soul of blues is a very real religious crisis that needs resolution, or, at least, constant exploration: "in light of the existence of an omnipotent, omniscient, and omnibenevolent God . . . why [is] the suffering of the oppressed . . . not arrested or at least lessened." The blues approach to this question, which is fashioned from the biblical narratives learned by bluespeople during their upbringing in the African American church, lies, Spencer argues, in two biblically derived themes: "work of the devil" and "reaping what you sow."

The Devil is a frequent visitor to blues music, but with somewhat different purpose depending on the song. Indeed, in our assessment, at least three different "devils" can be found in the blues repertoire. The first, seen in

Lonnie Johnson's "Devil's Got the Blues" (cited in Spencer 1989: 34), is the dark object of the blues lament, the personal sadness, depression, and agony borne of hard times and harsh lives. Johnson identifies the blues explicitly with the devil, indicates that it comes upon a person without warning, and leaves a mind full of hell.

The second devil is the church (and its hypocritical ministers and holier than thou congregants), as reflected in the following blues song (cited in Spencer 1989: 43):

> Some of the Good Lord's children, some of them ain't no good
> Some of them are the devil and won't help you if they could.
> Some of the Good Lord's children kneel upon their knees and pray
> You serve the devil in the night and serve the Lord in the day.

Finally, as expressed in J. T. "Funny Papa" Smith's "Fool's Blues," blues-people liken their own behavior (usually involving insobriety, fornication, hurt-fulness and other acts condemned by the church) to the work of the devil:

> Some people tell me God takes care of old folks and fools
> But since I been born he must have changed the rules. . . .
> You know this must be the devil I'm serving, I know it can't be Jesus Christ
> Because I asked him to save me and look like he's trying to take my life.

In sum, the devil is a multivocal symbol that is used in blues music to represent painful experience and unrighteousness on the one hand and both religious people, and bluespeople, on the other. One interpretation of the complex devil symbol in this musical genre is that it signifies human frailty and suffering, traits that unite all humans, friend and foe, alike. In this, blues music reflects what William Jones (1979: 59) has referred to as "humanocentric theism, a key feature of African American theology generally."

Despite this broadside for shared humanity, blues music also reflects an internalization of the religious critique of the blues lifestyle, as evidenced in the "reap what you sow" theme commonly found in blues songs. For example, in "Going Down Slow" (cited in Spencer 1989: 26) Jimmy Odgen describes his sinful ways and the consequences he must endure:

> I have had my fun if I don't get well no more
> My health is failing me and I'm going down slow.
> Please write my mother, tell the shape I'm in
> Tell her to pray for me, forgive me my sin.
> Tell her don't send no doctor, doctor can't do no good
> It's all my fault, didn't do things I should.

Similarly, in "Cypress Grove Blues," Skip James (cited in Spencer 1989: 27) proclaims:

> *Well the old people told me baby but I never did know*
> *The Good Book declares we got to reap just what we sow.*

Argues Spencer (1989: 20), the "reap what you sow" theme affirms that upon final analysis blues is a "secular religion," sung by victim/pilgrims who "seek wholeness that arrives through imperfection." While they defiantly reject organized religion, bluespeople, he (1989: 20) argues, do not reject God; rather, they disregard "the God they perceive as indifferent to them, and fashion a new God." This new God, which has been called "the blues god" by Neal (1978), offers plain-spoken, undisguised honesty and emotional salvation through music. In the words of Will Weldon's "Red Hot Blues":

> *All you got to do is just swing and sway*
> *When you're feeling low just dance these blues away*
> *(cited in Spencer 1989: 20).*

Adds Rev. Rubin Lacy (quoted in Evans 1967: 13), a bluesman turned preacher: "I used to be a famous blues singer and I told more truth in my blues than the average person tells in his church songs. . . . The blues is just more truer than a whole lot of the church songs that people sing."

One of the most significant progeny of blues was jazz, a product of the melting of blues notes with ragtime syncopation (and the use of a piano) as well as with the brass-band musical texture and instrumentation. In its early years, in the 1920s, jazz directly appropriated the plaintive voice of blues, but expressed it instrumentally by using scooping, sliding, and other effects. In addition to the impact it had on other forms of church music, in time, jazz was invited directly into the church in the African American community. A key figure in this movement was Duke Ellington. Composer of the "Soda Fountain Rag" at age 14, Ellington went on to be a leader in the big band movement and in 1932 wrote a song called "It Don't Mean a Thing If It Ain't Got That Swing," which provided a label for the big band swing jazz style. Thirty years later, he helped to launch the religious jazz movement in response to a growing popular desire for modernizing church music. Ellington produced three Concerts of Sacred Music, beginning with the Grace Cathedral Church of San Francisco in 1965, followed by the second at the Cathedral of St. John the Divine in New York in 1966, and concluding with a concert at Westminster Abbey in London in 1973. Interweaving gospel and spiritual songs using full orchestra, choir and solo performers with instrumental numbers, these concerts, while performed at predominantly white churches, affirmed the deep religiosity at the heart of jazz music.

Another child of the blues was R & B, which emerged after the Second World War by combining blues forms, harmonic patterns, call and response formatting, and earthy lyrics for stage performance by a small ensemble that tended to include electric guitar, drums, and possibly string bass and piano. In the late 1950s, the formation and rapid expansion of Motown Records in Detroit marked the ascension of this musical genre. The dynamic religious tension of R & B is exemplified, in constrasting ways, in the lives and work of Marvin Gaye and Al Green (both of whom also recorded more socially conscious songs that would be classified as Soul). The son of a Pentecostal minister, Gaye was "imbued with a deep spiritual sensitivity anchored in a Christ- centered ethic of love" (West 1988: 174). This upbringing shaped his music, which "remained in the Afro-American Christian tradition" (West 1988: 175), as reflected in his song "Wholly Holy," which refers to the Second Coming of Christ and the need for living in fidelity with the teachings of the Bible.

Despite his faith, Gaye brought to his music a raw, gritty realism, which, ultimately, can be seen as a conflicted syncretism of "his fundamental love for God and his preoccupation with the worldly opiates of drugs and sex" (Jones 1989: 69). His hit song "Sexual Healing," which effectively combines vastly discordant elements, including a blues focus on "feelin' down" (in this case, perhaps influenced by the experience of drug withdrawal), a Christian belief in spiritual healing, the unblushing impudence and bravado that characterizes urban street culture, and oceanic symbolism, well expresses the material world/spiritual world contradictions of Gaye's life.

In tragic irony, Gaye's life ended at his own father's hands, affirming thereby the troublesome religious question at the heart of African American secular music, which is well expressed by the restless title of another of Gaye's hit songs: "What's Going On?"

Like Gaye, Al Green came from a religious family, one in which singing gospel music was a daily occurrence. Green began his public singing career as a tenor in his father's gospel group, but, like many African American singers, he felt an insatiable attraction to popular music. Forming his own Soul group, he hit the Midwest "chitlin' circuit" of small clubs, dining spots, and dives. Then in 1971, a song he recorded, "I'm So Tired of Being Alone," unexpectedly sold over a million copies and Green was catapulted to the top of the Pop Music charts. Over the next five years, he had a total of 15 different songs reach the Top 10 singles list, confirming Green vast popularity. Yet, material success proved unsatisfying for Green and at the height of his popularity he abandoned his secular musical career for the church. Green explained his dramatic change as the result of "coming into the knowledge of Christ and being transformed in mind and spirit on a particular morning" (quoted in

Broughton 1984: 125). The occurrence of a "born again" experience in a secular African American singer is, in fact, not a rare event. As Pollard (1989b: 88) suggests, "countless other popular singers have acknowledged their indebtedness to and returned to the basic givens of African American religiosity." What is noteworthy, in fact, and as Green's case re-affirms, is that despite the frequent exchange of critical barbs between the African American church and the worldly secular musical scene, the boundaries dividing the two remain highly permeable. Ultimately, within the context of a racist society, commonalities of experience and the realization of a shared oppressor, as well as recognition of a collective history and an appreciation of the powerful rhythms at the core of African American identity, provide the building blocks for the erection of bridges across even the most hostile waters.

Beyond Christianity: The Role of African American Music in Messianic Nationalism

Without doubt, the heart of African American religious music lies within the bosom of Christianity rather than in any of the other religious traditions found in the African American community. However, religious music does appear among some of the non-Christian messianic nationalist groups, especially those with a Hebraic orientation, while elements of Elijah Muhammad's Islamic ideology have had their influence on African American secular music.

Among the Hebraic groups, the black Hebrew Israelites have evolved a brand of Gospel music that reflects their ideology and historic circumstance. Following the messianic nationalist emigrationist urge, as reported in Chapter 4, members of this group migrated to Liberia in 1967 and to Israel in 1969. In Israel, where they have now lived for over three decades (Singer 1999), the black Hebrews have developed a communal lifestyle that has sustained the group through various hardships. Music plays a central role in the social life of the black Hebrews, during both religious and recreational activities. The group supports numerous bands and choirs, among both the adults and children, and they exhibit a range of styles including R & B, rock and roll, and gospel music. Music is performed at most black Hebrew gatherings, including Sabbath and holiday services, dances, and cultural programs, and the group's premier band, the Soul Messengers, regularly plays outside of the black Hebrew community as Israeli weddings, Bar Mitzvahs, and parties, and to entertain the troops at Israeli military bases.

The black Hebrew understanding of the traditional African American religious songs that they sing is seen in the changing relationship between performers and their music as a result of their conversion to and socialization in the black Hebrew messianic nationalist ideology. An important gospel singer during the early years following the black Hebrew migration to Israel was known as Sefia Bat Israel. Born in a small North Carolina town in 1938, she began her involvement with religious music early in life. According to Sefia (quoted in Singer 1985: 134): "I've been singing around the house all my life, mostly spiritual songs. They had a meaning to me. I always sang from when I was a little girl . . . . Most churches, they always have a choir and if you want to get in the choir you just tell them you want to sing. . . . I'd sing in the choir and in the little groups. . . . I'd sing with different churches. I'd be traveling with singing groups from the church." Growing from these experiences and the affirmation she received, Sefia developed a desire to become a professional singer. But her efforts were thwarted by the clash between her church-oriented values and the personal sacrifices and moral compromises demanded of her in the music industry: "You got to know somebody and you got to do crooked things, dirty things, things against your morals." She reacted to this dilemma by joining the black Hebrew Israelites, and at once affirmed her rejection of the immorality she experienced in American society and was embraced as a highlighted performer in a community that supported her religious values.

Sefia believes that traditional music has been a source of strength and sustenance for the oppressed African American masses, but her attitude toward and her understanding of her music has changed since joining the black Hebrews. She observed (quoted in Singer 1985: 135):

Most of our songs is basically the same as our forefathers sang them. The same soul. It is spiritual. That is the only thing that kept us living. . . . You see, gospel songs is taken mostly from the Bible and different things that's happened to you and then you just put it together. . . . But it's different [among the black Hebrews] because now I know what the songs mean! There is a meaning to the songs. Like the song "River Jordan." We've been singing that since we was in slavery, but we didn't know what it meant. . . . The songs was talking about Black people, but we didn't know that. . . . You know, I read the Bible all my life, but I didn't know that it was us that was in there. . . . When I was a child . . . we sing the song "I want to Walk the Streets of Jerusalem" . . . to me it was always just a dream. Jerusalem was so far off, so mythical. Back then when I was singing it, I was meaning after I die. So the song seemed sad to me. . . . But here I am now, I'm alive and I've walked the streets of Jerusalem. . . . So when I sing about Jerusalem, it is with an entirely different spirit.

As Sefia's remarks suggest, the black Hebrews believe they have discovered and are fulfilling the *true meaning* of gospel songs. This meaning, they assert, was known to the slaves but was lost to subsequent generations of

African Americans raised in the White-dominated Christian church. In short, in the black Hebrew view, the imagery of black religious music is not an adaptation of Biblical characters, places, and events to fit the North American experience of African Americans. Rather, it is a direct and accurate expression of their treasured memories of a distant homeland in Israel. In this sense, the black Hebrews understand African American traditional religious music not as symbolic or metaphoric communication about the blight of enslavement in America, but as an accurate historic reading of the history of their ancestors in Israel.

Growing out of their "discovery" of the "true meaning" of spiritual music, the black Hebrews have had to modify some traditional songs to conform to group ideology and their contemporary situation. As one singer in the group explained (quoted in Singer 1985: 137): "A song might have something in it that is not uplifting, so we might have to change that. Like the song 'Tedious Journey' has the line: 'I'm sometimes right, I'm sometimes wrong.' But we said, 'No, we're never wrong,' so we could not use that." Another adjustment concerns references to Jesus. Instead of praising Jesus, black Hebrew songs praise their messianic leader Ben Ami. In this way, the black Hebrews are able to adapt traditional African American songs to support and confirm their current messianic nationalist belief system and the social hierarchy and structure of social relations within their community.

Parallels to this use of music can be found in secular African American songs as well. Charise Cheney (1999: 1), for example, has analyzed the ways contemporary rap music has been "inspired and informed by the teachings of Elijah Muhammad" and has, in turn, promoted messianic nationalist beliefs among listeners. As Pinn (2000: 263) notes: "An accurate history of rap music must understand it in connection to the larger development of hip hop culture. Hip hop first emerged as a cultural and creative response to the matrix of industrial decline, social isolation, and political decay endemic to the Bronx in New York City. . . . In essence, hip hop culture and its musical voice—rap—signal both cultural resistance and . . . a continued dialogue with religious ideals and institutions."

Historically, while rap has gone through a number of developmental phases since its appearance, and several distinct varieties are identifiable (e.g., Dyson 1989, Schensul et al. 2000), its staccato beat, rapid rhyme schemes, hip language, "in your face realism," anger, and bravado are notable characteristics of the genre which derives its rhetorical style from traditional African American religious chanting and from the "Jamaican tradition of toasting or speaking over extended beats" (Pinn 2000: 263). Found in the lyrics of some rappers, those Cheney (1999) has termed "rap nationalists," is a political message, and it is here that the influence of Islamic nationalism is most evident. Cheney (1999: 1), for example, points to the music of the West Coast rapper Paris, a self-proclaimed Muslim and member of Louis Farrakhan's Nation of Islam, and to his 1989 song "Brutal." Paris explicitly says the song is meant to teach Farrakhan's "science," and "Brutal" underscores the relationship between the Nation of Islam and Paris's confrontational assertion of African American identity. Moreover, she (1999: 1) asserts that "From East Coast groups such as Public Enemy, KRS-One and Boogie Down Productions, and X-Clan to West Coast artists like Ice Cube, Paris and Kam, rap nationalists intentionally conjure a tradition of model, and militant, black manhood. They idolize he words and works of political personalities—men like Marcus Garvey, Malcolm X and Minister Louis Farrakhan. . . ." Similarly, Cheney (1999) points out Sara Webb's song, "Dial 7," which refers to whites as the devil, to African Americans as the "sun, moon and star," and to the fact that "It's Nation Time," all symbolic constructs borrowed from Elijah Muhammad's teachings. Additionally, she notes that number of well-known rap artists have joined one or another of the several Islamic groupings in the African American community.

Rap music also contains an intense indictment of Christianity. In "The Real Holy Place," for example, KRS-One claims that the reason that African Americans embrace Christianity is because their former masters had. These lines express a belief, found elsewhere in the music of rap nationalists, that African American adoption of Christianity exemplifies submission to white dominance. Like African American messianic nationalists generally, KRS-One challenges the conventional Euro-centric interpretation of the Bible. In the song "The Eye Opener," KRS-One emphatically asserts that Christ, Abraham, Noah, King Solomon, and John the Baptist were black.

Reflecting the influence of Elijah Muhammad, "The Eye Opener" goes on to declare that the "whitewashing" of biblical figures "Is the work of Satan, egotistical, and negatively psychological." Rap anger in response to white oppression, as well as a militant view of God, is captured in Ice Cube's "When I Get to Heaven." The song identifies a contemporary white cop with church bombings in Alabama, claims that God wouldn't mind the killing of such oppressors, and indicates that Noah had to build his Ark to escape such domination.

Additionally, some rap music is openly critical of the African American Christian church. For example, in their song "Fishin' 4 Religion," Arrested Development criticizes the passivity in the contemporary church, asserting that mainstream African American churches are praising a God that encourages only self-pity, not self-defense. Moreover, the lyrics of this song openly question the relevance of preaching in effecting change.

Praise and Protest

Rap music, in short, contains within its wide embrace a message of religious nationalism that Cheney (1999: 2) has labeled "hip hop gnosticism." The message, like that of messianic nationalism generally, is the psychological, and perhaps the physical, liberation of the African American masses. Ironically, also within its domain, rap music includes a celebration of various behaviors, such as drug use, that most African American churches view as a modern enslaver of the African American people. Like African American religious music, in other words, rap is both burdened and enlivened by contradictions, contradictions that, as with its religious counterpart, find expression and at least temporary resolution in the participatory act of a musical presentation and performance.

It has been argued throughout this chapter that music is at the core of the religious experience, as well as at the core of church practice, in the African American community, and, further, that this relationship, although constantly evolving, dates to the earliest days of the African American presence in the New World. The roots of African American religious music lay both in Africa and in the often harsh yet clearly at times (i.e., within the context of the church and other religious activities) spiritually uplifting experience of life in America. The origin of a distinctly African American religious musical tradition dates to slavery and to the synergistic blending of African musical styles and approaches with biblical images and aspirations. Since its emergence, religious music in the African American community, like its secular counterpart, has been on the move, with new genres appearing continually along the way; while older styles have undergone changes, they often do not disappear but retain their vibrancy and meaningfulness to African American audiences. Just as the secular music of the slaves was a source of religious music for them, so, too, religious music in the African American community has been a forge for the production of new types of secular music. The latter, in turn, has had its influence, directly and indirectly, on religious music, affirming thereby a key element of African American religious music: it is a musical tradition that is in constant motion, responding continually to enduring and new challenges in a changing world. In this process, religious music has reflected a double nature. It is a vehicle for mediating the gap between spiritual aspiration and worldly experience, on the one hand, and between accommodation to the powers that be and protest against inequality and oppression, on the other. Moreover, religious music is a force of unity of feeling and sentiment within the African American community, and hence a cultural domain of tremendous power for uplifting the individual spirit, pulling together the masses, and helping to create a distinctly African American experience.

Conclusion

$\mathcal{A}$frican American religion exhibits a wide variety of forms and trajectories. To a greater or lesser degree, all African American religious movements and groups form complex syncretic ensembles. As Bourguignon (1970: 190) points out, "Afro-American religions, in their many forms, represent a mixing and merging of African and European traditions and often the formation of a new growth of belief and ritual, quite different from the sources from which they started." In fact, as with groups that identify themselves as Islamic, or black Spiritual churches in New Orleans that incorporate Native American elements (e.g., the use of Black Hawk), the source of elements found in particular African American religions extends beyond Africa or Europe. The Spiritual movement, the leading representative of the thaumaturgical sect, probably constitutes the most explicit manifestation of syncretism in the African American religious experience in the United States. Rich patterns of syncretic blending also exist, however, within messianic-nationalist sects as well as conversionist sects and mainstream congregations belonging to the black Baptist and Methodist denominations and even in African American congregations affiliated with the white-controlled denominations. Given the importance of syncretism in the religions under consideration, it must be better understood if we are to better comprehend the nature and variety of religious forms created by African Americans.

Attempting to understand religious syncretism necessitates addressing two questions: why does syncretism occur, and how does it operate? The starting point for answering the first question lies in recognizing that religion is a cultural system, a socially patterned set of meanings and behaviors. Culture enables survival through coordinated activity, structured and meaningful social interaction, and a minimization of cognitive dissonance or metaphysical anxiety. Like other aspects of cultural systems, religious beliefs and rituals, whatever their spiritual or other dimensions, are directly and immediately about "this world," the world of the living, the world of social relationships, physical hardships, and human feelings. Religion endlessly is constructed and reconstructed in response to human experience, emotion, cognition, and need in the context of changing social realities.

In this light, the emergence of new religious forms reflects the appearance of new needs, dilemmas, social arrangements, and social contexts. Under these circumstances, brought into being through cultural contact, migration, natural disaster, epidemics, changing employment patterns, environmental degradation, imperial conquest, changing demographics, and similar social restructuring, old beliefs and ritual patterns are drained of credibility. As Wallace asserts, "[R]eligious belief and practice always originate in situations of social and cultural stress and are, in fact, an effort on the part of the stress-laden to construct systems of dogma, myth, and ritual which are internally coherent as well as true descriptions of a world system and which thus will serve as guides to efficient action" (Wallace 1966: 30).

In this sense, new religions can be said to address "consequent dilemmas," palatable threats to human emotional satisfaction and cognitive coherence wrought by the development of social and cultural stress. New religions tend to be like sponges in absorbing new elements and practices because they emerge in the contest of creative restructuring. Old cultural configurations have proven unworkable and unsatisfying, the intensity of experiential distress is heightened, and the resulting hunger for coherence produces an openness to new cultural formulations. In this creative environment, cultural input from diverse sources is possible at a level unknown during periods of relative stability.

The source of new ideas and practices, however, is not unlimited. It is conditioned always by the social milieu in which new religions arise. Emergent religions draw readily from available conceptual and ritual fields, picking and choosing compatible elements. For example, the black Hebrew Israelites, described in chapter 4, emerged in the United States during a period of notably increased awareness and concern about pollution and environmental damage, renewed interest in vegetarianism and communalism, leftist critique of American social structure and imperialism, and African American concern with black culture and nationalism. Aspects of all of these contemporary yet socially unrelated ideas that were, so to speak, "in the air" during the formation of the Black Hebrew Israelite Nation found their way into the belief system of the group. The compatibility of these assorted elements lies in their ability to be woven by the black Hebrews into the larger tapestry of messianic-nationalist alienation from the social and cultural practices dominant in American society.

Conclusion

Religious syncretism, in short, reflects the capacity, indeed the regularity, of cultural innovation. Although culture has commonly been defined as the traditional aspects of a people's or group's way of life, as Wagner (1981) stresses, invention *is* culture. In his view, "We live our lives by ordering and rationalizing, and re-creating our conventional controls in creative swoops of compulsive invention. . . . Because we 'use up' our symbols in the course of using them, we must forge new symbolic articulations if we are to retain the orientations that make meaning itself possible" (Wagner 1981: 59). Thus the invention of culture is a constant process, marked by periodic episodes of concentrated innovation.

This general pattern is of note because, of all cultural spheres, religion presents itself as the least affected by innovation—the most traditional, most fundamental, and most stable component of culture. But this emphasis on tradition is, in a sense, a ruse. Religion is not so much traditional as it is "traditionalizing" in its nature. Religion in Hobsbawm's (1963: 1) terms is "invented tradition," that is, "a set of practices, normally governed by overtly or tacitly accepted rules and of ritual or symbolic nature, which seek to inculcate certain values and norms of behavior by repetition, which automatically implies continuity with the past." Tellingly, Hobsbawm adds,

> *[W]e should expect [the invention of tradition] to occur more frequently when a rapid transformation of society weakens or destroys the social patterns for which "old" traditions had been designated, producing new ones to which they were not applicable, or when such old traditions and their institutional carriers and promulgators no longer prove sufficiently adaptable and flexible or are otherwise eliminated; in short, when there are sufficiently large and rapid changes on the demand or the supply side.* (Hobsbawm 1963: 4)

Barnett (1953) emphasized several components of cultural invention that are relevant to the process of religious syncretism, including *screening*, *recasting*, and *integration*. In the course of social life, especially during periods of heightened tension, novel cultural elements are evaluated for their ability to carry culturally salient meanings and to provide some advantage for the innovator. Unless new ideas or behavior can be: (1) seen as bearing cultural significance (that is, reenforcing a broader cultural message) and (2) meeting particular group needs as solutions to consequent dilemmas, they are not likely to be adopted.

Elements that pass this screening test rarely move "as is" into the receptor cultural system. Rather they are modified by the recipients so as to "make sense" in the new system, that is, so as to blend with the preexisting or emergent cultural configuration. For example, as argued in chapter 6, Spiritual beliefs were not adopted directly from white Spiritualism. Instead, African

Americans borrowed and reworked various components of Spiritualism in light of their own needs, experiences, and culture. Consequently, there is now a considerable difference between white Spiritualism and African American Spiritual practice but a close resemblance between the ritual structure of Spiritual churches and patterns found in black Holiness and Pentecostal groups. Similarly, as seen in chapter 1, the Jesus of black Christianity was constructed as a living and knowable personage, a process congruent with the African American emphasis on multistranded, face-to-face personal relationships. Jesus could only be appealing to African Americans if he were recast as a familiar, personable, and immanent God. By contrast, although Spiritual churches adopted many conventional Catholic rituals, such as genuflection in front of the altar, elements like the Catholic mass were ignored because their formal structuring of behavior did not fit with the preexisting African American emphasis on ecstatic experience.

Finally, integration of new cultural elements requires interdigitation with aspects of the existing culture. Areas of similarity between old and new culture are identified and linked, thereby masking the knots that might otherwise reveal the constructed character of culture. This joining occurs at the symbolic level. For example, the adoption of a vegetarian diet among the black Hebrew Israelites was not presented in terms of the American health food movement but rather with reference to a Biblical passage (Genesis 1: 29), even though it is clear from Leviticus that the Biblical Hebrews were not vegetarians. Without linking the new dietary practice with a preexisting component of group ideology (acceptance of the Bible as a literal account of divine will), acceptance of the new element might be resisted. With the establishment of symbolic linkage between old and new cultural components, novel elements can be experienced as both familiar and meaningful by group members.

In sum, it is likely that the criteria for the adoption of new elements into a syncretic configuration includes

(1) a felt need for consequent dilemma solutions (CDSs),

(2) exposure in some fashion to a potentially adoptable novel element,

(3) perceived utility of the element as a culturally meaningful CDS,

(4) limited incongruity between the new element and the existing cultural system,

(5) arenas of similarity or overlap between new and old elements that allow the symbolic interweaving of the two, and

(6) ability to "age" and modify the new element so that it does not seem entirely novel or uncomfortably foreign.

Over time, this process of cultural invention can lead to the creative integration of ideas and behaviors of quite diverse origin without the appearance of a product composed of disparate threads and patches. As Benedict (1934: 47) pointed out long ago, "The [cultural] whole . . . is not merely the sum of its parts, but the result of a unique arrangement and interrelation of parts that has brought about a new entity."

Prophetic figures like Elijah Muhammad, Father Divine, Reverend Ike, or many others mentioned in preceding chapters play an especially important role in the invention and borrowing process. These religious innovators have

(1)   the ability to identify pressing dilemmas and felt distress;

(2)   the imagination, creativity, and experience to fashion or borrow elements;

(3)   the authority to introduce novel conceptions and activities; and

(4)   the sensitivity to gauge the reaction of group members to the new patterns and to retool them accordingly.

Wallace (1956) has referred to the process of religious creativity on the part of prophetic figures as "mazeway resynthesis." As used by Wallace, "mazeway" refers to the individual's conception of reality and mental construction of self, other, and the world. During periods of heightened social and cultural stress, when the built-in stress-reducing strategies have been exhausted without a satisfactory improvement in life experience, one or more individuals may undergo a sudden restructuring or resynthesis of mazeway information. This new picture of reality can then be presented to the group as a more satisfying cultural alternative. Obeyesekere, who uses the term "subjectification" to label this phenomenon, notes that it involves

> *a process whereby cultural patterns and symbol systems are put back into the melting pot of consciousness and refashioned to create a culturally tolerated set of images . . . [called] subjective imagery. Subjective imagery is often protoculture, or culture in the making. While all forms of subjective imagery are innovative, not all of them end up as culture, for the latter depends on the acceptance of the subjective imagery by the group and its legitimation in terms of the larger culture.* (Obeyesekere 1981: 169–70)

Beyond the presence of a prophet figure and the birth of a new religious system, several other factors promote syncretism in particular groups, including

(1)   a decentralized organizational structure,

(2)   institutionalization of individual communication with the spirit realm,

(3) culture contact and acculturation,

(4) internal threats to group existence, and

(5) competition among parallel groups in a local context.

Decentralization allows the local adoption of new elements by eliminating an important barrier to religious innovation: the existence of a centralized leadership authorized to establish and regulate official beliefs and practices. With the kind of decentralization seen in many African American religious groups, elements adopted in one locale are free to diffuse among sister groups as local need arises, such as appears to have occurred with Catholic practices and symbols in Spiritual churches. Maintenance of a belief in direct spiritual communication after the initial prophetic period provides a vehicle for the socially legitimated introduction of new elements in response to changing conditions. Acceptance of lay contact with the spiritual realm makes every believer a potential innovator. In the absence of centralized regulation of individual religious experience, innovation can be both rapid and a potential challenge to group integrity.

Culture contact provides the arena for exposure to new religious elements as well as the common context for disruption of preexistent religious patterning. Religious innovation is especially frequent under conditions of social domination in which "religions of oppressed" (Lanterari 1963) emerge as revitalization movements among subordinated peoples. Internal threat to group structure, such as the appearance of a challenge to the existing leadership of a church, promotes the adoption of the new patterns designed either to distract members or to eliminate the challenge outright. For example, among the black Hebrew Israelites, the introduction of a more rigid group structure and set of governmental offices was a response to an internal threat to Ben Ami's leadership.

Finally, the existence of similar groups in the same setting produces pressure to innovate as a means of marking social distinctiveness. Thus, breakaway groups from the Nation of Islam have tended to stress areas of difference with the Nation so as to promote their uniqueness. Under Elijah Muhammad, this often meant an adoption of more orthodox Muslim belief, while under Wallace Muhammad—who stressed orthodox Islam—it has meant the reverse. Often, conflicts of this sort are waged over the authenticity or divine sanction of group beliefs and practices.

In light of this discussion, the high level of syncretism found among African Americans can be explained by:

(1) long-term social subordination producing various periods of enhanced social and cultural stress;

(2) exposure to a wide range of cultural experiences, religious and social patterns, and local environments;

(3) ready acceptance of direct spiritual communication and structural decentralization rooted in Baptist influence; and

(4) openness to prophetic figures based on early and enduring identification with the Old Testament.

These factors underlie the syncretic urge in African American religion and have contributed enormously to the rich diversity outlined in this book.

Beyond syncretism, as we have argued, the multifarious forms of African American religion juxtapose elements of protest and accommodation to racism and social stratification in various ways. Along with others, we see this dynamic tension as the heart and soul of African American religion. It expresses the deep desire for full acceptance as women and men and as equal beneficiaries of the material, political, and social rewards generated by the toil of the multicultural working classes of American society. However, this desire has never been expressed as accommodation on any terms. Rather, African American religion has retained and developed a firm emphasis on resisting, at both the individual and collective levels, the ugliest expressions of racist ideology and behavior. At times, and under particular circumstances, the resistive strain in African American religions has crystallized into a bold rejection of all forms of accommodation; however, this orientation, as we have seen, can quickly develop, with changing circumstances, into a more accommodative stance.

Within each of the four African American sectarian types discussed in this volume, the juxtaposition of protest and accommodation changes over time in response to both external and internal forces. Historically, messianic-nationalist sects have emphasized the protest dimension, at least rhetorically, while conversionist and thaumaturgical sects have been more likely to select accommodationist responses. Yet protest against the larger society in these latter groups is not absolute but rather is couched in such beliefs as their rejection of the myth that hard work itself guarantees material prosperity. Like American religion in general, African American religion has become one of privatization or individuation. In this regard, black religious groups serve as hegemonic agencies. Nevertheless, the strong sense of group identity expressed in black evangelical churches of the rural South was kept alive in the economic enterprises of various messianic-nationalist sects and the religious inspiration that leaders of the mainstream congregations in the black community provided for the civil rights movement. While not overlooking the transcendental features of African American religion, we are most struck by the "this-worldly" and instrumental quality of this multidimensional religious tradition. The "pragmatic spirituality" (Wilmore 1983a) of African American religion, as we have argued, has its roots in the African American response to the harsh, yet always changing, realities of life in America. These changing conditions, in their varying regional, historical, and class expressions, help us to understand the rich diversity that constitutes African American religion. The constants of racial and class oppression, conversely, have contributed to uniformities that unify the African American religious tradition.

Despite the presence of hegemonic elements, Wilmore views African American religion as intrinsically radical because of its preoccupation with liberation from oppression:

> *Black religion has always concerned itself with the fascination of an incorrigibly religious people with the mystery of God, but it has been equally concerned with the freedom of man—freedom from the religious, economic, social and political domination which white men have exercised over Black men since the beginning of the African slave trade. It is this radical thrust of Black people for human liberation expressed in theological terms and religious traditions which is the defining characteristic of Black Christianity and of Black religion in the United States.* (Wilmore 1983a: ix–x)

Since the civil rights era, the emancipatory potential of African American religion has been manifested in various developments that transcend sectarian or denominational affiliations. In the wake of the Black Power movement, progressive black clergy created the National Conference of Black Christians (NCBC) and black caucuses in the National Council of Churches and many white-controlled denominations. The NCBC supported the Black Manifesto presented by James Forman, the former international affairs director of the Student Nonviolent Coordinating Committee, at the Riverside Church in New York City on April 26, 1969. In addition to a half-billion dollars as reparation for racial injustices to be paid through the Black Economic Development Conference (a subsidiary of the interracial Interreligious Foundation for Community Organization) by the white-controlled mainstream Protestant and Catholic churches and Jewish synagogues, the manifesto espoused solidarity with African nations and denounced capitalism and imperialism. Forman stated, "We are dedicated to building a socialist society inside the United States . . . led by Black people . . . concerned about the total humanity of the world" (quoted in Wilmore 1983a: 204). For the most part, the leaders of the NCBC belonged to white-controlled denominations rather than the historically black denominations. Furthermore, although NCBC continued to convene into the 1980s, like the larger Black Power movement, by 1972 it had lost much of its momentum (Sawyer 1988: 155). In contrast to NCBC, the various other black ecumenical organizations—such as the Congress of National Black Churches, Partners in Ecumenism, the National Black Pastors Conference, and the National Black Evangelical Association—that emerged during the 1960s and 1970 "empower only insofar as the limits of reform permit" (Sawyer 1988: 159–160).

The term "Black Theology" emerged in the late 1960s among various radical African American clerics involved in the civil rights and Black Power movements. James Cone (1938–) quickly emerged as the leading proponent of Black Theology (Chapman 1996: 100–119; Cone 1999; Hopkins 1999). He had been reared in the AME church in rural Arkansas. After entering Garrett Theological Seminary in Evanston, Illinois, he encountered opposition from his white professors when he attempted to analyze racism as a theological problem (Chapman 1996: 110). While teaching at Philander Smith College, a black institution affiliated with the United Methodist church in Little Rock, he increasingly felt dissonance in his efforts to relate systematic theology to the African American experience. During a teaching stint at Adrian College in Michigan, he found inspiration in the NCBC statement on Black Power in July 1966 and went on to publish *Black Theology and Black Power* (1968) and *A Black Theology of Liberation* (1970). Following a short teaching stint at the Interdenominational Theological Center in Atlanta, Cone accepted a position at Union Theological Seminary in New York City that continues his base of operations. Other major figures in the Black Theology movement have included Albert Cleage, J. Deotis Roberts, Major Jones, Gayraud Wilmore, Joseph Washington Jr., and C. Eric Lincoln. Despite their differences, African American theologians agree that Jesus Christ acted as a liberator against human oppression and that consequently the black struggle against racism is inherently Christian. Most black theologians remain uncritical of the class structure and foreign policy of American society, but some proponents of Black Theology argue that the adoption of a Marxist critique is essential to the development of an African American revolutionary Christianity. Cornel West (1982: 121), for example, argues that black theologians need to "discover and discern what aspects of Afro-American culture and religion can contribute to a counter-hegemonic culture in American society." During the early 1970s, some black theologians, such as James H. Cone, came in contact with other forms of liberation theology in Africa, Latin America, and Asia, and began to seriously consider socialism as an alternative to capitalism. Despite its roots in the struggle of African Americans for racial justice, Black Theology remains by and large an academic pursuit of black scholars teaching in white-controlled seminaries and universities. In their survey of 1,531 urban clergy affiliated with the seven historic black denominations (including COGIC),

Lincoln and Mamiya (1990: 169) found that 34.9 percent answered in the affirmative and 65.1 answered in the negative to the question, "Have you been influenced by any of the authors and thinkers of black liberation theology?"

> *The liberation motif . . . showed wide variation among the denominations, especially between the A.M.E. (66.2 percent positive) and COGIC (17.9 percent positive). . . . [B]lack liberation theology is still a pioneer area not yet subscribed to by many black urban clergy. In short, the denominations with higher educational levels among their clergy such as the A.M.E., along with the intellectual elite of the Black Church (theologians, scholars, and divinity school students), are the major proponents of this view. The fact that the Pentecostal ministers of the Church of God in Christ, which has the largest sector of lower-class members among the seven denominations, have been scarcely influenced by the theological perspective suggests some of the class limitations of this movement.*
(Lincoln and Mamiya 1990: 179–80)

Nevertheless, Cone (1984: 114), who was strongly influenced in his thinking by Cornel West—a former colleague at Union Theological Seminary—exhorts his colleagues to work with the "many genuinely committed black pastors and lay persons who transcend the limitations of their denominational identity by becoming identified with Christ through a commitment to the poor," despite his fear that the major black denominations are not yet ready for a radical critique of American capitalism.

Female black theologians have developed a Womanist Theology that challenges the sexism not only in the larger society but also in the black churches and Black Theology (Grant 1993). Dolores Williams, a professor at Union Theological Seminary, draws parallels between the experiences of Hagar in the Old Testament and those of African American woman and has expressed solidarity with Palestinian and Native American women who identify with the Caanites rather than the Israelites (Chapman 1996: 157). She has also examined how the work of African American writers, such as Alice Walker, Margaret Walker, and Zora Neale Hurston, exemplify the experiences of women in black churches. Other Womanist theologians include Jacquelyn Grant, a professor at the Interdenominational Theological Center in Atlanta, and Cheryl Townsend Gilkes, who is both a Baptist minister and a sociology professor at Colby College in Maine.

The Rainbow Coalition under the leadership of Rev. Jesse Jackson constitutes the most recent counterhegemonic manifestation of African American religion. Jackson, a minister affiliated with the Progressive National Baptist Convention, USA, became one of Martin Luther King, Jr.'s chief lieutenants during the Southern Christian Leadership Conference's desegregation campaign in Chicago in 1966. He was placed in charge of the SCLC's Operation Breadbasket, which he utilized for his own political base after making a break with the SCLC several years following King's assassination in 1968. Operation PUSH emerged out of Operation Breadbasket in 1971 as a national religious reform-oriented movement. Jackson's PUSH congregation in Chicago reportedly has over five thousand members and meets on Saturdays, apparently permitting its members to attend services at other churches on Sundays (Washington 1985: 98). Although Jackson initially espoused a variant of black capitalism during the 1970s, the federal government's minimal efforts to promote black entrepreneurial activities prompted him to adopt consumer rights tactics.

On November 3, 1983, Jackson announced his decision to run as a Democratic candidate for the U.S. presidency. While Jackson's agenda has been largely reformist in a social democratic vein rather than a revolutionary one, many progressives, not only among African Americans but also among whites, Hispanics, Asian Americans, and Native Americans have rallied around his agenda under the organizational umbrella of the Rainbow Coalition. Jackson inspired millions of African American voters in the 1984 and 1988 presidential campaigns. By utilizing the sermonic folk discourse of black political revivalism, as James Washington (1985: 105) observes, "Jesse has steered progressive black Christians into new, uncharted waters." As in the civil rights movement, black churches have served as the support base of the Rainbow Coalition. Jackson's political rallies are well attended by black ministers and are conducted in a style modeled after black religious services. People affiliated with local branches of Operation PUSH, the majority of whom were ministers, served as the coordinators of about half of the viable state operations of the Rainbow Coalition in the 1984 presidential campaign (Collins 1986: 132).

The vast majority of the black churches responded to the campaign's appeal, and competed for a place on Jackson's itinerary. Well over 90 percent of the black clergy endorsed the campaign within two months of Jackson's announcement speech. They were helped by the endorsement of such nationally known figures as T. J. Jemison, president of the National Baptist Convention, with a membership estimated at 6.5 million. It was no doubt Jemison's endorsement and active participation in the campaign that turned out the large Louisiana vote for Jackson, enabling him to win in that state. Jemison's predecessor had not supported Martin Luther King nor endorsed the civil rights movement, but Jemison belonged to a new generation. He was the beneficiary of changes that had occurred in black theological thinking between the black power movement and the 1980s—changes that were equipping the black church to reassert the role it

had played at an earlier time in its history as the nurturer not only of the spir-
itual hopes of the black masses, but of their political hopes as well. The support
of the pentecostal churches—especially the Church of God in Christ (the fastest-
growing black denomination)—also marked this period as different from the
civil rights era. Collins 1986: 134)

During the 1988 presidential campaign, Jackson considerably broadened his appeal outside the African American community. The Rainbow Coalition had regarded itself as the voice of the powerless—the poor, small farmers, women, gays and lesbians, and ethnic minorities (Reynolds 1997). As a result of his coalition-building abilities, Jackson received 18.2 percent of all the votes in the 1984 Democratic primaries and 19.3 percent of all the votes in the 1988 Democratic primaries. Jackson called for a defense budget freeze, full employment, self-determination for Palestinians, and political empowerment of African Americans and other working-class people. He also criticized the exploitative practices of American-based multinational corporations. Despite his popular appeal and that fact that Jackson trailed only Michael Dukakis in delegate votes at the 1988 Democratic convention, the Democratic presidential nominee chose Lloyd Bentsen, a conservative U.S. senator from Texas, as his running mate.

In 1989, Jackson moved the headquarters of the Rainbow Coalition from Chicago to Washington, D.C. Since that time, he has focused on addressing inner-city crime, violence, drug abuse, teenage pregnancy, voter registration, health care reform, affirmative action policies, the anti-apartheid movement, and the struggle for democracy in Haiti. Since its highpoint in 1988, the Rainbow Coalition has undergone decline due to serious organizational and financial problems. Some critics have argued that Jackson has functioned in a top-down mode that has shut the membership of the Coalition out of decision-making and that has made it difficult to distinguish him from the larger organization. As Marable (1992: 177) so astutely observes, "Jackson's frenetic, larger-than-life personality and his chaotic organizational style, consisting of a coterie of loyalists who rarely disagree with the boss, works against genuinely democratic decisionmaking." In reality, this is a pattern not unique to Jackson but rather one inherent in the role of the black minister and perhaps that of ministers, priests, and other religious leaders around the world.

Efforts by various proponents of Black Theology to incorporate radical political theory and organizations such as the National Conference of black Christians and Jackson's Rainbow Coalition illustrate the continued potential of black religion to serve as a liberating force. While African American religion undoubtedly will continue to manifest both hegemonic and counter-

Conclusion

hegemonic qualities, its more progressive expressions can be expected to be part of any vanguard for radical social-structural change emanating from the black community. As Marable (1983: 214) asserts, "it is entirely possible that the most decisive ally of the black working class in its struggle for democratic socialism, at least among the black elite, will be the Black church." Ironically, because of its dialectical character, African American sectors within religion can be expected to stand as stalwart opponents of this struggle.

References

Abrums, Mary
  1999. "'Jesus Will Fix It After Awhile': Meanings and Health." *Social Science and Medicine* 50:89–105.

African Methodist Episcopal Church
  1984. "Toward a More Effective A.M.E. Church." Final Report to the General Board and the 1984 General Conference.

Ahlo, Olli
  1980. *The Religion of the Slaves: A Study of the Religious Tradition and Behavior of Plantation Slaves in the United States, 1830–1865*. Helsinki: Academia Scientiarum Fennica.

Ahlstorm, Sydney E.
  1975. *A Religious History of the American People* 2. Garden City, N.Y.: Image.

Albuquerque, de, Klaus
  1981. "Folk Medicine in the South Carolina Sea Islands." *Review of Afro-American Issues and Culture* 2, no. 2: 44–74.

Alland, Alexander, Jr.
  1962. "'Possession' in a Revivalistic Negro Church." *Journal for the Scientific Study of Religion* 1: 204–13.
  1981. *To Be Human: An Introduction to Cultural Anthropology*. New York: John Wiley.

Allen, Jr., Ernest
  1998. "Identity and Destiny: The Formative Views of the Moorish Science Temple and the Nation of Islam." In *Muslims on the Americanization Path?*, ed. Yvonne Yazbeck Haddad and John L. Esposito, 163–214. New York: Oxford Univ. Press.

Allen, Robert
  1969. *Black Awakening in Captialist America: An Analytic History*. New York: Doubleday.

Allen, William, Charles Ware, and Lucy Garrison

    1967. *Slave Songs of the United States.* New York: A Simpson. [Originally published in 1867.]

Alston, Jon P., Letitia T. Alston, and Emory Warrick

    1971. "Black Catholics: Social and Cultural Characteristics." *Journal of Black Culture* 2: 245–55.

Alston, John P., Charles W. Peck, and C. Ray Wingrove

    1972. "Religiosity and Black Militancy: A Reappraisal." *Journal for the Scientific Study of Religion* 11: 252–61.

Anderson, John Q.

    1960. "The New Orleans Voodoo Ritual Dance and Its Twentieth-Century Survivals." *Southern Folklore Quarterly* 24:135–143.

Anderson, Robert Mapes

    1979. *Vision of the Disinherited: The Making of American Pentecostalism.* New York: Oxford Univ. Press.

Aptheker, Herbert

    1943. *American Negro Slave Revolts.* New York: International.

Austin, Diane J.

    1981. "Born Again . . . and Again and Again: Communitas and Social Change among Jamaican Pentecostalists." *Journal of Anthropological Research* 37: 226–46.

Babbie, Earl

    1966. "A Third Civilization: An Examination of Sokagakkai." *Review of Religious Research* 7, no. 2: 101–20.

Baer, Hans A.

    1981. "Prophets and Advisors in Black Spiritual Churches: Therapy, Palliative, or Opiate?" *Culture, Medicine, and Psychiatry* 5: 145–70.

    1982. "Toward a Typology of Black Folk Healers." *Phylon* 43: 327–43.

    1984. *The Black Spiritual Movement: A Religious Response to Racism.* Knoxville: Univ. of Tennessee Press.

    1985. "Black Spiritual Israelites in a Small Southern City: Elements of Protest and Accommodation in Belief and Oratory." *Southern Quarterly* 23, no. 3: 103–24.

    1988. "The Metropolitan Spiritual Churches of Christ: The Socio-Religious Evolution of the Largest of the Black Spiritual Associations." *Review of Religious Research* 30: 162–76.

Baer, Hans A., and Merrill Singer

    1981. "Toward a Typology of Black Sectarianism as a Response to Racial Stratification." *Anthropological Quarterly* 54: 1–14.

References

Baldwin, Lewis V.

1980. "'Invisible Strands' in African Methodism: A History of the African Union Methodist Protestant and Union African Methodist Episcopal Churches, 1805–1980." Ph.D. diss. Northwestern Univ.

1983. *"Invisible" Strands in African Methodism*. Scarecrow. Metuchen, N.J.: Scarecrow Press.

Barnett, Homer

1953. *Innovation: Inventing Traditions*. New York: McGraw-Hill.

1964. "The Acceptance and Rejection of Change." In *Explorations in Social Change*, ed. G. Zollschan and W. Hirsch, 345–67. Boston: Houghton Mifflin.

Baron, Harold M.

1971. "The Demand for Black Labor: Historical Notes on the Political Economy of Racism." *Radical America* 5, no. 2: 1–46.

1976. "The Demand for Black Labor." In *Racial Conflict, Discrimination and Power: Historical and Contemporary Studies*, ed. William Barclay, Krishna Kumar, and Ruth P. Simms, 190–202. New York: AMS.

Bass, Ruth

1981. "Mojo." In *Mother Wit from the Laughing Barrel: Readings in the Interpretation of Afro-American Folklore*, ed. Alan Dundes, 380–87. New York: Garland.

Bauman, Zygmunt

1976. *Socialism: The Active Utopia*. London: George Allen & Unwin.

Beck, Carolyn Stickney

1989. *Our Own Vine and Fig Tree: The Persistence of the Mother Bethel Family*. New York: AMS.

Benedict, Ruth

1934. *Patterns of Culture*. Boston: Houghton Mifflin.

Bennett, Robert

1974. "Black Episcopalians: A History from the Colonial Period to the Present." *History Magazine of the Protestant Episcopal Church* 43: 231–36.

Bentley, William H.

1975. "Bible Believers in the Black Community." In *The Evangelicals*, ed. David F. Wills and John D. Woodbridge, 108–21. Nashville, Tenn.: Abingdon.

Benyon, E. D.

1938. "The Voodoo Cult among Negro Migrants in Detroit." *American Journal of Sociology* 43: 894–907.

Berger, Graenum

1978. *Black Jews in America*. New York: Commission on Synagogue Relations.

Berry, Jason

1995. *The Spirit of Black Hawk: A Mystery of Africans and Indians.*
Jackson: Univ. Press of Mississippi.

Bethel, Elizabeth Rauh

1981. *Promiseland: A Century of Life in a Negro Community.* Philadelphia:
Temple Univ. Press.

Billingsley, Andrew

1999. *Mighty Like a River: The Black Church and Social Reform.* New
York: Oxford Univ. Press.

Blackwell, James Edward

1949. "A Comparative Study of Five Negro 'Store-front' Churches in
Cleveland." M.A. thesis. Western Reserve Univ.

Bobock, Robert

1986. *Hegemony.* London: Tavistock.

Boggs, Beverly

1977. "Some Aspects of Worship in a Holiness Church." *New York
Folklore* 3: 29–44.

Boggs, Carl

1984. *The Two Revolutions: Gramsci and the Dilemmas of Western Marxism.*
Boston: South End.

Boles, John B.

1983. *Black Southerners, 1619–1896.* Lexington: Univ. Press of
Kentucky.

Bonacich, Edna

1976. "Advanced Capitalism and Black/White Race Relations in the
United States: A Split Labor Market Interpretation." *American
Sociological Review* 41: 34–51.

Bontempts, Arna, and Jack Conroy

1966. *Any Place But Here.* New York: Hill and Wang.

Bourguignon, Erika

1970. "Afro-American Religions: Traditions and Transformation." In
Black America, ed. John Szwed, 190–201. New York: Basic Books.

Brandon, George Edward

1983. "The Dead Sell Memories: An Anthropological Study of Santeria
in New York City." Ph.D. diss. Rutgers Univ.

Broom, Jack

1966. "The Negro Church and the Movement for Equality." M.A.
thesis. Univ. of California at Berkeley.

Brotz, Howard

1970. *The Black Jews of Harlem: Negro Nationalism and the Dilemma of
Negro Leadership.* New York: Schocken.

Broughton, Viv

1984. *Black Gospel: An Illustrated History of the Gospel Sound.* Poole, Eng.: Blandford Press.

Brown, Audrey Lawson

1994. "Afro-Baptist Women's Church and Family Roles: Transmitting Afrocentric Cultural Values." *Anthropological Quarterly* 67: 173–86.

Brown David H.

1990. "Conjure/Doctors: An Explanation of a Black Discourse in America, Antebellum to 1940." *Folklore Forum* 23, nos. 1/2: 3–46.

Brown, Hugh S.

1965. "Voodooism in Northwest Louisiana." *Folklore Miscellany* 2: 74–86.

Brown, Karen McCarthy

1991. *Mama Lola: A Vodou Priestess in Brooklyn.* Berkeley: Univ. of California Press.

Brown, Lawrence

1978. *Garveyism as a Religious Movement: The Institutionalization of a Black Civil Religion.* Metuchen, N.J.: Scarecrow.

1990. "Black Indigenous Drug Users: Prospects for Intervening in the Transmission of Human Immunodeficiency Virus Infection." In *AIDS and Intravenous Drug Use: Future Directions for Community-Based Prevention Research*, eds. Carl Leukefeld, Robert Battjes, and Z. Amsel, 53–67. Rockville, Md.: National Institute on Drug Abuse.

Burkett, Randall K.

1994. "The Baptist Church in the Years of Crisis." In *African-American Christianity: Essays in History*, ed. Paul E. Johnson, 134–58. Berkeley: Univ. of California Press.

Burnham, Kenneth E.

1979. *God Comes to America: Father Divine and the Peace Mission Movement.* Boston: Lambeth.

Burnim, Mellonee

1980. "The Black Gospel Music Tradition: Symbol of Ethnicity." Ph.D. diss., Indiana Univ.

Burns, Thomas A., and J. Stephen Smith

1978. "The Symbolism of Becoming in the Sunday Service of an Urban Black Holiness Church." *Anthropological Quarterly* 51: 185–204.

Campbell, Augustus P.

1951. "Amity Baptist Church: The Natural History of a Church as an Urban Institution." M.A. thesis. Atlanta Univ.

Campbell, James T.

1995. *Songs of Zion: The African Methodist Episcopal Church in the United States and South Africa*. New York: Oxford Univ. Press.

Cantril, Hadley, and Muzafer Sherif

1938. "The Kingdom of Father Divine." *Journal of Abnormal and Social Psychology* 33: 147–67.

Carlisle, Rodney

1975. *The Roots of Black Nationalism*. Port Washington, N.Y.: Kennikat.

Carter, Sandy

1999. "Move On Up: The Politics of Gospel." *Z Magazine* 12, no. 9: 53–56.

Cartwright, John Henderson

1993. "Martin Luther King, Jr., and Modern African American Religion. In *Encyclopedia of African American Religions*, ed. Larry G. Murphy, J. Gordon Melton, and Gary L. Ward, xxxvii–xlvi. New York: Garland Publishing Company.

Chapman, Mark L.

1996. *Christianity on Trial: African-American Religious Thought Before and After Black Power*. Maryknoll, N.Y.: Orbis Books.

Cheney, Charise

1999. "Representin' God: Rap, Religion and the Politics of Culture." *The North Star* 3, no. 1: 1–10.

Chicago Tribune

1977. "It Was a 'Holy War' in Washington, Complete with POWs." 11 Mar., 17.

Childs, John Brown

1980. *The Black Political Minister*. Boston: G. K. Hall.

Clark, Elmer T.

1965. *The Small Sects in America*. Nashville, Tenn.: Abingdon.

Clark, William A.

1937. "Sanctification in Negro Religion." *Social Forces* 15: 544–51.

Cleage, Albert, Jr.

1972. *Black Christian Nationalism: New Directions for the Black Church*. New York: Sheed and Ward.

Clegg III, Claude Andrew

1997. *An Original Man: The Life and Times of Elijah Muhammad*. New York: St. Martin's Press.

Cobbins, Otho B.

1966. *History of Church of Christ (Holiness) U.S.A., 1895–1965*. New York: Vantage.

Cohen, Cathy
  1999. *The Boundaries of Blackness: AIDS and the Breakdown of Black Politics*. Chicago: Univ. of Chicago Press.
Cohen, Daniel
  1972. *Voodoo, Devils, and the Invisible World*. New York: Dodd, Mead.
Cohn, Norman
  1970. *The Pursuit of the Millennium*. New York: Oxford Univ. Press.
Collins, Daniel F.
  1971. "Black Conversion to Catholicism." *Journal for the Scientific Study of Religion* 10: 208–18.
Collins, Sheila D.
  1986. *The Rainbow Coalition: The Jackson Campaign and the Future of U.S. Politics*. New York: Monthly Review.
Cone, James H.
  1972. *The Spirituals and the Blues*. San Francisco: Harper and Row.
  1984. *For My People: Black Theology and the Black Church*. Maryknoll, N.Y.: Orbis.
  1999. *Risks of Faith: The Emergence of a Black Theology of Liberation, 1968–1998*. Boston: Beacon Press.
Conkin, Paul L.
  1997. *American Originals: Homemade Varieties of Christianity*. Chapel Hill: Univ. of North Carolina Press.
Cooley, Gilbert E.
  1977. "Root Doctors and Psychics in the Region." *Indiana Folklore* 10: 191–200.
Cooper, Lee R.
  1974. "'Publish or perish': Negro Jehovah's Witness Adaptation in the Ghetto: " In *Religious Movements in Contemporary America*, ed. Irvin I. Zaretsky and Mark P. Leone, 700–721. Princeton, N.J.: Princeton Univ. Press.
Cornelius, Janet Duitsman
  1999. *Slave Missions and the Black Church in the Antebellum South*. Columbia: Univ. of South Carolina Press.
Cowing, Cedric B.
  1971. *The Great Awakening and the American Revolution: Colonial Thought in the 18th Century*. Chicago: Rand McNally.
Cox, Oliver C.
  1976. *Race Relations: Elements and Dynamics*. Detroit: Wayne State Univ. Press.

Crowder, Ralph L.

    1980. "Black Physicians and the African Contribution to Medicine." *Western Journal of Black Studies* 4, no. 1: 2–17.

Csordas, Thomas J.

    1987. "Health and the Holy in African and Afro-American Spirit Possession." *Social Science and Medicine* 24: 1–11.

Cummings, Judith

    1985. "Diverse Crowd Hears Farrakhan in Los Angeles." *New York Times*, 16 Sept., 10.

Dalton, Harlon

    1989. "AIDS in Blackface." *Daedalus* 118, no. 3: 205–27.

Davis, Alison

    1940. "The Negro Church and Associations in the Lower South." Research Memorandum, Carnegie-Myrdal Study. New York.

Davis, Alison, Burleigh Gardner, and Mary Gardner

    1965. *Deep South: A Social Anthropological Study of Caste and Class.* Chicago: Univ. of Chicago Press.

Davis, Arnor

    1970. *Churches in Shaw: A Report on a Survey of the Churches in Shaw Urban Renewal Area of Washington, D.C.* Washington, D.C.: Redevelopment Land Agency of the District of Columbia.

Davis, Cyprian

    1990. *The History of Black Catholics in the United States.* New York: Crossroad.

    1991. "History of the African American Catholic Church in the United States: Evangelization and Indigenization." In *Directory of African American Religious Bodies*, ed. Wardnell J. Payne, 257–63. Washington, D.C.: Howard Univ. Press.

Davis, Rod

    1987. "Children of Yoruba." *Southern Magazine* 1, no. 5: 35–41, 85–85.

DeCaro, Louis A.

    1996. *On the Side of My People: A Religious Life of Malcolm X.* New York: New York Univ. Press.

    1998. *Malcolm and the Cross: The Nation of Islam, Malcolm X, and Christianity.* New York: New York Univ. Press.

Deveney, John Patrick

    1997. *Paschal Beverly Randolph: A Nineteenth-Century Black American Spiritualist, Rosicrucian, and Sex Magician.* Albany: State Univ. of New York Press.

Djedje, Jacqueline
    1983. "An Expression of Black Identity: The Use of Gospel Music in a Los Angeles Catholic Church." *Western Journal of Black Studies* 7, no. 3: 148–60.
Dobrin, Arthur
    1975. "A History of the New Jews in America." Manuscript. Schomburg Public Library. New York City.
Dollard, John
    1937. *Caste and Class in a Southern Town*. Garden City, N.Y.: Anchor.
Dougherty, Molly C.
    1978. *Becoming a Woman in Rural Black Culture*. New York: Holt, Winston, and Rinehart.
    1982. "Southern Midwifery and Organized Health Care: Systems in Conflict." *Medical Anthropology* 6:114–26.
Douglass, Frederick
    1962. *Life and Times of Frederick Douglass*. New York: Collier Books Edition. [Originally published in 1892.]
Doyle, Dorothy, and Bill Doyle
    1985. "Farrakhan Challenges Support for Israel." *Guardian*, 16 Oct., 19.
Drake, St. Clair, and Horace R. Cayton
    1945. *Black Metropolis*. New York: Harcourt, Brace.
Du Bois, W. E. B.
    1903a *The Souls of Black Folk: Essays and Sketches*. Chicago: A. C. McClurg.
    1903b *The Negro Church in America*. Atlanta: Atlanta Univ. Press.
    1967. *The Philadelphia Negro: A Social Study*. New York: Schocken.
    1972. *The Souls of Black Folk*. New York: Fawcett.
Dupree, Sherry Sherrod
    1997. *African-American Holiness-Pentecostal Movement: An Annotated Bibliography*. New York: Garland Publishing Company.
Dvorak, Katherine L.
    1991. *An African-American Exodus: The Segregation of the Southern Churches*. Brooklyn: Carlson Publishing.
Dyson, Michael Eric
    1989. "Rap, Race and Reality: Run-D.M.C." In *The Theology of American Popular Music*, a special issue of *Black Sacred Music: A Journal of Theomusicology*, ed. Jon Michael Spencer, 142–45.
    1995. *Making Malcolm: The Myth and Meaning of Malcolm X*. New York: Oxford Univ. Press.

Ebony
    1960. "Spiritual Churches: Sect Marks 35 Years of Growth." Oct., 69–70, 75.

Eddy, G. Norman
    1952. "Store-Front Religion." In *Cities and Churches: Readings on the Urban Church*, ed. Robert Lee, 177–94. Philadelphia: Westminister.

Embry, Jessie L.
    1994. Black Saints in a White Church: Contemporary African American Mormons. Salt Lake City: Signature Books.

Embry, Jessie L. and Cardell K. Jacobson
    1995. "Middle-Class African-American Mormons." *Research in Race and Ethnic Relations* 8: 223–40.

Essien-Udom, E. U.
    1962. Black Nationalism: A Search for Identity in America. Chicago: Univ. of Chicago Press.

Evanzz, Karl
    1999. The Messenger: The Rise and Fall of Elijah Muhammad. New York: Pantheon.

Fairclough, Adam
    1993. "The Southern Christian Leadership Conference and the Second Reconstruction, 1957–1973." In *Modern American Protestantism and Its World—Native Americans and Black Protestantism*, ed. Marty E. Marty, 188–205. Chicago: Univ. of Chicago Press.

Fauset, Arthur H.
    1971. Black Gods of the Metropolis. Philadelphia: Univ. of Pennsylvania Press.

Feagin, Joe R.
    1968. "Black Catholics in the United States: An Exploratory Analysis." *Sociological Analysis* 29: 186–92.

Felton, Ralph Almon
    1952. Go Down Moses: A Study of 21 Successful Negro Rural Pastors. Madison, N.J.: Dept. of the Rural Church, Drew Theological Seminary.

Femia, Joseph
    1975. "Hegemony and Consciousness in the Thought of Antonio Gramsci." *Political Studies* 23: 29–48.
    1981. Gramsci's Political Thought: Hegemony, Consciousness and the Revolutionary Process. Oxford: Clarendon.

Ferris, William R., Jr.
    1972. "The Rose Hill Service." *Mississippi Folklore Register* 6: 37–55.

References

First Church of Deliverance
1979. *50th Anniversary, 1929–1979*. Chicago.
Fisher, Miles Mark
1922. "The Olivet Baptist Church." M.A. thesis. Univ. of Chicago.
Fishman, Robert Gray
1979. "Spiritualism in Western New York: A Study in Ritual Healing." *Medical Anthropology* 3: 1–22.
Fitts, Leroy
1985. *A History of Black Baptists*. Nashville, Tenn.: Broadman.
Flora, Cornelia Butler
1976. *Pentecostalism in Columbia: Baptism by Fire and Spirit*. Cranbury, N.J.: Associated Univ. Presses.
Foner, Philip S.
1974. *Organized Labor and the Black Worker, 1619–1973*. New York: Praeger.
1976. *Blacks in the Revolution*. Westport, Conn.: Greenwood.
Foner, Philip S., ed.
1983. *Black Socialist Preacher: The Teachings of Reverend George Washington Woodbey and His Disciple, Reverend G. W. Slater, Jr.* San Francisco:
Synthesis.
Fontenot, Wonda L.
1994. *Secret Doctors: Ethnomedicine of African Americans*. Westport, Conn.: Bergin & Garvey.
Fowler, Robert Booth
1985. *Religion and Politics in America*. Metuchen, N.J.: Scarecrow.
Fox, Kenneth
1995. "Anthropology's Hoodoo Museum." *Culture, Medicine and Psychiatry*
19: 409–21.
Franklin, Robert M.
1997. *Another Day's Journey: Black Churches Confronting the American Crisis*. Minneapolis: Fortress Press.
Frazier, E. Franklin
1949. *The Negro in the U.S.* New York: Macmillan.
Frazier, E. Franklin
1963. *The Negro Church in America*. New York: Schocken.
1974. *The Negro Church in America*. New York: Schocken.
Friedman, Samuel et al.
1987. "The AIDS Epidemic among Blacks and Hispanics." *Milbank Quarterly* 65: 455–89.

Fullinwider, S. P.

    1969. *The Mind and Mood of Black America: 20th Century Thought.* Homewood, Ill.: Dorsey.

Gallagher, Jim

    1977. "Wallace D. Muhammed: Reviver of Muslim Faith." *Chicago Tribune*, 21 Feb., 1 and 4.

Gallatin, Martin V.

    1979. "Rev. Ike's Ministry: A Sociological Investigation of Religious Innovation." Ph.D. diss. New York Univ.

Gardell, Mattias

    1996. *In the Name of Elijah Muhammad: Louis Farrakhan and the Nation of Islam.* Durham, N.C.: Duke Univ. Press.

Garon, Paul

    1975. *Blues and the Poetic Spirit.* New York: Da Capo.

Garrison, Vivian

    1979. "The Inner-City Support Systems Project (ICSS): An Experiment in Medical Anthropology and Community Psychiatry, A Preliminary Report." College of Medicine and Dentistry of New Jersey.

Gelman, Martin

    1965. "Adet Beyt Moshe—The Colored House of Moses." Ph.D. diss. Univ. of Pennsylvania.

Gennep, Arnold van

    1960. *The Rites of Passage.* London: Routledge and Kegan Paul.

Genovese, Eugene D.

    1970. "The Legacy of Slavery and the Roots of Black Nationalism." In *For a New America*, ed. James Weinstein, 394–420. New York: Random House.

    1974. *Roll, Jordon, Roll: The World the Slaves Made.* New York: Vintage.

    1979. *From Rebellion to Revolution: Afro-American Slave Revolts in the Making of the Modern World.* Baton Rouge: Louisiana State Univ. Press.

George, Carol V.

    1973. *Segregated Sabbaths: Richard Allen and the Emergence of the Independent Black Churches, 1790–1840.* New York: Oxford Univ. Press.

Gerlach, Luther

    1970. "Corporate Groups and Movement Networks in Urban America." *Anthropological Quarterly* 43: 123–45.

Gerlach, Luther P., and Virginia H. Hine

    1970. *People, Power, and Change: Movements of Social Transformation.* Indianapolis: Bobbs-Merrill.

Geschwender, James A.

    1978. *Racial Stratification in America*. Dubuque, Iowa: Wm. C. Brown.

Gilkes, Cheryl Townsend

    1990. "To Sit and Die or to Stand and Live: Understanding AIDS and Responding Redemptively as Christians to Its Victims." *Journal of Religious Thought* 47, no. 2: 56–63.

    1994. "The Politics of Silence." In *African-American Christianity: Essays in History*, ed. Paul E. Johnson, 80–110. Berkeley: Univ. of California Press.

Goldsmith, Peter D.

    1985. "Healing and Denominationalism on the Georgia Coast." *Southern Quarterly* 23, no. 3: 83–102.

    1989. *When I Rise Cryin' Holy: African-American Denominationalism on the Georgia Coast*. New York: AMS.

Good, Bryon J., and Mary-Jo DelVecchio Good

    1980. "Spiritualist Realities: A Symbolic Analysis of Spiritualist Clinical Practice." Paper presented at 79th Annual Meeting of American Anthropological Association. Washington, D.C.

Gosnell, Harold

    1937. *Machine Politics: Chicago Model*. Chicago: Univ. of Chicago Press.

Gottlieb, Pete

    1987. *Making Their Way: Southern Blacks' Migration to Pittsburgh, 1916–1930*. Urbana: Univ. of Illinois Press.

Gramsci, Antonio

    1971. *Selections from the Prison Notebooks*. New York: International Publishers.

Green, Charles

    1999. "The Black Church in the Struggle for Housing and Neighborhood Revitalization." *Research in Social Policy* 5: 81–96.

Green, Vera

    1970. "The Confrontation of Diversity within the Black Community." *Human Organization* 29: 267–72.

Gregg, Robert

    1992. *Sparks from the Anvil of Oppression: Philadelphia's African Methodists and Southern Migrants, 1890–1940*. Philadelphia: Temple Univ. Press.

Greisman, H. C., and Sharon S. Mayers

    1977. "The Social Construction of Unreality: The Real American Dilemma." *Dialectical Anthropology* 2: 57–67.

Gregg, Howard D.

    1980. *The A.M.E. Church and the Current Negro Revolt*. Nashville, Tenn.: AME Sunday School Union.

Hall, Arthur L., and Peter G. Bourne

1973. "Indigenous Therapists in a Southern Black Urban Community." *Archives of General Psychiatry* 28: 137–42.

Hamilton, Charles V.

1972. *The Black Preacher in America*. New York: William Morrow.

Hamilton, C. Horace, and John M. Ellison

1930. *The Negro Church in Rural Virginia*. Blacksburg: Virginia Agricultural Station, Virginia Polytechnic Institute.

Hannerz, Ulf

1969. *Soulside: Inquiries into Ghetto Culture and Community*. New York: Columbia Univ. Press.

Harding, Vincent

1969. "Resistance and Religion among Ante-Bellum Negroes." In *The Making of Black America*, ed. August Meier and Elliot Rudwick. New York: Atheneum.

Harper, Nile et al.

2000. *Urban Churches, Vital Signs: Beyond Charity Toward Justice*. Grand Rapids, Mich.: William B. Eerdmans Publishing.

Harrell, David Edwin

1971. *White Sects and Black Men*. Nashville, Tenn.: Vanderbilt Univ. Press.

1975. *All Things Are Possible: The Healing and Charismatic Revivals in Modern America*. Bloomington: Indiana Univ. Press.

Harris, Michael

1992. *The Rise of Gospel Blues: The Music of Thomas Andrew Dorsey in the Urban Church*. New York: Oxford Univ. Press.

Harris, Sara

1971. *Father Divine*. New York: Collier.

Harrison, Ira E.

1971. "The Storefront Church as a Revitalization Movement." In *The Black Church in America*, ed. Nelsen, Yokley, and Nelsen, 240–50.

1992. "Community AIDS Education: Trials and Tribulations in Raising Consciousness for Prevention." In *African Americans in the South: Issues of Race, Class, and Gender*, ed. Hans Baer and Yvonne Jones, 79–93.

Harvey, Paul

1997. *Redeeming the South: Religious Cultures and Racial Identities among Southern Baptists, 1865–1925*. Chapel Hill: Univ. of North Carolina Press.

Haskins, James

1978. Voodoo and Hoodoo: Their Tradition and Craft as Related by Actual *Practitioners*. New York: Stein and Day.

Haywood, Carol Lois

> 1983. "The Authority and Empowerment of Women among Spiritualist Groups." *Journal for the Scientific Study of Religion* 22: 157–66.

Herron, Leonora and Alice M. Bacon

> 1979. "Conjuring & Conjure-Doctors." In *Mother Wit from the Laughing Barrel*, ed. Alan Dundes, 359–79. New York: Garland Publishing Company.

Herskovits, Melville J.

> 1941. *The Myth of the Negro Past*. New York: Harper.

Higginbotham, Evelyn Brooks

> 1993. *Righteous Discontent: The Women's Movement in the Black Baptist Church, 1880–1920*. Cambridge, Mass.: Harvard Univ. Press.

Hill, Carole E.

> 1973. "Black Healing Practices in the Rural South." *Journal of Popular Culture* 6: 848–53.

Hill, Richard Child

> 1980. "Race, Class and the State: The Metropolitan Enclave System in the United States." *Insurgent Sociologist* 10: 45–59.

Hindess, Barry, and Paul Q. Hirst

> 1975. *Pre-Capitalist Modes of Production*. London: Routledge and Kegan Paul.

Hobsbawm, Eric

> 1963. "Introduction: Inventing Traditions." In *The Invention of Tradition*, ed. Eric Hobsbawm and Terance Ranger, 1–14. Cambridge: Cambridge Univ. Press.

Hollenweger, W. J.

> 1974. *Pentecost Between Black and White*. Belfast, Northern Ireland: Christian Journals Ltd.

Holt, J. B.

> 1940. "Holiness Religion: Cultural Shock and Social Reorganization." *American Sociological Review* 5: 740–47.

Hopkins, Dwight N.

> 1999. *Introducing Black Theology of Liberation*. Maryknoll, N.Y.: Orbis Books.

Hoshor, John

> 1936. *God in a Rolls-Royce*. New York: Hillman-Carl.

Howard, John

> 1972. "The Making of a Black Muslim." In *Down to Earth Sociology*, ed. James Henslin, 244–55. New York: Free Press.

Hraba, Joseph

> 1979. *American Ethnicity*. Itasca, Ill.: F. E. Peacock.

Huberman, Leo
1960. *We, the People: The Drama of America*. New York: Monthly Review.

Hudson, Winthorp
1973. *Religion in America: An Historical Account of the Development of American Religious Life*. New York: Scribner's.

Hunt, Larry L., and Janet G. Hunt
1975. "A Religious Factor in Secular Achievement Among Blacks: The Case of Conversion." *Social Forces* 53: 595–605.
1976. "Black Catholicism and the Spirit of Weber." *Sociological Quarterly* 17: 369–77.
1977. "Religious Affiliation and Militancy Among Urban Blacks: Some Catholic/Protestant Comparisons." *Social Science Quarterly* 57: 821–34.

Hurston, Zora Neale
1931. "Hoodoo in America." *Journal of American Folklore* 44: 317–417.
1981. *The Sanctified Church*. Berkeley, Calif.: Turtle Island.

Jackson, George Pullen
1943. *White and Negro Spirituals*. New York: Dover.

Jackson, J. H.
1980. *A History of Christian Activism: The History of the National Baptist Convention, U.S.A., Inc.* Nashville, Tenn.: Townsend.

Jackson, Jacquelyne Johnson
1981. "Urban Black Americans." In *Ethnicity and Medical Care*, ed. 37–219. Cambridge, Mass.: Harvard Univ. Press.

Jacobs, Claude F.
1989. "Spirit Guides and Possession in the New Orleans Black Spiritual Churches." *Journal of American Folklore* 102: 45–67.
1990. "Healing and Prophecy in Black Spiritual Churches: A Need for Reexamination." *Medical Anthropology* 12: 349–70.

Jacobs, Claude F., and Andrew J. Kaslow
1990. *The Spiritual Churches of New Orleans: Origins, Beliefs, and Rituals of an African-American Religion*. Knoxville: Univ. of Tennessee Press.

Jacquet, Constant H., Jr.
1989. *Yearbook of American and Canadian Churches 1989*. Nashville, Tenn.: Abingdon.

Jemison, Cecil Charlene Gentry
1972. "A Study of Two Black Baptist Churches in a Metropolitan Area." M.A. thesis. Fisk Univ.

Johnson, Benton
1961. "Do Holiness Sects Socialize in Dominant Values?" *Social Forces* 39: 309–16.

Johnson, Charles S.

    1934. *Shadow of the Plantation*. Chicago: Univ. of Chicago Press.

    1941. *Growing Up in the Black Belt: Negro Youth in the Rural South*. Washington, D.C.: American Council on Education.

Johnson, Charles S., and A. P. Watson

    1969. *God Struck Me Dead: Religious Conversion Experiences and Autobiographies of Ex-Slaves*. Philadelphia: Pilgrim.

Johnson, Guy

    1930. *Folk Cultures on St. Helena Island, South Carolina*. Chapel Hill: Univ. of North Carolina Press.

Johnstone, Ronald L.

    1971. "Negro Preachers Take Sides." In *The Black Church in America*, ed. Nelsen, Yokley, and Nelsen, 275–86.

Jones, Charles Edwin

    1987. *Black Holiness: A Guide to the Study of Black Participation in Wesleyan Perfectionist and Glossolalic Pentecostal Movements*. Metuchen, N.J.: Scarecrow.

Jones, Diane, and William H. Matthews, eds.

    1977. *The Black Church: A Community Resource*. Washington, D.C.: Institute for Urban Affairs and Research, Howard Univ.

Jones, Lawrence Neale

    1975. "The Black Pentecostals." In *The Charismatic Movement*, ed. Michael P. Hamilton, 145–58. Grand Rapids, Mich.: Eerdmans.

Jones, LeRoi (Amiri Baraka)

    1968. *Black Music*. New York: William Morrow.

Jones, Oliver

    1983. "The Black Muslim Movement and the American Constitutional System." *Journal of Black Studies* 13: 414–37.

Jones, Orea

    1989. "The Theology of 'Sexual Healing': Marvin Gaye." In *The Theology of American Popular Music*, a special issue of *Black Sacred Music: A Journal of Theomusicology* (Fall) 3, no. 2, ed. Jon Michael Spencer, pp. 68–74.

Jones, Raymond

    1939. "A Comparative Study of Religious Cult Behavior among Negroes with Special Reference to Emotional Conditioning Factors." *Howard University Studies in the Social Sciences* 2, no. 2.

Jones, William

    1973. *Is God a White Racist? A Preamble to Black Theology*. Garden City, N.Y.: Anchor/Doubleday.

Jordan, Lewis G.

    1930. *Negro Baptist History (1750–1930)*. Nashville, Tenn.: Sunday School Publishing Board.

Jordan, Wilbert C.

    1979. "The Roots and Practice of Voodoo Medicine in America." *Urban Health* (Dec.): 38–41.

Jordan, Winthrop D.

    1968. *White Over Black*. Chapel Hill: Univ. of North Carolina Press.

Jules-Rosette, Bennetta

    1980. "Creative Spirituality from Africa to America: Across Cultural Influences in Contemporary Religious Forms." *Western Journal of Black Studies* 4: 273–85.

Kanter, Rosabeth Moss

    1972. *Commitment and Community: Communes and Utopias in Sociological Perspective*. Cambridge, Mass.: Harvard Univ. Press.

Kaplan, Howard M.

    1969. "The Black Muslims and the Negro American's Quest for Communion." *British Journal of Sociology* 20: 164–77.

Kartzman, David M.

    1973. *Before the Ghetto: Black Detroit in the Nineteenth Century*. Urbana: Univ. of Illinois Press.

Kaslow, Andrew J.

    1981. "Oppression and Adaptation: The Social Organization and Expressive Culture of an Afro-American Community in New Orleans." Ph.D. diss. Columbia Univ.

Kaslow, Andrew J., and Claude Jacobs

    1981. *Prophecy, Healing, and Power: The Afro-American Spiritual Churches of New Orleans*. A Cultural Resources Management Study for the Jean Lafitte National Historical Park and the National Park Service. Dept. of Anthropology and Geography, Univ. of New Orleans.

Katz, Bernard

    1969. *The Social Implications of Early Negro Music in the United States*. New York: Arno Press.

Keber, Helen Phillips

    1971. "Higher on the Hog." In *The Not So Solid South: Anthropological Studies in a Regional Subculture*, ed. J. Kenneth Morland, 4–15. Athens: Univ. of Georgia Press.

Kenyon, Robert S.

    1949. "Sociological Analysis of a Religious Cult: The Temple of Israel Spiritualist Church." M.A. thesis. Atlanta Univ.

King, K. J.

1972. "Some Notes on Arnold J. Ford and New World Black Attitudes to Ethiopia." *Journal of Ethiopian Studies* 10: 81–87.

King, Willis J.

1969. "The Negro Membership in the (Former) Methodist Church in the (New) United Methodist Church." *Methodist History* 7, no. 3: 32–43.

Kinney, John William

1979. "Adam Clayton Powell, Sr., and Adam Clayton Powell, Jr.: A Historical Exposition and Theological Analysis." Ph.D. diss. Columbia Univ.

Kirkwood, Cynthia

1992. "The Black Church and AIDS. *Christianity and Crisis*, Sept. 21.

Kosman, Barry A. and Seymour P. Lachman

1993. *One Nation Under God: Religion in Contemporary American Society.* New York: Crown Trade Paperbacks.

Kostarelos, Frances

1994. *Feeling the Spirit: Faith and Hope in an Evangelical Black Storefront Church.* Columbia: Univ. of South Carolina Press.

Kuna, Ralph R.

1974–1975. "Hoodoo: The Indigenous Medicine and Psychiatry of the Black American." *Ethnomedizin* 3, nos. 3/4: 273–95.

Kusmer, Kenneth L.

1976. *A Ghetto Takes Shape: Black Cleveland, 1870–1930.* Urbana: Univ. of Illinois Press.

Laguerre, Michel S.

1981. "Haitian Americans." In *Ethnicity and Medical Care*, ed. Alan Harwood, 172–210. Cambridge, Mass.: Harvard Univ. Press.

1984. *American Odyssey: Haitians in New York.* Ithaca, N.Y.: Cornell Univ. Press.

Lakey, Othal Hawthorne

1995. *The History of the CME Church* (Revised). Memphis: CME Publishing House.

Landes, Ruth

1967. "Negro Jews in Harlem." *Jewish Journal of Sociology* 9: 175–89.

Landing, James

1974. "The Spatial Expression of Cultural Revitalization in Chicago." *Proceedings of the Association of American Geographers* 6: 50–53.

Lanterari, Vittorio

1963. *The Religions of the Oppressed.* New York: New American Library.

Leacock, Seth, and Ruth Leacock
　　1975. *Spirits of the Dead*. Garden City, N.Y.: Doubleday.
Lee, Martha F.
　　1996. *The Nation of Islam: An American Millenarian Movement*. Syracuse: Syracuse Univ. Press.
Levine, Lawrence
　　1973. "Slave Songs and Slave Consciousness: An Exploration in Neglected Sources." In *American Negro Slavery*, ed. Allen Weinstein and Frank Otto Gatell. New York: Oxford Univ. Press.
　　1977. *Black Culture and Black Consciousness*. New York: Oxford Univ. Press.
Levinsohn, Florence Hamlish
　　1997. *Looking for Farrakhan*. Chicago: Ivan R. Dee.
Lewis, Hylan
　　1955. *Blackways of Kent*. Chapel Hill: Univ. of North Carolina Press.
Lewis, Oscar
　　1966. "The Culture of Poverty." *Scientific American* 215: 19–25.
Lincoln, C. Eric
　　1962. *The Black Muslims of America*. Boston: Beacon.
　　1973. *The Black Muslims in America*. Rev. ed. Boston: Beacon.
　　1984. *Race, Religion and the Continuing American Dilemma*. New York: Hill and Wang.
Lincoln, C. Eric, and Lawrence H. Mamiya
　　1990. *The Black Church in the African American Experience*. Durham, N.C.: Duke Univ. Press.
Lockley, Edith A.
　　1936. "Spiritualist Sect in Nashville." M.A. thesis. Fisk Univ.
Loescher, Frank S.
　　1971. *The Protestant Church and the Negro*. Westport, Conn.: Negro Universities Press.
Long, Charles H.
　　1971. "Perspectives for a Study of Afro-American Religion in the United States." *History of Religion* 11: 54–65.
MacAdam, Doug
　　1982. *Political Process and the Development of Black Insurgency, 1930–1970*. Chicago: Univ. of Chicago Press.
MacRoberts, Omar M.
　　1999. "Understanding the 'New' Black Pentecostal Activism: Lessons from Ecumenical Urban Ministries in Boston." *Sociology of Religion* 60: 47–70.

Maduro, Renaldo J.

    1975. "Hoodoo Possession in San Francisco: Notes on Therapeutic Aspects of Regression." *Ethos* 3: 425–47.

Magida, Arthur J.

    1996. *Prophet of Rage: A Life of Louis Farrakhan and His Nation.* New York: Basic.

Malcolm X

    1965. *The Autobiography of Malcolm X.* New York: Grove.

Mamiya, Lawrence H.

    1982. "From Black Muslim to Bilalian: The Evolution of a Movement." *Journal for the Scientific Study of Religion* 21: 138–52.

Marable, Manning

    1981. *Blackwater: Historical Studies in Race, Class Consciousness and Revolution.* Dayton, Ohio: Black Praxis.

    1983. *How Capitalism Underdeveloped Black America.* Boston: South End.

    1984. *Race, Reform and Rebellion: The Second Reconstruction in Black America, 1945–1982.* Jackson: Univ. Press of Mississippi.

    1985. *Black American Politics: From the Washington Marches to Jesse Jackson.* London: Verso.

    1994. *The Crisis of Color and Democracy: Essays on Race, Class, and Power.* Monroe, Maine: Common Courage Press.

    1997. *Black Liberation in Conservative America.* Boston: South End Press.

Marks, Carole

    1985. "Black Labor Migration: 1910–1920." *Insurgent Sociologist* 12, no. 4: 5–24.

Marsh, Clifton E.

    1984. *From Black Muslim to Muslim: The Transition from Separation to Islam, 1930–1980.* Metuchen, N.J.: Scarecrow.

Martin, Sandy Dwayne

    1999. *For God and Race: The Religious and Political Leadership of AMEZ Bishop James Walker Hood.* Columbia: Univ. of South Carolina Press.

Marx, Gary T.

    1967. "Religion: Opiate or Inspiration of Civil Rights Militancy among Negroes." *American Sociological Review* 32: 64–72.

Marx, Karl, and Friedrich Engels

    1964. *On Religion.* New York: Schocken.

Mathews, Holly F.

1992. "Killing the Medical Self-Help Tradition among African Americans: The Case of Lay Midwifery in North Carolina." In *African Americans in* the *South: Issues of Race, Class, and Gender*, eds. Hans A. Baer and Yvonne Jones, 60–78. Athens: Univ. of Georgia Press.

Maultsby, Portia

1983. "The Use and Performance of Hymnody, Spirituals and Gospel in the Black Church." *Western Journal of Black Studies* 7, no. 3: 161–71.

Mauss, Armand L.

1981. "The Fading of the Pharoh's Curse: The Decline and Fall of the Priesthood Ban Against Blacks in the Mormon Church." *Dialogue: A Journal of Mormon Thought* 14, no. 3: 10–45.

Mays, Benjamin E.

1968. *The Negro's God as Reflected in His Literature*. New York: Atheneum.

Mays, Benjamin E., and Joseph R. Nicholson

1933. *The Negro Church*. New York: Institute of Social and Religious Research.

McCall, Emmanuel L.

1973. "American, National, and Southern Baptists—Partners?" *Review and Expositor* 70: 365–74.

McCall, George J.

1963. "Symbiosis: The Case of Hoodoo and the Numbers Racket." *Social Problems* 10:361–70.

McCloud, Aminah Beverly

1995. *African American Islam*. New York: Routledge.

McDonogh, Gary Wray

1993. *Black and Catholic in Savannah, Georgia*. Knoxville: Univ. of Tennessee Press.

McGreevy, John T.

1996. *Parish Boundaries: The Catholic Encounter with Race in the Twentieth-Century Urban North*. Chicago: Univ. of Chicago Press.

McGuire, Meredith B.

1987. *Religion: The Social Context*. Belmont, Calif.: Wadsworth.

Mead, Frank S.

1975. *Handbook of Denominations in the United States*. Nashville, Tenn.: Abingdon.

Mead, Frank S., and Hill, Samuel S.

1995. *Handbook of Denominations in the United States* (10th edition). Nashville: Abingdon Press.

Meier, August

    1952. "The Emergence of Negro Nationalism." *Midwest Journal* 4: 95–111.

    1966. *Negro Thought in America, 1880–1915: Racial Ideologies in the Age of Booker T. Washington*. Ann Arbor: Univ. of Michigan Press.

Melton, J. Gordon

    1978. *The Encyclopedia of American Religions* 1 and 2. Wilmington, N.C.: McGrath.

Metraux, Alfred

    1972. *Voodoo in Haiti*. New York: Schocken.

Michael, Ethan

    2000. "Another Exodus: The Hebrew Israelites from Chicago to Dimona," ed. Yvonne Chireau and Nathaniel Deutsch, 73–90. New York: Oxford Univ. Press.

Miller, Jon L.

    1980. "The Failed Mission: The Catholic Church and Black Catholics in the Old South." In *The Southern Common People: Studies in 19th-Century Social History*, ed. Edward Magdol and Jon L. Wakelyn, 37–54. Westport, Conn.: Greenwood.

Mintz, Sidney W., and Richard Price

    1976. *An Anthropological Approach to the Afro-American Past: A Caribbean Perspective*. Philadelphia: Institute for the Study of Human Issues.

Mitchell, Henry H.

    1975. *Black Belief*. New York: Harper & Row.

Mongeau, Beatrice, Harvey L. Smith, and Ann C. Maney

    1961. "The 'Granny' Midwife: Changing Roles and Functions of a Folk Practitioner." *American Journal of Sociology* 66: 497–501.

Montgomery, Callie Mae

    1937. "Some Social Aspects of the Reed Street Baptist Church, Atlanta." M.A. thesis. Atlanta Univ.

Montgomery, William E.

    1993. *Under Their Own Vine and Fig Tree: The African-American Church in the South, 1865–1900*. Baton Rouge: Louisiana State Univ. Press.

Moore, Sidney Harrison

    1975. "Family and Social Networks in an Urban Black Storefront Church." Ph.D. diss. American Univ.

Morris, Aldon D.

    1984. *The Origins of the Civil Rights Movement: Black Communities Organizing for Change*. New York: Free Press.

Morris, Calvin S.

    1990. *Reverdy C. Ransom: Black Advocate of the Social Gospel.* Lanham, Md.: Univ. Press of America.

Morrison-Reed, Mark D.

    1984. *Black Pioneers in a White Denomination.* Boston: Beacon.

Moses, Gregg

    1997. *Revolution of Conscience: Martin Luther King, Jr., and the Philosophy of Nonviolence.* New York: Guildford Press.

Moses, Wilson J.

    1982. *Black Messiahs and Uncle Toms: Social and Literary Manipulations of a Religious Myth.* University Park: Pennsylvania State Univ. Press.

Muhammed, Raquel

    1980. "Black Muslim Movement After the Death of Elijah Muhammad." Ph.D. diss. United States International Univ.

Mukenge, Ida Rousseau

    1983. *The Black Church in Urban America: A Case Study in Political Economy.* Lanham, Md.: Univ. Press of America.

Murphy, Joseph M.

    1988. *Santeria: An African Religion in America.* Boston: Beacon.

Murphy, Larry G., J. Gordon Melton, and Gary L. Ward, eds.

    1993. *Encyclopedia of African American Religions.* New York: Garland Publishing.

Murphy, Robert F.

    1979. *An Overture to Social Anthropology.* Englewood Cliffs, N.J.: Prentice-Hall.

Murray, Andrew E.

    1966. *Presbyterians and the Negro—A History.* Philadelphia: Presbyterian Historical Society.

Myrdal, Gunnar

    1962. *An American Dilemma: The Negro Problem and Modern Democracy.* New York: Harper & Row.

Naison, Mark

    1983. *Communists in Harlem during the Depression.* New York: Grove.

Neal, Larry

    1978. "Aesthetics and Culture." *The Drum* 9: 11–12.

Nelsen, Hart M., and L. Dickson

    1972. "Attitudes of Black Catholics and Protestants: Evidence for Religious Identity." *Sociological Analysis* 33: 152–65.

Nelsen, Hart M., and Anne Kusener Nelsen

    1975. *Black Church in the Sixties.* Lexington: Univ. Press of Kentucky.

Nelsen, Hart M., Raytha L. Yokley, and Anne K. Nelsen, eds.
　1971. *The Black Church in America*. New York: Basic Books.
Nelson, Geoffrey K.
　1969. *Spiritualism and Society*. London: Routledge and Kegan Paul.
Nelson, Timothy J.
　1996. "Sacrifice of Praise: Emotion and Collective Participation in an African-American Worship Service." *Sociology of Religion* 57: 379–96.
　1997. "The Church and the Street: Race, Class, and the Congregation." In *Contemporary American Religion: An Ethnographic Reader*, ed. Penny Edgel Becker and Nancy L. Eiesland, 169–90. Walnut Creek, Calif.: Altamira Press.
Newman, Richard
　1997. "'Warrior Mother of Africa's Warriors of the Mother High God': Laura Adorkor Kofey and the African Universal Church." In *This Far by Faith: Readings in African-American Women's Religious Biography*, eds. Judith Weisenfeld and Richard Newman, 110–21. New York: Routledge.
New Orleans City Guide
　1938. Federal Writers Project. Boston: Houghton Mifflin.
Newsweek
　1966. "The Black Jews of New York." 26 Dec., 44.
New York Amsterdam News
　1931. 31 July.
Norwood, Frederick A.
　1974. *The Story of American Methodism*. Nashville, Tenn.: Abingdon.
Obeyesekere, Gananath
　1981. *Medusa's Hair*. Chicago: Univ. of Chicago Press.
Oh, Hohn Kie-Chang
　1973. "The Nichiren Shoshu of America." *Review of Religious Research* 14, no. 3: 169–77.
Osofsky, Gilbert
　1965. *Harlem: The Making of a Ghetto: Negro New York, 1890–1930*. New York: Harper & Row.
Ottenberg, Simon
　1959. "Leadership and Change in a Coastal Georgia Negro Community." *Phylon* 20: 7–18.
Parenti, Michael
　1964. "The Black Muslims from Revolution to Institution." *Social Research* 31: 175–94.
Paris, Arthur E.
　1982. *Black Pentecostalism: Southern Religion in an Urban World*. Amherst: Univ. of Massachusetts Press.

Paris, Peter J.

    1978. *Black Leaders in Conflict: Joseph H. Jackson, Martin Luther King, Jr., Malcolm X, Adam Clayton Powell, Jr.* New York: Pilgrim.

    1985. *The Social Teaching of the Black Churches.* Philadelphia: Fortress.

Parker, Robert A.

    1937. *The Incredible Messiah.* Boston: Little, Brown.

Parkin, Frank

    1971. *Class Inequality and Political Order: Social Stratification in Capitalist and Communist Societies.* New York: Praeger.

Parsons, Anne

    1965. "The Pentecostal Immigrants: A Study of an Ethnic Central City Church." *Journal for the Scientific Study of Religion* 4: 183–97.

Patterson, Daniel

    1988. "'Going Up to Meet Him': Songs and Ceremonies of a Black Family's Ascent." In *Diversities of Gifts: Field Studies in Southern Religion,* ed. R. Tyson, James Peacock, and Daniel Patterson, pp. 91–102. Chicago: Univ. of Chicago Press.

Patterson, James Oglethorpe

    1984. *"The Mother Church."* Memphis: Pentecostal Temple Institutional Church of God in Christ.

Patterson, J. O., German R. Ross, and Julia Atkinson, eds.

    1969. *History and Formative Years of the Church of God in Christ with Excerpts from the Life and Works of Its Founder—Bishop C.H. Mason.* Memphis: Church of God in Christ Publishing House.

Payne, Ward J., ed.

    1993. *Directory of African American Religions.* Washington, D.C.: Howard Univ. Press.

Payne-Jackson, Arvilla, and John Lee

    1993. *Folk Wisdom and Mother Wit: John Lee—An African American Herbal Healer.* Westport, Conn.: Greenwood Press.

Peck, Gary R.

    1982. "Black Radical Consciousness and the Black Christian Experience: Toward a Critical Sociology of Afro-American Religion." *Sociological Analysis* 43: 155–69.

Pelt, Owen D., and Ralph Lee Smith

    1960. *The Story of the National Baptists.* New York: Vantage.

Perrow, Charles and Mauro Guillen

    1990. *The AIDS Disaster: The Failure of Organizations in New York and the Nation.* New Haven: Yale Univ. Press.

Perry, Bruce

    1991. *Malcolm: The Life of a Man Who Changed Black America.* New York: Station Hill Press.

Piepkorn, Arthur Carl
    1971. "The Primitive Baptists of North America." *Concordia Theological Monthly* 42: 297–314.

Pinn, Anthony B.
    1998. *Varieties of African American Religious Experience.* Minneapolis: Fortress Press.
    2000. "Rap Music and Its Message." In *Religion and Popular Culture in America*, ed. Bruce Forbes and Jeffrey Mahan, pp. 268–76. Berkeley: Univ. of California Press.

Pitts, Walter F.
    1997. *Old Ship of Zion: The Afro-Baptist Ritual in African Diaspora.* New York: Oxford Univ. Press.

Ploski, Harry A., and Warren, eds.
    1976. *The Negro Almanac: A Reference Work on the Afro-American.* New York: Bellwether.

Pollard, Alton
    1989a "Religion, Rock, and Eroticism: Prince." In *The Theology of American Popular Music*, a special issue of *Black Sacred Music: A Journal of Theomusicology* (Fall) 3, no. 2, ed. Jon Michael Spencer, pp. 133–41.

Pope, Liston
    1957. *The Kingdom Beyond.* New York: Friendship.

Powdermaker, Hortense
    1967. *After Freedom.* New York: Schocken.

Raboteau, Albert J.
    1978. *Slave Religion: The "Invisible Institution" in the Antebellum South.* New York: Oxford Univ. Press.
    1983. "Black Catholics: A Capsule History." *Catholic Digest*, June, 32–38.
    1986. "The Afro-American Traditions." In *Caring and Curing: Health and Medicine in the Western Religious Tradition*, ed. Ronald L. Numbers and Dareel W. Amundsen, 539–81. New York: Macmillan.

Ransom, R. C.
    1950. *Pilgrim of Harriet Ransom's Son.* Nashville, Tenn.: AME Sunday School Union.

Raper, Arthur F.
    1936. *Preface to Peasantry: A Tale of Two Black Belt Counties.* Chapel Hill: Univ. of North Carolina Press.

Rawick, George
    1977. *The American Slave: A Composite Autobiography, Volume 4: Texas.* Westport, Conn.: Greenwood Press.

Regis, Helen

    1999. "Second Lines, Minstrelsy, and the Contested Landscapes of New Orleans Afro-Creole Festivals." *Cultural Anthropology* 14, no. 4: 472–504.

Reid, Ira De A.

    1926. "Let Us Prey." *Opportunity* 4: 274–78.

Reich, Michael

    1971. "The Economics of Racism." In *The Capitalist System*, ed. Richard Edwards, et. al., 313–21. Englewood Cliffs, N.J.: Prentice Hall.

Reinders, Robert C.

    1961. "The Church and Negro in New Orleans, 1850–1860." *Phylon* 22: 241–48.

Reinhoid, Robert

    1982. "Years of Tension Preceded Arizona Confrontation." *New York Times*, 26 Oct.

Reynolds, Barbara

    1976. "Changes in Black Muslims: Why the Surprise." *Chicago Tribune*, 7 Apr., 38.

Reynolds, David

    1997. *Democracy Unbound: Progressive Challenges to the Two Party System.* Boston: South End Press.

Richardson, Harry V.

    1947. *Dark Glory: A Picture of the Church Among Negroes in the Rural Church.* New York: Friendship.

    1976. *Dark Salvation: The Story of Methodism as It Developed Among Blacks in America.* New York: Doubleday.

Richardson, James T.

    1980. "People's Temple and Jonestown: A Corrective Comparison and Critique." *Journal for the Scientific Study of Religion* 19: 239–55.

Roberson, Mildred

    1985. "The Influence of Religious Beliefs on Health Choices of Afro-Americans." *Topics in Clinical Nursing* 7, no. 3: 57–63.

Roberts, Hugh

    1989. "Improvisation, Individuation, and Immanence: Thelonious Monk." In *The Theology of American Popular Music*, a special issue of *Black Sacred Music: A Journal of* Theomusicology (Fall) 3, no. 2, ed. Jon Michael Spencer, pp. 50–56.

Roberts, John H.

    1989. *From Trickster to Badman: The Black Folk Hero in Slavery and Freedom.* Philadelphia: Univ. of Pennsylvania Press.

Robinson, David M.
  1974. "A Song, a Shout, and a Prayer." In *The Black Experience in Religion*, ed. C. Eric Lincoln, 212–34. New York: Doubleday.
Robinson, Robert
  (n.d.) *An Introduction to Church of God in Christ: History, Theology, and Structure*. Little Rock, Ark.: Robert Robinson.
Rose, Arnold
  1948. *The Negro in America*. New York: Harper & Row.
Rushing, Byron
  1972. "A Note on the Origin of the African Orthodox Church." *Journal of Negro History* 57: 37–39.
Sackey, Charles
  1973. *The Political Economy of Urban Poverty*. New York: Norton.
Salanini, Leonardo
  1981. *Sociology of Political Praxis: An Introduction to Gramsci's Thought*. London: Routledge & Kegan Paul.
Samuels, William H.
  1981. "The Recovery and Revitalization of the Black Church." D. Ministry diss. Univ. of Chicago.
Sanders, Cheryl Jeanne
  1996. *Saints in Exile: The Holiness-Pentecostal Experience in African American Religion and Culture*. New York: Oxford Univ. Press.
Sawyer, Mary
  1988. "Black Ecumenical Movements: Proponents of Social Change." *Review of Religious Research* 30: 151–61.
  1994. *Black Ecumenism: Implementing the Demands of Justice*. Valley Forge, Pa.: Trinity Press.
Saxon, Lyle, Edward Dreyer, and Robert Tallant
  1945. *Gumbo Ya-Ya*. Louisiana Writers Project Publications. Cambridge, Mass.: Riverside.
Scheiner, Seth M.
  1965. *Negro Mecca: A History of the Negro in New York City, 1865–1920*. New York: New York Univ. Press.
Schensul, Jean, Christina Huebner, Merrill Singer, Marvin Snow, Pablo Feliciano, and Lorie Broomhall
  2000. "The High, the Money, and the Fame: The Emergent Social Context of 'New Marijuana' Use among Urban Youth. *Medical Anthropology* 18, no. 4: 389–414.
Schwimmer, Eric
  1987. "Gramsci, History and the Future Economy." In *Beyond the New Economic Anthropology*, ed. John Clammer, 78–117. New York: St. Martin's.

Scott, James C. Scott

1990. *Domination and the Arts of Resistance: Hidden Transcripts*. New Haven, Conn.: Yale Univ. Press.

Semmes, Clovis E.

1995. *Racism, Health, and Post-Industrialism: A Theory of African-American Health*. Westport, Conn.: Praeger.

Seraile, William

1998. *Fire in His Heart: Bishop Benjamin Tucker Tanner and the A.M.E. Church*. Knoxville: Univ. of Tennessee Press.

Sernett, Milton C.

1975. *Black Religion and American Evangelicalism*. Metuchen, N.J.: Scarecrow.

1997. *Bound for the Promised Land: African American Religion and the Great Migration*. Durham, N.C.: Duke Univ. Press.

Shack, William A.

1974. "Ethiopia and Afro-Americans: Some Historical Notes." *Phylon* 25: 142–55.

Shapiro, Deanne Ruth

1970. "Double Damnation, Double Salvation: The Sources and Varieties of Black Judaism in the United States." M.A. thesis. Columbia Univ.

Shaw, Talbert O.

1973. "A Tentative Profile of the Black Clergy in Chicago." *Journal of Religious Thought* 30: 39–51.

Shriver, Peggy L.

1989. *Having Gifts That Differ: Profiles of Ecumenical Churches*. New York: Friendship.

Shockley, Grant S., and Leonard Haynes

1964. "The A.M.E. and the A.M.E. Zion Churches." In *The History of American Methodism* 2, ed. Emory Stevens Burke, 526–82. Nashville, Tenn.: Abingdon.

Shopshire, James Maynard

1975. "A Socio-Historical Characterization of the Black Pentecostal Movement in America." Ph.D. diss. Northwestern Univ.

Silberman, Charles E.

1964. *Crisis in Black and White*. New York: Vintage.

Simpson, George Eaton

1978. *Black Religions in the New World*. New York: Columbia Univ. Press.

Simpson, Robert

1970. "A Black Church: Ecstasy in a World of Trouble." Ph.D. diss. Washington Univ.

Singer, Merrill

> 1979. "Saints of the Kingdom: Group Emergence, Individual Affiliation and Social Change among the Black Hebrews of Israel." Ph.D. diss. Univ. of Utah.

> 1981. "The Social Meaning of Medicine in a Sectarian Community." *Medical Anthropology* 5: 207–32.

> 1982. "Life in a Defensive Society: The Black Hebrew Israelites." In *Sex Roles in Contemporary American Communes*, ed. Jon Wagner, 45–81. Bloomington: Indiana Univ. Press.

> 1985. "'Now I Know What the Songs Mean!': Traditional Black Music in a Contemporary Black Sect." *Southern Quarterly* 23, no. 3: 125–40.

> 1988. "The Social Correlates of Conversion to a Black Religious Sect." *Review of Religious Research* 30: 177–92.

> 1992. "The Southern Roots of Judaism." In *African Americans in the South: Issues of Race, Class, and Gender*, ed. Hans A. Baer and Yvonne Jones, 123–38. Athens: Univ. of Georgia Press.

> 1999. "Symbolic Identity Formation in an African American Religious Sect: The Black Hebrew Israelites. In *Black Zion: African American Religious Encounters with Judaism*, ed. Yvonne Chireau and Nathaniel Deutsch, pp. 55–72. Oxford: Oxford Univ. Press.

Singer, Merrill, Lani Davidson, and Gina Gerdes

> 1988. "Culture, Critical Theory, and Reproductive Illness Behavior in Haiti." *Medical Anthropology Quarterly* 2: 370–85.

Singer, Merrill, and Margaret Weeks

> 1996. "Preventing AIDS in Communities of Color: Anthropology and Social Prevention." *Human Organization* 55: 488–92.

Singer, Merrill, and Maria Borrero

> 1984. "Indigenous Treatment for Alcoholism: The Case for Puerto Rican Spiritism." *Medical Anthropology* 8: 246–47.

Singer, Merrill, and Roberto Garcia

> 1989. "Puerto Rican Espiritista: Life History of a Female Healer." In *Women as Healers*, ed. Carol Shepherd McClain, 157–85. New Brunswick, N.J.: Rutgers Univ. Press.

Singleton, George A.

> 1952. *The Romance of African Methodism*. New York: Exposition.

Smith, C. S.

> 1922. *A History of the A.M.E. Church*. Philadelphia: AME Book Press.

Smith, Joan

> 1981. *Social Issues and the Social Order: The Contradictions of Capitalism*. Cambridge, Mass.: Winthrop.

Snook, John B.

1973. *Going Further: Life-and-Death Religion in America.* Englewood Cliffs, N.J.: Prentice-Hall.

Snow, Loudell F.

1973. "'I Was Born just Exactly with the Gift': An Interview with a Voodoo Practitioner." *Journal of American Folklore* 86: 272–81.

1974. "Folk Medical Beliefs and Their Implications for Care of Patients." *Annals of Internal Medicine* 81: 82–96.

1977. "Popular Medicine in a Black Neighborhood." In *Ethnomedicine in the Southwest*, ed. Edward H. Spicer, 19–95. Tucson: Univ. of Arizona Press.

1978. "Sorcerers, Saints, and Charlatans: Black Folk Healers in Urban America." *Culture, Medicine and Psychiatry* 2: 69–106.

1979. "Mail Order Magic: The Commercial Exploitation of Folk Belief." *Journal of Folklore Institute* 16: 44–73.

1994. *Walkin' Over Medicine: Traditional Health Practices in African-American Life.* Boulder, Colo.: Westview Press. Sobel, Mechal

1979. *Travelin' On: The Slavery Journey to an Afro-Baptist Faith.* Westport, Conn.: Greenwood.

Southern, Eileen

1973. *The Music of Black Americans: A History.* First edition. New York: W. W. Norton and Co.

1983a *The Music of Black Americans: A History.* Second edition. New York: W. W. Norton and Co.

1983b *Readings in Black American Music.* New York: W. W. Norton and Co.

Spear, Allan H.

1967. *Black Chicago: The Making of a Negro Ghetto, 1890–1920.* Chicago: Univ. of Chicago Press.

Spector, Rachel E.

1998. *Cultural Diversity in Health and Illness* (4th edition). Stamford, Conn.: Appleton & Lange.

Spencer, Jon

1992. *Black Hymnody: A Hymnological History of the African-American Church.* Knoxville: Univ. of Tennessee Press.

Spencer, Jon, ed.

1989. *The Theology of American Popular Music.* A special issue of *Black Sacred Music: A Journal of Theomusicology* (Fall) 3, no. 2.

Stark, Rodney, and William Sims Bainbridge
  1985. *The Future of Religion: Secularization, Revival, and Cult Formation*. Berkeley: Univ. of California Press.
Stavrianos, L. S.
  1981. *Global Rift: The Third World Comes of Age*. New York: Morrow.
Sutton, Joel Brett.
  1983. "Spirit and Polity in a Black Primitive Church." Ph.D. diss. Univ. of North Carolina.
Swift, David E.
  1989. *Black Prophets of Justice: Activist Clergy Before the Civil War*. Baton Rouge: Louisiana State Univ. Press.
Synan, Vinson
  1971. *The Holiness-Pentecostal Movement in the United States*. Grand Rapids, Mich.: Eerdmans.
Tallant, Robert
  1946. *Voodoo in New Orleans*. New York: Collier.
Taylor, Clarence
  1994. *The Black Churches of Brooklyn*. New York: Columbia Univ. Press.
Tinney, James S.
  1978. "A Theoretical and Historical Comparison of Black Political and Religious Movements." Ph.D. diss. Howard Univ.
  1979. "Exclusivist tendencies in Pentecostal self-definition." *Journal of Religious Thought* 36: 32–49.
  1982. "Pentecostals: A Change in Name." *National Leader*, July 29.
Tucker, David M.
  1975. *Black Pastors and Leaders: Memphis 1819–1972*. Memphis: Memphis State Univ. Press.
Turner, Richard Brent
  1997. *Islam in the African American Experience*. Bloomington: Indiana Univ. Press.
Turner, Ronny E.
  1973. "The Black Minister: Uncle Tom or Abolitionist?" *Phylon* 24: 86–95.
Turner, Victor
  1969. *The Ritual Process*. Chicago: Univ. of Chicago Press.
Turner, William Clair, Jr.
  1984. "The United Holy Church of America: A Study in Black Holiness-Pentecostalism." Ph.D. diss. Duke Univ.
Tyms, James Daniel
  1938. "A Study of Four Religious Cults Operating among Negroes." M.A. thesis. Howard Univ.

Valentine, Charles A.

    1968. *Culture and Poverty: Critique and Counter-Proposals*. Chicago: Univ. of Chicago Press.

Vincent, Theodore G.

    1972. *Black Power and the Garvey Movement*. Berkeley, Calif.: Ramparts

Valentine, Charles A.

    1968. *Culture and Poverty: Critique and Counter-Proposals*. Chicago: Univ. of Chicago Press.

Vincent, Theodore G.

    1972. *Black Power and the Garvey Movement*. Berkeley, Calif.: Ramparts.

Wagner, Roy

    1981. *The Invention of Culture*. Chicago: Univ. of Chicago Press.

Walker, Clarence

    1982. *A Rock in a Weary Land: The African Methodist Episcopal Church during the Civil War and Reconstruction*. Baton Rouge: Louisiana State Univ. Press.

Walker, James Perry

    1985. "Rev. Louis Cole, Black Baptist Circuit Preacher, 1901–1981." *Southern Quarterly* 23, no. 3: 49–69.

Walker, Sheila S.

    1972. *Ceremonial Spirit Possession in Africa and Afro-America*. Leiden: Brill.

Wallace, Anthony F. C.

    1956. "Revitalization Movements." *American Anthropologist* 58: 264–81.

    1966. *Religion: An Anthropological View*. New York: Random House.

Wallerstein, Immanuel

    1979. *The Capitalist World-Economy*. Cambridge: Cambridge Univ. Press.

Walls, William

    1974. *The African Methodist Episcopal Zion Church*. Charlotte, N.C.: A.M.E. Zion Publishing House.

Walters, Raymond

    1970. *Negroes and the Great Depression*. Westport, Conn.: Greenwood.

Warburton, T. Rennie

    1969. "Holiness Religion: An Anomaly of Sectarian Typologies." *Journal for the Scientific Religion* 8: 130–39.

Washington, James Melvin

    1985. "Jesse Jackson and the Symbolic Politics of Black Christendom." *Annals of the American Academy of Political and Social Science* 480: 88–105.

1986. *Frustrated Fellowship: The Black Baptist Quest for Social Power*.
Macon, Ga.: Mercer Univ. Press.

Washington, Joseph J., Jr.

1960. *Black Religion: The Negro and Christianity in the United States*.
Boston: Beacon.

1973. *Black Sects and Cults*. Garden City, N.Y.: Doubleday.

Washington, Paul M.

1994. *"Other Sheep I Have": The Autobiography of Father Paul M.
Washington*. Philadelphia: Temple Univ. Press.

Watson, Andrew Polk

1932. "Primitive Religion among Negroes in Tennessee." M.A. thesis.
Fisk Univ.

Watson, G. Llewellyn

1973. "Social Structure and Social Movements: The Black Muslims in
the U.S.A. and the Rastafarians in Jamaica." *British Journal of Sociology*
24: 188–204.

Watson, Wilbur H.

1984. "Folk Medicine and Older Blacks in Southern United States." In
Black Folk Medicine: The Therapeutic Significance of Faith and Trust, ed.
Wilbur H. Watson, 53–66. New Brunswick, N.J.: Transaction Books.

Watts, Jill

1994. *God, Harlem, U.S.A.: The Father Divine Story*. Berkeley: Univ. of
California Press.

Webb, Beatrice Larson

1973. "A Study of Voodoo Mail-Order Advertising in Louisiana."
Louisiana Review 2: 65–71.

Webb, Lillian Ashcraft

1981. *About My Father's Business: The Life of Elder Michaux*. Westport,
Conn.: Greenwood.

Weidman, Hazel et al.

1979. *Miami Health Ecology Projects, Volume 1*. Univ. of Miami.

Weisbrot, Robert

1983. *Father Divine and the Struggle for Racial Equality*. Urbana: Univ. of
Illinois Press.

West, Cornel

1982. *Prophecy Deliverance! An Afro-American Revolutionary Christianity*.
Philadelphia: Westminister.

1988. *Prophetic Fragments*. Grand Rapids, Mich.: Eerdmans.

1990. "The New Cultural Politics of Difference." In *Out There:
Marginalization and Contemporary Cultures*, ed. R. Ferguson, M. Gever,
T. Minh-ha, and C. West, 19–36. Cambridge, Mass.: MIT Press.

Wheeler, Edward L.

    1973. "Beyond One Man: A General Survey of Black Baptist Church History." *Review and Expositor* 70: 309–19.

White, Gavin

    1978. "Patriarch McGuire and the Episcopal Church." In *Black Apostles: Afro-American Clergy Confront the Twentieth Century*, ed. Randall K. Burkett and Richard Newman, 151–80. Boston: G. K. Hall.

White, Newman

    1928. *American Negro Folk-Songs*. Cambridge, Mass.: Harvard Univ. Press.

White, O. Kendall, and Daryl White

    1980. "Abandoning an Unpopular Policy: An Analysis of the Decision Granting the Mormon Priesthood to Blacks." *Sociological Analysis* 41: 231–45.

    1985. "Integrating Religious and Racial Identities: An Analysis of LDS African-American Mormon." *Review of Religious Research* 36: 289–311.

Whiting, Albert N.

    1952. "The United House of Prayer for All People: A Case Study of a Charismatic Sect." Ph.D. diss. American Univ.

Whitten, Jr., Norman E.

    1962. "Contemporary Patterns of Malign Occultism among Negroes in North Carolina." *Journal of American Folklore* 75: 311–25.

Williams, Eric

    1944. *Capitalism and Slavery*. New York: Russell & Russell.

Williams, Melvin D.

    1974. *Community in a Black Pentecostal Church*. Pittsburgh: Univ. of Pittsburgh Press.

Wilmore, Gayraud S.

    1983a. *Black Religion and Black Radicalism*. Maryknoll, N.Y.: Orbis.

    1983b. *Black and Presbyterian: The Heritage and the Hope*. Philadelphia: Geneva.

Wilson, Bryan R.

    1969. "A Typology of Sects." In *Sociology of Religion*, ed. Roland Robertson, 361–83. Baltimore: Penguin.

    1973. *Magic and the Millennium: A Sociological Study of Religious Movements of Protest Among Tribal and Third-World Peoples*. New York: Harper & Row.

Wilson, James Q.

    1960. *Negro Politics: The Search for Leadership*. New York: Free Press.

Wilson, John

    1978. *Religion in American Society: The Effective Presence*. Englewood Cliffs, N.J.: Prentice-Hall.

Wimberly, Ricard

    1989. "Prophecy, Eroticism, and Apocalypticism in Popular Music." In *The Theology of American Popular Music*, a special issue of *Black Sacred Music: A Journal of* Theomusicology (Fall) 3, no. 2, ed. Jon Michael Spencer, pp. 125–32.

Winslow, David J.

    1969. "Bishop E.E. Everett and Some Aspects of Occultism and Folk Religion in Negro Philadelphia." *Keystone Quarterly* 14: 59–80.

Woodman, Harold, ed.

    1966. *Slavery and the Southern Economy*. New York: Harcourt, Brace & World.

Woodson, Carter Goodwin

    1945. *The History of the Negro Church*. 2d ed. Washington, D.C.: Associated Publishers.

Wynia, Elly M.

    1998. *Church of God and Saints of Christ: The Rise of Black Jews*. New York: Garland Publishing.

Yinger, J. Milton

    1970. *The Scientific Study of Religion*. New York: MacMillan.

Index

National Colored Spiritualist
Association, 194
National Conference of Black
Christians, 95, 280
National Conference of Black
Churchmen, 95
National Primitive Baptist Convention,
174
New Thought, 221, 228
Nirchiren Shoshu, 109

Olivet Baptist Church, 47–48, 65, 73
Organization of Afro-American Unity,
149
Original Hebrew Israelite Nation, xiii,
115, 133–35, 151, 268–70, 274
Oyotunyu Village, 206

Parham, Charles Fox, 155
paternalism, 23
Patterson, James O., 166, 168, 179
Peace Mission, 49, 217–22, 231. *See*
Father Divine
Pentecostal, 153
Pentecostal Assemblies of the World,
156, 163
Pentecostal Temple Institutional
Church, 166, 179, 182
politico-religious organization, polity,
30–32, 62–73, 75–77, 83–86, 136–41,
162–66, 168–70, 192–95, 197-99
polygamy, 135
Powell, Adam Clayton, Jr., 87
Presbyterians, black, 25, 104–5
Prince, 258–59
prison song, 261
Progressive National Baptist
Convention, 67, 92, 95
Prophet Jones, 27
Prosser, Gabriel, 21
protest and accommodation,
juxtaposition of, xvii; in African
American mainstream churches,
86–100; in black congregations in

white-controlled mainstream
denominations, 110–12; in black
religious music, 249–50; in
conversionist sects, 175–82; in
messianic-nationalist sects, 143–51;
in thaumaturgical sects, 210–15

Quakers, 6, 102

racism, role of, 43
Rainbow Coalition, 282–84
Ransom, Reverdy, 47, 70, 87, 95, 99
rap, 259, 271
Redeeming Christian Spiritualist
Church, 188
revitalization movement, 50
revivals, 12, 34, 41
rhythm and blues (R&B), 267
Richlieu, Leon, 117
Robinson, Ida, 170
rootwork, rootworkers, 238

Sanctified churches, 152–72. *See* black
Holiness-Pentecostal movement
santeria, 205
Seals, Mother Catherine, 187
séance, 228
Second Awakening, 5, 7, 14, 250
Second Cumberland Presbyterian
Church in the United States, 55
sect, concept of, xvii
Seymour, William J., 155
Sharpton, Al, 180
Shrines of the Black Madonna, 57, 132
Shuttlesworth, Fred, 40
Silver Bluff Church, 15
slave religion, 3–12, 20–23
slavery, 3–12
Smith, Lucy, 158
socialism, 281, 285
Society for the Propagation of the
Gospel, 4–5, 103
Southern Baptist Convention, 9, 64,
68, 103

Southern Christian Leadership
Conference, 81, 91, 97, 99–100
Speaking-in-tongues, 153. *See*
glossolalia
Spiritual advisors and prophets, 243–44
Spiritual churches, Spiritual movement,
xiii, 49–51, 59–60, 184–202, 208,
210–15, 273
Spiritualist Church of the Southwest,
187
Spiritualists, 237–38
Spirituals, 251–55
split labor market, 43, 97
St. George's Methodist Episcopal
Church, 17, 83
St. Thomas African Episcopal Church,
103
storefront churches, 45–52, 88, 172–73
Sullivan, Leon, 98, 180
syncretism, 246–48, 273–79

Taylor, William F., 187–89
thaumaturgical sect, African American,
59–60, 183–215
Turner, Nat, x, 9, 14, 21, 25
typology of African American folk
healers, 234–38

typology of African American sects, xxii,
52–60

Union American Methodist Episcopal
church, 72
Unitarians, black, 102
United Church and Science of Living
Institute, 60, 183, 203–5, 208–10
United House of Prayer for All People,
222–24
United Methodists, black, 105
Unity Holy church, 154
Universal Hagar's Spiritual church, 187,
229
Universal Negro Improvement
Association, 118, 130–31, 220

Vesey, Denmark, 9, 21
Voodoo, Vodou, *vodun*, 22, 59, 184–85,
200–201, 205, 211–12, 228, 233,
239–40

Watson, Thomas B., 187
Womanist Theology, 282
Woodbey, George Washington, 87, 95
World Community of al-Islam in the
West, 128, 150

This book was designed and typeset on a PC computer system using QuarkXpress software. The text is set in Janson, and display type is set in EddaCaps and Officina Sans. This book was designed and typeset by Bill Adams and manufactured by Thomson-Shore, Inc.